LIBRARY
H.S. PERF. & VIS.
ARTS

PHOTO BY TALBOT-GILES

TIME OUT FOR GINGER

ACTING EDITION

★

═ COMEDY IN THREE ACTS ═
═ BY RONALD ALEXANDER ═

★

812
Ale

DRAMATISTS
PLAY SERVICE
INC.

COPYRIGHT, 1953, BY RONALD ALEXANDER (REVISED)

COPYRIGHT, 1948, BY RONALD ALEXANDER
(under the title "Season With Ginger")

CAUTION: Professionals and amateurs are hereby warned that TIME OUT FOR GINGER, being fully protected under the copyright laws of the United States of America, the British Empire, including the Dominion of Canada, and all other countries of the Copyright Union, is subject to a royalty. All rights, including professional, amateur, motion picture, recitation, lecturing, public reading, radio broadcasting, television, and the rights of translation into foreign languages, are strictly reserved. Particular emphasis is laid on the question of readings, permission for which must be secured from the author's agent in writing.

All inquiries concerning rights (other than amateur and stock rights) should be addressed to the author's agent, MCA Artists, Ltd., 598 Madison Avenue, New York 22, N. Y.

Inquiries on stock productions should be addressed to Samuel French, 25 West 45th Street, New York, N. Y.

The amateur acting rights of TIME OUT FOR GINGER are controlled exclusively by the Dramatists Play Service, Inc., 14 East 38th Street, New York 16, N. Y., without whose permission in writing no amateur performance of it may be made.

TIME OUT FOR GINGER was first produced by the Alley Theater in Houston, Texas. It was produced in New York by Shepard Traube and Gordon Pollock in association with Don Hershey at the Lyceum Theater on November 26, 1952. Scenery and lighting were by Eldon Elder, and the play was directed by Shepard Traube. The cast was as follows:

LIZZIE, *the maid*	Laura Pierpont
AGNES CAROL	Polly Rowles
HOWARD CAROL	Melvin Douglas
JOAN, *their daughter, age 18*	Mary Hartig
JEANNIE, *their daughter, age 16*	Lois Smith
GINGER, *their daughter, age 14*	Nancy Malone
EDDIE DAVIS, *an athlete, Joan's boy friend*	Conrad Janis
TOMMY GREEN, *Ginger's boy friend*	Larry Robinson
MR. WILSON, *the high school principal*	Roland Wood
ED HOFFMAN, *bank president, Howard Carol's boss*	Philip Loeb

SYNOPSIS OF SCENES

ACT I

The living-room of the home of Mr. and Mrs. Howard Carol. Early Fall, 4:30 one afternoon.

ACT II

SCENE 1. Four weeks later.
SCENE 2. A Saturday afternoon. Four weeks later.

ACT III

The same evening.

TIME OUT FOR GINGER

ACT I

The scene is the home of Mr. and Mrs. Howard Carol, upper middle-class residents of a typical American town or small city. The living-room, where the action passes, is bright, cheery, and roomy. At the back of the stage, above the living-room proper, is the entrance hallway, which runs from about Center-stage to the extreme Right. At extreme Right of this hallway, up-stage, is the front door, unseen by the audience. This door is heard slamming each time anyone uses it, and each time the doorbell is heard when anyone wants to enter. Just visible to the audience, to the Left of the unseen front door is a small clothes closet, in the up-stage wall of the set, and coats, hats, and the like, are perceived when the door opens. The hallway extends to the L. about half-way across the upper part of the stage. Standing near the wall are, immediately to the L. of the clothes closet door, a chair and L. of that an oblong table, with flowers or a potted plant on it. A flight of stairs, about C. stage, comes down (presumably) from the second floor. The actors enter from what is supposed to be the top of the stairs, unseen by the audience. Three or four steps below the entrance to the stairway is a small landing, from which the lower two or three steps, down to stage level, turn to stage R. These last steps are provided with a banister, and two newel posts form the extremities of the stairway. The R. wall of the stage, starting from below where the invisible front door is supposed to be, and somewhat to its L., is a large window, a bit over half-way down-stage. Below this, not far from the curtain-line, is a radio-console. A small mirror hangs on the wall over it. Against the up-stage wall, L. of the bottom

of the stairway, is a flat-topped sideboard, in which is at least one drawer. A wastebasket stands nearby. To the R. of the sideboard, a little below the stairs, is a small phone table with a phone on it. Small chairs to R. and L. of the phone table. The L. wall of the room includes the door to the kitchen, preferably a swinging door. Just below this, against the wall, a small table, with a lamp and a few framed family photos. Below this is a corner, described hereafter as D. L. corner. On two sides of this, facing the audience, are bookshelves, some of which have a few books, and one of which has bottles, cans, jars, paint brushes. A little further down-stage to the L. is a bench, in which is a practical drawer or lift-top. Standing out a little from this corner is a small work table, described hereafter as Ceramic Table, on this a small potter's wheel. A few prints and small pictures on the walls of the corner. At the extreme down-stage extremity of the corner is a small chair, described as a child's chair. Above the window at stage R. is a jog in the room formed by part of the set; this masks the R. extremity of the hallway leading to the front door. In this jog is a small table, on which is a lamp. Opposite the down-stage part of the window, and somewhat more than half-way down stage, is a sofa, big enough for three people. On it are sofa pillows. There is a curtain thrown over the back of the sofa, and another on the floor, to its R. Directly above the sofa is a small table with a lamp. Directly below it a coffee table. To L. of this, about C., a small ottoman. A little U. L. of this an armchair, and just U. L. of this, a medium-sized drum table. Pictures, curtains, drapes, may be added to complete the scene. NOTE FOR THE USE OF DIRECTORS PRODUCING THE PLAY. A diagram of the stage will be found on p. 81. This shows the arrangement of the scene substantially as used in the professional production. However, it should be pointed out that certain details of the set itself and certain articles of furniture may be omitted and altered for purposes of simplification. For example, the hallway U. L. need not be quite so large as is indicated on the diagram, and possibly the front door might be in view

of the audience. The large window to R. is scarcely used and may be easily omitted. While the stairs are necessary for a good deal of stage business, and the platform is most effective, a little ingenuity in arranging business might provide an easy substitute for the business now indicated as taking place on the landing. The L. wall of the set might be somewhat straighter than indicated on the diagram. The console-radio D. R. is not used. That was used in the original production simply as "dressing" and may be omitted. The hall table may also be omitted and a chair put in its place.

AT RISE: *Lizzie, the maid, known as Liz, is on-stage, holding a flower pot. After a second the front door slams, off U. R., and Agnes appears U. R. in hallway. She has been shopping and carries packages and a newspaper. Packages are two stocking boxes, which are never unwrapped, and a bag or larger package, in which are a small unglazed pot or pitcher, and a round can of smoking tobacco. The moment the door slams Liz turns up to see who is entering.*

AGNES. (*As she enters.*) Hiya, Liz. (*Liz puts flower pot on table above sofa.*)
LIZ. Hello, Mrs. Carol.
AGNES. (*Crossing down to table behind sofa. Puts packages on it.*) Curtains look nice. (*Crosses L. to chair R. of sideboard. Drops purse and gloves on chair.*)
LIZ. I think so. How was shopping? (*Folds curtain on back of sofa. Puts it back on sofa.*)
AGNES. (*Crossing L. to D.L. corner.*) Not bad—I only got one small dent on the right front fender.
LIZ. Your fault?
AGNES. Of course not. Men drivers!
LIZ. Did you call a cop?
AGNES. I didn't have to. It was a police car.
LIZ. Who was it?
AGNES. (*Putting can of tobacco on shelf D. L. corner.*) Murray Beck and Al Rocco. I told them. I said, "If you'd been cruising around the way you're supposed to instead of parking, I wouldn't have hit you." (*Crosses R. to above sofa.*)

LIZ. You were right, but don't tell me what they said!

AGNES. I hate men who laugh at logic. It's so anti-feminist.

LIZ. (*Picks up curtain from floor* R. *of sofa, folds it.*) Get all your shopping done?

AGNES. (*Crossing down to sofa. Sits.*) Well, I got the tobacco for Howard, and the paint for my ceramics, but then I lost the list, so I just took pot luck. (*Holding up newspaper.*) Did you see what Barney White put in the paper today?

LIZ. (*Leaning over* R. *side of sofa to see.*) She takes a nice picture. What does it say?

AGNES. It says, "Joan Carol, daughter of Mr. and Mrs. Howard G. Carol, who has been chosen to play the title role in this year's high school production of Victoria Regina. (*Liz crosses* L. *to up* L. *of sofa.*) The cast will meet today for the first time to read the play under the watchful eye of Mr. Guy Thompson, well-known New York actor."

LIZ. You mean the school got a New York actor to come out here and put on the play?

AGNES. Yes. The English teacher coaches the football team and both practices fall at the same time.

LIZ. Oh, by the way, did Mr. Carol make another speech today?

AGNES. Yes, at the high school for the children. Why?

LIZ. Barney White called and said, "Ask Mr. Carol if I can quote him on his speech."

AGNES. Oh, dear.

LIZ. Well, don't worry yet. It may not be one of his major speeches.

AGNES. Let's hope not.

LIZ. I don't understand why people keep asking him to speak.

AGNES. (*Rises, crosses* D. L. *with box of paint and newspaper.*) Well, Howard looks perfectly rational, and he is normally, but when he gets on a platform and looks down at that vast sea of faces, something happens to him.

LIZ. (*Crossing down* L. *to above drum table.*) Have you ever been able to figure out what?

AGNES. It's mixed up with a lot of things. Howard's worked very happily at the bank for a number of years. He leaves here every morning with his brief-case, comes home every night with his brief-case and a bag of jelly beans for me. . . . (*Sits* D. L. *bench.*) But he has never had a creative outlet.

LIZ. Having three daughters is pretty creative.

AGNES. Yes, but he's a man, and I guess every man wants a son.

LIZ. (*Crossing R. to table behind sofa to pick up flowers.*) Would you like some coffee?

AGNES. Love some. (*Front door slams, and Howard Carol enters. He carries brief-case and hat in one hand. Wears coat.*)

HOWARD. Hello, everybody. (*Crosses down L. to drum table. Puts brief-case on it. Agnes rises, crosses R. to Howard.*)

LIZ. Hello, Mr. Carol.

AGNES. (*Crossing R., carrying newspaper.*) Hello, dear. Have you seen this? (*Hands Howard newspaper.*)

HOWARD. Yeah, cute. Saw it at the office. (*Starts to put coat over back of armchair.*) I was just going to hang it up, Liz. (*Crosses up to closet, hangs coat.*)

LIZ. (*Crossing up, carrying flowers. Turns to Howard.*) You'd better, if you want some coffee.

HOWARD. That's a very good basis for mutual understanding.

LIZ. (*Crossing down L. to above drum table.*) He seems happy.

AGNES. Yes, that's sometimes a bad sign. (*Howard re-enters from closet. Agnes crosses up R. to C.*) How did the speech go, dear? (*Liz crosses L. to ceramic table L. Gets cardboard box.*)

HOWARD. The kids seemed to love it. (*Crosses L. to drum table.*)

LIZ. What was the speech about, Mr. Carol?

HOWARD. Manners, Liz.

LIZ. I'll get the coffee. (*Liz exits into kitchen L. Howard reaches into his brief-case, takes from it a bag of jelly beans.*)

HOWARD. (*Crossing R. to Agnes with jelly beans.*) For you, lady.

AGNES. Thank you. (*Takes bag. Howard and Agnes embrace.*)

HOWARD. You know I had to go to four places to get those today, and they don't make jelly beans the way they used to, either.

AGNES. Why do you suppose that is?

HOWARD. It's a lost art. There are no craftsmen left who hand roll them the way they used to. And have you noticed, black ones seem to be disappearing like buffalo.

AGNES. It's kind of sad to see the world change like this, isn't it?

HOWARD. It certainly is. (*Howard kisses Agnes.*)

AGNES. Darling, are you sure you spoke about manners?

HOWARD. (*Crossing L. to above drum table.*) Of course.

AGNES. What did you say?

HOWARD. Would you like to hear the speech?

AGNES. No, no. I don't want to hear the whole speech, just a brief résumé.

HOWARD. I said that most boys today are crude, unkempt, aggressive little monsters who have no respect for the opposite sex.

AGNES. Howard!

HOWARD. (*Crossing D. L. to small table. Puts brief-case on it. Agnes sits on R. arm of armchair.*) Well, it's the truth. But I don't blame this on the boys.

AGNES. You don't?

HOWARD. No, the girls are just as bad. They compete with the boys on every level. They race around, slapping them on the back, shouting at them on the street. No wonder the boys have no manners.

AGNES. Then the fault is with the girls?

HOWARD. No, the fault is with the parents; with the whole co-educational system that breeds this competition between boys and girls.

AGNES. Oh, now I see where this is leading. (*Rises.*) Girls are forced to compete and take exercise forty-five minutes twice a week and boys come to regard them as physical equals.

HOWARD. Well, that's part of it.

AGNES. Then you mean you don't think girls should be forced to take exercise?

HOWARD. I mean I don't think any of those kids should be forced to do anything that infringes on their dignity as human beings. They should be allowed the freedom of being themselves, of making their own decisions.

AGNES. Well, this smacks of progressive parenthood!

HOWARD. I've always thought of myself as a free-thinker as far as our kids are concerned.

AGNES. I know. I've got the scars to prove it. (*Howard pats Agnes' back. Agnes crosses up to chair R. of sideboard, takes off her jacket, puts it and jelly beans down.*) But, Howard, isn't there a contradiction here somewhere?

HOWARD. What do you mean? (*Crosses L. to table, takes papers from brief-case.*)

AGNES. On the one hand you complain about the lack of manners in young people and on the other you say, "If they don't

want manners, they shouldn't be forced to have them. Let them run wild."

HOWARD. (*Crossing R. to Agnes.*) No, no, no. If those kids weren't so beset by restrictions and taboos they wouldn't feel the need to break loose and run wild later on.

AGNES. How do you account for your youngest child?

HOWARD. Virginia?

AGNES. Yes.

HOWARD. There is no accounting for her. She's the exception that proves the rule.

AGNES. Cliché, darling.

HOWARD. Well, maybe, but it's true. (*Crossing L. to above drum table.*) I don't know why she is such a roughneck.

AGNES. Maybe if you showed as much interest in her as you do in Joan and Jeannie, you'd find out why.

HOWARD. I spend as much time on her as I do on the other two girls.

AGNES. (*Crossing L. to Howard.*) But not with the same attitude, Howard. You've never treated Virginia the way you did the two older kids.

HOWARD. (*Crosses down L. around table to armchair, sits.*) Oh, darling, let's not get off on that again.

AGNES. Well, if you don't practice what you preach, do you think it's wise to launch your theories from a public platform to a group of impressionable youngsters?

HOWARD. Listen. Those kids are perceptive and very mature. They knew exactly what I was trying to say, even if you don't. (*Agnes looks at Howard, shrugs.*)

JOAN. (*Off.*) Mom. . . . Mom! (*Front door slams.*)

AGNES. Yes, dear. Trouble?

JOAN. (*Enters front door U. R.*) Mom, it's terrible.

HOWARD. Hya, beautiful.

JOAN. (*Running down L. to Howard. Kisses him.*) Hello, Dad.

HOWARD. What's the matter?

JOAN. (*Crossing R. to sofa, puts her coat over L. back of sofa.*) I'm so mad I could die! (*Liz enters from kitchen, carrying coffee service, small cream pitcher, 2 cups and saucers. She crosses R. above armchair to coffee table and puts tray down on it.*)

AGNES. About what? (*Sits on sofa.*)

JOAN. She's an ugly old hag.

LIZ. Who is? (*Crosses up to* R. *of sofa.*)

JOAN. *Victoria Regina.* We just read the play. I won't do it, I won't, I won't!

LIZ. Hang up your coat.

JOAN. I'll do it in a minute.

LIZ. Right now.

JOAN. I'm going out again in a little while.

AGNES. Right now.

JOAN. But, gee, Mom.

HOWARD. Right now. (*Joan turns to look at Howard.*)

JOAN. Parents! (*Picks up coat. Crosses up to closet, hangs coat.* (*Agnes pours cup of coffee.*)

LIZ. (*Crossing* L.) Want a coke?

JOAN. Please, Liz, I need one. (*Liz, crossing* L. *to kitchen, takes one final look back at Agnes before she exits into kitchen.*) I don't see why Helen Hayes would take an old part like that. (*Crosses down to* C.)

AGNES. (*Rises. Crossing* L. *to Howard with cup of coffee.*) And mislead you.

JOAN. She keeps getting older in every scene. Do I have to do it?

AGNES. (*Crossing* R. *to Joan.*) Did you say you would? (*Crosses* R. *to sofa, sits. Pours herself cup of coffee.*)

JOAN. But there are girls at school so much better equipped to play old women. (*Liz enters from kitchen with a bottle of coke. Crosses* R. *to Joan, takes Joan's* L. *hand and puts bottle in it. Liz crosses to kitchen, exits.*)

AGNES. If you gave your word, there is only one honest course for you to follow. (*Liz, crossing* L. *to kitchen, nods approval.*)

JOAN. But I only took the part so I could get out of gym twice a week.

HOWARD. Huh? I don't quite follow that.

JOAN. (*Turns* L. *to Howard.*) Practice for the play and gym periods come at the same time every week.

HOWARD. And all this time I thought you were seeking culture.

JOAN. (*Crossing* L. *to Howard.*) So in view of that I don't think I should be forced to do Victoria, do you, Dad?

HOWARD. Unless you or this Mr. Thompson can find someone to take over the part before practice starts, you most certainly have to do what you promised. Right, dear?

AGNES. Right.

JOAN. (*Crossing* R. *to sofa. Sits on* L. *arm.*) Well. (*Front door slams.*) I don't understand that reasoning.
HOWARD. I'm sorry. (*Jeannie enters front door, carrying schoolbooks.*)
JEANNIE. Hello, everybody. (*Puts books on hall table, crosses down fast to Howard in armchair, puts her arm around his neck. She carries folded sheet of paper.*)
HOWARD. Hello, kitten.
JEANNIE. Hello, Daddy. Your speech today was simply wonderful.
HOWARD. I'm glad you liked it.
JEANNIE. All the girls at school say you must be the most terrific man in the world.
JOAN. Everybody adores you. They say they wish all their fathers were as liberal-minded as you are.
HOWARD. Well, it's just a question of saying the right thing at the right time.
JEANNIE. But it was such a courageous stand to take.
HOWARD. Oh, not really.
JEANNIE. (*Crosses* R. *to* C.) Well, we want you to know that every girl in the junior and senior classes support your stand and was moved to action by your stirring words.
HOWARD. You see, dear?
JEANNIE. (*Crossing* R. *above sofa.*) Will you sign this, Mother?
AGNES. What is it?
JEANNIE. (*Hands sheet of paper to Agnes.*) A petition.
JOAN. (*Turns to Jeannie.*) How many signatures have we got?
JEANNIE. Over a hundred. (*Crosses* L. *to* C.) And, Daddy, we want you to know, we'll back you against any and all opposition, regardless of the consequences.
AGNES. Howard, have you seen this?
HOWARD. What?
AGNES. (*Rises, crosses* L. *to* C. *and reads.*) "We the undersigned do herewith subscribe to the statement of Howard G. Carol—quote—'I would abolish gymnasium for girls because it infringes on their rights as individuals, and no one should be forced to do anything he doesn't want to do.'" Unquote. (*Unrolls paper, hands it to Howard. Crosses* L. *to* L. *of armchair.*)
HOWARD. Who put out this petition?
JEANNIE. The girls of the junior and senior classes.

HOWARD. But, kitten, you had no right to circulate a petition without asking me.
JOAN. We only quoted you. (*Crosses up to sideboard, puts coke bottle on it.*)
JEANNIE. (*Crossing L. to armchair.*) And you don't mind, do you?
HOWARD. Well, I didn't mean to make an issue out of it.
AGNES. Howard, you'd better do something to stop this.
JOAN. You mean you said it and didn't mean it? (*Crosses down to R. of Howard.*)
HOWARD. Well, I didn't mean to abolish gym for girls.
JEANNIE. Daddy!
JOAN. Daddy!
HOWARD. Basically it was a speech on manners.
JOAN. You mean you approve of gym for girls?
HOWARD. Well, not exactly.
AGNES. Howard, what did you say?
HOWARD. (*Hands petition to Joan and takes speech from his R. breast pocket and reads. Joan folds up petition and hands it to Jeannie, who puts it on table.*) I said, "perhaps one reason that young men do not conform to the rules of etiquette is that they see girls playing volley ball and basketball, thus losing sight of their femininity."
JOAN. (*Crossing down R. to D. R. of ottoman.*) And then you said it.
HOWARD. Yeah. Huh? Well, extemporaneously I may have said that perhaps one idea might be to change the method of gym for girls.
AGNES. What sort of change, dear?
HOWARD. Instead of those rough sports let them take long walks during those periods.
JEANNIE. I agree with you, Daddy.
JOAN. So do I. (*Sits on ottoman.*)
HOWARD. It stands to reason, Agnes, that competitive sports are too violent for young girls. (*Looks at Joan.*)
AGNES. (*Crossing R. to coffee table.*) I'll bet the school board is looking for the highest tree in town right now. (*Sits on sofa.*)
JEANNIE. I think Daddy absolutely put his finger on the root of the problem. (*Front door slams.*)

JOAN. I think your speech was positively breath-taking. (*Ginger enters front door, carrying school books.*)
GINGER. (*Looking off* R.) I think all men stink. (*Crosses down to sofa. Drops books on table behind sofa, drops coat over* L. *back of sofa.*) Hello, Pop.
HOWARD. Don't retract that remark just because I'm here.
GINGER. I wasn't going to.
AGNES. What's wrong between you and Tommy today?
GINGER. He always wants me to do something I don't want to do, because he doesn't want me to do something he doesn't want me to do. That's the trouble with men.
AGNES. Now you know that's true, Howard.
HOWARD. Yeah, it's confused enough to be.
JEANNIE. (*Crosses* L. *one step.*) What does Tommy want you to do?
GINGER. (*Crosses* L. *to* C.) Be a cheer leader.
HOWARD. What's wrong with that?
GINGER. Nothing, if you want to be a cheer leader. I just don't want to be a cheer leader.
AGNES. Then don't do it, darling. Don't let anyone infringe on your basic right.
GINGER. I won't.
JOAN. (*Turns to Ginger.*) Why don't you put a washer on that drip?
GINGER. (*Crosses* L. *a step.*) He's not a drip. He just frightens you because he's got brains.
JOAN. (*Turns* R. *on ottoman.*) He doesn't frighten Eddie, though, does he?
GINGER. Oh, your big four-letter man—b-o-r-e.
HOWARD. All right, that's enough. (*Ginger smirks at Joan, who turns front.*)
GINGER. (*Crossing* R. *to sofa.*) Where's Lizzie, Mom?
AGNES. Try the kitchen.
GINGER. (*Crosses* L. *to* U. R. *of ottoman.*) Ask Eddie what happened yesterday. (*Joan turns to Ginger. Ginger crosses* L. *to kitchen, exits.*)
JOAN. Gee, she gripes me. (*Jeannie looks at Howard, shrugs.*)
AGNES. Why? (*Jeannie crosses to* D. L. *corner, and sits on bench. She takes small jar from ceramic table, looks at it.*)
JOAN. (*Rises, crossing* R. *to* L. *of sofa.*) She has no dignity. She

runs around the halls at school like a wild gazelle. (*Crosses* L. *to* C. *To Howard.*) Yesterday during lunch hour she was wrestling with two boys—sophomores.

HOWARD. She's just high spirited, that's all.

JOAN. Everybody laughs at her, and it reflects on my standing among the seniors.

AGNES. That means you live in reflected laughter. I should think that would be a very happy situation.

JOAN. (*Crossing* R. *to sofa.*) I can see you don't understand, Mom.

AGNES. Take it up with your father. He's very understanding.

JOAN. (*Turns* L., *crosses to Howard.*) Daddy, do I have to do Victoria?

HOWARD. How did we get back to that?

JOAN. (*Sits on ottoman.*) I have to circulate petitions and I won't have time now that you've endorsed your stand.

JEANNIE. Don't you want to do it?

JOAN. No.

JEANNIE. Do you think maybe I could do it?

JOAN. (*Rises, runs* L. *to Jeannie upstage of armchair.*) Oh, you'd be much better than I would and you'd save my life.

JEANNIE. All right, I'll try. Let's go upstairs and read a couple of scenes. (*Joan and Jeannie cross* R. *to stairs.*)

JOAN. (*Crossing* R. *to table, behind sofa. Picks up books.*) Good. Then we'll tell Mr. Thompson about it tomorrow before classes.

JEANNIE. (*Joan and Jeannie begin to climb stairs.*) He's going to be down at the drug store later. Let's tell him then.

JOAN. All right.

AGNES. Just a minute, girls. (*Joan and Jeannie stop. Agnes rises, crosses up to* R. *of bottom of stairs.*) It seems to me you're both riding roughshod over a moral issue.

JOAN. What do you mean, Mother?

AGNES. Joan, Mr. Thompson chose you and you have no right to pass the part on to your sister or anybody else without his knowledge and consent.

JOAN. (*Crosses downstairs to Agnes.*) Even if I don't want to do it, and Jeannie does?

AGNES. That decision is not for you and Jeannie to settle between you.

JOAN. (*Crosses down to* U. R. *of ottoman. Jeannie crosses downstairs.*) But Daddy said nobody should be forced ——
AGNES. Howard. . . .
HOWARD. I know what I said, but that has nothing to do with this.
JOAN. You mean you were wrong?
HOWARD. No, but you can't apply one rule to every issue.
JEANNIE. (*Crossing down to* L. *of Howard.*) Not even if they're related issues?
HOWARD. Sometimes, kitten, but not this time.
JOAN. Why not, Daddy?
HOWARD. Well, because, darling, you gave your word before I made the speech. (*Agnes crosses down to behind* L. *end of sofa.*)
JEANNIE. But I want the part and I don't want to take gym.
JOAN. So doesn't that make everything all right?
HOWARD. Agnes . . .
AGNES. (*Sits on* L. *back of sofa.*) Don't drag me into this.
JOAN. If I ask Mr. Thompson and he says yes, is it all right then, Daddy?
HOWARD. Oh, all right, ask him. But be sure you don't force him.
JOAN. Oh, Daddy, we won't.
JEANNIE. Thank you, Daddy.
JOAN. You're wonderful. (*Joan and Jeannie kiss Howard. Jeannie musses Howard's hair. Girls run up to foot of stairs.*) Oh, call me when Eddie comes, will you, Mom? (*Joan and Jeannie exit upstairs, giggling.*)
AGNES. All right. Well, dear, you're certainly developing a great sense of organized chaos.
HOWARD. It's just that social relationships are a little difficult at times.
AGNES. (*Crosses* L. *Sits on ottoman.*) You know, Howard, there are times when everybody does things they don't want to do.
HOWARD. Did you get a dent on the right front fender of my car today?
AGNES. (*Rises.*) Yes.
HOWARD. How?
AGNES. Doing something I didn't want to do. (*Crossing* L. *above armchair to* D. L. *corner.*) I ran into a police car. (*Howard groans.*) Oh, Barney White's been calling you. (*Sits on bench* D. L.)

HOWARD. What did he want?

AGNES. It seems he wants to quote you on your speech.

HOWARD. Oh. . . . (*Rises, crosses up to phone on phone table* U.)

AGNES. He'll probably want a picture, too.

HOWARD. I haven't got a picture. (*Dials number.*)

AGNES. Maybe you ought to have some made?

HOWARD. Maybe I should. You get so upset over these things. (*Into phone.*) Hello, Barn. . . . Howie . . . did you call me? . . . Well, it was nothing.

AGNES. Oh, come now.

HOWARD. (*Into phone.*) Well, the kids sort of amplified it. . . . You what? . . . Where'd you get ahold of a copy of the petition? . . . They did, huh? (*Looks upstairs. Sits in chair* R. *of phone table.*) Well, I suggested that they go for long walks during those periods. You know what George Washington said, "Long walks are the best exercise."

AGNES. He must have said something else.

HOWARD. (*Into phone.*) Sure, Barney, go ahead and print it. Can't do any harm. (*Rises.*) Thanks for calling. (*Hangs up.*) Seems to have created quite a stir. (*Crosses down to above drum table. Picks up petition, reads it.*)

AGNES. Uh-huh.

HOWARD. (*Crosses* L. *to Agnes.*) You don't understand this, darling, because you're not as close to the problems of the young people as I am.

AGNES. No. I'm in the house all day. (*Front doorbell rings.*) I'll get it, Liz. (*Rises, crosses* U. R., *stopping behind Howard.*) You know, Howard, this kind of reasoning can lead to a terrible disease called "Hoof-in-the-mouth." (*Crosses* U. R. *to front door.*)

HOWARD. (*Following Agnes.*) Even boys aren't as aggressive and overt as some girls today. (*Looks upstairs.*)

AGNES. (*Off* U. R.) Now really, Howard.

EDDIE. (*Off* U. R.) Hya, Mrs. Carol. (*Howard winces, crosses down to armchair.*)

AGNES. (*Off. Mimicking Eddie.*) Hya, Eddie. . . . Come in. (*Eddie enters from front door, followed by Agnes.*)

EDDIE. Hya, Mr. Carol.

HOWARD. Hello, Eddie. Sit down. (*Sits in armchair.*)

EDDIE. Thanks. (*Sits on sofa.*)

AGNES. (*Calling upstairs.*) Joan, Eddie is here.

JOAN. (*Off, upstairs.*) I'll be down in a minute, Mother.

AGNES. (*Imitating Joan.*) All right. (*Crosses down to* C. *Howard puts petition on drum table.*)

EDDIE. (*Sprawled comfortably on sofa.*) What do you think of a guy coming all the way from New York to try and steal my girl?

AGNES. (*Stops* R. *of Howard.*) I beg your pardon?

EDDIE. This actor. That's why he gave my girl the part in the play. But he better not fool around with my girl. (*Settles back on sofa.*) I guess he doesn't realize I'm the big man in this school. (*Howard picks up Time magazine from drum table, looks into it.*)

AGNES. (*Looks at Howard.*) I guess not. (*Crosses to* D. L. *corner below armchair. Sits on bench, begins working on her ceramic. Eddie sits up on sofa, crosses and recrosses his legs.*)

EDDIE. (*Rises.*) Hey, Mr. Carol, that was some speech you made in school today.

HOWARD. (*Smiles at Eddie, looks at Agnes.*) Thanks, Eddie.

EDDIE. (*Crosses to* C.) After school all the guys were bowing to the girls—(*Bows.*) and holding their coats. (*To Agnes.*) It was a regular eighteenth century ball.

AGNES. I'll bet.

EDDIE. (*Crossing* L. *above armchair to Agnes.*) I got so swept away I opened the car door for Joan. (*To Howard.*) I never did that before in my life. (*To Agnes.*) She was so shocked she staggered.

HOWARD. She's just not accustomed to gentility. (*Reads magazine. Eddie does a take.*)

EDDIE. Oh. (*Eddie looks from Howard, who is reading, to Agnes, who is painting. Folds arms and brushes his hair. Then he runs up* R. *to foot of stairs, looks up. Crosses down* C. *to* U. L. *of sofa, and bursts into several hot licks of music—humming bits of jazz—at the end of which, he falls on his back on sofa. Howard takes a drink of his coffee, his hand shaking nervously. Eddie sits up.*) That always makes my father nervous.

HOWARD. Yeah. How's your father's ulcer, Eddie?

EDDIE. (*Rises. Crosses* L. *to ottoman, puts* L. *foot on it.*) Mr. Carol, I knew there was something I had to tell you.

HOWARD. What is it?

EDDIE. Football practice starts tomorrow.

HOWARD. (*To Agnes.*) Did you hear that, dear?

AGNES. No, I'm tuned out.
EDDIE. (*Takes foot off ottoman.*) Sure does. So get your tickets early or you'll never see me run.
HOWARD. How's the team going to be this year?
EDDIE. Well, as I said to the coach this afternoon, I said, "Just put ten other kids on the field and give me the ball."
AGNES. That was nice of you.
EDDIE. (*Looks at Agnes.*) I'm murder on a field.
AGNES. I think you're murder off.
EDDIE. Thanks. (*Howard looks at Eddie. Eddie looks at Agnes. Howard looks away, amused.*) Did I tell you how many colleges are trying to get me?
HOWARD. Not yet.
EDDIE. (*Starts L. to Howard.*) I got the list right here. (*Ginger and Liz enter from kitchen. Ginger crosses to U. R. of ottoman, Liz crosses to U. L. of drum table.*)
GINGER. Hya, muscle-head.
AGNES. Virginia.
EDDIE. Hya, kid. (*Breaks R., crosses to sofa.*)
GINGER. What are you doing, showing Mom and Pop your scrap book?
EDDIE. Why don't you stop? (*Sits on sofa.*)
LIZ. Tell them what happened yesterday.
GINGER. No. It will embarrass him.
EDDIE. It was an accident.
GINGER. It was not.
HOWARD. What happened?
GINGER. He insulted me.
EDDIE. I did not.
GINGER. You did so, you reactionary.
HOWARD. Never mind that. What happened?
GINGER. (*Turns back to Howard.*) He called Tommy Green a sissy.
HOWARD. I don't see how that concerns you.
LIZ. (*Crossing D. R. to L. of drum table.*) Let her finish.
HOWARD. Finish.
GINGER. Every time one boy wants to insult another, he calls him a sissy. And by that they imply that girls are inferior to boys.
LIZ. And they're not.
AGNES. I see your point.

HOWARD. Pass.

GINGER. So yesterday after school, when the track team was out I challenged him to a hundred yard dash.

EDDIE. I didn't want to race a girl.

GINGER. At first he just laughed, but after I needled him for a while, he said he'd show me.

HOWARD. Well, what happened?

GINGER. (*Looking at Eddie.*) I ran him into the ground.

AGNES. You mean you beat him?

GINGER. By five yards.

EDDIE. Three yards. (*Howard laughs. Ginger crosses down to Howard.*)

AGNES. Howard.

HOWARD. That's the funniest thing I ever heard.

EDDIE. I had a bad foot. (*Joan and Jeannie come downstairs. Joan descends to floor level, Jeannie stays a step or two above her.*)

GINGER. You did not.

JOAN. I'm ready, Eddie.

EDDIE. (*Rises, crosses up to arch, limping.*) Come on, let's go.

JOAN. (*Stops Eddie.*) Eddie, what's wrong with your foot?

EDDIE. I sprained it.

JOAN. When?

EDDIE. Yesterday.

JOAN. But you weren't limping this afternoon.

EDDIE. Come on, it's late. (*Exits to front door.*)

JEANNIE. (*Crossing downstairs and down L. to Howard.*) 'Bye, Daddy. (*Kisses Howard. Joan takes her coat from closet, puts it on.*)

HOWARD. 'Bye, darling, and, Joanie, you get back here in time for dinner.

JOAN. All right.

HOWARD. 'Cause if you don't I'll send Virginia out to run you and your athlete down. (*Howard, Jeannie, Ginger, Liz and Agnes laugh.*)

JOAN. Daddy. (*Exits to front door.*)

JEANNIE. (*Crossing up to closet, blows Howard a kiss.*) 'Bye. (*Gets coat from closet, exits to front door. Howard, Agnes and Ginger ad lib. good-byes.*)

HOWARD. (*Looks at Ginger, stops laughing.*) As for you, Miss . . .

GINGER. What?

HOWARD. Don't ever do a thing like that again.

GINGER. Why not?

HOWARD. It's unladylike.

GINGER. But, Pop, I *can* beat him.

HOWARD. Never mind that. From now on try to remember you're a girl.

GINGER. (*Crossing* L. *to above drum table.*) I wish I were a man.

LIZ. (*Crosses* D. R. *a step.*) Would you rather have him live with the delusion girls are inferior and be disillusioned later in life? (*Ginger picks up Ms. of Howard's speech from drum table.*)

HOWARD. I don't care anything about him, Elizabeth. I'm talking about her.

GINGER. Is this a copy of your speech?

HOWARD. Yes, it is.

GINGER. May I read it?

HOWARD. Sure, if you want to.

GINGER. Thanks. (*Takes Ms., crosses* R. *to* U. R. *of armchair. Stops.*) Pop?

HOWARD. Huh?

GINGER. Do you love me?

HOWARD. Of course I love you.

GINGER. I'm glad, 'cause you're really going to have to. (*Runs up and exits upstairs. Liz crosses* R. *to sofa, gets Ginger's coat, crosses up to closet, hangs up coat. Then crosses down* C.)

HOWARD. What do you suppose that means?

AGNES. I don't know, but they're going to have to take Virginia for very long walks.

HOWARD. Oh, Lizzie . . .

LIZ. (*Stops* U. R. *of armchair.*) Yeah?

HOWARD. This is mere curiosity, but didn't I just see you hang up Virginia's coat?

LIZ. Yes, you did. Why?

HOWARD. I don't mean to offend you, but I just wondered. Her above all?

AGNES. "She," dear.

HOWARD. "She"—doesn't sound right. She above all?

LIZ. Why shouldn't I hang up her coat?

HOWARD. I just don't want you to spoil her.

AGNES. Nobody is spoiling her, Howard.

LIZ. You spoiled the other two.
HOWARD. That's silly.
LIZ. It's not silly.
AGNES. She's right.
HOWARD. How?
LIZ. They kiss you and bully you into doing anything they like.
AGNES. But the minute Virginia tries to do something, then you become the father.
LIZ. And I don't see why she should be handicapped just because she wasn't a boy.
AGNES. That's why she hung up her coat.
LIZ. So there.
HOWARD. (*Waves his hand in despair.*) I never seem to win one of these things. (*Liz crosses* U. L. *to sideboard and sets something—doily—straight.*) What is it, my choice of words or lack of phrasing, or what? Elizabeth—(*Liz crosses down to* U. L. *of drum table.*) from here on out, she has my consent to run against five horses at Hialeah Park every day.
LIZ. She'd win. (*Front doorbell. Liz crosses* R. *to front door.*)
HOWARD. (*To Agnes.*) If you'd listen to me we wouldn't have had all this trouble about gym for girls and running foot races.
AGNES. What do you mean?
HOWARD. I told you three times, have a son, but no, you wouldn't listen. (*Front door slams. Liz and Tommy Green enter.*)
LIZ. (*Crossing* L. *to foot of stairs.*) It's Tommy Green.
HOWARD. Hello, Tommy. Come in.
AGNES. Hello, Tommy.
TOMMY. (*Crossing down to* C.) Hello, Mrs. Carol . . . Mr. Carol.
LIZ. (*Crossing upstairs a few steps.*) Ginger . . .
GINGER. (*Off.*) Will you come up for a minute, Liz?
LIZ. Tommy's here.
GINGER. (*Off.*) Tell him to wait.
LIZ. (*To Tommy.*) Wait. (*Exits upstairs.*)
TOMMY. Yes, ma'am.
HOWARD. Sit down, Tommy.
TOMMY. Thank you, sir. (*Crosses down to* L. *end of sofa, sits.*) I heard your speech today, Mr. Carol.
AGNES. Everybody did.
TOMMY. And I must say it was quite fascinating.

HOWARD. Thanks, Tommy. I understand football practice starts tomorrow.
TOMMY. Yes, sir.—There are a few points in that speech I'd like to discuss with you.
HOWARD. You don't play football, do you, Tommy?
TOMMY. No, sir. Mr. Carol, you said . . .
HOWARD. I wish I were back in school. I'd run that Eddie Davis ragged. Did I ever tell you about my football days?
TOMMY. Not recently.
HOWARD. Oh. (*Liz enters downstairs, followed by Ginger, who carries a small book. Liz crosses L. to sideboard, picks up coke bottle, and exits into kitchen.*)
GINGER. Hya, Tommy. (*Tommy rises, crosses up to Ginger, below foot of stairs.*)
TOMMY. Hya, Ginger.
GINGER. What do you want?
TOMMY. Well, I thought maybe you'd like to walk down to the drug store and take a look at the New York actor.
GINGER. (*Indicating her book.*) No, thanks. I'm doing some research on individual rights.
TOMMY. Oh. Well, there's something I want to tell you.
GINGER. Well, tell me.
TOMMY. You don't have to be a cheer leader if you don't want to.
GINGER. Thanks.
TOMMY. I believe everyone should be allowed to do what he wants to do.
HOWARD. Hey, hey, hey! Just a minute, young man.
TOMMY. (*Turns L. to Howard.*) Yes, sir?
HOWARD. (*Rises, crossing U. to L. of Ginger.*) Are you the one responsible for teaching this human dynamo she's the equal of anyone, anywhere?
GINGER. No one had to teach me that.
HOWARD. I wasn't talking to you, Flash.
GINGER. Go ahead, Tommy. Tell him what you believe.
TOMMY. Well, sir, in principle I believe anyone should be allowed to compete on any level they choose.
HOWARD. I see. . . .
TOMMY. (*Ginger looks at Tommy admiringly.*) To deprive any person, man or woman, of his constitutional rights is to infringe upon the fundamental law of the land and deny them their basic

freedom as set down by our founding fathers, when they said, "We hold these truths to be self-evident; that all men are created equal . . ."

HOWARD. Well, thanks, Tommy. (*Crosses down to* R. *of armchair. Tommy follows Howard. Ginger moves down* R., *sits on* L. *arm of sofa.*)

TOMMY. In other words, it is the privilege and the responsibility of every American to think the way he likes, act the way he likes, talk the way he likes, vote the way he likes, and to worship as he pleases.

HOWARD. That's very true, but . . . (*Crosses down, Tommy following.*)

TOMMY. And I would like to say, regardless of race, color, creed or sex, there are no second-class citizens of these United States, and we, as liberty-loving people, must seek out the evil, never retreat from the heat of battle, and destroy the forces of reaction that impede progress. (*Howard turns back to see if more speech is coming.*) That speech got me last year's debating medal. (*Ginger rises, crosses* R., *sits in* C. *of sofa.*)

HOWARD. I can see why. (*Crosses* L. *to* D. L. *corner, sits on bench.*)

TOMMY. (*Crossing* L. *to above armchair.*) I wrote it myself.

AGNES. Tommy . . .

TOMMY. Yes, ma'am?

AGNES. You prefaced all that by saying, "in principle, I believe . . ." but the point is how do you feel about Virginia running foot races against Eddie?

TOMMY. Mrs. Carol, I don't feel she should do it.

GINGER. What?

TOMMY. I can't help it. That's the way I feel.

GINGER. Then you don't believe what you've always said.

TOMMY. (*Crossing* R. *to* C.) Yes I do.

GINGER. But you mean I shouldn't compete against Eddie?

TOMMY. (*Crossing* R. *to sofa.*) Sure you should with Eddie, or with any other man. (*Sits on* L. *of sofa.*) But you should compete as a girl, not a boy.

GINGER. If everybody is equal what difference does it make how I compete?

TOMMY. It makes a difference because men and women are

equal, but not the same. (*Front.*) If there weren't any difference I'd go out on dates with Eddie Davis.

GINGER. What for? I can run faster than he can.

TOMMY. Look, Ginger, that's not why I like you.

GINGER. Why do you like me?

TOMMY. Because you're a girl.

GINGER. And that's why you don't want me to compete against Eddie?

TOMMY. Yes.

GINGER. (*Rises, backs* R. *to* R. *end of sofa.*) Then you don't think of me as an equal.

TOMMY. Sure I do, but I think of you as a girl first.

GINGER. Well, I want to be an equal first. (*Crosses* U. *and* L. *above sofa to* U. L. *of it.*)

TOMMY. (*Rises, crosses* U. L.) Then go ahead, I don't want to talk about it any more.

GINGER. (*Crossing* L. *to Tommy.*) You don't want to talk about it because you know you're wrong.

TOMMY. (*Front.*) I want to go home and think. 'Bye, Mrs. Carol . . . Sir. (*Tommy crosses* U. R. *and exits front door.*)

HOWARD and AGNES. 'Bye, Tommy.

GINGER. (*Following Tommy.*) Wait a minute. You can't get out of it that easy. (*Exits front door.*)

HOWARD. (*Rises, crosses* R. *above armchair.*) Virginia seems to have discovered a new sex—boys, girls, and equals. (*Sits in armchair. Ginger re-enters front door.*)

GINGER. (*Crossing down to* U. L. *of sofa.*) I worry about that boy. (*Agnes rises.*) He's terribly confused. (*Crosses down to sofa, sits on* L. *arm.*)

AGNES. (*Crossing* R. *to* U. C.) Well, never mind, darling. One of you will straighten out.

GINGER. Pop, don't you think it's wonderful I can run faster than anyone else in the whole school?

HOWARD. No, I don't, Virginia. I agree with Tommy. You shouldn't be trying to run faster than anyone else. (*Agnes crosses* R. *to sofa and chucks Virginia under chin, then sits on sofa.*)

GINGER. (*Looks at Agnes, then back to Howard.*) Oh, Pop, did you really mean all the things you said in that speech today? (*Front doorbell.*)

HOWARD. If I didn't mean them I wouldn't have said them. (*Liz enters from kitchen, crosses* R. *to front door.*)
GINGER. You heard what he said, Mom. (*Rises, crosses* L. *to Howard, musses his hair. Crosses up to stairs, exits. Howard rises, crosses up to sideboard.*)
HOWARD. That kid will be the death of me. (*Liz enters from front door.*)
LIZ. It's Mr. Wilson, the high school principal. (*Liz crosses* L., *exits into kitchen. Agnes rises.*)
HOWARD. Hello, Bob, come on in.
WILSON. (*Entering from front door.*) Hello, Agnes . . . Howie. (*Wilson and Howard shake hands.*)
HOWARD. Can I take your coat?
WILSON. I can only stay a minute. (*Drops hat on table behind sofa.*)
HOWARD. How about a drink?
WILSON. Thanks, no.—Let's get right to the point, shall we?
HOWARD. Yeah, fine.
WILSON. (*Crossing* L. *two steps.*) First, I would like you to do me a favor. If in some wild moment, I should ever ask you to speak again—please turn me down. (*Takes coat off, crosses* R., *drops coat over* L. *back of sofa. Agnes sits in* C. *of sofa.*)
HOWARD. I will be delighted.
WILSON. Thank you. Now on that disagreeable note, let's go forward, shall we? (*Takes Ms. petition from pocket.*) Have you seen this petition? (*Unrolls petition a little.*)
HOWARD. Yes, I have.
WILSON. Doesn't it make you shudder? (*Folds petition, puts it back in pocket.*)
HOWARD. No, it doesn't. (*Crosses* D. L. *to* L. *of drum table.*)
WILSON. Obviously you haven't heard about Virginia. (*Howard turns* R.) This afternoon she reported for the boys' football team.
AGNES. (*Rises.*) Oh, no!
WILSON. Oh, yes.
HOWARD. (*Crossing* R. *to Wilson.*) Football? Agnes, call her down here. (*Wilson crosses* L. *to above armchair.*)
AGNES. (*Crosses up to foot of stairs. Calling.*) Virginia.
HOWARD. (*Crossing* R. *to Wilson.*) We'll settle this in five minutes.
GINGER. (*Off.*) Yes, Mom?

HOWARD. (*Crossing up to foot of stairs.*) Come down here.

AGNES. But surely even if she insists on playing, there is no problem about stopping her.

WILSON. (*Leaning on back of armchair.*) Unfortunately, Agnes, there's no rule that says she can't play.

HOWARD. Well, you can declare girls ineligible.

AGNES. On what grounds? (*Wilson crosses down to L. of drum table.*) I'm not defending her, Howard, I'm just asking.

HOWARD. Do me a favor and don't ask questions like that in front of her. (*Ginger enters downstairs.*)

GINGER. Did you call me, Pop?

HOWARD. I certainly did. Sit down, Virginia.

GINGER. (*Crossing down to L. end of sofa.*) Yes, sir. Hello, Mr. Wilson. (*Sits C. of sofa. Agnes crosses D. R. to R. end of sofa, stands.*)

HOWARD. (*Crosses D. to L. of sofa.*) Virginia, what is this foolishness about your playing football?

GINGER. You mustn't shout at children, Pop. You must reason with them.

AGNES. (*Sitting on sofa R. of Ginger.*) Darling, what on earth made you do a thing like this?

GINGER. Pop's speech. I've always wanted to play football and he said, "Everybody should be allowed to do what they want to do."

HOWARD. No, no. No, I said, "Nobody should be forced to do what they don't want to do."

WILSON. What's the difference?

HOWARD. There is a great deal of difference.

GINGER. Well, I don't want to not play football.

HOWARD. Well, you're not going to.

GINGER. You're being arbitrary, Pop.

AGNES. But, darling, don't you realize it's a dangerous game? You might get hurt.

GINGER. I'd make a great half-back.

HOWARD. Virginia, what makes you think you can play football?

GINGER. (*Rises. To Howard.*) I can run, I can kick. You were a great half-back, and there's no reason why I can't be just as good as you were.

AGNES. Look, Virginia. Your father . . . (*Pulls Ginger down to sofa.*)
HOWARD. Virginia, you're not going to play football, and that's final.
GINGER. You didn't object to Jeannie playing in *Victoria*.
HOWARD. That's different.
GINGER. It's not different.
WILSON. Young lady, you'll force me to pass a regulation forbidding girls to partake in any sport.
GINGER. (*Rises. Crossing* L. *to* C.) All right, Mr. Wilson, go ahead. But if I'm denied my athletic rights I'll refuse to attend classes.
WILSON. Then I'll have you expelled.
GINGER. (*Crossing* L. *to above armchair.*) Let me remind you, sir, the Constitution and the Bill of Rights guarantee every American citizen life, liberty and the pursuit of happiness.
WILSON. Are you going to let her talk to me like that?
HOWARD. What? No. (*Crossing* L. *to Ginger.*) Virginia, surely you understand we're only thinking of you. (*Sits on back of armchair.*)
GINGER. It's not really me you're thinking of, Pop. It's yourself.
HOWARD. What do you mean by that?
GINGER. You're afraid if I go out for the team people will laugh at you.
HOWARD. Why should they laugh at me?
WILSON. Because of that preposterous speech you made this afternoon. (*Howard rises.*)
GINGER. You're putting your vanity above my freedom of choice.
HOWARD. I'm doing no such thing.
WILSON. Yes, you are.
HOWARD. Whose side are you on?
WILSON. My side. I think you're both wrong.
GINGER. Sure, because you're afraid this change will lead to a lot of other changes in school.
AGNES. Believe me, Virginia, that is not what I'm worried about. (*Howard turns* R.)
GINGER. (*Crossing* R. *below Howard to* L. *end of sofa.*) Mom, you're being old-fashioned.
AGNES. I am?

GINGER. Yes. You've accepted the theory that women shouldn't compete with men. (*To Howard.*) Well, *I* haven't.

HOWARD. (*Crossing R. to Ginger.*) Virginia, if you persist in this nonsense, I'll cut off your allowance.

GINGER. I don't need any money, I'm in training. (*Wilson holds hand to his face.*) You see, Pop, I don't ask to be on the team. All I ask is a chance to try out for it.

AGNES. (*Holding hand out to Ginger. Pulls her down to sofa.*) But, darling, I don't think you're equipped to play football.

GINGER. (*Sits on sofa L. of Agnes.*) You can't say that until you've given me a chance.

AGNES. But you're a girl.

GINGER. Lots of athletes are.

HOWARD. (*Kneels L. of Ginger.*) They don't play football against men.

GINGER. Because men won't let them. You're supposed to be sports, and all the time you're afraid we'll be equal to you.

AGNES. Or better than you. (*Howard rises, crosses L. to R. of ottoman.*)

HOWARD. Well, there seems to be only one solution.

WILSON. And what, may I ask, is that?

HOWARD. Go upstairs, Virginia, if you don't mind. We'll discuss this later.

GINGER. Yes, sir. Thanks, Mom. (*Kisses Agnes on cheek.*)

AGNES. You're welcome, Virginia.

GINGER. (*Rises.*) Good evening, Mr. Wilson. (*To Howard.*) I'm going to bed tonight at eight o'clock, just like the coach ordered. (*Agnes rises. Ginger exits toward front door, and returns carrying pair of football pants stuffed with a jersey and shoulder guards in one hand, and a football helmet in other.*)

HOWARD. (*Crossing up C.*) What have you got there? (*Agnes crosses up to stairs.*)

GINGER. My football equipment. (*Exits upstairs, followed by Agnes.*)

HOWARD. Virginia, you can't practice in the house.

WILSON. Well, what's your solution?

HOWARD. (*Crossing down to behind sofa.*) I think some of the things she says make a great deal of sense.

WILSON. I might have expected you to say that.

HOWARD. What does the coach think?

WILSON. (*Crossing down to armchair.*) We don't pay the coach to think. (*Sits in armchair.*) We pay the coach to teach English.

HOWARD. (*Crossing down to sofa. Sits.*) That's fine talk from an educator, Bob.

WILSON. Howie, you certainly don't believe what you said this afternoon.

HOWARD. Bob, don't you think that a child should be allowed to seek his own fulfillment?

WILSON. (*Rises. Crossing R. behind sofa to R. arm of sofa.*) Not if it means complete chaos.

HOWARD. If chaos in your school is the result of the searching and probing of a fourteen-year-old, then your foundations are rotten.

WILSON. Now, wait a minute. (*Sits on R. end of sofa.*) I would like to follow your reasoning through to its illogical conclusion. If she wanted to burn down the house, would you let her do it?

HOWARD. No. Of course not. I'd try to show her why it was wrong.

WILSON. Why?

HOWARD. Because if she burned down the house she'd have no place to live.

WILSON. Suppose she only wanted to burn out one room?

HOWARD. It would depend upon which room. If she felt she had to do it, I might just let her. And if she believes she can play football, I think she deserves a chance to try.

WILSON. You do?

HOWARD. I certainly do. I made a statement, and by gosh, I'll stick to it.

WILSON. You don't think that's wrong?

HOWARD. That's not for you or me to decide, Bob. It's for her to find out. Maybe when she has her nose rubbed in the dirt a couple of afternoons, she'll emerge a normal, healthy girl.

WILSON. You realize, of course, I could stop this by expelling her.

HOWARD. Sure you could, if you'd get a kick out of demonstrating naked authority.

WILSON. Oh, I'm not going to. (*Rises. Stands by R. arm of sofa. Agnes enters downstairs, stands on them.*) I don't blame Virginia. It's been my experience that in dealing with people like you, the parent is in much greater need of education than the child.

AGNES. (*Crossing downstairs to below newel post.*) Well, how are we doing down here?

HOWARD. Fine, darling, just fine.

WILSON. (*Crossing L. above sofa to Agnes.*) Oh, yes. The girls demand that gym be abolished. Virginia wants to play football. I have been plagued by boys who want to smoke in class. I caught two kids necking in the corridor. Because of *his* little speech my life has become a model of exquisite misery.

HOWARD. Well, Bob, the problems of modern education aren't simple, you know.

WILSON. (*In great anger, picks up his hat from table above sofa.*) Agnes, it is my considered opinion that your husband is a blight on the American academic scene—(*Crosses up C. To Howard, over his shoulder.*) and a full-grown juvenile delinquent. (*Slaps hat on his head and exits to R. front door.*)

HOWARD. (*Rises, laughing.*) I'd better go after him. He forgot his coat.

AGNES. (*Takes coat. Crossing up to closet. Hangs coat.*) Don't be silly. He won't get cold for a long time. (*Howard crosses L. to phone table.*) I'll have one of the kids take it to school tomorrow.

HOWARD. Did you hear the way that kid talked to Bob Wilson?

AGNES. (*Crossing down to arch.*) Do you think maybe Virginia really is part gazelle? (*Ginger enters downstairs, wearing football pants.*)

GINGER. Mom.

AGNES. Yes, dear.

GINGER. Where's the sewing box?

AGNES. Ask Lizzie.

GINGER. (*Crossing L. to kitchen.*) I've got to take a tuck in these pants. (*Exits into kitchen.*)

HOWARD. (*Crosses L. to below sideboard. Calling off into kitchen.*) Hold that line. (*Crosses R. a few steps.*) I hope Eddie Davis tackles her so hard her teeth rattle for a week.

AGNES. (*Crossing D. L. to D. L. corner.*) I hope she beats Eddie Davis out for his position, is elected Captain of the team, and makes the All American.

HOWARD. You can't make the All American till you're in college.

AGNES. Excuse me. (*Sits on D. L. corner bench. Ginger, followed by Liz, enters from kitchen, glass of milk in her R. hand, holding her pants up with her L. hand, a carrot in her teeth. They walk in*

step, Liz carrying sewing box. As Ginger passes Howard she makes a haughty toss of the carrot greens over her shoulder. They cross R. and upstairs. On lower landing Liz makes the three ring sign to Agnes and exits.)

HOWARD. (*Crossing R. to foot of stairs.*) Isn't that ridiculous? (*Agnes laughs.*) What are you laughing at? (*Crosses down to armchair, sits.*)

AGNES. You know perfectly well you're proud and delighted and would give your elk's tooth to see her play. (*Howard picks up Time magazine from drum table.*)

HOWARD. You must think I'm insane.

AGNES. I do. I think you're the most wonderfully insane man I know, and I wouldn't have any one else for the father of my children.

HOWARD. I hope not. (*Laughs.*) You know, this might just make the front page of the paper in the morning.

AGNES. Right next to your famous last words.

HOWARD. Oh, my gosh! (*Throws magazine in the air. As Howard rises*)

CURTAIN FALLS

ACT II

SCENE 1: *The same.*

AT RISE: *Front door slams. Liz enters from front door, crosses to closet, hangs up her coat.*

LIZ. Mrs. Carol.
AGNES. (*Entering from kitchen.*) Liz? (*Crosses to D. R. of sideboard.*)
LIZ. (*Crossing L. to Agnes.*) How's the roast?
AGNES. They'll eat it. Any news?
LIZ. Not yet. They just finished their last scrimmage.
AGNES. But she must know by now whether or not she made the team?
LIZ. (*Crossing down to sofa, sits on L. arm.*) No. Mr. Blake doesn't tell any one he's cut until after they hit the locker room today.
AGNES. Tell them they're what?
LIZ. Cut. When the coach walks up to you and says, "You're cut," it means you are no longer a member of the team.
AGNES. (*Taking off her apron.*) How do you know all these things?
LIZ. I'm an authority. (*Agnes laughs, crosses up to sideboard, puts her apron down.*) I've been to all the practice sessions and know every play by heart.
AGNES. So does Howard. (*Liz rises, crosses L. to ottoman.*)
LIZ. Pretty good coach, that Blake. (*Puts L. foot up on ottoman.*) Fast running game from the "T" but not much razzle-dazzle.
AGNES. That's a shame.
LIZ. Good ground game. No air arm. (*Front door slams. Liz steps down from ottoman.*) Maybe this is her. (*Liz and Agnes cross up C. Joan from front door, carrying petition.*)
JOAN. Hello.
LIZ. Have you heard any news?
JOAN. (*Crossing L., stops at kitchen door.*) How could I? This was gym day. (*Exits into kitchen.*)

LIZ. (*Looks at Agnes. Crossing* L., *shouting off to kitchen.*) Don't you take gym during school?
AGNES. No, dear, she upholds her father's ideals by cutting gym in protest, and spends two afternoons a week in detention. She fixes them.
LIZ. (*Shouting off to kitchen.*) Didn't you go over to the football field to cheer Ginger on?
JOAN. (*Off.*) I most certainly did not.
LIZ. Why not?
JOAN. (*Entering from kitchen with coke, her coat over her arm.*) The girls in the senior class have declared the football field "off limits." (*Crosses* R., *puts coke and petition on table behind sofa. Then crosses up to closet, hangs up coat.*)
AGNES. Sounds like the senior class of 1890.
JOAN. You can laugh if you like, but if Daddy lets Ginger get on the squad we'll boycott the games. (*Agnes crosses* R. *to window, looks out.*)
LIZ. (*Crosses down to behind drum table.*) You ought to be ashamed of yourself, acting like a twelve-year-old child.
JOAN. (*Crossing down to sofa.*) Well, I'm not. (*Sits on* C. *of sofa.*)
LIZ. I go down and watch every day, and let me tell you, Ginger can kick and she can run.
JOAN. We'll see how much good she does the team in the face of an economic embargo.
AGNES. Does this mean war?
LIZ. (*Starts* L. *toward kitchen.*) Call me as soon as she comes in, Mrs. Carol. (*Front door slams.*)
AGNES. All right, Liz.
LIZ. (*Turns* R., *crossing* U. *to* R. *of sideboard.*) Maybe this is her. (*Jeannie enters from front door, crosses* L. *to kitchen.*)
AGNES. Hello, Jeannie.
JEANNIE. Hello.
AGNES. What's the matter?
JEANNIE. (*Off.*) Nothing.
JOAN. How's the play coming?
JEANNIE. (*Entering from kitchen door with a coke in her hand, coat over her arm. She slaps kitchen door.*) I hate that guy Thompson. He's nothing but an unmitigated bore. (*Crossing* R.,

35

sets coke on table behind sofa and crosses up to closet, hangs coat in it.)
AGNES. (*Crossing* L. *to sideboard.*) Jeannie.
JEANNIE. Well, he is. He says cruel, vicious, insulting things to me. Everybody laughs. (*Slams closet door.*) And it's all Dad's fault. (*Crosses* D. L. *to Agnes.*)
AGNES. How do you arrive at that, dear?
JEANNIE. (*Crossing down to* L. *of sofa.*) If he hadn't let Ginger go out for the team, I wouldn't have had all this humiliation.
AGNES. Like what?
JEANNIE. Today Guy said, "Miss Carol, this is a love scene, not an off-tackle smash." (*Liz crosses up to sideboard, picks up apron.*)
AGNES. Oh. (*Joan laughs.*)
JEANNIE. (*Crossing* R. *to sofa.*) It's not funny, Joan.
JOAN. I'm sorry.
JEANNIE. (*Sits on* L. *of sofa.*) I could die. (*Front door slams.*)
LIZ. (*Crossing* R. *to* R. *of sideboard, Agnes crosses up to* R. *of foot of stairs.*) This must be her. (*Howard enters from front door with brief-case.*)
AGNES. (*Standing ready for a kiss.*) Hello, darling. (*Howard crosses* D. L. *slowly to behind drum table.*)
JEANNIE and JOAN. Hello, Daddy!
LIZ. (*Crossing down to* U. R. *of ottoman.*) Hello, Mr. Carol. Would you like some coffee?
HOWARD. (*Puts brief-case on drum table.*) No, thank you. Save it for Virginia Carol, girl athlete. (*Joan and Jeannie exchange looks, then look at Howard.*)
LIZ. She's not allowed to have coffee.
HOWARD. Then throw it out.
LIZ. Okay, I will. (*Liz exits into kitchen. Howard takes bag of jelly beans from brief-case and drops it on drum table. Then takes copy of Life magazine from brief-case, hiding its cover from audience.*)
AGNES. (*Crossing down to* U. R. *of ottoman.*) How come so late, darling? (*Jeannie and Joan set down their cokes on coffee table.*)
HOWARD. I was detained at the bank. Has anyone seen this? (*Holds Life magazine up, revealing its cover of Virginia in a football helmet, to the audience and to his family.*)
AGNES. Oh, no! (*Agnes crosses* L. *to Howard, takes magazine*

from him. She then crosses back to C. *Jeannie rises, crosses* L., *stands* L. *of Agnes. Joan rises, crosses* L., *stands* R. *of Agnes.*)
JOAN. It's Ginger.
HOWARD. It says, "The New Look in Football." Pictures start on Page 103. (*Jeannie and Joan open magazine.*) There's a whole lay-out.
JEANNIE. Isn't this exciting?
HOWARD. It's hysterical.
JOAN. Here's the page.
AGNES. That's a wonderful picture of Virginia.
HOWARD. Read what it says.
JEANNIE. (*Takes magazine. Reads.*) "Virginia Carol, daughter of town banker, as she appears after a hard two-hour scrimmage."
AGNES. (*To Howard.*) She could have combed her hair.
JOAN. Here's a picture of Mr. Wilson. (*Howard grimaces, takes off coat.*)
JEANNIE. And here's a picture of the bank.
AGNES. What's this?
JOAN. Why, it's a photostatic copy of the petition against gym for girls.
JOAN and JEANNIE. Aw, Daddy! (*Howard takes his coat and hat, slowly crosses up to closet, hangs his coat. Joan and Jeannie cross* R. *to sofa and sit, Joan in* C. *and Jeannie on* L. *Agnes crosses* R., *sits on* L. *arm of sofa.*)
JEANNIE. (*Reading.*) "Petition circulated day she reported for first practice quotes banker-father who said, 'I would abolish gymnasium for girls because no one should be forced to do anything he doesn't want to do.'" (*Howard crosses down* L. *slowly to armchair, sits.*) I still agree with you, Daddy.
JOAN. So do I.
JEANNIE. (*Reading.*) "In a quiet, straight-laced town, a beautiful 14-year-old redhead"—(*Takes.*) beautiful 14-year-old redhead? (*Agnes nudges Jeannie to continue reading. Jeannie reads.*) "—Daughter of ultra conservative banking stock"—(*Agnes, Joan and Jeannie giggle. Howard looks at them sourly.*) "—kicks over the traces by reporting as a football candidate."
AGNES. Howard, have you seen this? (*Joan takes magazine, moves* R. *on sofa.*)
HOWARD. Yes, and so will 27 million other people this week. (*Jeannie climbs to her knees on sofa.*)

JOAN. (*Reading.*) "Father, Howard G. Carol, is a victim of such remarks as, 'We'd never have to worry about depression here if he could run a bank like she can run a ball.' Rival bank has printed blotters which say . . ."

HOWARD. ". . . which say, 'if you're looking for a half-back, you've got the wrong bank.'" (*Agnes, Joan and Jeannie laugh. Howard rises, crosses up to sideboard.*)

AGNES. Howard, this is fantastic.

JEANNIE. They don't even mention my playing in *Victoria*.

HOWARD. Jeannie, will you and Joan go upstairs for a few minutes? I want to talk to your mother alone.

JEANNIE. Sure. (*Rises, takes coke, crosses up to stairs, exits.*)

JOAN. (*Rises.*) Daddy . . .

HOWARD. (*Crossing down to stage L. wall table.*) Yes.

JOAN. (*Crossing L. to Howard.*) Would you sign this petition against Ginger playing football? (*Agnes crosses down, sits on C. of sofa.*)

HOWARD. Not unless you can guarantee me international notoriety.

JOAN. Very well. But it's all your fault I have to take gym twice a week. (*Agnes picks up Life from coffee table.*)

HOWARD. I'm sorry. Now would you mind getting out of here for about five minutes? (*Crosses down to drum table.*)

JOAN. All right. (*Crosses R. to sofa.*) May I take this? (*Agnes holds magazine away from Joan.*)

HOWARD. No, you may not.

JOAN. (*To Howard.*) I want to read about the Movie of the Week.

HOWARD. Agnes . . .

AGNES. Joan, will you please do as you are told.

JOAN. Very well, Mother. (*Crossing up to stairs.*) But I think everybody's being very selfish.

HOWARD. About what?

JOAN. (*On lower landing.*) No one's thought of what a blow these pictures will be to Eddie's morale, have they? He's only the captain of the team. (*Joan exits upstairs. Agnes sets magazine down on coffee table.*)

HOWARD. (*Crossing R. to L. of sofa.*) Agnes, I've had a rough day.

AGNES. Down at the bank? (*Howard nods.*) Because of the pictures?

HOWARD. There's one you didn't get to, on the next page. (*Agnes picks up magazine, but hesitates to turn page. Howard signals her to turn it, and she does so.*)

AGNES. (*Gasps.*) Howard!

HOWARD. Read what that says.

AGNES. (*Reading. Howard crosses* U. *as she reads.*) "Virginia Carol, girl football player, and father roll around in the dirt during hard scrimmage after she had knocked him down." Howard . . .

HOWARD. (*Crossing* D. R. *to sofa.*) I was standing around on the field during practice a couple of weeks ago. They had an end sweep toward me at one point. She threw a block, missed the end, hit me, and down we went. (*Breaks* L., *then turns back.*) It just happened to be the day the photographers were there.

AGNES. Oh, dear!

HOWARD. It was a bad block, too high. After it was over, she picked me up, looked me straight in the eye, and said, "Spectators." (*Takes magazine from Agnes, crosses* L. *to behind drum table.*)

AGNES. Was she hurt, dear?

HOWARD. (*Stops.*) No, darling, she got right off me. (*Puts magazine on drum table, open.*)

AGNES. You weren't hurt, were you?

HOWARD. (*Crossing* R., *slowly.*) Aside from a few minor cuts and bruises, slight giddiness, a lack of focus, and their having to carry me to a bench and give some water, I was fine. (*Crosses* R. *above sofa to* R. *of it.*)

AGNES. (*Laughs silently.*) Well, you're too old to be playing football anyway. What did Ed Hoffman say?

HOWARD. (*Turns to Agnes.*) Nothing. He just kept looking at me—(*Shakes head.*) and shaking his head.

AGNES. What does that mean?

HOWARD. Oh, he's probably disappointed because I missed the ball carrier.

AGNES. I'm serious.

HOWARD. (*Crossing* L. *below coffee table to above armchair.*) I don't know. He said he'd be over later to talk to me.

AGNES. Well, Ed may be president of the bank but he's got a sense of humor.

HOWARD. (*Stops.*) He certainly has. (*Crossing* L.) Oh, Lord, it was just a simple little speech on manners.
AGNES. (*Rises. Crossing* L. *to Howard.*) Well, darling, don't feel badly about it. When Virginia gets home, we'll simply explain the situation to her and that will be . . .
HOWARD. Oh, no, we won't. (*Turns to Agnes.*)
AGNES. What?
HOWARD. I absolutely forbid you to tell your daughter the possible consequences of her madness.
AGNES. Now, darling, that's silly.
HOWARD. I mean it. I wouldn't dream of suppressing this child.
AGNES. Howard, you're being stubborn and ridiculous.
HOWARD. That's the last word. If we lose the house we can all go down and live under the bleachers, right next to her beloved football field.
AGNES. (*Looking around* R.) And on Saturday I can sell peanuts.
HOWARD. Anyway, if I did ask her to quit, she'd probably claim I'm putting selfish interests like home, family, and security above her individual rights. (*Sits on edge of drum table.*)
AGNES. (*Crossing* L. *to* L. *of Howard. Puts arms around him.*) Howard, I love you.
HOWARD. Where *is* she?
AGNES. Now, darling, don't get nervous.
HOWARD. She's taking the longest way home just to keep me in suspense. (*Front doorbell.*) That's probably Ed Hoffman now. I was hoping she'd get here before he did, but no, she'd rather sit in some dirty old locker room. (*Liz enters from kitchen, laughing, carrying a copy of Life, which she is reading.*)
LIZ. (*Crossing* R. *to* R. *of Howard.*) Oh, Mr. Carol, you're famous. (*Agnes signals Liz to "Sh."*)
HOWARD. Would you mind answering the door, Liz?
LIZ. Not at all. (*Liz exits to front door.*)
HOWARD. (*In Agnes' arms.*) Oh, Agnes, why couldn't she have been a boy?
AGNES. Ohhhh . . . darling. (*Liz enters from front door.*)
LIZ. It's Mr. Hoffman. (*Crosses* L. *to below sideboard. Ed Hoffman enters from front door.*)
ED. Hya, Howie . . . Agnes.
HOWARD. (*Rises, crossing* U. R. *to Ed.*) Hya, Ed. Come in.
AGNES. Can I take your coat?

ED. (*Takes off coat.*) No, thanks, I'll just throw it across a chair. (*Crosses D. L. to armchair, starts to drop coat over back.*)
HOWARD. (*Crosses R. to Ed, takes coat from him.*) I'll get it, Liz. Sit down, Ed. (*Crosses U. to hallway chair, puts coat and hat on it.*)
ED. Thank you. I'm sorry, Liz.
LIZ. It's all right, Mr. Hoffman. (*Liz exits into kitchen.*)
ED. Well, Ag, how does it feel to be the wife of a national figure?
AGNES. Pretty awesome. (*Crosses R. to sofa, sits.*)
ED. I'm sure. You must be very proud of him.
AGNES. I am. (*Howard re-enters, crosses down to behind sofa.*)
ED. You certainly put this town on the map.
HOWARD. Yeah, and myself, too.
ED. Yes. (*Crossing slowly down around ottoman to armchair.*) Did he tell you, since Life magazine came out, people have been streaming into the bank?
AGNES. No.
ED. Not to do business, you understand, just to make jokes. (*Sits in armchair.*)
AGNES. Well, that will pass.
ED. At one point I was closing a deal with old man Bryant, and I heard what sounded like an uprising of savages in a Hollywood movie. Into the bank burst a group of our most respected merchants doing a snake dance and shouting, "Booma lacka, booma lacka, sis boom bah. Howard Carol, rah rah rah!"
AGNES. What did you do?
ED. I'm president of the bank. What could I do? (*Rises.*) I rushed out of my office and got on the end of the line. (*Snake-dancing R. above table to C.*) "Booma lacka, booma lacka, sis boom bah. Howard Carol, rah, rah, rah." (*Howard sits on L. back of sofa.*) I wonder what ever happened to old man Bryant? I lost him in the snake dance.
AGNES. Sounds like a Legion convention.
ED. Practically. By the way, I met Mrs. Claude Brackett on the street. She said, "Young man." You know how old she is. I said, "Yes, Mrs. Claude Brackett." She said, "What is an anarchist?" I said, "Why?" She said, "I want to know if it's dangerous."
AGNES. What does she mean by anarchist, Ed?
ED. (*Crossing L. to behind drum table.*) Didn't you read Bob Wilson's statement in *Life*?

AGNES. Statement?
HOWARD. Well, he's a stuffed shirt, anyway.
ED. (*Picks up magazine.*) Let me read it to you. Right under his picture they have a caption that reads, "Irate principal Robert Wilson," and then a quote which says, "I do not blame the poor child. I blame her father, who told me he would let her burn down the house." (*Agnes leans forward on sofa, stares at Howard. Howard catches her glance.*)
HOWARD. No, no, he misquoted me. I said if she felt she had to do it, I might let her burn out one room in the house.
ED. Well, that's different. I knew you'd never let her burn down the whole house. (*Agnes leans back.*)
AGNES. Which room?
HOWARD. Her own room.
AGNES. That's right next to ours.
HOWARD. I can't help that. Change her room.
ED. Well, that's settled. Anyway, Bob goes on to say, "Any parent who preaches anarchy to his children is either a complete idiot or has no regard for law and order. (*Crossing R. to Howard.*) In any case he hardly seems qualified to hold an advisory position at a bank."
AGNES. He has some nerve.
ED. (*Crossing R. below coffee table.*) He certainly has. Every bank has to have at least one lunatic to deal with the depositors. (*Drops magazine on coffee table, crosses R. to R. of sofa.*)
AGNES. Howard, I don't suppose anybody will take him seriously.
HOWARD. And if they do, they can just go jump in the river so far as I'm concerned.
ED. What are you getting so upset about?
HOWARD. I'm getting a little tired of all these jokes.
ED. It's just fun, Howie.
HOWARD. I know, but a lot of people were kidding on the level today. (*Tommy Green bursts into the room from kitchen, looking back at Liz, who follows him from kitchen.*)
TOMMY. (*Rushing by Howard.*) Hello. . . . (*Crosses R. to below foot of stairs.*)
AGNES. Hello, Tommy.
LIZ. (*In kitchen doorway.*) He sneaked past me. (*Liz exits into kitchen.*)
TOMMY. Is Ginger home yet?

AGNES. No, she is not.
TOMMY. Do you mind if I sit and wait? (*Crosses* U., *sits in chair* R. *of phone table.*)
AGNES. (*Crossing up to Tommy.*) I'm sorry, Tommy, but we're having a very important discussion.
TOMMY. I'll be completely unobtrusive.
HOWARD. (*Crosses* R. *to Tommy.*) I'm terribly sorry, but you can't stay.
TOMMY. (*Rises. To Howard.*) Maybe this doesn't mean anything to you, but if Ginger makes the football team, she and I are through.
ED. (*Steps down to* R. *of coffee table, turns* U. L. *to Tommy.*) Young man, do you know who I am?
TOMMY. Of course, Mr. Hoffman.
ED. If you don't go, right now, the first thing I'll do when I leave here is—(*Turning slowly front.*) foreclose the mortgage on your father's house. (*Leers. Tommy crosses* L. *fast, exits into kitchen. Ed, Howard and Agnes laugh. Ed, crossing* L. *to armchair.*) Ah, kids. I've got two of my own and every day I grow to hate them more. (*Looks at Howard. Sits in armchair.*) Shall we get back to our scrimmage?
HOWARD. (*Crosses down to* C.) You heard what Tommy just said. He doesn't want to have anything to do with my daughter because I let her play football.
ED. Howie, he's just a kid.
HOWARD. (*Crossing* L. *to ottoman.*) He's probably heard a lot of other people talking like that.
ED. Don't be silly. (*Agnes crosses down to* L. *of sofa.*)
HOWARD. That's just the beginning. (*Crossing* L. *to above drum table.*) Now I suppose because of that idiotic statement Bob Wilson gave out, I'll be subject to all kinds of pressure.
ED. Nobody is putting any pressure on you.
HOWARD. No, not yet. But I know how these things work. One simple remark starts a whole chain reaction.
ED. You're making yourself angry.
HOWARD. (*Crossing* R.) I *am* angry.
ED. There's no reason to be.
HOWARD. (*Crossing* R. *to Agnes.*) Maybe you don't think so, but I can see where this is leading.
ED. Where?

HOWARD. It starts with jokes. Then it develops into serious discussions. The first thing you know there is criticism, (*Crossing L. to above ottoman.*) and I suppose the next thing, the board of directors will be telling me if I don't behave in a certain way, they won't renew my contract.
ED. Howie . . .
HOWARD. Well, let me tell you that I will not change my behavior pattern to satisfy the whim of some guy like Bob Wilson.
ED. What's the matter with you?
HOWARD. And what's more, if the Board thinks I'm too irresponsible to hold an advisory position, I'll resign right now.
AGNES. (*Crossing L. to Howard.*) Howard . . .
HOWARD. (*Crossing R. above sofa to window.*) I don't have to live in this town. I can go some place where people aren't so smug and provincial.
ED. Now look, Howie. I came over here to talk this over as a friend, but you're blowing it up all out of proportion.
HOWARD. I don't think so. (*Turns L.*) And what's more I don't think this is just a friendly visit.
AGNES. Now, Howard. (*Crosses R. above sofa to above Howard.*)
ED. Hey, now wait a minute. (*Rises. Crossing R. to L. end of sofa.*) If this is the way you're going to behave maybe we ought to examine this a little bit further.
HOWARD. I don't know what's so friendly about . . .
ED. Just a minute. I'm not talking to you now as a friend. I'm talking to you as the president of the bank.
HOWARD. Okay, Mr. President. Let's have it. (*Sits on R. end of sofa. Agnes sits on R. arm.*)
ED. Maybe you're right. When it was only a question of Virginia playing football, we all laughed. But if these jokes are going to make you so hot under the collar that you start to behave publicly the way you've been behaving in this room, Bob Wilson's statement is apt to seem more logical every day.
HOWARD. (*To Agnes.*) Aha. What did I tell you? (*To Ed.*) What do you suggest I do?
ED. All I had in mind when I came here was to suggest that you stop making any more speeches for a while. But now I suggest, first, that you stay away from the football field. Ask Barney White to print a retraction of your stand on gym for girls. And tell Virginia she can't play football. (*Crosses L. to C.*)

HOWARD. And if I won't?

ED. (*Turns* R.) Is there some great big moral issue involved here?

HOWARD. Yes, I think there is.

ED. Well, I don't. And for your own good I suggest you take my advice.

AGNES. (*Rises.*) Ed, you make this sound sort of serious.

ED. I think that's entirely up to Howie. In six weeks we both have contract renewals. If Virginia's still playing football and Howie is still the clown of the town, then our bank becomes a First National Laughing place, and I don't think we can afford that.

AGNES. (*Crossing* L. *to Ed, above table.*) Ed, if what you just described were actually to happen, where would you stand—I mean as far as Howard's concerned?

ED. Agnes, I love you both, but I'm a banker. The only thing I stand behind is money.

AGNES. Well, I certainly don't have to tell you what I think of that statement.

ED. (*Turns front.*) No, and I hope you won't. (*Turns back to Agnes.*) But I'm not going to tie up my security with yours over the right of Howie to pretend he's back in school, or the right of Virginia to play football.

AGNES. Now let me tell you . . .

HOWARD. (*Rises.*) Darling, would you leave Ed and me alone for a minute? (*Crosses* U. *and* L. *above sofa* L. *of it.*)

AGNES. Sure. (*To Ed.*) Excuse me. (*Crosses* L., *exits into kitchen.*)

HOWARD. (*Crossing* L. *to Ed.*) Ed, the reason I asked Agnes to leave us alone was so I could thank you privately for your charity and understanding in this instance.

ED. You're very welcome.

HOWARD. I don't know what kind of an old bone you or the board of directors might throw at me where you feel I can't get into any trouble. (*Crossing* L. *above Ed.*) Why don't you lock me up in the vault in the morning and let me out at night? That way I won't have a chance to talk to anyone. (*To Ed's back.*)—A sort of golden solitary confinement. (*Crosses* D. L. *to* D. L. *of drum table.*)

ED. Look, Howie, this problem has a very simple solution. You're being totally unreasonable.

HOWARD. I don't think so. (*Crossing* U. R. *to* L. *of sofa.*) And let me tell you I will not retract any statement I ever made. I'll say

whatever I like, whenever I like. (*Crossing* R. *below sofa.*) And what's more, under no circumstances will I ask Virginia to stop playing football.

ED. Why not?

HOWARD. (*Crossing* R. *below sofa to* R. *of it.*) Because I believe everyone should be allowed to do what they want to do.

ED. Howie, she's a girl, not a boy!

HOWARD. I'm quite well aware of that fact.

ED. Sometimes I don't think you are, any more. (*Front door slams. Ginger enters from it.*)

HOWARD. Hello, Virginia.

GINGER. Hello, Pop. Hello, Mr. Hoffman. (*Crosses* L. *to stairs, starts to go up.*)

ED. Hello, Virginia. (*Crosses* L. *to armchair, sits.*)

GINGER. (*Starting upstairs.*) Excuse me.

HOWARD. (*Crossing to foot of stairs.*) Virginia, did you make the team?

GINGER. I'd rather not talk about it now.

HOWARD. I'm sorry but I've got to know.

GINGER. Oh, Pop! (*She cries, turns* L., *away from Howard, holding on to banister. Ed hears her cry, looks at Howard, who glares at him.*)

HOWARD. Don't cry, darling.

GINGER. I can't help it. I wasn't given a fair chance. (*Ginger runs upstairs. Ed rises, crosses* R. *to* R. *end of sofa.*)

HOWARD. (*Crossing* L. *to kitchen door. Calling off.*) Agnes. (*Crosses* R. *to above armchair. To Ed.*) Well, there's your answer. (*Liz enters from kitchen, followed by Agnes. Liz stands above drum table, Agnes stands down stage of sideboard.*)

AGNES. What is it?

HOWARD. Virginia's upstairs.

AGNES. Did she make the team?

HOWARD. No.

LIZ. (*Crossing* R. *to stairs, going up.*) That's an outrage. She was the best thing on the field yesterday.

HOWARD. Just not good enough.

LIZ. She's a better half-back than most full-backs. (*Exits upstairs.*)

ED. (*Crossing* L. *to Howard above sofa.*) Well, I guess I'll be running along. So long, Howie. (*Extends* R. *hand to Howard.*)

HOWARD. So long, Ed. (*Shakes hands with Ed, looking away*

from him. Agnes crosses R., *glaring at Ed, to hall chair. She gets Ed's coat and hat, crosses down to him, hands him coat and hat. Then moves* R. *and stands, arms folded. Howard crosses* L.)

ED. I'm glad my little visit here didn't create any hard feelings. (*Ed exits to front door.*)

AGNES. (*Crossing* L. *to* L. *of Howard.*) I'm so mad at Ed Hoffman, I'd like to open a bank across the street and give away money.

HOWARD. (*Crossing* R. *to foot of stairs.*) If there is one thing I can't stand, it's unfairness. Why, she could run better than half the other kids on the field.

AGNES. You were hoping she'd get on the team, weren't you?

HOWARD. (*Crossing* L. *to Agnes.*) You darn right, I was.

AGNES. So was I. Liz and I knelt in front of the lighted oven and prayed she'd make it. (*Howard pats Agnes' hand. Ginger enters downstairs.*)

GINGER. (*Crossing downstairs to* U. C.) Pop, I want to ask you something.

HOWARD. What, darling?

GINGER. Is there a difference between boys and girls?

HOWARD. Well, in what way? (*Crosses* R. *to Ginger. Agnes follows.*)

GINGER. One day I heard you say nobody takes the ball down the field as fast as me. And then the coach said I play smarter heads-up football than Eddie Davis.

HOWARD. He did, huh?

GINGER. So what I'd like to know, is it because he's a boy and I'm a girl that he made the first team, and I only made the scrub team?

HOWARD. No, no. . . . What did you say?

AGNES. You made the scrub team?

GINGER. Yes, and he made Varsity.

HOWARD. Is that what you were crying about a little while ago?

GINGER. Sure.

HOWARD. (*Arms around Ginger.*) Oh, Baby, you're wonderful! Did you hear that, Ag? She made the team.

AGNES. (*Holding out* R. *hand as though offering peanuts. Crossing* L.) Peanuts. . . . Get your hot roasted peanuts!

CURTAIN

ACT II

Scene 2

AT RISE: *The same. A shopping bag stands against* L. *side of coffee table, and its contents, tied bundles of mail, are scattered on coffee table. A framed copy of Life magazine cover hangs over sideboard on wall. More bundles of mail are scattered on drum table, bench in corner* D. L., *and floor nearby.*

Curtain rises on an empty stage. Joan comes downstairs carrying a big bundle of laundry. Starts toward kitchen. —Front doorbell. Joan crosses back up-stage, drops laundry bundle at foot of stairs, and goes to answer bell. When she is out of sight—

JOAN. (*Off.*) Oh, thank you. (*Front door slams.*)
AGNES. (*In kitchen.*) Who was it, Joan?
JOAN. (*Off.*) More mail. (*Enters, dragging two mail sacks.*)
AGNES. (*Off.*) How many sacks?
JOAN. Two.
AGNES. (*Off.*) Well, you can handle that.
JOAN. (D. R. *of phone table.*) Where shall I put them?
AGNES. (*Off.*) Where do they look best, dear? (*Joan stacks mail sacks one on top of the other sack in front of phone table.*)
JOAN. (*Crossing* U. *to get bundle of laundry.*) House work. (*Crosses* L. *to kitchen.*) You'd think Lizzie would clean on Friday, being she insists on going to the football game every Saturday. (*Exits into kitchen.*)
AGNES. (*Enters from kitchen.*) Sure. (*Crosses to drum table.*)
JOAN. (*Enters from kitchen. Crossing* R. *to foot of stairs.*) Why isn't Jeannie helping today?
AGNES. (*Crossing* R. *to sofa.*) She is an actress. Her play opens tonight and she's resting. Shall we try to do something about this fan mail?
JOAN. I don't understand why everybody in America sends Ginger letters.
AGNES. Maybe because Yale named her First Lady of the Gridiron.

JOAN. (*Crossing* L. *to drum table, picks up mail. Crossing* L. *to* D. L. *corner.*) You'd think Daddy would stay home on Saturday to help us. (*Starts putting mail on bench in* D. L. *corner.*)
AGNES. (*Putting mail into shopping bag. Leaves two packets on table.*) How do you figure that, dear?
JOAN. If he'd kept Ginger off the squad, he and Lizzie wouldn't be at the football game today, and I would.
AGNES. I see.
JOAN. And I think he might at least assume some responsibility for changing my whole life.
AGNES. I'll tell him when he comes in.
JOAN. (*Crossing* R. *below armchair to* C.) Another thing I don't understand about Daddy . . .
AGNES. Joan, please relax. It's four o'clock in the afternoon. (*Crosses up behind sofa, sets shopping bag down.*) What's the matter with you, anyway? (*Joan sits* C. *of sofa.*)
JOAN. I've got a big problem.
AGNES. (*Crossing down to sofa.*) What is it?
JOAN. Well, ever since Ginger got on the football team, I've been having a lot of trouble with Eddie, every Saturday night.
AGNES. What sort of trouble? (*Sits on* L. *of sofa. Picks up two packets of mail from coffee table.*)
JOAN. Well, it used to be we'd have a date, go to a movie or a dance, have a soda, talk awhile, and then he'd kiss me good night.
AGNES. And now?
JOAN. Now he wants to start kissing me good night as soon as we get out.
AGNES. Well, believe me when I tell you that has nothing to do with Ginger playing football. (*Agnes and Joan laugh.*)
JOAN. What am I going to do?
AGNES. Well, there are several things you can do. First, I'd suggest you develop a kind of attitude and not allow yourself to get into compromising situations.
JOAN. Have you ever been in the front seat of a car with a man?
AGNES. Yes, with your father.
JOAN. What did you do?
AGNES. I managed to fend him off with dignity and the illusion of superiority.
JOAN. It's kind of hard to be more superior than Eddie.
AGNES. I'm sure.—I'll tell you a little secret. I think you're going

to have to bend his ego a little. Once you get the upper hand with a kid like Eddie, it's down-hill all the way.
JOAN. Suppose Eddie gets the upper hand with me?
AGNES. Oh. That's what you're really worried about, isn't it? *(Joan nods.)* Well, I know that you're intelligent enough to realize the difference between what's good and real for you, and what isn't, because if you didn't, you wouldn't be sitting here telling me your troubles.
JOAN. I guess that's right.
AGNES. There are times when that choice may be rather difficult, Joan, but speaking as a woman who knows you very well, I have absolute confidence in your judgment.
JOAN. *(Embracing Agnes.)* Thanks, Mom.
AGNES. Don't worry, Joanie, everything will work out fine. *(Laughs.)* And it better.
JOAN. I hope it works out like you and Daddy.
AGNES. So do I. *(Looks at bundles of mail in her hand.)*
JOAN. Mom, how did you meet Daddy?
AGNES. Oh, he picked me up on the street one day.
JOAN. Mom!
AGNES. Yeah. I heard a whistle, and I turned and there was this guy. I said, "Did you whistle at me?" He nodded, and I said, "What for?"
JOAN. What did he say?
AGNES. He didn't say anything. He just put out his hand. He was holding two black jellybeans. That's how it started. He was seven and I was five.
JOAN. And you've loved him ever since?
AGNES. *(Rises. Crossing up to sideboard.)* Ever since and always will. *(Puts bundles of mail into sideboard drawer. Jeannie enters downstairs, to lower landing.)*
JEANNIE. *(To Joan, not seeing Agnes.)* Where's my mother?
AGNES. *(Crosses down three steps. Looking at Jeannie.)* What? I must be tired. *(Joan and Agnes laugh.)*
JEANNIE. *(To Agnes.)* Hello, darling.
AGNES. *(The actress.)* Hello.
JOAN. *(Rises. Crossing L. to kitchen.)* How's the play going to be tonight—*(Strikes pose.)* Miss Bernhardt?
JEANNIE. Guy says I look better than Helen did dress rehearsal night. *(Joan exits into kitchen.)*

AGNES. (*Crosses down to drum table.*) Helen who?
JEANNIE. (*Crossing downstairs and down to* U. C.) Helen Hayes, Mother.
AGNES. Excuse me.
JEANNIE. (*Crossing* L. *to* U. R. *of armchair.*) He's the most fascinating man.
AGNES. He is? Just a week ago you hated him. (*Sits in armchair.*)
JEANNIE. That's before I understood the theater. He wasn't being mean, he was simply being caustic.
AGNES. Oh, I see.
JEANNIE. (*Crossing* D. R., *sits* R. *of ottoman.*) He says I have all the makings of a great actress.
AGNES. He does!
JEANNIE. He says I should come to New York.
AGNES. Don't lie down on that pink cloud with those dirty shoes on.
JEANNIE. (*Sits on ottoman.*) Don't you think I'll be a great actress, Mother?
AGNES. I'll come backstage tonight and tell you, Jeannie. (*Joan enters from kitchen, carrying a coke.*) One thing I do think, is you and your sister show very poor taste in not being at the football game today. (*Jeannie rises, crosses* R. *to sofa.*)
JEANNIE. Oh, no!
JOAN. (*Crossing down to above drum table, gives Agnes coke.*) Nobody goes to the games this year.
AGNES. Thank you, Joan. You're wrong. Your father tells me the stands are packed every week, and most people come just to see your sister kick a ball around before the game begins.
JEANNIE. (*Turns* L.) They'll get tired of that when she doesn't play.
AGNES. Are those grapes terribly sour, girls?
JEANNIE. (*Crossing* L. *to ottoman.*) Anyway, it's all Daddy's fault we can't see the games.
AGNES. What? (*Puts coke down on table.*)
JEANNIE. If he hadn't let Ginger play, we juniors would be allowed to go.
JOAN. That's right.
AGNES. Now listen just a minute, girls. Joan, when you thought that gymnasium for girls was being abolished your father allowed you to give up the part in the play, didn't he?

JOAN. Yes.
AGNES. Jeannie, he allowed you to play in *Victoria,* didn't he?
JEANNIE. Yes, Mother.
AGNES. So, basically you were both permitted your free pursuits. Is that right? (*Jeannie and Joan nod Yes. Agnes rises, crosses up R. of Jeannie.*) Then why do you feel that your father is wrong in not denying Virginia the same right you had? (*Picks up shopping bag behind sofa. Jeannie crosses R. to L. of Agnes.*)
JOAN. (*Crossing R. to C.*) We don't believe a girl should be allowed to play football.
JEANNIE. It's just not right, Mother.
AGNES. In other words, anything you disagree with is wrong and should be stopped. Is that it?
JOAN. Well, not exactly that.
AGNES. Exactly what?
JEANNIE. Well, we feel Ginger should be allowed to do whatever she wants to do, as long as it's not playing football. (*Agnes crosses L. above armchair to D. L. corner, carrying shopping bag.*)
JOAN. (*Looks at Jeannie. Crossing L. to behind armchair.*) That's the resolution passed by the girls of the senior and junior classes.
AGNES. By majority vote?
JEANNIE. Of course, Mother.
AGNES. I see. By democratic procedure, you have both decided to tear up the Bill of Rights. That's very interesting. (*Puts shopping bag on bench D. L. corner.*)
JOAN. (*Crosses L. two steps.*) Mother, we haven't.
AGNES. If you hadn't, you'd defend Virginia's right to play whether you disagreed with it or not. (*Joan crosses R. to behind armchair.*) Any questions? (*Crosses R., picks up coke bottle from drum table. Crosses R. to between Jeannie and Joan.*) You know you could both take a very good lesson from your father. He stands to lose his job, but he'd rather take that chance than deprive your sister of her freedom of choice.
JEANNIE. Gee! Daddy is a kind of Joan of Arc character. Isn't he?
AGNES. (*Crossing down to armchair. Sits.*) Yeah. Voices and all.
JEANNIE. (*Crossing D. R. to L. arm of sofa.*) Well, from now on, I'm going to the games.
JOAN. Jeannie!
JEANNIE. I'm going over to Ginger's side, and if Eddie Davis

makes one more remark about her or Dad, I'll kick him all over the school. (*Agnes takes shoes off.*)
JOAN. What?
JEANNIE. He started this whole thing about the boycott because he was mad at Ginger.
JOAN. (*Crossing R. to Jeannie.*) Well, why shouldn't he be?
JEANNIE. Why should he be?
JOAN. She ruined his prestige as captain of the track team.
JEANNIE. Well, from now on, I go along with Ginger.
JOAN. How dare you?
AGNES. All right, girls, that's enough. Go to a neutral corner. (*Joan crosses L. to behind drum table.*)
JEANNIE. You're upsetting me emotionally, and I have a performance tonight. (*Sweeps around to R., exits upstairs.*)
JOAN. (*Over Agnes's L. shoulder.*) She's a traitor to American womanhood, per se. (*Joan exits into kitchen.*)
AGNES. (*Putting shoes on.*) It was a simple little speech on manners.
HOWARD. (*Off U. R.*) Agnes.
AGNES. Yes, dear.
HOWARD. (*Off U. R.*) Agnes. (*Front door slams and Howard enters, wearing raccoon coat and felt hat pushed back on his head.*) Where is she? (*Crosses down to U. L. of sofa.*)
AGNES. Where is who?
HOWARD. My daughter.
AGNES. (*Rises.*) Which one?
HOWARD. (*Crossing up to stairs. Yells up.*) Ginger! Ginger!
AGNES. (*Crossing up R. to C.*) Good Lord, what's happened to you?
HOWARD. (*Crossing down to Agnes.*) I tore down the goal posts.
AGNES. Why?
HOWARD. You mean you haven't heard?
AGNES. No.
HOWARD. (*Takes Agnes in his arms.*) She scored a touchdown in the last two minutes of play.
AGNES. What did they do, throw her over the goal post?
HOWARD. Sit down and let me tell you all about it.
AGNES. (*Crossing D. R. to sofa.*) Try and stop you. (*Howard takes off coat and hat, puts them over back of armchair.*) Are you going to start from the opening kick-off? (*Sits on C. of sofa.*)

HOWARD. No, just the last two minutes.
AGNES. What happened before that?
HOWARD. Nothing. That's the first time she got in the game.
AGNES. Howard, either you're coloring this or it was an awfully dull afternoon.
HOWARD. Please, dear, let me talk.
AGNES. Carry the ball.
HOWARD. (C.) It was the last two minutes of the game. The Varsity 11 was playing its heart out down on the field. We had possession of the ball on our own thirty-yard line. It was the third down and four to go. Should they run it for the four yards, or should they—(*Gestures.*) throw a pass, with their backs to the goal?
AGNES. Run it.
HOWARD. They elected to kick.
AGNES. They're so young, didn't you know they would?
HOWARD. (*Points* D. L.) The kick went deep into coffin corner.
AGNES. Where's that?
HOWARD. The two-yard line.
AGNES. Why do they call it the coffin corner?
HOWARD. (*Crossing* D. L. *to below armchair.*) Agnes, please!
AGNES. All right, so it's down in coffin corner. Now what?
HOWARD. The enemy takes possession. He smashes at the line. No gain. Second and ten on their own two. What should they do? (*Crossing* U. L. *to above drum table*.) The right half drops back into the end zone, and shoots a long pass out into the flat. Three men are down there. It looks like it will be completed, but Eddie Davis smashes through and knocks it down.
AGNES. Good old Eddie!
HOWARD. Third and ten. Now what? The right half takes it on a wide end sweep. He's going wide, wide. The end is out. It looks like the ball carrier is in the clear, but no . . .
AGNES. No?
HOWARD. No! They bring him down with a yard loss.
AGNES. I thought he was going to break through.
HOWARD. Yeah, everybody did. (*Crosses* R. *to* L. *of sofa.*) Okay, it's the fourth and ten.
AGNES. Fourth and eleven! They just lost a yard.
HOWARD. Yeah. You're getting good. (*Crosses* R. *and pats*

Agnes's back. Crosses back to C.) Okay, they're going to kick. They go into punt formation.
AGNES. Where's your daughter?
HOWARD. On the bench.
AGNES. Howard, there's not much time left.
HOWARD. (*Crossing* L. *to above drum table, rubbing hands.*) Yeah, isn't it wonderful? (*Crossing* R. *to* C.) Okay, they're going to kick. Suddenly the whistle blows. Our team calls a time-out. (*Crouches down.*) They go back into a huddle. The fans sense something momentous is going to happen. One man breaks away from the huddle and—(*Points* L.) trots towards the bench. It's Eddie Davis, the Captain. The crowd cheers, he was pretty good today. (*Crossing* L. *to above drum table.*) But who are they putting in his place?
AGNES. Whom!
HOWARD. My daughter! (*Crosses* L. *to* U. L. *of drum table. Then, trotting down stage* R. *and* U. *to* C.) She trots away from the bench, across the field. The fans go mad. They scream, they whistle, they cheer. They're yelling, (*Shaking his fists and jumping in the air.*) "It's her. It's her!" (*Crosses* D. *to* R. *of ottoman.*) I am completely calm and silent.
AGNES. I can just imagine!
HOWARD. (*Crossing up to* C.) Now I know we will see some football. The referee greets her . . . she greets him. . . .
AGNES. At least they're on friendly terms.
HOWARD. (*Goes into a huddle.*) She joins the circle of her teammates. They're glad she is in the game.
AGNES. Howard, get to the play!
HOWARD. Don't you want the mood?
AGNES. No.
HOWARD. Okay. Fourth and eleven. They're going to kick. (*Points upstage.*) My daughter is sent back to the safety position to receive the punt. (*Crosses* D. *to below ottoman.*) The ball is—(*Indicates.*) snapped. He gets the—(*Indicates.*) kick away. (*Crosses* U. *to* C.) It's a long one, down the field, past the fifty-yard line. (*Backing up to newel post of stairway.*) She's going back, back! (*Indicates receiving kick.*) She takes it in her own territory and starts up the field. The ends try to box her in but she slips them, and starts for the right side. The stands are on their feet. She has no interference. (*At* L. *end of sofa.*) She's at

the fifty, the forty, she shakes off a tackler at the thirty-five. She's down to the thirty, and is trapped.

AGNES. Big boys?

HOWARD. (*Through cupped hands.*) Reverse your field, I scream. (*Stamping foot four times.*) Reverse your field! (*Direct to Agnes.*) She hears me, (*Crosses* U.) cuts back to the thirty-five, (*Crosses* L.) swings over to the left side, (*Crosses* U.) crosses back to the center, and streaks off into the clear, with only three men between her and the goal line.

AGNES. Three men?

HOWARD. (*Crossing* D. *three steps slowly, grimacing.*) They start up after her. (*Agnes puts hands over her face.*) They think they've got her in a trap —— (*Stops.*) But she doesn't yield. She tries to feint them out of position, but they keep coming. Suddenly she does a—(*Spins up* R.) half spin, (*Crosses down* L.) straight-arms a man, (*Side-steps* R.) hurdles the man who tries to knock her out of bounds, and then—(*Prances down stage.*) dances down the sideline stripe and—(*Goes down on his knees.*) over the goal-line for a touchdown. (*Kisses floor.*) Pay dirt!

AGNES. Well, I'm glad that's over.

HOWARD. (*Sits up.*) No-o-o, then the extra point!

AGNES. (*Puts hands over her ears.*) I don't want to hear about that.

HOWARD. What a game, what a game! (*Falls back on floor.*) I'm exhausted. (*Sits up.*) After it was over the team carried her around on their shoulders. The crowd surged out onto the field and that modest little hero kept shouting, "Put me down! Put me down!"

AGNES. Did they?

HOWARD. At last. Agnes, I don't want you to feel you've completely missed one of the great moments in the history of this town.

AGNES. Don't worry, dear, I'm certain we shall relive that moment many times. (*Howard laughs.*) And as the years roll by, it will get even more graphic.

HOWARD. (*Rises.*) Anyway, I've brought you something.

AGNES. Jellybeans!

HOWARD. A piece of that historic goal post. (*Takes small piece of wood from pocket, hands it to Agnes.*)

AGNES. I shall treasure this always.

HOWARD. (*Reaches for piece of wood.*) You don't have to take it if you don't want to.
AGNES. (*Holding it away from Howard.*) No, no. I wouldn't be without it.
HOWARD. (*Crossing L. to drum table. Picks up coke.*) He's a shrewd man, that Blake.
AGNES. He's shrewd?
HOWARD. One of the smartest coaches I've ever known.
AGNES. That's interesting.
HOWARD. (*Crosses U. R. to above armchair.*) Do you realize what he's been doing these past two weeks?
AGNES. No, I'm afraid I don't.
HOWARD. He's been keeping her under wraps. (*Drinks coke.*)
AGNES. Well, it's been getting awfully cold, Howard.
HOWARD. (*Crosses U. to sideboard, slams coke down on it. Crossing R. to C.*) What is the use of talking to you! "Under wraps" means he's kept her on the bench because he didn't want anybody to know how good she was.
AGNES. (*Rises. Crossing L. to Howard.*) Why not?
HOWARD. Because if they didn't know, she's a secret weapon.
AGNES. That's very clever.
HOWARD. Oh, golly, I wonder where that kid learned to run like that?
AGNES. (*Crossing D. L. to L. of Howard.*) I used to be able to run.
HOWARD. (*Crossing down to Agnes.*) Yeah, I remember. (*Embraces her.*)
AGNES. Now, Howard, suppose the children come through here.
HOWARD. I think the kids know about us by now. (*Kisses Agnes. Urging Agnes R. to sofa.*) I haven't been this excited since you and I were eighteen.
AGNES. (*Stops.*) I was sixteen. (*Howard sits on C. of sofa, Agnes to his L.*)
HOWARD. I think you're more attractive now that you were then. (*Embraces Agnes.*)
AGNES. You do?
HOWARD. I certainly do. (*Arm round Agnes.*)
AGNES. I wish Virginia played football every day.
HOWARD. Do we have to go to that play tonight?
AGNES. We certainly do.

HOWARD. Let's come right home after it's over.

AGNES. Darling, it's a very long play.

HOWARD. Oh. Where are the kids now?

AGNES. All over. (*Joan enters from kitchen, looks at her parents. Crosses R. to U. C. Agnes jumps up, crosses R. to mirror, fixes hair. Then crosses up to U. R. of sofa. Howard spots a piece of lint on carpet to R. of coffee table and bends over to pick it up.*) Feeling better?

JOAN. Uh-huh. Hello, Daddy.

HOWARD. Hya, beautiful. Did you hear about the game today?

JOAN. No.

HOWARD. Well, it was the last two minutes of play. Your sister . . .

AGNES. (*To Howard.*) Howard, you're going to get all excited again. (*Looks up, sees Joan.*)

JOAN. Excuse me. (*Crosses U., goes upstairs to lower landing.*) Oh, Mom.

AGNES. Yes?

JOAN. Thanks for the advice. (*Exits upstairs.*)

HOWARD. (*Rises. Crosses U. to the framed Life picture hanging on wall. Agnes crosses down around coffee table and L. to D. L. corner.*)

Fight 'em, Ginger,
Fight 'em, fight 'em.
Beat 'em, Ginger,
Beat 'em, beat 'em.
Rush right down that field like thunder.

(*Rushes L. toward Agnes. Agnes sees him coming, runs L. to D. L., protesting.*)

Show them that you are a wonder!

(*Howard catches Agnes, embraces her. Liz enters from front door, crosses down to L. of sofa.*)

LIZ. Mrs. Carol. Mrs. Carol. Have you heard about the —— (*Sees Agnes and Howard embracing.*) Oh, excuse me. (*Howard breaks away from Agnes.*)

AGNES. It's all right, Liz. We have no secrets.

LIZ. (*Crossing L. to C.*) Did you hear the news?

AGNES. I've been through it.

HOWARD. (*Crossing R. to Liz.*) I told her, Liz, but she doesn't know anything about football.

LIZ. Isn't it wonderful, and wasn't she cute?
HOWARD. Cute? (*Picks up Liz.*) She was magnificent!
LIZ. She certainly was. (*Howard puts Liz down.*)
AGNES. This certainly has been an emotional experience.
HOWARD. You know what Blake will do with her now, Liz?
AGNES. Put her back under wraps, I hope.
HOWARD. Exactly, if he doesn't need her. He'll probably save her for the traditional Thanksgiving Day game. (*Running down around drum table and* U. R. *to foot of stairs, singing.*)
Fight 'em, Ginger,
Fight 'em, fight 'em.
Beat 'em, Ginger,
Beat 'em, beat 'em.
Oh, Liz. (*Stops at foot of stairs.*)
LIZ. Yes?
HOWARD. Hang up my coat. (*Exits upstairs, running and singing.*)
Run right down that field like thunder.
Show them that you are a wonder!
LIZ. (*Picks up Howard's coat from back of armchair. Crossing* U. C.) I've never seen him so happy. (*Puts coat and hat down on hallway chair.*)
AGNES. I guess that counts for something.
LIZ. (*Crossing* L. *to above drum table.*) Did he tell you everything that happened this afternoon?
AGNES. Everything.
LIZ. (*Crossing* L.) Would you like to hear my version?
AGNES. No, thank you. (*Front door slams, Ginger enters from front door.*) Hello, baby. (*Crosses* R. *to below phone table.*)
GINGER. (*Crossing* U. *to behind* L. *end of sofa, taking off coat.*) Hello, Mom. (*Throws coat over* L. *back of sofa. Agnes and Liz exchange looks.*)
LIZ. Hello, Virginia.
GINGER. Hello, Liz.
AGNES. What's the matter?
GINGER. Nothing.
LIZ. (*Looks at Agnes, then at Ginger.*) Ginger, you were wonderful. (*Looks at Agnes, then crosses* L. *below Agnes to kitchen door, where she takes one more look at Agnes, and exits to kitchen.*)

AGNES. (*Crossing* R. *to* C.) I've just had an excited recounting of your adventure.
GINGER. Where is Pop?
AGNES. He's upstairs. (*Ginger looks upstairs, then crosses* D. *to sofa.*) What's the matter, baby?
GINGER. Everything. (*Sits on* C. *of sofa.*)
AGNES. But you scored a touchdown this afternoon.
GINGER. Oh, Mom, I'm miserable.
AGNES. (*Crossing* R. *to sofa. Sits next to Ginger.*) Darling, what happened? (*Puts arm around Ginger.*)
GINGER. Well, the last few seconds of the game the boys called time out. They wanted me to play, so they told Eddie to walk off quietly or they'd throw him off bodily. They knew the other team had to punt. The kicker went back to his end zone. Our line crashed through. He had to rush the kick. It was a bad punt that wobbled down to the twenty. They let me take it, they opened a hole up the center that a slow freight could have gone through. They were determined I'd score.
AGNES. Well, isn't that the purpose of the game?
GINGER. But, Mom, they all treated me like something special, not just like anybody carrying the mail.
AGNES. What about those three men who had you trapped?
GINGER. When I got to them, I slowed up. By that time I didn't want the touchdown. I wanted them to tackle me.
AGNES. And they didn't?
GINGER. They were laughing so hard, they fell flat on their faces. I had to score.
AGNES. But didn't that touchdown win the game?
GINGER. Mom . . .
AGNES. That's what I understood.
GINGER. By the time I got into the game we were leading thirty-four to nothing.
AGNES. (*Looks around upstairs, then looks front.*) Well, I've been had!
GINGER. (*Rises, crosses* L. *to* C.) Then they picked me up on their shoulders, like a curio, and marched me around the field. Both teams. With Daddy leading them. I was furious. I kept shouting, "Put me down! Put me down!"
HOWARD. (*Off.*) Do I hear the small voice of my great conquering hero?

GINGER. Yes, Pop. (*Crosses* L. *to behind armchair. Holds on to armchair, facing front.*)
AGNES. Stand your ground, dear, or he'll run right through you.
HOWARD. (*Off.*)
Fight 'em, Ginger,
Fight 'em, fight 'em.
Beat 'em, Ginger,
Beat 'em, beat 'em.
(*Enters downstairs to lower landing.*) There's the little star. Five feet two-and-a-half inches of greased lightning. Welcome home, son. (*Ginger bears, runs off to kitchen.*)
AGNES. (*Rises.*) Son? (*Crosses* L. *to kitchen.*) Howard!

CURTAIN

ACT III

The same.

AT RISE: *Howard is seated in armchair, writing on pad of paper.*

HOWARD. (*Reading.*) "Mayor Green, Commissioners, Ladies and Gentlemen. No, no. Mayor Green, Principal Wilson, Commissioners, Ladies and Gentlemen."
AGNES. (*Off. Upstairs.*) Lizzie. . . . Lizzie. . . . Howard.
HOWARD. Yes, dear?
AGNES. (*Off.*) Howard, where's Lizzie?
HOWARD. In the kitchen, I guess.
AGNES. (*Off.*) Would you call her, please?
HOWARD. Lizzie.
LIZ. (*In kitchen.*) What do you want, Mr. Carol?
HOWARD. What do you want, Agnes?
AGNES. (*Off.*) Ask Liz if Jeannie's petticoat is pressed.
HOWARD. Liz, is Jeannie's petticoat pressed?
LIZ. (*Off.*) Yes, it is.
HOWARD. Yes, it is.
AGNES. (*Off.*) Oh, that's good. Would you bring it up, darling?
HOWARD. Why can't Liz bring it up?
AGNES. (*Off.*) She's busy.
HOWARD. Can't you come down?
AGNES. (*Off.*) I'm getting dressed.
HOWARD. (*Rises. Crossing up to foot of stairs.*) Look, Agnes, I'm trying to write a speech.
AGNES. (*Off.*) This is more important.
JOAN. (*Off upstairs.*) Will you get my dress, too, Daddy?
HOWARD. Why can't you come down and get your own dress?
AGNES. (*Off.*) Howard, you're wasting time.
JOAN. (*Off.*) I'll come half way. (*Joan and Agnes giggle, off. Howard crosses* L. *to kitchen, tossing pencil on drum table and echoing the women's laughter as he exits into kitchen. He re-enters, carrying petticoat and Joan's dress on hangers as Joan enters downstairs to lower landing, brushing her hair. Howard crosses* R.

to foot of lower landing and hands Joan clothes over railing.) Thank you, Daddy.
HOWARD. (Crossing down to armchair.) You're welcome.
JOAN. Hey, that's a real smooth suit.
HOWARD. (Stops.) It should be. I've been wearing it for years. (Joan laughs, exits upstairs. Howard sits in armchair, picks up pad, resumes writing. Doorbell.)
AGNES. (Off.) Howard, would you please answer the front door?
HOWARD. (Puts pad and pencil down on drum table. Rises. Crossing R. to answer door.) I don't know why. I'm always the first one dressed. (Howard exits to front door.)
VOICE. (Off.) Mr. Carol's residence?
HOWARD. (Off.) Yeah. Oh, thank you. Here you go. (Front door slams and Howard re-enters carrying corsage box.)
AGNES. (Off.) Who was it, dear?
HOWARD. Nobody.
AGNES. (Off.) It must have been somebody.
HOWARD. It was the florist. (Sets corsage box on phone table, open. Starts to cross down to armchair.)
AGNES. (Off. Giggles.) I knew it was somebody. (Howard stands C., silently counts to ten. Then crosses down to armchair, sits. Agnes enters downstairs, carrying small white towel in which is wrapped nail polishing equipment. On stairs.) Howard.
HOWARD. Yes, dear. (Turns and sees Agnes. Rises.) Hey, you look sensational.
AGNES. Thanks. (Crosses downstairs and down to coffee table. Puts nail kit on table.) It's probably the last dress I'll be able to afford. (Howard sits on R. arm of armchair.)
HOWARD. Hey, come here. (Agnes crosses L. to Howard. Howard puts arms around Agnes.) I think you are more attractive than any of our kids.
AGNES. You do?
HOWARD. I certainly do. Say, do we have to go to that play tonight?
AGNES. (Breaking embrace, crossing U. a few steps.) Howard . . . (Howard sits in armchair, resumes writing. Agnes crosses L. to over Howard's L. shoulder, looks at speech.) Darling, I don't like to invade your fantasy but how much further away from the bank is that speech going to take you?
HOWARD. Stop worrying, darling.

AGNES. (*Crossing* R. *to* R. *of ottoman.*) What I don't understand is, the bank is probably furious—what makes you so happy?

HOWARD. I got a wife who loves me and the prettiest half-back ever to put on football equipment.

AGNES. (*Crossing* R. *two steps.*) Howard, that prettiest half-back is a very unhappy little girl.

HOWARD. Oh, darling, you exaggerate things.

AGNES. (*Crosses a step* R.) *I* exaggerate things? You don't think calling her "son" this afternoon was a slight exaggeration?

HOWARD. I'm sure she understands I was excited and it just slipped out.

AGNES. (*Crossing* L. *to ottoman.*) Don't you think it would be wise if you went upstairs and tried to explain that to her? I don't think she's even going to the play.

HOWARD. All right, darling, I will. And don't worry. Everything's going to be all right.

AGNES. My intuition tells me "No." (*Front doorbell.*)

HOWARD. Why does your intuition always have to be so negative?

AGNES. (*Crossing up to answer front door.*) It had a very unhappy childhood. (*Off.*) Hello, Ed. (*Howard hears, rises, quickly crosses* L. *to* D. L. *corner. Sits on bench, begins painting ceramic on potter's wheel.*)

ED. (*Off.*) Hello, Ag.

AGNES. (*Off.*) Come in. (*Ed enters from front door, followed by Agnes. Crosses* L. *to below phone table, she stands to his* R. *Ed looks at Howard, who ignores him. Then looks back at Agnes.*)

ED. Is your husband at home?

AGNES. (*Crossing down to sofa. Sits* C.) Ed's here to drop the other shoe, dear.

HOWARD. Hello, Ed.

ED. Hya, Howie.

HOWARD. Sit down. I'll be with you in a minute.

ED. (*Crossing down to* L. *of sofa.*) You're very kind. (*Takes off his coat, drapes it over* L. *back of sofa.*) Well, Ag, how are you?

AGNES. I don't know, but I hate being called Ag.

ED. Phyllis hates being called Phyl. Insists the children call her Phyllis. I hate being called Edward. (*Crossing* L. *to Howard. To Howard.*) Human nature is a funny thing.

AGNES. How true. (*Ed glances back at Agnes.*)

ED. (*Observing Howard painting ceramic.*) Occupational therapy? (*Howard and Agnes laugh.*)
HOWARD. What's on your mind, Ed?
ED. All kinds of things. Tonight I was sitting around reminiscing about the scenes of my childhood. And were they harrowing! Remember them?
HOWARD. I certainly do.
ED. I said to Phyllis, "Phyl . . . Phyl—(*Crosses down R. to drum table.*) Phyllis, I'm talking to you. Thank you. Remember the kid who failed English 2 because he turned in a paper expounding the economics of whatever it was?" (*Howard laughs.*) She said, "H'mmmmm." I said, "Whatever happened to him?" She said, "He married that handsome Hosenmacher girl." (*To Howard.*) I said, "Oh, Howie Carol."
HOWARD. Yeah, Howie Carol.
ED. (*To "Phyllis" again.*) I said, "Well, he made a great success today at the football game." She said, "Oh, is he back in school?" (*To Howard.*) I said, "I guess so." (*Crosses L. to Howard.*) Here are your contracts. (*Hands Howard contracts, which he takes from pocket.*) The Board meets Tuesday. I don't think it will do much good, but sign them and turn them in. We'll see what happens.
HOWARD. Okay, thanks, Ed.
ED. Don't be so casual. I talked to some of the boys. If you are still running wild on Monday and Virginia's still on the team, you may not get approval.
HOWARD. Then there's no sense leaving the contracts, Ed, because we both will be.
ED. Howie, you made a one-man show of yourself this afternoon.
AGNES. How do you mean, Ed?
ED. (*Crossing R. to C.*) Well, first of all, he didn't sit in the stands with the people. He sat on the bench with the squad.
HOWARD. The coach invited me.
ED. When Virginia got into the game, he warmed up with her, running up and down the side-lines. He led cheers. He even tried a back flip and landed flat on his raccoon coat. When she took the ball—(*Crossing L.*) he ran the whole thirty yards with her and was waiting for her in the end zone. (*Crossing R. to C.*) Took *her* in his arms, and kissed the left half-back.
HOWARD. What a game! What a game!
ED. I turned to say something to Barney White—he was rolling

in the aisle. (*Crossing L. to Howard.*) Later at the club I talked to Barney. He showed me a picture he was going to print Monday morning of Howard tearing down the goal post. Howie, you're becoming a character. More people will be coming to the games to see you than her.

HOWARD. You're just jealous, Ed.

ED. (*To Agnes.*) Jealous! (*To Howard.*) I'm jealous. Yes, I'm jealous. I'm jealous because little kids don't point at me on the street and go . . . (*Points at Howard, jumps up and down, laughs.*)

HOWARD. I'm sorry, Ed, but I believe everyone is entitled to the sanctity of his own privacy.

ED. Privacy? (*To Agnes.*) There were twelve thousand people at that game today.

HOWARD. You know what I mean, Ed.

ED. Is that why you agreed to make a speech at the football dinner next week? What's so private about that?

HOWARD. I don't want to argue with you, Ed.

ED. You know, Ag, he's really beginning to worry me.

AGNES. Why, Ed?

ED. Any man who can construct a whole crusade on absolutely nothing is either crazy or so far ahead of his time, none of us understands him. (*To Howard.*) Is everybody wrong except you?

HOWARD. Could be.

ED. (*Points to Agnes.*) Talk it over with Ag. (*Crossing R. to sofa.*) I'll pick you up in my car later and we'll go to the play. (*Picks up his coat, puts it on.*) It may help if we're seen together. (*To Agnes.*) You've been like a little mouse. See you later, Ag.

AGNES. All right, Edward.

ED. (*Hat over heart, singing.*) Boola, boola. Boola, boola. (*Starting to front door.*) Howie Carol, you're a foola. (*Exits front door.*)

AGNES. (*Rises, crosses L. to C.*) Howard, I admire your integrity. I always like the way you feel on small important issues.

HOWARD. Thanks. What is there about me you don't admire? (*Rises, crosses R. to Agnes.*)

AGNES. I hate putting maternal instincts and security above your honor, but Ed's right.

HOWARD. (*Crosses R. to armchair, puts contracts on drum table.*) No, darling.

AGNES. Howard, I understand you've been hurt, but you're being proud and unwise. You heard what Ed said.
HOWARD. Ed Hoffman doesn't frighten me.
AGNES. He frightens *me*.
HOWARD. Did you see how upset he got? He doesn't want to lose me. He knows he'll be left holding the bag.
AGNES. With *us* in it.
HOWARD. No.
AGNES. Darling, would you take the advice of a life-long friend and sign those contracts?
HOWARD. (*Turns R. to Agnes.*) You mean you agree with Ed?
AGNES. Yes.
HOWARD. Well, you're both wrong.
AGNES. In this discussion there are seeds that will blossom into a real quarrel.
HOWARD. Not tonight. (*Goes to grab Agnes.*)
AGNES. (*Breaks R.*) You'll find out.
HOWARD. (*Crossing R. to Agnes.*) Now, darling —— (*Ginger appears on stairs wearing a bathrobe and slippers, carrying Jeannie's cape.*)
GINGER. (*Crosses down to foot of stairs.*) Mom . . . look. . . . (*Ginger crosses D. R. around sofa to D. R. of Agnes. Agnes and Howard watch as Jeannie enters downstairs dressed as young Queen Victoria.*)
JEANNIE. Hello.
HOWARD. Well, . . . Your Highness!
AGNES. Oh, Jeannie!
JEANNIE. (*Crossing downstairs to U. C.*) You like it, Daddy?
HOWARD. It's majestic, isn't it, darling? (*Howard turns Jeannie around, then crosses up to phone table for corsage.*)
GINGER. I helped her dress, Mom.
AGNES. You did? (*Puts arm round Ginger.*)
GINGER. Uh-huh. I was her lady-in-waiting. (*Hands Agnes Jeannie's cape.*)
HOWARD. (*Presenting corsage to Jeannie.*) Your majesty. (*Howard kisses Jeannie. Ginger crosses L. slowly to chair in D. L. corner, and sits, observing the scene.*)
JEANNIE. (*Taking flowers. Curtseys.*) Thank you.
HOWARD. Kitten, you look enchanting. (*Pats Jeannie. Calling off to kitchen.*) Lizzie. (*To Jeannie.*) You nervous?

JEANNIE. Something's happened to my stomach. (*Liz enters from kitchen dressed for play. Crosses* R. *to* D. C. *near sideboard.*)
LIZ. Did you call me, Mr. Carol? (*Howard, Jeannie, and Agnes ad lib. admiration.*)
AGNES. (*Crossing* U. *to* D. R. *of Jeannie.*) Liz, we called you in to take a look at our little star, but I'm not sure you're not more attractive. (*Winks at Ginger.*)
LIZ. I always dress for opening nights.
HOWARD. (*Crossing* L. *to Liz.*) We have so many here in town. (*Hands Liz keys.*) Here are the keys to the car, Liz. (*Helps Liz on with cape.*) Don't worry about getting it back. We're going down with Ed Hoffman.
AGNES. I'll take the car out of the garage for you, Lizzie.
LIZ. Okay. (*Crosses* R. *to above ottoman. To Jeannie.*) Are you ready? (*Jeannie looks at Liz, who crosses* R. *to below* R. *corner of arch.*)
JEANNIE. Uh-huh.
AGNES. Good luck, now. (*Kisses Jeannie.*)
JEANNIE. Thank you. (*Agnes begins hooking Jeannie's cape.*) Mom, just a couple of very important things. Don't forget to applaud the scenery when the curtain goes up. Guy says that's important. Only don't applaud me when I first come on the stage, just because I'm the star of the play. He says that's amateurish. Even Helen Hayes insists they don't applaud her.
LIZ. What does she do, hold up her hands? (*Ginger's head drops down.*)
JEANNIE. (*To Liz.*) If they applaud, she kills it.
AGNES. Kills what?
JEANNIE. (*Turns* L. *to Agnes.*) Don't you know what that means?
AGNES. No, dear, I don't.
JEANNIE. Neither do I, but Guy does.
LIZ. Anything else?
JEANNIE. (*To Liz.*) Yes. There are some places where you're not supposed to laugh, but I don't have time to tell you about them now.
AGNES. We'll sit very quietly.
JEANNIE. But there are other places where you are supposed to laugh.
HOWARD. We'll watch the other people.

AGNES. Be awfully regal, Jeannie. (*Embraces Jeannie.*)
JEANNIE. I will. (*Crossing L. to Howard.*) 'Bye, Daddy.
HOWARD. 'Bye, kitten. And remember what I told you—don't lope. (*Kisses Jeannie. Agnes crosses U. C.*)
JEANNIE. I won't. (*Jeannie exits through front door, head high. Agnes looks at Howard, follows Jeannie off.*)
LIZ. (*Crosses up to C.*) Makes me feel like the Dowager Queen. (*Exits. Howard turns L., sees Ginger sitting in small chair D. L., stops a moment. Crosses down to armchair. Ginger rises, crosses U. R. as though to exit upstairs.*)
HOWARD. Virginia . . . (*Sits in armchair.*)
GINGER. (*Stops below phone table.*) Yes, Pop?
HOWARD. (*Holding R. hand out.*) Come here. (*Ginger crosses down to Howard, hands behind back.*) You mad at me?
GINGER. No.
HOWARD. I'm sorry I called you "son" this afternoon.
GINGER. That's all right, Pop.
HOWARD. What's the matter?
GINGER. Nothing, Pop.
HOWARD. Oh, sure there is. Come on, tell me. (*Ginger sits on ottoman next to armchair.*)
GINGER. I don't know, Pop. I feel kind of funny and unhappy.
HOWARD. I think maybe I know what that is.
GINGER. You do? What?
HOWARD. Growing pains. Every kid goes through that.
GINGER. Did you go through it?
HOWARD. Sure. When I was your age I felt funny all the time. (*Ginger smiles.*)
GINGER. Pop, when you were my age didn't you ever have dates?
HOWARD. Only with your mother.
GINGER. Did you take long walks together and just talk?
HOWARD. No. I wasn't much of a talker then.
GINGER. What did you do?
HOWARD. Oh, we sat . . . and just sat mostly, I guess.
GINGER. Did you go dancing?
HOWARD. Not until she asked me to go to the junior prom.
GINGER. I'll bet you were a wonderful dancer.
HOWARD. I was not. I couldn't dance at all. It took your mother four weeks to teach me a two-step, which we still do.
GINGER. (*Dreaming.*) Was the prom fun, Pop?

HOWARD. I remember she led all night.
GINGER. (*Dreaming.*) Was it romantic?
HOWARD. Naah, the dance was dull. . . . But . . . (*Chuckles.*) I remember that was the night your mother and I got in my old jalopy and drove over to the . . . No, not very romantic.
GINGER. I'd like to have dates and go dancing and sit and just talk.
HOWARD. Is that what's troubling you?
GINGER. Sorta. . . .
HOWARD. You miss seeing Tommy, don't you? (*Ginger rises, crosses R. two steps.*) Well, let me tell you something, darling. (*Howard rises, crosses R. to Ginger.*) Don't let this momentary loneliness keep you from doing anything you want to do. Two to one this separation is much tougher on him than on you.
GINGER. You think so?
HOWARD. Uh-huh.
GINGER. Oh, maybe I better go call him. (*Breaks up toward phone. Howard stops her.*)
HOWARD. No, no. You sit tight and when he does come around you make him accept you, (*Pulling Ginger down to him.*) not only as a girl but as anything else you want to be.
GINGER. But suppose he won't accept me as a football player?
HOWARD. Don't you worry. If Tommy is half the boy that you and I know he is, he'll see the justice of your cause, and you'll have a much better time together.
GINGER. All right, Pop. I'll take your word.
HOWARD. Thata girl. Listen to me and you'll learn how to deal with men. (*Crosses down to armchair.*)
GINGER. Thanks, Pop.
HOWARD. Feel better? (*Sits in armchair.*)
GINGER. Much.
HOWARD. That's good.
GINGER. (*Crosses U. to foot of stairs, stops.*) Pop.
HOWARD. Huh?
GINGER. Would you do me a favor?
HOWARD. What, darling?
GINGER. Would you take me to the play tonight? (*Crosses down two steps.*) I want to get dressed up and have a date.
HOWARD. I'll be honored.
GINGER. What time will you call for me?

HOWARD. About 8:15.
GINGER. I won't keep you waiting.
HOWARD. You'd better. It's one of the first rules of being a girl.
GINGER. If I do will you be awful mad?
HOWARD. Sore as a boil.
GINGER. It's going to be some date.
HOWARD. We'll make it up over a soda. (*Agnes enters from front door.*)
GINGER. (*Backs up R. a step. Blows Howard a kiss.*) That's all I can say. (*Crosses up backward to foot of stairs. Collides with Agnes.*) Excuse me, Mother.
AGNES. What are you so excited about?
GINGER. I got a date.
AGNES. With whom?
GINGER. A real dream boat. (*Exits upstairs joyously.*)
AGNES. (*Crossing D. to C.*) Whom does she have a date with?
HOWARD. Me.
AGNES. (*Crossing L. to Howard.*) Well, dream boat, you're really sailing tonight, aren't you?
HOWARD. I certainly am. (*Agnes sits on ottoman.*)
AGNES. Hey . . . hey . . . remember when I acted in the senior play?
HOWARD. Yeah, and I rehearsed all the love scenes with you.
AGNES. And most of them weren't in the play. (*Rises. Crossing R. to L. end of sofa.*) I'm more excited than Jeannie.
HOWARD. (*Writing on pad he used before.*) Every man should be allowed his own faith.
AGNES. What was that?
HOWARD. A faith he can share with his fellowmen.
AGNES. (*Crossing D. to above coffee table.*) Howard, please don't write out loud. It makes me nervous.
HOWARD. You know, darling, I think this speech should be eloquent, but terse. Don't you?
AGNES. The terser the better. I'd like to see you keep it under wraps. (*Phone rings.*)
HOWARD. In this very precarious situation you're supporting me like a pillar of jello. (*Phone again. Agnes crosses U. to answer it.*)
AGNES. (*Into phone.*) Hello. . . . Yes, she is. Will you hold on for a moment?
GINGER. (*Off upstairs.*) Mom, was that call for me?

AGNES. No, dear, it's Eddie for Joan. (*Crosses slowly* D. R. *to* L. *of sofa.*)
GINGER. (*Off.*) Oh. . . . Joan, phone.
HOWARD. (*Writing.*) "Every man should have a dream and every dream should have a purpose."
AGNES. That's pretty fancy.
HOWARD. Thomas Jefferson said that.
AGNES. (*Crosses* D. *to sofa.*) Well, he wouldn't have if he'd known what it was going to be used for. (*Sits* C. *of sofa. Joan enters downstairs, dressed for the play. Crosses to phone table, picks up phone.*)
JOAN. (*Into phone.*) Hi . . . uh-huh . . . sure. . . . (*Howard looks up. Joan laughs.*) Uh-huh. . . . (*Howard echoes her giggle.*) Yeah. . . . (*Howard listens.*) Right. . . . (*Howard turns away.*) 'Bye.
HOWARD. (*Chuckles.*) That's the least informative telephone conversation I've ever overheard. (*Joan crosses* D. *to* C.)
AGNES. She does that all the time.
JOAN. (*To Howard.*) Like my dress?
HOWARD. Lovely. Where did you get the talent for such telephone discretion?
JOAN. I'm glad I have talent for something. Mom, will you fix this bow? (*Crosses* R. *to Agnes. Faces down* L.)
AGNES. (*Fixing bow.*) You poor free soul. You're the only completely irresponsible and carefree member of the clan tonight.
JOAN. (*Crossing around to* U. L. *of sofa.*) Well, when Ginger gets as old as I am she'll learn that you either compete with men or go out with them.
AGNES. And what have you decided is the wisest course?
JOAN. Eddie's picking me up in a few minutes.
AGNES. Collaborationist!
JOAN. One of the best there is. I'm going to borrow some of your "Intoxication," Mom. (*Exits upstairs.*)
AGNES. Oh, yes. Every once in a while I realize how big that girl is getting. (*Front doorbell.*) No wonder he's captain of the track team. (*Rises, crosses up to front door.*)
HOWARD. He must have phoned from the lawn.
AGNES. (*Off.*) Oh, hello. Come in. (*Agnes enters from front door.*) It's someone for Virginia. (*Agnes crosses* L. *to below newel post of stairs. Tommy Green enters from front door, stands* U. R.)

HOWARD. Oh, hello, Tommy.
TOMMY. Hello, Mr. Carol.
HOWARD. Come in.
TOMMY. Thank you. (*Crosses down to* C.)
JOAN. (*Off.*) Tell him I'll be down in a minute, Mother.
AGNES. It isn't for you.
TOMMY. Is Virginia at home?
AGNES. Yes, she is. Sit down, Tommy. I'll call her. (*Starts* R. *to go upstairs.*)
HOWARD. Just a minute, darling. I'd like to talk to Tommy first.
AGNES. (*Takes step toward Howard.*) Dear . . .
HOWARD. Sit down, Tommy. (*Tommy sits on* L. *end of sofa.*) What do you want to see my daughter about?
TOMMY. Well . . .
AGNES. Darling, it's getting awfully late.
HOWARD. This won't take long.
TOMMY. Well . . .
AGNES. If you two gentlemen will excuse me—(*Crossing* L. *to kitchen.*) I'm going into the kitchen for no reason. (*Exits into kitchen.*)
HOWARD. Well, we got as far as "well" twice.
TOMMY. Mr. Carol, I came here to ask Virginia to the play tonight.
HOWARD. And in asking her, do you think you'll get back in her good graces?
TOMMY. Yes, sir.
HOWARD. How?
TOMMY. I have my whole speech planned. (*Rises. Orates.*) "This is not the time to be emotional."
HOWARD. I don't want to hear the whole speech, Tommy.
TOMMY. Oh. Well, the main theme is reason and logic.
HOWARD. (*Rises. Crossing* R. *to Tommy.*) Tommy, I would like to give you some advice out of my rich personal experience. In dealing with women a man must shun reason and logic—(*Pushes Tommy down on* L. *arm of sofa.*) for time has shown the male of the species has never been able to turn these two weapons to his own advantage. They are the heritage and birthright of the sex, made of gentle steel, who oppose us. Thus every man must forge a weapon of his own design in the fires of this eternal struggle and pray that when he does go to ~~do battle~~, he will not be reasonably

or logically slain more than sixty percent of the time. A simple man can ask no more.

TOMMY. What weapon do you use, sir?

HOWARD. (*Looks up* L., *then back.*) Confusion. In my twenty years of married life I have confused more issues than a liberal, and have emerged the victor over reason, logic, and my wife, forty percent of the time . . . (*Crosses* L. *to armchair.*) I think.

TOMMY. Congratulations.

HOWARD. (*Crosses* R., *back to Tommy.*) As you get older and your duplicity increases, so will your admiration for this—(*As though sprinkling dust over Tommy*) dust of wisdom I have sprinkled upon you.

TOMMY. Mr. Carol, you mean I should try to confuse Ginger?

HOWARD. No, no. I don't think you'd better try that, Tommy.

TOMMY. If I can't use reason and logic, and I can't use confusion, what's left?

HOWARD. (*Pulls Tommy to his feet.*) Action. . . . Dedication. Tommy, at fourteen a woman is impressed by shining knights and holy grails. At eighteen they start to smile indulgently and when they reach my wife's age, they laugh openly. Tommy, if you're going to win Virginia back you've got to prove you're willing to fight for her.

TOMMY. I'm not a fighter, sir.

HOWARD. You can't ask her to that play. You've got to tell her she's going with you.

TOMMY. She'd hit me. (*Howard crosses* L. *to below drum table, then crosses back to Tommy above it.*)

HOWARD. You've got to be strong and dominant, yet at the same time you've got to let her know no matter what she is or does, she's your girl.

TOMMY. I'm sorry, sir, but I disagree with you.

HOWARD. You do?

TOMMY. Yes. We've never had to resort to intrigue. Our relationship has always been more mature than that.

HOWARD. (*Crossing up to foot of stairs.*) Well, you're the victim. (*Calling upstairs.*) Virginia.

GINGER. (*Off.*) Yes, Pop?

HOWARD. Will you come down here for a minute? (*Tommy crosses* R. *below sofa.*)

GINGER. (*Off.*) Sure.

HOWARD. (*Crossing* L. *to drum table.*) I'll be sitting right here with pad and pencil—(*Picks up pad and pencil from drum table. Crossing* L. *to* D. L. *corner*) just in case you have any last words for posterity. (*Howard turns off wall lamp over* D. L. *corner, sits on upstage bench, concealed from sight. Ginger enters downstairs dressed for play, wearing cape.*)

GINGER. (*Coming down.*) Yes, Pop. (*On lower landing.*) Hello, Tommy.

TOMMY. Hi. . . . (*Crosses up* L. *two steps.*)

GINGER. What do you want?

TOMMY. (*Crosses* L. *a step.*) I came to ask you to the play.

GINGER. You did?

TOMMY. Yes.

GINGER. (*Crossing downstairs to below newel post.*) Well, no, thank you.

TOMMY. (*Crossing* L. *to Ginger.*) Why not?

GINGER. Because you're just like every other man. (*Howard listens attentively.*) You're not big enough in character to accept me as a real equal.

TOMMY. What do you mean?

GINGER. If you recognize me as a football player, then you feel you must discriminate against me as a woman.

TOMMY. Now, just a minute.

GINGER. Don't interrupt. (*Tommy, exasperated, crosses* D. *to* L. *arm of sofa.*) I've got six weeks to make up for. (*Crossing* D. *to* L. *of Tommy.*) I've always liked you because you talked freedom and equality, but when the time came, you couldn't practice it.

TOMMY. I talked about social problems.

GINGER. (*Turns front.*) This is a social problem. (*To Tommy.*) It's all your fault I'm not accepted as a girl.

TOMMY. My fault?

GINGER. Yes, your fault. If you hadn't been so petty and narrow-minded, you would have taken me out these past six weeks and said, "This is my girl."

TOMMY. (*Front.*) "She plays football."

GINGER. Why not?

TOMMY. (*To Ginger.*) People laugh.

GINGER. And you're afraid they're laughing at you. You're a coward, Tommy Green.

TOMMY. That's not true.

GINGER. You're passive instead of active—(*Sobs.*) and I never want to see you again! (*Runs upstairs.*)

TOMMY. (*Crossing U. to foot of stairs.*) All right, if that's the way you feel about it. (*Front doorbell.*)

HOWARD. How are you doing with reason and logic?

TOMMY. (*Crossing L. to U. R. of part of D. L. corner.*) She never gave me a chance. She wants to be both the dominated and dominant figures.

HOWARD. That's because you let her be.

TOMMY. What can I do about it?

HOWARD. I told you. (*Agnes enters from kitchen to answer front door. Crosses R. to U. C.*) The secret of my success with women is that I never let any of them dominate me. (*Agnes stops, looks at Howard, smiles. Howard looks at her.*)

TOMMY. I'm so angry I could go up and drag her down here bodily.

HOWARD. Would you like to try?

EDDIE. (*Off U. R.*) Hya, Mrs. Carol.

AGNES. (*Off U. R.*) Hello, Eddie, come in.

TOMMY. (*Crosses R. to bar.*) No. I guess I better go. (*Agnes enters, followed by Eddie Davis, crosses L. to foot of stairs.*)

AGNES. I'll get Joan.

EDDIE. Hey, did you hear about the touchdown we set up for your daughter this afternoon?

AGNES. Multiple versions. Excuse me, please. (*Exits upstairs.*)

EDDIE. (*Crossing L.*) Hello, Greenie. (*Slaps Tommy on L. shoulder as he passes.*) Hya, Mr. Carol. You sure were excited out there on the field today. I thought you were going to have a heart attack. (*Howard chokes. Eddie turns R., crosses up to Tommy.*) Hey, Greenie, what are you doing here?

TOMMY. Why?

EDDIE. I thought Ginger gave you the brush.

TOMMY. You did?

EDDIE. That's what I heard.

TOMMY. Well, she did. (*Crosses R. to down R. of phone table.*)

EDDIE. Oh, I get it. She asked you over to tell you how to lead her cheers next week. (*Tommy stops below newel post.*) Or maybe she invited you to the play, huh?

TOMMY. What does that mean?

EDDIE. (*Crossing R. to below Tommy.*) Well, all the guys on the

squad are taking their best date, so why shouldn't she take pretty little you? (*Tommy turns L. and hits Eddie, standing directly down-stage of him, on the jaw. Eddie falls flat between ottoman and L. arm of sofa. Tommy stands with his eyes closed a second, then opens them. Howard crosses R. to drum table. Ginger, carrying cape, enters downstairs, followed by Joan carrying coat, followed by Agnes, who remains on upper landing.*)

GINGER. (*Crosses D. to R. of Tommy.*) Tommy.

JOAN. (*Crosses down to above armchair.*) Eddie.

AGNES. Howard.

HOWARD. Yes, dear?

AGNES. Why didn't you stop them from fighting? (*Crosses down to lower landing.*)

HOWARD. Eddie wasn't fighting.

TOMMY. I hate violence.

HOWARD. I can see that.

TOMMY. (*To Ginger.*) But some place a man must take an active stand. (*Eddie rises, crosses suddenly U. to L. of Tommy. Ginger steps back to behind L. back of sofa. Agnes crosses downstage.*)

EDDIE. (*Picks up Tommy's R. fist, looks at it.*) You all right? (*Agnes crosses L. to above Howard.*)

TOMMY. Fine. (*Eddie breaks L.*) And from now on, this girl can do whatever she wants to do. She was right and we were all wrong. Is that clear?

EDDIE. Yeah, Tom. . . .

TOMMY. Okay.

JOAN. (*Turns L. to Howard and Agnes.*) So long, Mom . . . (*Kisses Agnes.*) Dad. (*Kisses Howard over Agnes' L. shoulder.*)

HOWARD. 'Night, Joan.

AGNES. Have a good time, Joan.

JOAN. Yeah. (*Turns to Eddie, who reaches for her coat, which she does not give him.*) You coming, athlete?

EDDIE. Well, yes, dear, I am. (*Joan exits to front door. Eddie shrugs, smiles, follows her off.*)

TOMMY. Well, good night, Mrs. Carol. . . . Mr. Carol. (*To Ginger.*) What I wanted to say before was that I am sorry about the way I acted the past six weeks.

GINGER. (*Crossing L. to Tommy.*) Tommy Green, aren't you going to ask me to the play?

TOMMY. I did ask you.

GINGER. Don't you want to ask me again?

TOMMY. All right. Want to go to the play with me?

GINGER. Sure. (*Hands Tommy cape. He puts it on her. Crossing L. to Agnes.*) I'm ready if you are, Tommy.

TOMMY. Okay, let's go.

AGNES. (*Crossing R. to Ginger.*) Have a nice time, Virginia.

TOMMY. 'Night, Mrs. Carol. (*Crosses L. to Howard. Extends R. hand.*) Thanks, Dad. (*Howard crosses up away from Tommy, considers a moment, then crosses down to Tommy, shakes his hand.*)

HOWARD. All right, son.

TOMMY. (*Crossing R. to below Ginger.*) Come on, Virginia, let's go.

HOWARD. Oh, Tommy . . . (*Tommy and Ginger stop.*) can I have a minute alone with your girl?

TOMMY. (*Looks at his wrist-watch.*) It's getting pretty late.

AGNES. (*Crossing R. to Tommy, takes Tommy by arm.*) Come along, Mr. Green. I'd like to know your intentions. (*Agnes and Tommy exit to front door.*)

HOWARD. I just had to tell you, you're very beautiful, little girl.

GINGER. Thanks, Pop. Oh, I'm sorry I had to break our date.

HOWARD. (*Crossing R. to Ginger.*) I understand.

GINGER. (*Looks over to window R. and back.*) You were right about Tommy.

HOWARD. What do you mean?

GINGER. You said he'd come back, and he did.

HOWARD. I only knew that because that's what I always did.

GINGER. And you said he'd accept me for what I am.

HOWARD. He had no other choice. (*Crossing D. to L. of sofa with Ginger, who sits C. on sofa.*) You know, I may have been right about Tommy, but there was something I was very wrong about. (*Sits on L. end of sofa.*)

GINGER. What?

HOWARD. You and me.

GINGER. What do you mean, Pop?

HOWARD. When you said to Tommy a little while ago, "You're just like every other man," you meant me, didn't you?

GINGER. No, Pop.

HOWARD. Oh, yes, you did. I certainly made an unholy spectacle of myself this afternoon, didn't I?

GINGER. (*Laughs.*) Sort of.

HOWARD. Yeah, but there were a lot of reasons for it. First of all, when I saw you run out on the field I didn't care what anybody thought. I had a football player in the family. You see . . . and this is a secret, just between us and your mother . . . when I was in high school I wasn't a very good football player. (*Sits back.*) As a matter of fact, I never got into any of the games.

GINGER. You didn't?

HOWARD. No, so this was my first game, as well as yours. You know, when I heard the coach say, "Send Carol in," I almost ran out onto the field myself. (*Ginger laughs, then becomes serious.*)

GINGER. Pop?

HOWARD. What, darling?

GINGER. Are you sorry I'm not a boy?

HOWARD. I wouldn't trade you for any boy in the world. (*Howard embraces Ginger, with her head over his R. shoulder.*)

GINGER. May I tell you a secret now, Pop?

HOWARD. You sure can. (*Howard breaks embrace.*)

GINGER. Being a girl is so much fun, I've decided to give up football. (*Howard releases Ginger, turns L.*)

HOWARD. Is that what you want to do most in the world, Miss Carol?

GINGER. Yes, Daddy.

HOWARD. All right. (*Ginger rises, picks up her bag and gloves from coffee table.*)

GINGER. Oh, can I always tell you my secrets?

HOWARD. I hope you will, but I know you won't.

GINGER. Why not?

HOWARD. Because today I'm the man you love, but one of these days I'll just be your father.

TOMMY. (*Off.*) Virginia. (*Ginger crosses R. to window, looks out. She looks back to Howard, who smiles and nods at her. She crosses L. above sofa to U. C., and stands facing Howard while she fixes her dress. He looks at her once more, and she exits to front door, stepping off with a determined stride. Howard rises, crosses up to "Life" picture on wall, takes it down. He looks at it a moment, then places it face down on chair R. of sideboard. Crosses to D. L. corner, picks up his pad from bench.*)

HOWARD. (*Reading.*) "Every man should have a dream, and every dream should have a purpose." (*Crossing R. to drum table.*) Thomas Jefferson. (*Tears speech off pad, crumples it, puts it on*

table.) No wonder he died broke! (*Crosses u. around armchair, sits. Picks up contracts, signs them with a pen from tray on drum table.*)
GINGER. (*Off.*) Good night, Mom.
TOMMY. (*Off.*) Good night, Mrs. Carol.
AGNES. (*Off.*) Have fun, kids. (*Agnes enters from front door.*) Ed and Phyllis are waiting for us out front in the car, Howard. (*Gets her cape, bag and gloves from chair R. of phone table, puts cape on.*)
HOWARD. All right.
AGNES. You ready?
HOWARD. In a minute.
AGNES. Howard, will you please stop writing that speech?
HOWARD. I'm not writing any speech. I'm signing the contracts for the bank.
AGNES. (*Turns L.*) What? When did that happen?
HOWARD. Just now.
AGNES. But why? How?
HOWARD. Agnes, come here.
AGNES. We haven't got much time.
HOWARD. No, no. I want to ask you something. (*Agnes crosses L. to R. of ottoman.*) When did you buy that dress for Virginia?
AGNES. When the season began. I thought she'd need it.
HOWARD. You did, huh?
AGNES. Yes.
HOWARD. She certainly is a little girl now.
AGNES. (*Looking R.*) She certainly is. Howard, I've got a wonderful idea.
HOWARD. What?
AGNES. (*Crossing R. to down C.*) It's something I've been thinking about for a long time.
HOWARD. What?
AGNES. Why don't you and I have a son, huh? (*Howard laughs, rises, crosses to Agnes, takes her in his arms.*)
HOWARD. Say, do we really have to go to that play tonight?
AGNES. Howard! (*They cross u. toward front door as*)

CURTAIN FALLS

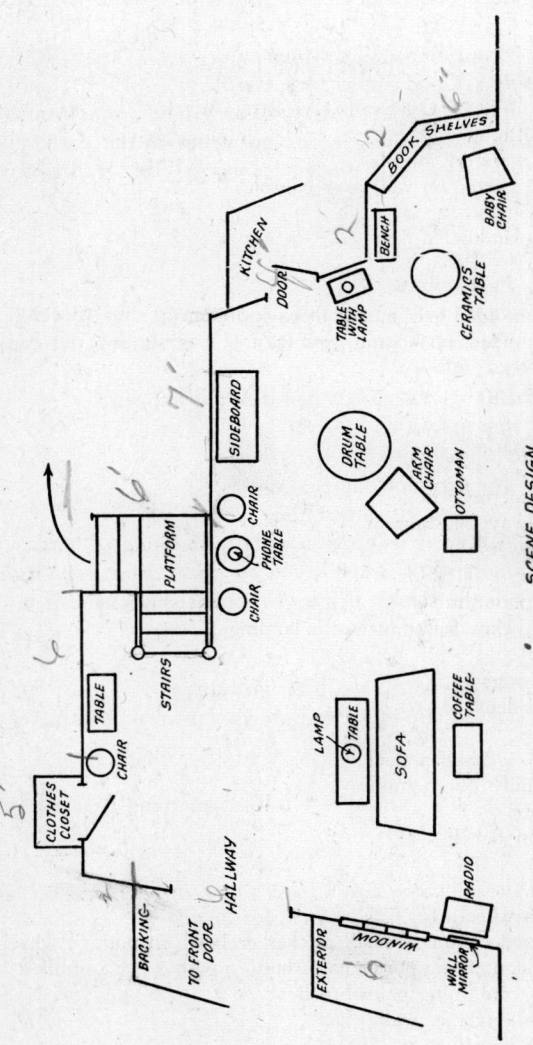

PROPERTY LIST

On Stage, At Rise, Act I

Radio console, D. R.
   Bowl of flowers on console
Small framed mirror on wall over console
Drapes on window
Curtains on window
Sofa
   2 pillows on sofa
   1 curtain unfolded over R. side of back of sofa
1 curtain, unfolded, on floor D. R. sofa
Coffee table D. S. sofa
Table behind sofa
   Magazines
Table S. R. arch
   Lamp
Picture on wall over table
Table in hallway, R. stairway
   Vase of flowers
Hallway chair, S. R. table
Chair, R. of phone table
Phone table, below lower staircase landing
   Telephone
   Vase of flowers
Chair R. of sideboard
Sideboard
Small table D. S. kitchen door
   Framed family photographs
In D. L. corner
   Cushions on bench
   Small chair
Table
Small potter's wheel
Baked, unglazed ceramic—small pitcher or bowl on potter's wheel
   Small rack containing poster paint bottles, with 1 place unfilled
   Small glass containing paint-brushes
Small pictures on D. L. wall
Bookcase over bench, D. L. corner
Armchair, L. C.
Table, L. armchair

Small platter with 3 sharpened pencils and fountain pen, filled
Ottoman, R. armchair
In Hallway Closet
  Old hats
  Galoshes and Rubbers

OFF R.

For HOWARD:
Typed speech
Brief case
  Act I
    1/4 pound jelly beans in paper bag
    Time magazine
    Banking papers in folder
  Act II—Scene 1
    1/4 pound jelly beans in paper bag
    Special *Life* magazine
Small piece goalpost—Act II—Scene 2
Bunch of keys in case—Act III
Corsage in box—Act III

For AGNES:
2 empty stocking boxes, wrapped and tied—Act I
Cardboard box containing jar of poster paint, tied to open easily—Act I
1 section full-sized newspaper—Act I
Black bag and gloves—Act I

For GINGER:
School books—Act I
Football pants, stuffed with jersey, shoulder pads and helmet—Act I

For JEANNIE:
School books—Act I
1 petition, folded—Act I

For JOAN:
1 petition, folded—Act II—Scene 1
2 mail sacks—Act II—Scene 2

For EDDIE:
1 typed list—Act I

For WILSON:
1 petition, folded—Act I

For HOFFMAN:
3 contracts, folded—Act III

TO BE PRESET, ACT II—SCENE 1

1 blue bowl
2 books

To Be Preset, Act II—Scene 2
Framed *Life* cover, on wall over sideboard
Shopping bag, against L. side coffee table, with several bundles of mail, scattered on coffee table

To Be Preset, Act III
Pitcher of flowers on sideboard
Agnes' evening wrap, bag and gloves, on chair R. of phone table

Off L.
For AGNES:
Small towel, wrapped around nail buffer and empty nail cream jar—Act III
For HOWARD—*Act III*:
1 petticoat on hanger
Joan's evening dress on hanger
For GINGER:
Glass of milk—Act I
Raw carrot—Act I
For LIZ:
Coffee service—Act I
  tray
  coffee pot filled with coffee
  2 cups and saucers
Wicker sewing basket—Act I
1 coke—Act I
Special *Life* magazine—Act II—Scene 1
For JOAN:
1 coke—Act II—Scene 1
1 coke—Act II—Scene 2
Laundry bundle, Act II—Scene 2
Hair brush—Act III
For JEANNIE:
1 coke—Act II—Scene 2

To Be Preset, Act II—Scene 2
30-odd packets of letters and telegrams, scattered on D. L. bench and drum table

To Be Preset, Act III
Legal size yellow pad of paper, on L. C. table
New ceramic—small pitcher or jar on potter's wheel

PROPERTY PLOT

Act I

As indicated in property list

Act II—Scene 1

Strike:
Ceramic from potter's wheel on the ceramic table
Brief-case from L. wall table
Glass from drum table
Petition from drum table
Time magazine from drum table
Newspaper from drum table
Cup and saucer from drum table
Coffee service from coffee table
Cup and saucer from coffee table
Jelly beans from chair R. of the sideboard
Flowers from phone table
Set:
Move ceramic table against the downstage bench
Special *Life* magazine in brief-case, off R.
Jelly beans in brief-case, off R.
2 books on console.

Act II—Scene 2

Strike:
Brief-case from L. wall table
Coke bottle from coffee table
Life magazine from coffee table
Glass from drum table
Set:
Shopping bag, against L. side of coffee table
18 packets of mail scattered on coffee table
Hang framed *Life* picture on wall over sideboard
Scatter 36 packets of mail on bench in D. L. corner and on drum table

Act III

Strike:
Mail from inside bench
Shopping bag from platform
Mail bags from below phone table

Piece of goal-post from coffee table
2 books from console
Set:
Unscrew caps of red and blue paint jars in rack, in D. L. corner
New ceramic on potter's wheel
Pad on drum table
Agnes' evening wrap, bag and gloves on chair R. of phone table
Petticoat and Joan's Act III dress on hanger off L.

Successful Plays for Amateurs

THE CURIOUS SAVAGE
FATHER OF THE BRIDE
HARVEY
MISTER ANGEL
JUNIOR MISS
STAGE DOOR
ARSENIC AND OLD LACE
SEVEN SISTERS
YEARS AGO
THE MAN WHO CAME TO DINNER
GEORGE WASHINGTON SLEPT HERE
CUCKOOS ON THE HEARTH
YOU CAN'T TAKE IT WITH YOU

(Most of the titles above are available everywhere, but in order to make certain of availability write direct to the Dramatists Play Service, Inc.) Each play is available in a paper-bound acting edition. *Price, 90c each.*

Send For Free Descriptive Catalogue

Popular Plays
IN 90c ACTING EDITIONS

- THE CHILDREN'S HOUR
- MISTER ROBERTS
- THE SHRIKE
- A SLEEP OF PRISONERS
- TWO DOZEN RED ROSES
- VENUS OBSERVED
- BE YOUR AGE
- IN ANY LANGUAGE
- THE LADY'S NOT FOR BURNING
- FLIGHT INTO EGYPT
- ONE BRIGHT DAY
- THE CHASE
- THE BRASS RING
- SEE THE JAGUAR

DRAMATISTS PLAY SERVICE, Inc.

14 East 38th Street   New York 16, N. Y.

New Plays
For Community Theaters

BE YOUR AGE

THE BRASS RING

IN ANY LANGUAGE

I'VE GOT SIXPENCE

MR. PICKWICK

THE LOVE OF FOUR COLONELS

SEE THE JAGUAR

FLIGHT INTO EGYPT

THE CHASE

ONE BRIGHT DAY

THE CLIMATE OF EDEN

Send for free list of plays

DRAMATISTS PLAY SERVICE, Inc.

14 East 38th Street　　　　　　　New York 16, N. Y.

92 27

[LIBRARY
H.S. PERF. & VIS.
ARTS]

DATE DUE

MAR 2 0 2002
JAN 1 8 2005

40.5811

Lily's Mechanic

THE WOMEN OF WORTHY SERIES - BOOK 6

A SECOND CHANCE ROMANCE

SERALYNN LEWIS

This is a work of fiction. Names, characters, places, and incidents either are the product of the author's imagination or are used fictitiously. Any resemblance to actual persons, living or dead, events, or locales is entirely coincidental.

To the extent the image or images on the cover of this book depict a person or persons, such person or persons are merely models, and are not intended to portray any character or characters featured in the book

All rights reserved. No part of this book may be reproduced or used in any manner without written permission of the copyright owner except for the use of quotations in a book review. For more information, address: info@seralynnlewis.com.

Copyright © 2022 by TimiDio Press, LLC

First paperback edition February 2022

Edited by Carla Rossi
Book cover & Formatting by Qamber Designs

ISBN 978-1-952953-12-5 (paperback)
ISBN 978-1-952953-11-8 (ebook)

www.seralynnlewis.com

ACKNOWLEDGEMENTS

Writing any book is difficult at best, but without friends who have expertise in certain areas, it would be even more difficult.

Dr. Paul Dorinsky was kind enough, once again, to lend his expertise as a physician to verify research on Nils's illness. Huntington's disease, while rare, does exist, is hereditary, and has no cure. For those who suffer with this disease, I pray you find comfort in the Lord and his almighty wisdom. Thank you, Doctor.

Kendal Smeeth, a retired environmental public relations expert, assisted with the research on fuel tanks. Thank you, Kendal.

Laura Volpini, an attorney in Cleveland, Ohio, answered legal questions for the state of Ohio. Thank you, Laura.

For my writing partner and friend, Cheryl Kramarczyk. She's been with me since my first book was published and we've been meeting regularly to review every chapter. Her willingness to take time away from her own writing and her remarkably busy homelife is much appreciated. Thank you, Cheryl.

"Forgiveness does not mean die mean ignoring what has been done or putting a false label on an evil act. It means, rather, that the evil act no longer remains as a barrier to the relationship. Forgiveness is a catalyst creating the atmosphere necessary for a fresh start and a new beginning."

—Martin Luther King

Chapter 1

Carson Brown's back stiffened, and he had a death grip on the wheel as he turned his truck into the entrance of the narrow road that led to his uncle's small airstrip. He slowed to a halt and got out of the truck to remove the chain. The gravel lane would take him to the hangar, terminal, and farmhouse.

The airport's sign dangled from one rusty bolt. Stiff May breezes slapped the faded marquee against the equally neglected pole. The other pole was bent at an odd angle and led him to believe someone, or something, hit it and caused the sign to break off on one end.

Except for his uncle's funeral, he'd been to Worthy, Ohio, only a half dozen times since he left for the Navy, and he hadn't even had time to visit the homestead after the funeral.

A keen sense of loss enveloped him when thoughts of his jovial uncle poured into his brain. He should have made more of an effort to visit.

Uncle Patrick had been instrumental in his life's profession, but now his uncle was dead, and re-visiting the airport and farmhouse gave him a sense of homecoming and peace. It wouldn't last and would be bittersweet. Soon the airport and his childhood home would be owned by someone else, and it pained him.

Lily's MECHANIC

He drove along the narrow lane, eager to see the Cessna and prop plane his uncle kept in the hangar near his farmhouse. The two beauties heightened his love affair with aircraft, and it never waned in the ensuing years. They launched memories of the times he spent working on them with Uncle Patrick.

A sadness smashed him in the chest, and he idly rubbed the area around his heart to ease the pain of loss for the uncle he loved so much. And for the land and planes both he and his uncle loved so much. Carson had spent the bulk of his grade school and high school years here when he and his mother came to live with Uncle Patrick. The sense of loss overpowered him, knowing the place would be sold and everything torn down to make way for housing developments. His gut burned with frustration.

Larger than life, his uncle had been the only male influence he'd ever had—or wanted—when he was a boy. His mother's brother epitomized the man he had wanted to become.

What had happened to the place since the last time he'd been here? Had it really been five years ago? When he spoke to his uncle on the occasions he was stateside, Uncle Patrick told him everything was wonderful. Had he not wanted Carson to worry?

Not that he could have done anything about it while he was at sea, but he could have made an effort to visit more regularly after he'd left the military. At a minimum, he could have come to town before his uncle died. Regret clawed at his gut.

The strong breezes pushed the unkempt tall grasses until they were almost parallel to the land. Stately pines beyond the left side of the lane and the thick swath of trees to the far right past the field created a wind tunnel of sorts. He inhaled deep of their clean, fresh scent. The expansive oak and elms ran the length of his uncle's property and formed a

2

barrier between the airport and the Sandburg Farm just on the other side.

As a kid and even as a teenager, he flew kites in the football-sized tract. He recalled the wind as it rushed in his face and the joy of a fun afternoon. Uncle Patrick told him the location of the trees made the area an ideal spot for it.

On other occasions, Carson laid in the grass and relished staring at the blue sky. When the planes took off, he gazed with wonder at the underbellies of the small aircraft.

A heartfelt sigh filled his lungs. Time to see how the rest of his uncle's place fared.

As he pulled into the makeshift driveway at the old farmhouse, and got out of his truck, he whipped off his sunglasses and rubbed his jaw. His gaze wavered from one building to the next.

The old homestead wasn't in great shape, with its less-than-level front porch and green peeling paint. Could it be his uncle had never painted the place since he was a teenager?

The hangar seemed in better condition than the terminal, and there were two additional outbuildings. They hadn't been there the last time he visited. No surprise his uncle added new buildings but hadn't painted the house. Uncle Patrick's priorities were always about the planes and never about his living space. Carson couldn't disagree with his thought process.

Air punctuated by cow manure wafted around him. The smell wasn't unwelcome, but he'd forgotten the pungent aroma and how it made his nose wrinkle.

Where am I headed? The question wrapped around his chest like a vise as he remembered his uncle's funeral six weeks ago. What would he do now that he found himself without a wife or a job? Rudderless in a sea of confusion. That's what he was.

Lily's MECHANIC

Uncle Patrick made it clear he planned to give his estate to charity, but Carson longed for the place that held so many wonderful memories.

The eerie silence gripped him until a rumble of an engine caused him to squint toward the end of the lane. He glanced at his phone. The attorney was right on time.

William Bottleson had been one of his uncle's many close friends. He vaguely remembered Uncle Patrick's legal counsel, but he had little contact with him back then and only briefly saw him at the funeral. There were so many folks who wanted to extend their condolences and tell wonderful stories of his uncle that Carson hadn't spent a lot of time with any one person.

The attorney leveraged his more than portly figure out of his late model SUV and waddled to him with the strap of his satchel slung over his shoulder. He extended his beefy hand for a hardy shake. "It's good to see you, Carson. After the funeral, you left before I had a chance to speak with you, and your uncle insisted I talk to you in person."

His shoulders bowed and more regret piled on his already weighted conscious. "I had a family emergency and had to leave." It still left a bitter taste in his mouth.

"No matter. I have the keys to the house and the hangar padlock. We'll go inside and discuss Patrick's estate."

The attorney handed Carson the keys, and he unlocked the door.

He preceded the attorney and wiped his feet on the outside mat like his uncle had taught him all those years ago. Some habits were ingrained. The place reeked of dust and grime in the stagnant air.

The attorney coughed and wiped his mouth with displeasure. "We should open some windows."

Bottleson led him to his uncle's kitchen and opened the back door and window above the sink. The peeling and cracked wallpaper was in even worse shape than it had been in his boyhood days. It had a cluttered, lived-in look.

His uncle's attorney shifted in the uncomfortable chair. "The paperwork we need to go over won't take long."

"Uncle Patrick told me he'd planned on giving his estate to charity. I love this place, but wish I still had my uncle alive and well." Carson lowered his tall frame on the opposite side of the scuffed oak table.

A small smile played on the attorney's lips as if he had some secret. "Your uncle knew you loved him, and he loved you, too, which is why he left you his entire estate."

Carson rose and paced one end of the kitchen to the other, which took about four steps. His right hand gripped the back of his neck. "But he told me he was leaving the place to charity."

A pair of cheater lenses emerged from the attorney's breast pocket, and he perched them on the end of his nose. "Patrick changed his will less than a month before he died." Bottleson eyed him over the top of the lenses.

"But why?" He slumped into the chair, folding his arms over one another on the edge of the table. "He'd made it clear everything would be given to charity and never even hinted he'd changed his mind when I spoke to him three months ago. I even offered to buy the planes from him, but he refused."

The attorney squirmed and flipped through the pages in the thick file he'd pulled from his muddy brown case. "Your uncle decided you needed something other than the loss of your marriage to focus on. He was adamant, though, on the requirements for the transfer."

He leaned forward and clasped his hands, his breathing forced. "What do you mean?"

"Your uncle wanted to renovate and make it into a regional airport of substance. He planned to invite you to move here permanently and give you the position of head mechanic. No one could have imagined a blood clot would take his life."

"I don't understand." He slowly shook his head and pulled in his lips.

"Your uncle left specific instructions. To inherit the estate, you must complete the renovation, and demonstrate the airport's profitability. If you can't or refuse, the estate will go to auction with the proceeds distributed to his favorite charities. Except the land he bought from Nils Sandburg. It will revert to him or his heirs."

Bottleson pushed the paperwork toward him.

He snatched the three-page document and scanned its contents. "In less than six months?" His voice rose as he crumpled the edge of the document. "This is impossible. When did he buy land from Sandburg?"

The late spring sunshine warmed the old kitchen, but even with the door and window open, and the slight movement of air in the room, the walls closed in on him. Decades of aircraft oil filled his nostrils.

"Patrick bought the land some four years back. The deed is in the file. About a year ago, he hired an architect to re-design the airport and hangar. Meet with the architect and fulfill the terms of the will, and everything will be yours."

The attorney's matter-of-fact tone rankled, and the terms twisted his innards. But he'd play along.

"Did my uncle leave funds for the renovation?"

Beads of sweat dotted the attorney's high forehead and made him question what Bottleson wasn't saying. "There is some money in your uncle's accounts… but certainly not

enough to complete the entire renovation. It's my understanding Patrick planned to obtain a line of credit for the difference to complete the financing. You're free to do that, but it might be difficult since there are conditions to ownership. I don't think your uncle considered the final piece of financing needed when he changed his will. I hope you have personal funds to draw from for the renovation."

He'd have to partially finance the renovation? How much would he have to ante up? And if he failed? He'd lose his hard-earned savings.

His mind swirled with so many questions he blurted the foremost thing in his mind. "Why do you think he changed his will?"

The attorney took a deep breath and looked him straight in the eye. "I believe he sensed his death."

"What?" If smoke could have shot out of his ears, it would have filled the small room and obliterate the man before him. "You were one of his best friends, and you did nothing?"

The attorney's face became mottled with pinks and reds, and the sweat that had beaded earlier now made its way down the side of his cheek. "Now look here, Carson. Patrick never once gave any indication he had a notion his time was up. Sometimes people just know when the end is at hand. That was my gut feeling and why I think he changed his will."

A sense of remorse filled Carson's spirit. "I'm sorry. That was uncalled for."

Bottleson gave him a slight nod, lumbered to his feet, and handed Carson the folder. He shut the kitchen door and window. "Prayerfully consider it. The architect's contact information is listed in the file. I suggest you contact him sooner rather than later."

Carson held the folder close to his chest as if doing so

Lily's MECHANIC

would help him understand what had been going through his uncle's brain in the six months before he died.

"Patrick's savings and investments have been placed in an escrow account ready for when you make your decision." The attorney gave him an understanding look. "I rarely give a personal opinion, but I hope you decide to fulfill your uncle's dream. He would have liked that. I hope to see you in church on Sunday."

"Wouldn't miss it." He'd need the Lord's guidance with this entire situation, a step of faith if ever there was one. "I'll walk you to your car."

As he exited the farmhouse and locked the door, Carson looked up in time to see two young boys barreling across the field toward the trees.

He stepped off the porch and pointed. "Hey, you. Stop," he screamed and was about to run after them, but Bottleson grabbed his arm.

"Let them go. You have more important things to worry about than two kids crossing your uncle's land."

The little guys raced into the trees and looked over their shoulders to check if he chased them.

He gave the boys a thoughtful stare. "I don't remember Uncle Patrick saying there were young boys living nearby."

The attorney ambled to his car, opened the door, and chuckled. "They were probably treasure hunting."

His legs ate up the distance, and he put a hand on the attorney's arm. "Wait. Treasure hunting? Since when has there ever been any treasure on this land?"

"Your uncle caused quite a stir a few years back. Claimed there was treasure buried on his land." The man grasped his chin and the corner of his mouth lifted in a grin. "You know what a jokester he was. Told me he wanted to get people

interested in coming out to look at the airport. The folks of Worthy and even some people from Columbus came out and searched, but most folks believed your uncle had a few screws loose. Patrick laughed it off."

"What do you think?"

Attorney Bottleson heaved a sigh and gripped the car door. "I think it was a failed marketing ploy, and I told him so. He smirked, but never denied it."

He pointed to the trees. "Who do you think those kids were?"

"Check the Sandburg farm, they might know."

"I'll do that."

After the attorney drove away, he leaned his head back to stare at the cloud-streaked sky. "Great. If I take on Uncle Patrick's challenge, I'll have to worry about kids getting hurt on a construction site."

With hands propped on her hips, Lily Bennett looked around the old farmhouse kitchen in dismay. When did her childhood home turn into such a pit?

When her sons' grade school year ended in Austin, she consigned whatever was left of their family's furniture, loading her two boys and the meager possessions they could fit into her old SUV, and hightailed it back to her father's dairy farm in Worthy, Ohio. A place where she'd be able to regain normalcy and relax before she figured out her next steps.

By moving, she thought she had escaped the disaster that had become her life. But she was wrong. When she arrived yesterday, she stepped into a catastrophe she sensed might be worse than the last several years. Her father's jubilance

at their homecoming curtailed any questions about the farm and the house.

While she tackled the house one room at a time, she'd unravel the deplorable condition of her childhood home.

She blew out a breath and swiped stray hairs from her face and tucked them under her headband. "This house will take weeks to clean and organize and it doesn't even include the farm issues," she grumbled to herself.

Project management skills she acquired over the years would help with the overwhelming tasks, but she couldn't remain unemployed for too long.

The front door slammed, and she wiped her hands on her old apron as she stepped into the somewhat more organized version of the living room. Her sons ran inside and flopped onto the faded floral sofa, releasing plumes of dust in the air. Her nose wrinkled in disgust.

Despite the filth, her heart filled with joy as she looked at her two young sons, who seemed to have settled into farm life in less than a day. "You boys are all sweaty. What have you been doing?"

Evan, her youngest at nine, cast a swift glance at his older brother for direction.

"We just ran across the farm," twelve-year-old Lucas explained and shifted his eyes from her to his brother.

The head tilt toward Evan was a dead giveaway they'd been into something she wouldn't be happy about. But now wasn't the time to get into it when the old farmhouse needed a spring cleaning that should have been done ten years ago. They'd spill their secrets soon enough, and she didn't have the energy to play twenty questions.

"I see." She pointed her finger at the four super-sized trash bags next to the couch. "While you take those out to

the cans in the garage, I'll put lunch on the table."

Evan's red face scrunched with distaste. "Aw, Mom. Do we have to?"

She folded her arms across her chest and tapped her foot in her old running shoes. The muffled sound on the threadbare carpet hadn't given her the desired effect, so she resorted to *the look*.

Lucas poked his brother and shoved off the sofa. "Come on. Let's go. I'm starving."

They fisted the bags and dragged them out to the garage. She chuckled and stepped into the kitchen to pour three tall glasses of tangy lemonade.

The boys slid into the kitchen, sat in their chairs, and grabbed the glasses as she placed a sandwich, carrot sticks, and two cookies in front of each boy.

Lucas gulped the drink and wiped his mouth with the back of his hand. "Mom, you make the best lemonade."

"Use a napkin, son."

"And cookies." Evan crunched the sweet treats with crumbs falling out of the corners of his mouth.

Her lips twitched as she sipped the lemonade. Despite everything that had happened in the past six years, she sensed a new chapter of her life had begun. "Eat your sandwich."

Evan grabbed half and held it in mid-air. "Grandad told us there was buried treasure over at the old McClellan place." Her son's face got red, and he slapped the other hand over his mouth, then lowered his head to stare at the table. "Sorry, Lucas."

"Can't keep your trap shut," Lucas muttered and grabbed his sandwich and stuffed it in his mouth.

"Is that what you were doing? Looking for buried treasure?" She cocked her head and took a bite of her sandwich.

Evan's eyes grew wide, and he wiggled in his seat. "Gran-

Lily's MECHANIC

dad... er, Farfar told us all about it. He said we could look for it."

So little fun had existed in her sons' lives that she'd not begrudge them the intrigue of searching for non-existent buried treasure. Her father, however, should rein in the tall tales.

"He did, did he? You can look, but you will *not* dig anywhere over there, understood?"

Evan's brow furrowed and she could almost see the wheels flying around in his brain. He cupped his chin in his palms and frowned. "But Mom. How are we going to find it if we don't dig? It's buried, you know?"

"The land doesn't belong to Farfar, so you can't dig over there, OK?"

Lucas's shoulders drooped, and his breath came out in a whoosh. "It doesn't matter. The guys who showed up this morning didn't seem to want us there."

She sat up straight and forced her gaze from one son to the other. "What guys?"

Evan leaned toward her and lowered his voice as if he were on a super spy mission. "Two guys came out of the house just as we ran through the field to come home. The tall guy yelled for us to stop, but we kept running. He stared at us but didn't chase us."

Her mind whirred. It could only be Carson Brown. Who else could it have been? She'd relegated his name to the section of her brain marked lost love, but lately he invaded her dreams, and she couldn't figure out why. *I guess you never forget your first crush.*

What Carson was doing over at the airport was none of her business. She had too many of her own problems to worry about, but her mind remembered how her entire body trembled with hurt when her dad told her Carson had married.

"We were behind the hangar when they drove up. All the

12

buildings were locked." Evan's shoulders registered a dejection she hadn't seen since he lost his father to the justice system.

"I should hope so," she mumbled into her glass. A tiny frown forced its way to her lips.

Lucas grabbed another cookie. "After we got past the fence, we watched from behind the trees. The short guy got into the SUV and the tall guy watched the other guy drive off. Then he went inside the hangar. We watched for a while, but he didn't leave, so we came home."

Evan's eyes glittered with unshed tears. "Do you think Farfar told us about the treasure so we wouldn't bother him?"

They'd had so little male interaction since her husband had been imprisoned and even before, that she expected her father could fill the void. With deliberate movements, she set the glass on the table. She placed her elbow on the table and rested her chin on her fist. "Did he tell you to go, or did you ask him *if* you could go?"

"We asked," Lucas said.

"There you are. He didn't tell you *to* go. He said you *could* go. Big difference. I'm sure Farfar loves having you around. When you're through eating, go call him in for lunch."

When her dad came in, he reeked of cow. She'd have to reacquaint herself to the various animal smells. He washed up in the chipped farmhouse sink and sat to eat his lunch.

Her youngest son made a beeline to the chair next to her dad. "Tell us more about the buried treasure."

Her father grunted and chewed on his sandwich.

She placed a hand on her son's shoulder. "Go upstairs. You have one hour to play video games, then I'll need your help." The horror of doing chores always made them hide in their rooms.

Lucas jumped out of his chair and grabbed his brother's hand. "Come on, Evan. Mom wants to talk to Grandad."

Lily's MECHANIC

As the boys tromped up the steps, she sat and stared at her father. The years of farming had weathered his face with dark creases. His skin sagged, and he looked... unwell.

"Dad, are you OK?"

"I'm fine." Her father bristled and chomped on his sandwich. "Thanks for making lunch. I'm always so busy, I forget to eat."

"We won't let you forget to eat, Dad." She placed her hand on his veiny hand and he turned his palm up to curl his fingers around hers.

"You have your mother's hands." He gave her a wistful smile, as if he remembered the texture of her mother's touch in their clasped fingers. "I'm so glad you came home. I've missed you and the boys. They'll be a huge help around the farm."

She leaned forward and tilted her head. "I don't know how much help they'll be with your tall tales. Since when has there been a buried treasure over at the airport?"

A look of confusion passed over her father's face. "Patrick said there was. He died, you know." The comment brought a sadness to her father's faded blue eyes.

She squeezed his hand and pulled hers away to stack the dishes. "I know. He was your best friend."

"He was... And I miss him." His face brightened. "I hope Carson comes back and opens the airport."

For a moment, her mind traveled to a time when she and Carson spent all their summers and school days together. She remembered their last conversation before he left for the military. But he'd broken her heart, and she'd resigned herself that a relationship with him wasn't meant to be.

The sound of her father clearing his throat brought her back to the present.

He stilled and squinted at her. "Are you coming to church

14

on Sunday?"

The abrupt change of her father's demeanor caught her off guard.

"I'm not sure I'm ready to handle Worthy's gossip mill, Dad." She glanced around the room. "There's so much to do around here. When was the last time anyone cleaned? I threw out four big bags of trash and that was just from the living room."

Her admonishment made him hang his head. "I was going to clean, but I never got around to it. Since it was always just me, there didn't seem to be much point." His shoulders drooped and his voice trailed off to a whisper.

"Well, I'm not living in squalor, so I'll clean, paint, and make any necessary repairs."

Her father's head slowly shook from side to side. "That takes money, and I don't have it."

"I'll pay for the repairs and do the painting myself. I don't think any of the rooms have been painted since Mom died."

He frowned and lifted himself from the chair with a slight groan and took his plate to the sink. "The boys need to have the Lord in their lives."

"And you can take them with you on Sunday."

Her father exhaled softly, and he gave her a brief nod. "I'm headed out to the milking barn."

After her father shut the kitchen door with a quiet click, she rubbed her forehead with her fingertips. Why was her father interested if they went to church? It was another thing she'd have to tackle, and she wasn't ready for it. She hadn't set foot in church since she left home all those years ago when she'd decided to depend on herself for success.

How's that working out for you?

Chapter 2

After the attorney left, Carson found the hangar's key. It slid easily into the padlock, and it opened without a sound. He fumbled around on the wall to find the light switch.

When the cavernous room filled with sparse light, he frowned as he turned in a circle to take in every aspect of the huge area. Many of the overhead lights were burned out. It wasn't as organized or as clean as it had been the last time he'd visited.

Tools and airplane parts scattered across the floor in a haphazard way, almost as if an intruder had tossed the place. It wasn't like his uncle to leave the hangar in such disarray. Dank air and old motor oil permeated the room. How long had it been closed?

With careful movements, he stepped through the mess between the two planes and ran his hand over the Cessna's sleek fuselage. Before he could fly it or the prop plane, he'd have to check the licenses and ensure they were air worthy.

The amount of dirt on his hand told him neither aircraft had been flown in some time. It broke his heart. These planes were Uncle Patrick's pride and joy. What had happened? Had he begun to overhaul them?

His sudden death must have happened while he was in

the middle of it. "Well, at least no one stole anything," he mumbled to himself. "At least I don't think so."

Carson pulled out his phone to call Bottleson, but it went to voicemail, and he left a message. He wouldn't invest his time or savings until he had a better handle on what his investment would be. Any decision he'd make would require a call to the architect.

But first he'd visit his uncle's best friend.

He jumped into his truck and drove over to the Sandburg farm.

As he pulled up, Nils Sandburg and two of his farm workers came out of the barn. The farmhands made their way to the milking building, and the old man shuffled to the truck in his baggy overalls. His stooped back and gaunt face worried Carson.

He'd seen the man at his uncle's funeral, and was dismayed at how much he'd aged, but hadn't had enough time to have a heart to heart with Nils or with anyone else.

The timing of his uncle's burial coincided with yet another round of demands from his ex-wife, and he had to return to Virginia.

"Carson, my boy. Good to see you." Nils held out his hand and Carson shook it. The strength of the proud farmer had diminished quite a bit. "Are you here to take over the airport? Patrick planned for you to come back one day." The old man's blue eyes wavered, and a sadness enveloped them. "He's dead, you know, and I miss him."

He gripped his uncle's best friend's shoulder. "I know. I'm sorry for your loss."

Nils shaded his eyes from the late spring sun and a look of confusion covered his face. "What are you doing here?"

"I didn't get a chance to talk to you after the funeral and

I just stopped by the airport." He thumbed in the direction of his uncle's land. "Do you know if Uncle Patrick had been working on the planes when he died?"

The old man scratched his head. "I don't rightly know. We didn't talk about what he was doing over there." He leaned in and glanced from side to side as if there was someone in the vicinity to eavesdrop on their conversation. "He told me there was buried treasure somewhere on his land and he was going to find it."

His brow furrowed and his lips screwed up in displeasure. "When did he tell you that?"

Nils ran a hand through his sparse hair. "Don't know. I just know it's there, and he was looking for it." His face transformed with a huge smile. "Now that you're here, you can find it for Patrick… unless my grandsons beat you to it." He cackled like old women gossiping on their front porches, then coughed briefly.

Boys? Lily had sons? Was her husband here? A stab of something unknown ran through his chest, but he dismissed it.

Wondering about a woman from his childhood and teenage years wasn't something he wanted to dwell on. She was married, and he wasn't interested anyway. Women were nothing but trouble as far as he was concerned. Lily's father stood to regain the land if the renovation wasn't completed on time *and* the airport didn't demonstrate profitability.

Clearly Nils had already forgotten his uncle was dead. There'd be no useful information from the old man, and Bottleson would be no help because he hadn't believed the wild tale in the first place.

"Were your grandsons over at the airport this morning?"

Carson snatched a glance around the Sandburg farm, and it had been pretty much neglected, just like his uncle's

farmhouse. The barn's sagging roof and the buildings' faded paint told him the farm wasn't faring as well as it had been years ago. It hadn't looked this way when he was a boy.

He couldn't allow the kids to roam around the airport and house if he'd be renovating it, and he couldn't afford a lawsuit or to lose his inheritance. He needed to hold on to all the cash he had.

Nils's eyes brightened, and he bounced on his heels. A huge smile replaced the confusion of a minute ago. "Lily is here. You should go on over to the house and see her. Maybe she would know."

Those boys were her sons. A knot of longing and loss swirled through his belly. He'd wanted to start a family with his wife, Tanya, but she hadn't wanted children. At least not until she had found herself a better man. Women were trouble. A bitter lesson he'd learned from his ex-wife.

His jaw clenched as he watched Nils turn and shuffle to the barn.

He got into his truck and drove to the house.

It was time to face his past. A past that haunted him since he'd left Worthy.

As he walked past overgrown flower beds and a vegetable garden that hadn't been tended to in what he guessed was years, he stepped on the pitted wooden steps and knocked on the door. Clear packing tape covered three holes in the screen.

Carson's heart went out to the two young boys, but he couldn't afford to let himself become involved with Lily's family, not with the airport renovation hanging over his head. Besides, the boys had a father, a grandfather and... one another. Although with the spaced-out way Nils acted, the boys could at least depend on their father.

Lily's MECHANIC

Lily's steps faltered as she strode to the door, wiping her hands on a dishcloth, then hoisting it over her shoulder. The woman behind the screen door wasn't the girl he remembered. Fine lines creased her brow and her mouth pinched in a frown, but the pink tinges in her cheeks told him she recognized him.

She hadn't invited him in, but stood staring at him. He guessed she hadn't wanted him to see the condition of the interior. If it was anything like the exterior, he could understand her reluctance.

"Lily." Air rushed through his lungs and her name floated out of his mouth like a prayer.

The relationship he'd had with the woman in front of him crashed to a violent death a long time ago, and he wasn't interested anyway. "Can I talk to you for a moment?"

Wouldn't you know it? Lily's face had turned crimson in embarrassment. Scrubbing the kitchen in her ratty shorts and t-shirt hadn't prepared her for Carson when he appeared on her doorstep. She was face to face with a past she couldn't change.

What was the difference if she looked less than attractive? He was married, and she had a boatload of problems he couldn't possibly fathom. She absentmindedly pulled the dishcloth from her shoulder and held it in front of her and hoped to hold back the tide of emotion that threatened to overwhelm her. She hadn't wanted, nor had she needed him popping over at one of her many low points in the past fifteen years.

No doubt he was there about the boys. What other reason could Carson have to visit? He'd made it clear he hadn't been interested in pursuing their relationship a long time

20

ago. *Stop it.* Her only concern was for the boys, her father, and the farm, in that order.

She eased herself outside and quietly shut the screen door behind her and stood at an angle, hoping the boys were engrossed in their video games. But it wasn't meant to be when she heard them trouncing down the stairs to skid into the front hallway.

"It's him." Evan's voice rose, and he pulled at his brother's arm.

Lucas poked him in the ribs with his pointy elbow, leaned in, and whispered something, all the while keeping a close eye on Carson and her.

Both boys squeezed through the door and stepped around her to stand between her and Carson. Her heart melted at their confidence and courage.

Evan's little body shook as he tilted his head farther back to look at the tall man.

Carson's lips twitched, and he crouched in front of them with his forearms casually resting on his knees. "I think I saw you this morning running across the field at the airport."

Lucas pulled his shoulders back. "Yes, sir. That was us."

More than anything, her son's truthfulness made her heart swell with pride.

"We were—"

Lucas clamped a hand over Evan's mouth to shut him up.

Carson's lips lifted into a slight grin and his eyes danced as he cast a quick glance at Lily. "Looking for buried treasure, were you?" He uttered the words in the stilted silence.

Her mouth dropped open, and she snapped it shut. "You know about that?"

His eyes twinkled, and he gave her a barely there nod. "I heard." The soft response of those two words catapulted her

21

Lily's MECHANIC

back to another time.

Carson lifted to his feet and extended his hand. "I'm Carson, an old friend of your mother's."

The gentleness of his speech toward her sons gave her goosebumps. No man had ever treated them with the degree of respect Carson had shown in the course of two minutes. Not even their own father.

"You know our mom?" Lucas squinted at him but hadn't shaken Carson's hand. Instead, her son accused her with narrowed eyes.

She glared at her sons until they squirmed. "Carson and I haven't spoken since we graduated from high school."

Her childhood friend's face turned grim, and his entire body stiffened. "Perhaps I should speak to your husband."

Evan raised his chin. "He's dead."

A chasm opened in her stomach at the hollow quality of her young son's voice. The pain of the past rushed through her as Carson's gaze flickered from her sons to her. The grief counselors helped her boys to deal with the loss, but the pain and sadness remained.

His throat wobbled and his eyes grew dim. "I'm very sorry for your loss."

She gave a slight nod and placed a hand on each of her son's shoulders. "These are my sons, Lucas and Evan."

Anything to get the conversation away from her dead husband and back to the present.

Carson turned his attention to the boys. "Nice to meet you, but I don't think there's any buried treasure at the airport and even if there was, it would have been found long ago." His quiet voice softened the sternness of the words.

Lucas took a half step forward. "But Farfar said there was."

At the confused look on Carson's face, she lifted a corner

22

of her mouth. "Farfar is Swedish for grandfather."

He squatted to the boys' eye level again. "The thing is… there's equipment–"

Evan's bottom lip came out. "And we'll be in the way."

"That's not what I was going to say. My concern is for you and your brother's safety, Evan, not the fields or airport. If something were to happen to you, your mother would never forgive me, and I would never forgive myself."

A stark difference from their father when he was alive. She pondered if he had sons of his own that he could be so in tune to hers.

Her teenage heartthrob had turned into quite a man. He filled out as a man usually does at their age. She took in the perfectly creased khaki pants and blue and white pin-striped shirt. The sleeves had been rolled up and his muscled forearms caught her eye. He looked terrific as opposed to her washer woman outfit. No matter how good-looking Carson had become, they had a history she didn't wish to revisit. The pain of their last meeting spiraled and slammed into her chest.

Evan hopped from one foot to another. "Are there any planes in the hangar? Can we see them?"

Carson rose to his full height and his shoulders tightened. "The hangar has lots of sharp-edged stuff I need to corral, and you could get hurt, badly. When I get the place organized and cleaned up, I'll invite you to look at the planes. But I can't say when it will be. A lot has to happen before then."

He shifted his gaze from her to her sons and put his hands back in his pockets almost as if he hadn't known what to do with them.

From the expression on his face, she gathered he wanted to speak to her in private. "Boys, run to the barn and tell grandad Carson is here."

Lily's MECHANIC

"But Mom–" Lucas threw his arms across his chest, and she feared he'd refuse.

"No buts. Grandad needs to talk to Carson."

With reluctance, the boys clomped down the stairs, but all the way to the barn Lucas kept looking over his shoulder.

"What did you want to talk about?"

He grinned in the same way he had years ago, his eyes crinkled, and her heart fluttered. "You always could read me. It's great to see you, Lily. You look wonderful."

"Yeah, right. I'm exhausted and hip deep in dirt..." Her voice trailed and she was mortified at her words. She stared at his shoulder because she hadn't wanted him to see her thoughts. Out of the corner of her eye, she saw him wrinkle his brow in a thoughtful way.

"There's no treasure at the airport and I'm seriously worried they'll hurt themselves on a piece of equipment or something."

"I'd already told them they could look for treasure, but it was before..." She sighed and put her fists on her hips with the hand towel dangling on one side. "Are you renovating in preparation to sell?"

If he put the airport on the market, it might make the farm more valuable if her dad had to sell. It would also mean he'd be around for a while. Would his wife be there too? The last person she wanted to run into was Carson's wife. Lily was still angry at him for how he treated her. Over the years, her adeptness at professionalism kept her from lashing out at him.

She couldn't help herself and chanced a glance at his left hand, but there was no ring there and not even a shadow of one either. He probably hadn't ever worn one since he worked on planes. A lot of the construction workers she'd worked with hadn't worn them because they could lose a fin-

24

ger if it got caught on a piece of equipment.

His head jerked, and he narrowed his gaze. "How do you know the airport was to be renovated?

She tilted her head to the barn and crossed her arms. "Dad mentioned it a time or two when we talked on the phone."

He moved his gaze from her face to over her shoulder. "I'm not sure yet. I have some research to do before I'll commit to renovating."

"Are you staying at your uncle's house?"

His eyes met hers. "I'm at Amy's Bed & Breakfast. Do you remember Charlie Dillon? His little sister, Amy, owns it now."

"Dad told me Charlie passed away while in the military some years ago. So sad."

"That's right. But speaking of your dad… I stopped to see him first because I wanted to ask him about Uncle Patrick. He seemed out of it. Have you noticed?"

"I just arrived late yesterday afternoon and I'm getting acclimatized to farm life again." Her face crumpled, and she wrung her hands. She wasn't the only one who noticed her father's strange behavior. "Dad hasn't done much to the house in a long, long time."

"I'm sorry to hear. Uncle Patrick's place isn't in decent shape either."

She looked over Carson's shoulder to see her sons tearing through the yard. "The boys are on their way. Please don't mention Dad's lapses."

"I have to leave anyway."

She grasped the hand towel with both hands and gave him a hard glare. "I'll make sure the boys don't go anywhere near your place."

"I'm happy to give the boys a tour when I'm sure they won't get hurt." His mouth worked as if he wanted to say

Lily's MECHANIC

something more but thought better of it.

Lucas barreled up the stairs with his brother right behind him. "Mom, Farfar already spoke to him. Can we have a drink?"

She ruffled their heads as they wrapped their arms around her waist and leaned into her side.

Carson zipped down the steps and walked backward and kept his eye on her. "I'll call when the place is fit for you to visit, boys. Take care, Lily."

And he was gone just like the last time.

She'd have to guard her brain and her heart against Carson now that they were both in Worthy.

Chapter 3

Carson strode to the hangar's office late Friday afternoon and flopped into his uncle's rickety roll-around chair.

He leaned his head back and almost fell backward onto the floor. "First thing on the agenda… Get a new chair," he muttered as he leaned sideways and cast a frustrated glance at the offensive chair.

The generic ring tone of his phone made him scramble to pull it out of his pocket. Bottleson.

"Thanks for returning my call." Carson stared dejectedly at the list of repairs and maintenance needed to get the hangar operational again. "Yesterday, I took a peek at the planes, but the entire hangar was in disarray. It looked as though someone had torn through every piece of equipment, tool, and part. Do you know anything about that?"

The attorney raised his chin. "Patrick wanted to clear out the old junk, buy new tools, and reorganize so when you came to visit, you'd be more likely to make the move to Worthy. I never looked in the hangar after he died. I'm sorry it was left that way."

"It makes some sense although my uncle had been fastidious about the hangar and would not have left it the way I found it. All day I've been sorting through the mess and

have only been able to clear through a third of it. I'm making notes as I go along.

"So, you're planning on doing the renovation?" The eagerness in Bottleson's voice made him smile.

"Conditionally, yes."

"Explain." The attorney's gruff tone made him think there was something more to the attorney's interest than just closing out his old friend's estate.

"I haven't spoken to the architect, yet. Did my uncle leave any paperwork about the cost of the renovation?"

Dust swirled around the stale air in the office. With no windows and no air-conditioning, pleasant working conditions would be a priority if he were in here on a daily basis.

Bottleson's voice interrupted his train of thought. "If Patrick had preliminary pricing, it would either be in the hangar office or his den. Have you looked?"

"No, but I will. I have a general idea of my finances. My uncle's savings that were listed in the file doesn't seem like a lot and I have to see if I can stretch my savings far enough to get the ball rolling. If not, I'll have to take on inspection work to cover the shortfall."

"Right." Bottleson grunted and his chair creaked in the background. "I'd forgotten something yesterday. Patrick had a security system installed in the house and hangar. But the company was bought out, and no longer serviced residential systems. It angered your uncle for good reason, and he let the contract expire."

"Why would Uncle Patrick have a security system installed? He'd always padlocked the hangar and never had trouble before." Carson's voice rose, and he ran a dirty hand through his hair, stopping immediately when he became aware he'd done it. "You saw the house. There's nothing of

value in there."

The attorney sighed. "He had it installed when he tried to sell the idea of a hidden treasure."

"That buried booty will be the death of me." His irritated voice bounced through the room as he looked around the office. *What were you thinking Uncle Patrick, and why hadn't you ever discussed it with me?*

To be fair, Carson only had semi-regular contact with his uncle since he went into the military. When he got out, his focus was on his job and his wife. He worked to keep the grimace off his face. *It was a mistake to think she would replace Lily.*

"I believe the alarm controls are in the house's front hall closet, but I'm not sure where they are in the hangar."

Carson raised his head and squinted at the opposite wall. A new electrical panel caught his attention. He hadn't noticed it the last time he was here. It's here in the hangar office. It'll be something I have to think about if I... but right now questions must be answered for me to make a decision. I feel better knowing the state of the hangar was Uncle Patrick's handiwork and not an intruder. I'll search the den for the cost estimate."

"Understood. Let me know if you have any other questions."

"Will do."

After the call ended, he searched through the office. He was hungry and wanted to clean up. He lifted his tired posterior out of the chair, cast a quick glance at his work for the day, locked the door and left.

The late afternoon sun made his eyes water, and he slapped his aviators on. There had been no movement of air all day, and sweat and dirt streaked his arms and face. He put the chain back on the gate and his stomach grumbled.

Sneaking into the B&B in his filthy state with a bag of fried fast food would be tricky.

If he had stayed in a generic hotel in Columbus, it wouldn't have been a problem, but he'd have been farther away from the airport.

With a sigh of relief, he managed to avoid both Amy and her brother, Bryan, as well as the other guests in the B&B.

A hot shower and a full stomach later, he entered notes on his laptop and reviewed the work he'd done on his financial situation.

As he stared out the leaded glass window of his room, his mind traveled to Lily and her sons. He hadn't known Lily's husband died. Uncle Patrick never told him. In fact, they had never talked about his first girlfriend or her father, when he had visited. Later, their conversations had always been short, and Carson had done most of the talking.

What had happened to Lily in the dozen or so years since he'd last seen her? Where had she been living since she left Worthy? Did she return because she hadn't been able to afford to live where she was? And what had possessed him to offer to show her sons the planes?

He couldn't afford to be involved in her life right now, nor did he want to.

All the questions made his brain tired, so he focused his gaze on the B&B's charming room that would be his home until he made his decision.

The stately four poster bed was comfortable, and the elegant desk made his computer work easier. He loved the historical aspect of the old Victorian house and marveled at the state-of-the-art bathroom but had chuckled at the old skeleton key. It was quirky and quaint, and he loved it. The B&B reminded him of his uncle's farmhouse, but a more

well-kept version.

If he took a leap of faith, he'd move into his uncle's place. If he managed to keep the airport, he'd renovate the old farmhouse and add a few antiques, if he could afford them. Those were all big ifs.

A few hours later, the aroma of Amy's superb coffee drew him out of his room. Hopefully, she would offer one of her delicious pastries to go with a much-needed cup of Joe.

He stepped into the formal dining room and inhaled his favorite scent.

"Come on in and grab a mug and a snack." Amy placed the small urn on the buffet. The gangly child he remembered was long gone.

He grabbed a napkin and chose a danish, then filled his cup and layered it with cream and sugar. "Thanks. I had hoped there'd be some of your delicious treats. Where is everyone?"

She poured herself a cup and cradled it in her hands. "Most of the other guests have gone over to the fair on Main Street. Would you like to sit on the porch? We might be able to hear the music of the live band from there."

"Sure."

Her brother Bryan stepped in the room from the kitchen and grinned. "I could smell the coffee all the way over at the carriage house."

Amy cocked her head and gave it a tiny shake. "I'm surprised you're not cross-eyed with how much time you spend in front of your computer monitor."

Her brother rolled his eyes and sidestepped her. "Did I hear you say you can hear the music from the front porch?"

"Always have in the past," she said.

"Great." Bryan jerked his head. "Come on, Carson, join us. I need a break."

Lily's MECHANIC

The screen door slammed as Amy followed him and Bryan out. Carson sat on a comfortable wicker chair with soft cushions and leaned back and enjoyed the sounds of distant voices.

"Did you go out to the airport today?" Amy sipped her coffee, her blue eyes curious.

"Yeah, I started to put the hangar in order." He blew on his coffee before he took a sip.

Bryan chuckled. "Did you find the treasure?"

The cup halted and his body stilled before he could take a sip. "Does everyone know about it?" Even he could hear the disdain in his voice.

Amy settled more deeply in the rocker. "Yup. Everyone in town has been out there at one time or another." She stared thoughtfully into her cup. "Personally, I think your uncle was lonely, and that's why he told everyone there was a treasure." She turned her head toward her brother and grinned. "Remember when you had time off, and we went looking?"

Bryan's chin dipped, and he tilted his head. "You mean when you dragged me over there." He blew out an exasperated breath. "It was a ridiculous notion. Anything buried in those fields would have been long gone."

"Exactly. I don't understand it. Uncle Patrick never told me about any treasure buried on the land."

Amy's straightened in her chair and gave him a serene smile. "There's not one person in town that believes it's there, so I wouldn't worry about it."

Should he tell them about the security system? He didn't know them all that well although he remembered their grandparents, older brother Charlie and his best friend Zeke, Charlie's siblings were much younger, but the Dillon family had always been kind to him.

He stared into his cup. "I just don't understand why my

32

uncle installed a security system, though. It seems foolish." He hadn't realized he'd spoken until he looked up and stammered. "Except the planes should be secure in this day and age."

Brother and sister glanced at one another, and Bryan shrugged. "Maybe it was to propagate the myth."

"A fairly elaborate thing to do if that was the case, but you're probably right," he said.

"Listen." Amy cocked an ear to Main Street. "Do you hear it?"

"Barely." Bryan grunted and took a big bite of pastry.

Amy frowned at her brother. "You're no fun." She turned excited eyes on him. "Carson, you'll be at the Memorial Day parade on Monday, right?"

"I'm not sure. There's so much to do in the hangar." His voice wavered and he bit into the cherry Danish and almost let loose with a groan but caught himself. He'd have to visit Amy often when he moved out.

"Come on, man, it's an hour or two. It'll be a chance to connect with a lot of people and let them know you're in town." Bryan's voice cajoled and moved him at the same time.

The two siblings, who were almost strangers, encouraged him to hook up with old friends and have something fun to do and it filled his heart with joy. His mother and uncle had cared if he had an pleasant time, but both were gone. His old Navy buddy and best friend, Ben, was the only one left who made time for him. His ex-wife hadn't given two figs about him or his happiness.

"I suppose I could take a few hours off. I did get quite a bit done today and I'll go over after church tomorrow to make up for it."

"That's the spirit and a great plan. Would you like more coffee?" Amy stood and extended her hand for his cup.

Lily's MECHANIC

"Sure."

The distant sounds of people chattering, and the faint smell of fried foods wafted onto the porch. He sat with Bryan in companionable silence, the pinks and oranges of the late spring sunset washed over the sky to meld into inky darkness.

Amy returned and handed him a fresh brew.

"I have a question." His voice cut into the quiet evening.

"Shoot," Bryan chuckled. "Not literally, of course."

At Amy's brief nod, he leaned forward. "Do you have any recommendations for a security system firm?"

Bryan glanced at Amy and their mouths opened at the same time. "Eric Winters."

"Is he in Worthy?"

"He's the owner of Winters Security Systems. He'll take good care of you since you're former military too. He hires a lot of veterans."

"Great. I'm not ready for it yet, but when I am, I'll call him. I think I'll head in and have an early night. Where would you like me to put the cup?" He rose out of the chair a little stiff from the heavy lifting and moving equipment all day. His muscles would become accustomed to the strenuous work but in the meantime a couple of pain pills and that soft bed called to him.

Amy gave him a tiny smile and got on her feet. "I'll take it. Have a good sleep."

Carson nodded, then walked to his room. Would Lily and her family be at the parade on Monday? Forget it. His focus had to be on the airport and if he could swing the renovation.

He'd hadn't been in the mood to check for the cost estimate in his uncle's den before he left. It would be a top priority tomorrow.

34

SERALYNN LEWIS

Lily's sons bounced in the back seat in anticipation of what they would see and do. It was a way for Lily to get their minds off treasure hunting and a reprieve for her from the daunting tasks ahead. A time to relax for once.

Memorial Day dawned bright and clear without a hint of humidity as Lily parked her SUV on a side street and her family walked over to Main Street.

Evan pulled on her arm. "Mom, can we have a funnel cake?"

Lucas snatched the money she pulled from her jeans, and she watched as they stood in line.

Her dad motioned to a few older men sitting on benches under the square's old oak tree. "I'm headed over to talk to some of my church friends and watch the parade with them. Come find me when you're ready to leave."

He seemed more like himself today, but she'd have to watch him carefully. At breakfast this morning, he had been reluctant to let her take over the farm's administration. With the way he hemmed and hawed around the subject, it was certain there'd be a hornet's nest of issues and she'd have to deal with them, but she'd put it out of her mind for a few hours. She'd enjoy the day seeing the happiness on her sons faces.

"Lily?" A familiar voice pulled her out of her thoughts.

"Mia?" She grinned and embraced her high school friend. "Last we talked, you were in New York."

Lily hadn't seen her best friend since she'd gone away to college. They'd gone in different directions and had sporadic phone calls, but life got in the way, and they'd not been in contact.

35

Lily's MECHANIC

Mia introduced her husband, Sean, and their son Drew and their toddler, Devon. She, in turn, introduced her sons, but they'd already met at Sunday school.

"This looks like a good place to watch the parade," Mia commented as she looked around at the ever-growing crowds. "Sit on the curb, Drew."

All three boys sat and became better acquainted. She was happy they'd run into Mia and her family. It would ease her sons' loneliness and they'd have a new friend.

Sean pulled Devon from Mia's arms and hoisted him above his head and onto his shoulders as the toddler chortled with delight.

"I can't believe you're here. I'd heard you were back in town." Mia's blue eyes probed her.

She wrapped her arms around her middle and her body tensed. "Gossip still travels fast in Worthy."

Her friend cocked her head and frowned. "There wasn't any gossip, Lil. It was a simple statement that you were in town." She closed the gap between them. "I know it's been a long time, but I'd love it if we could get together and catch up."

Lily saw the sincerity in Mia's eyes. She needed a friend right now, but could she burden her old pal with every detail of her life? At least not in this very public place, she couldn't.

She inhaled and gazed at the boys in front of her. "I'm sorry. So much has happened since we lost track. I'd like to get together."

"No problem." Mia pulled a business card from her pocket, handed it to her and leaned closer. "You know who else is in town?" Her voice teased and her smile was mysterious.

"Who?"

She guessed where the conversation was going. Mia had been there when she went through the angst of her relation-

ship with Carson Brown. She'd never confided he'd broken her heart when he left.

"Carson Brown," she whispered and craned her neck around her husband and the other townsfolk who gathered there to watch the parade. "I saw him with Amy and Bryan a few minutes ago. He's divorced, you know."

She steeled herself not to show any emotion. She hadn't known Carson was divorced. Her father never mentioned it. When did it happen? No way would she entertain asking even though Mia would be relentless for information.

"I've already seen him."

Mia's gaze returned to her, and a look of astonishment covered her face. "Really?"

"He stopped over on Saturday. The boys were traipsing around the airport, and he was afraid they'd get hurt."

Lucas looked up and held his cup and napkin in the air. "Mom, what do we do with these?"

Sean grabbed the empty cups and moved away to find a trash receptacle before she could utter a word.

"What a nice guy." Her admiration for her friend's husband increased despite how quiet he was.

Mia turned soft eyes at her husband. "He is."

"Tell me about him."

"Another time. Right now, I want to know how it was to see Carson after so long."

She glanced at her sons, and they seemed focused on their conversation with Drew.

Lucas stood and turned his attention to her and Mia. "He's a friend of Mom's, but I'm not sure I like him."

Her friend stepped back and took in the situation quickly. "I'm sorry to hear that. Your mom, Carson, and I, and a few others were all friends growing up. Why don't you like him?"

Lily's MECHANIC

Lucas raised one shoulder, and he lowered his chin. "I don't know him." His eyes lifted, and his face lit up. "But he promised to show us his airplanes. I hope he keeps his promise."

Mia cast a quick glance at her and Lily could see questions popping up around her head like a cartoon balloon. She cleared her throat. "I'm sure he will, Lucas. Carson always kept his promises."

The words almost choked her, but she hadn't wanted to get into a discussion about Carson's reliability. She motioned to the street. "The parade is starting."

Her son turned and sat next to Drew as the first strains of the high school marching band started.

A sigh of relief rushed through her. The noise of the parade would keep her from a discussion about her lost love.

She couldn't afford to be interested in him, not that he would be interested in her. Even if they both happened to be single right now.

The sights and sounds brought memories of past parades and filled her with a homecoming warmth. A smile graced her lips. The boys commented on the various floats, and kids with decorated bikes in red, white, and blue caught the boys' attention.

Evan jumped up and tugged on her jeans. "Mom, do you think we could ride in the parade next year?"

In a year's time, they could be anywhere, and there was no way she'd promise them something and go back on her word.

"We'll see."

He scuffed his foot on the sidewalk and shoved his hands in his pockets. "That means no." Then he turned and dropped to the curb.

"I don't know why you bothered," Lucas whispered.

She stiffened when her friend hugged her side.

38

"Don't worry about it. I've learned boys can be quite moody," Mia whispered.

She wanted to say something, but she swallowed it when Sean frowned at his wife.

"How long is the parade?" Enthusiasm colored her words.

"It's just about over." Her friend sighed. "They're never long enough."

Mia's husband stroked his wife's hair. "Babe, we need to get back to the ranch. I just got a text. Old man Flint's horse needs attention."

"Can we at least get the boys some food before we leave?"

"Of course."

Sean looked at Mia as if the sun, moon, and stars rose because of her. The depth of love between her childhood friend and her husband took her breath away. A giant green eel of envy wrapped around her. Why couldn't she have had a marriage like Mia's instead of what she had?

She shook off those thoughts and hugged Mia goodbye. "I'll call you in a few days." It was a promise she'd keep.

After Lucas said bye to his new friend, he pulled on her hand. "I'm hungry, Mom."

She laughed and wrapped her arm around his shoulder. "Of course you are. Let's go get two of my favorite things here."

Evan grabbed her hand as they made their way through the crowd. "What, Mom?"

"Corndogs and apple dumplings."

They got their corndogs and ate them with lemonade splashes. Memories of the taste of the hot treat and cool drinks invaded her heart.

"Where are the apple dumplings?" Lucas looked around the food tents.

"I swear you must have a hollow leg." She laughed.

Lily's MECHANIC

She scanned the food tents for the sweet treat, but what caught her attention was Carson standing next to Amy and Bryan Dillon who had grown up to attractive adults.

Evan lifted his arm and pointed. "Mom, look... there's the guy from the airport." His voice carried enough that everyone around them looked their way.

She slid her hand over her son's finger and lowered it. "It's impolite to point." As she looked up, Carson's gaze pinned her in place, and she couldn't look away even if she wanted to. A warm sensation that hadn't felt her in years flowed through her. "I think it's time to find Grandad and go home."

Carson spoke to the Dillons, then made his way around the dwindling crowd and fixed his attention on her sons with a genuine smile. "Did you boys enjoy the parade?"

"Yes, sir," Lucas said.

Evan leaned his head as far back as he could to look at the tall man. "I'm sorry I pointed at you."

As Carson squatted, Evan followed his progress and adjusted his head. "It's OK, buddy. I didn't mind." After a hesitation, Carson added. "But your mom is right, you know."

"I know, but I forget."

"We all forget sometimes," Carson rose to his full height. "Have you boys had a chance to sample the food? I hear it's pretty good."

After her sons exhausted talk of the food and what they liked and didn't like, Carson turned to them. "Sounds like you all had a fun time. I'll see all of you around town. Enjoy the rest of your day."

With that, he tipped his chin and strode off almost as if there was a fire chasing him.

Chapter 4

A motor's rumble caught Carson's attention. He grabbed a rag and wiped his hands. As he stepped outside the hangar, he watched as a beat-up farm truck made its way up the lane and stopped right in front of him. Creaking hinges grated as the old man got out and slammed the door shut.

Lily's father hadn't been with her and the boys at the parade yesterday. At least Carson hadn't seen him.

Nils pulled the straw hat from his head and twisted it in his hands. "Is there somewhere we can talk?"

He gave a quick nod and led the way through the hangar, which was a tremendous improvement over what it had been the day he went to see Sandburg. He'd gotten all the tools labeled and organized. Later today, he'd begin maintenance on the planes, and excitement vibrated through him. He'd hadn't worked on small planes in a long time.

"Looks like you cleaned. Looks good." The old man nodded in approval. "Patrick would be happy you're back in Worthy."

He hadn't had the heart to tell Nils his uncle's terms for inheriting might prevent Carson from staying. He couldn't.

The voice message to Seth Blaine, the architect, was returned with a text to meet with him at the airport on

Wednesday morning. That was tomorrow. The message confounded him, and an uneasiness gripped his gut like a severe case of dysentery.

He moved into the office and sat behind the desk. He hadn't tidied up in there, but Nils wouldn't care. "What can I do for you, Mr. Sandburg?"

The farmer lowered his aging body into the chair and cleared his throat. "When Patrick was alive, he allowed me to graze my cows on the land I sold him anytime I wanted." The old man huffed out a breath. "But now you own the land and I need your permission to continue."

"I don't see why not. At least for the time being." He caught the old man's eye, willing him to tell the truth. "Why did you sell the land to Uncle Patrick if you needed it for grazing?"

The old man scratched his head and his gaze wandered around the tiny room. "It was a half-dozen years ago, but I don't rightly remember why I sold it."

Nils's skin turned a mottled red from his neck and traveled to his cheeks. Carson had the impression the farmer hadn't wanted to admit he'd been hard up for cash.

He smiled at Uncle Patrick's best friend. "Doesn't matter. I was just curious."

"Good. Lily is preparing a contract." His voice trailed and his chin trembled.

"Contract? We're friends. Why do we need a contract?"

"Lily is taking over the farm's finances." His uncle's friend clamped his mouth shut and looked at the floor. "She wants things by the book."

He leaned back and lifted his chin. "She does, does she?"

"Yup." Nils sighed, and he hung his head. "As much as I hate to admit it, I need her help. Do you think Patrick found the treasure?" The vacant look of the other day was back, and

42

he seemed out of it.

"I don't think Uncle Patrick found anything. There's no reason to believe he did. Lily came back to Worthy to take over for you, then?"

"No, no... my daughter didn't know anything about the farm." Nils crumpled the brim of his hat. "I never told her. She runs the farm now, and I take care of milking the cows."

He leaned forward. "How did her husband die?" Expectation made him hold his breath.

The old man cocked his head to the side and clenched his jaw. "Christopher? I never liked him. He's dead, you know."

Nils looked so lost, and it pained Carson to ask more questions, but he had to know what prompted Lily to come back.

"He went to prison and died there," Nils said without a trace of remorse.

His head shot up. *Prison?* The details of Lily's life just got worse and worse.

"Why was he in jail?"

"Don't know, but good riddance. He was never good enough for Lily."

It seemed he hadn't been either.

The conversation stunk like the manure that wafted from the Sandburg Farm every day since he'd returned.

If Lily's father hadn't warned Carson to stay away from her, Lily would have been his all those years ago, and he wouldn't have had the heartache of a divorce. Those boys would have been his too.

He couldn't go back, nor did he want to. Things change and a person had to move on. *Lord, why now?* After everything he'd been through with Tanya, why had Lily come back into his life?

Nils lifted his weary body from the chair. "I'll move the

cows tomorrow."

"That'll be fine."

He accompanied the farmer to his truck, and the old man gingerly climbed in and shut the door.

Nils grabbed his arm from inside the vehicle with a strength Carson hadn't expected. The old man's face cleared for a moment. "I'm glad you came home, Carson. You'll be good for Lily and the boys."

The old man wanted him to pursue his daughter? *Not happening.*

The farmer let go, pulled his hand inside the truck, and sped down the lane.

If ever there was an about face, the old man's change of heart where his daughter was concerned was it. Or was it because Nils hadn't been thinking clearly? He shook his head in disbelief.

It hadn't mattered. The change of heart came over a dozen years too late, and he was not about to go back in time. Not now, not ever.

He wouldn't trust either Nils or Lily. He simply couldn't risk losing land Uncle Patrick had earmarked for expansion later on. Other farms bordering the airport had sold out to developments, and it had been the only land available to his uncle.

What if Nils and Lily both found out if he failed to fulfill his uncle's terms, they'd get the land back?

Lily's nerves stretched thin, and her spine tingled with apprehension as she drove up the lane to the airport. She glanced at the contract sitting on the front seat, weighted by the corner of her purse.

44

The Memorial Day parade yesterday had balmy skies and perfect weather, but today the wind had picked up and clouds rushed in. A storm brewed, and it wasn't only the weather that threatened.

Carson had returned, and he'd turned her world upside-down and inside-out and she couldn't afford to think about him or any other man.

Her father's farm was in deep trouble. He was behind in the bills and behind in the taxes. She'd been to the tax office earlier and had agreed to make payments. It would take her five years to pay off the back taxes. That was if she got a job and another thing she had to worry about.

How could she leave her two boys with her father all day while she went to work? Should she convince her dad to sell, knowing how much the farm meant to him? It would surely kill him. And where would they go?

Something wasn't right with her father, and she couldn't put her finger on it.

As she pulled up to the hangar, the roar of an airplane engine nearly deafened her.

With the contract under her arm, she plugged her ears against the high-pitched whine and stepped into the hangar. Hearing protection gear was a must when Carson worked on the planes, otherwise, he'd be deaf in less than a year.

The sound died down to nothing as she rounded the sleek plane and Carson pulled off the communications headset.

She tugged the contract from under her arm. "Carson?"

He whipped around and propped his fists on his hips. "Lily?"

The gray t-shirt he wore stuck to his chest with grime and grease. His snug jeans looked terrific on his lanky frame. He threw the headset on the worktable and moved toward

Lily's MECHANIC

her, his steel-clad boots stomping past the various parts laid out on the floor.

"I want to talk to you about grazing our cows on the land Patrick bought from my dad." Her posture ramrod straight, and her chin lifted as she stepped closer to him.

The engine oil and perspiration from his oil-streaked t-shirt was a welcome change from the cow manure next door.

His forehead creased. "Nils was here this morning. I told him it was OK for him to use the pasture… For now."

"Dad was here?" She let her face go blank and made her voice neutral. The last thing she wanted was for Carson to figure out there was a lack of communication between her and her father where farm business was concerned. What had Dad done… and said?

"Yeah, he mentioned you'd be over with a contract for me to sign to make everything legit." He moved closer to her, and the protective eye gear disconcerted her. "Your dad and Uncle Patrick were best friends. Do we need a written agreement?"

She straightened to her full height. "Yes, we do. I want to protect the farm… and you, of course."

He pulled the safety glasses off and set them on the worktable. "Let's go into the office and talk. I'm afraid I can't offer you a beverage. Uncle Patrick's mini fridge breathed its last when I plugged it in."

She followed him, making note of the organized tool racks and part bins, but there were lights burned out and trash piled in the corner of the hangar. At least it appeared to be trash. How would she know?

Thankfully, she hadn't worn her business clothes, or the filthy office chairs would have ruined them.

He frowned and motioned for her to have a seat. "I hav-

en't gotten around to cleaning the office."

As if he could read her mind... but then, he always seemed to know her innermost secrets. *Let nothing show, Lily.*

"It's OK. These are old jeans anyway." She cleared her throat and set the contract on the desk between them. "It's just a simple one-page contract that says only Sandburg Farm has grazing rights. It stipulates the area. I've made it for one year, then we can see where we are at the end of the term."

He blinked, cocked his head, and pulled the contract to him. "It looks simple enough, but I still don't think we need it."

"Please."

He grabbed a pen from the desk, signed, and dated both copies. "There's a possibility I may not own the airport in six months. This contract would be useless then, and you'd have to get permission from the new owner."

His shoulders tensed and he pushed a copy to her.

She leaned forward and took it. "Are you selling the place?"

"Not if I can help it."

"Well, then, what are your plans?"

It was hotter than a Fourth of July picnic and the holiday was over a month away. Perspiration leaked from her pores, but Carson looked as cool as a freshly mowed lawn in the spring.

"I won't know until tomorrow."

"What's tomorrow?"

"I meet with the architect to see about the renovation. If it can or should be done. The place is in terrible shape. My uncle took care of the hangar fairly well and the other outbuildings, but not the terminal or the house. The meeting will determine what I can and can't do."

"I see. Why didn't you come back?" She blurted the question because that's what had been on her mind since she saw him at the parade. Good thing she hadn't said *to me* at the

Lily's MECHANIC

end. What was she thinking asking such a question? And did she really want to know? *Yes, she did.*

He squirmed in his seat. "Truth?"

She gave him a barely there nod, her stomach clenched.

"Nils took me aside two days before I left for the Navy and hadn't wanted me to stay in contact with you. Said I'd leave you for extended periods of time and he didn't want that life for you."

The shock of his words nearly made her catatonic. How could her dad have done that? Carson was who she'd wanted for a lifetime. Her father had never uttered a word.

Sadness outweighed anger as she contemplated what could have been. Bitterness swamped her. The vile taste it left made her want to heave. It didn't matter anymore. She had sons and responsibilities and Carson had changed. Big time.

"I see."

"Do you?" He jumped out of the chair and paced to the door and back, then flattened his hands on the desk and leaned into her. "I wanted to come back, Lily." He shook his head. "So many times. Then my uncle told me you got married." He stood straight up, and his tone became flat, his eyes hooded. "And I moved on. Why weren't you in church on Sunday?"

The subject change threw her. She was still stuck on the fact her father warned him to stay away. How could her sweet dad have done something like that? Had he not known how his interference could affect the course of her life? She'd married Christopher because she'd been so hurt. It didn't matter, not now.

"Church?" she squeaked out the word.

"Yeah, church."

She angled her body and crossed her arms in front of

her chest. "I see the gossip mills are alive and well in Worthy, Ohio." Her voice held disdain.

He sighed and drew a hand through his curly hair. "There wasn't any gossip, Lil. I saw your boys were there with Nils, but you weren't."

His childhood pet name for her, the one Mia used when they were youngsters, warmed her insides like chocolate melting in the microwave.

The oil and engine splatters across the floor drew her gaze. "I had things to do at the farm."

Out of the corner of her eye, she saw him give one tiny head shake, and then he plopped in the chair next to her and placed his hand on her bare arm. "You never missed church. What happened?"

She turned and narrowed her gaze. "I grew up."

"You're the one who first convinced *me* to go to church," he whispered.

The same discomfort she'd had when the police had carted her husband off to prison, pulled at her insides.

Her spiritual life was none of his business. It was because of him she'd stopped going to church when she'd left for college. "Tell me about your plans for the airport."

He crossed his arms. "What do you know about construction?"

Her response must have rankled.

Reluctant to tell him about her life in Austin, she figured it was best to respond with less detail.

She plucked at a thread on her torn pants. "I used to work with construction guys and on project sites."

"I won't know anything until tomorrow. The architect has the plans and he'll bring them in the morning. Was your husband a construction guy?"

49

Lily's MECHANIC

A nervous laugh left her lips. "No. He was in finance."

His gaze softened, and it nearly did her in. "How'd he die, Lil?"

Her head jerked, and she stared at him. "I'll tell you about my husband if you tell me about your wife."

"Deal."

The words left his mouth so fast she wasn't sure she'd heard him correctly.

He clasped his hands, and he appeared to be calm, but the tension in his arms and chest sailed over and slammed into her. "You know." He tried to belie the tension by lifting the corner of his mouth in a slight smirk. "Tanya cast a spell on me while I was in port almost seven years ago. I gave her a ring. It didn't work out, and we split." He made a shooing motion with his head. "Now you."

She blinked and considered what to include and what to exclude. "Christopher and I met my freshman year when I went away to college. We dated and eloped. When the boys were older, I got a job. A few years after he died, I came home."

That's all he'd get. No need to expose the incredible shame of what her husband had done.

"Your dad said he died in prison." Carson's voice was quiet.

Her head snapped, and she narrowed her gaze. "That's right. He died by suicide." She jumped out of the chair, grabbed the contract, and strode to her car with Carson in hot pursuit.

He grabbed her arm. "Wait."

She wouldn't look at him. "Let it go, Carson. You have your life and I have mine."

Dropping his hand, he rolled his shoulders. "You're right.

50

We have different lives now. I still want to give the boys a tour. I'll call when things are more settled."

He turned on his heel and walked back into the hangar.

She slid into the SUV and wanted to bang her head against the steering wheel, but she drove to the end of the lane, stopping for a moment to catch her breath.

Chapter 5

Discarded parts and rusted equipment crashed into the twenty-yard dumpster that had been delivered earlier. The bright June sunshine dampened Carson's t-shirt with sweat as he trudged another box of trash and hauled it over the top of the huge metal container. He could smell his body odor and didn't give a hoot if it offended his uncle's architect.

He glanced at his phone and down the lane. Where was Seth Blaine? Their meeting had been scheduled for eight, but it was almost nine.

If this was a sign of how this architect-builder conducted business, Carson was doomed. His annoyance expanded when he mused on all he could lose because he'd have to depend on this guy and his timeline. Courtesy of his years in the military, Carson expected, no, demanded timeliness. Lives depended on it.

The sound of a vehicle caught his attention. It was about time. He stood by the side of the dumpster with crossed arms, sweating like a Siberian husky in the deep south.

An average guy slid out of his late model SUV and grabbed a long cardboard tube. "Sorry I'm late. I had a family emergency." The preppy dressed architect motioned to the dumpster. "Did you order the roll-off?"

"Yes." He extended his hand, and Seth shook it. "Carson Brown."

"Condolences. I hadn't gotten to know your uncle all that well, but I looked forward to working with him."

Great. The situation was getting worse and worse. He eyed Blaine's light khaki pants and crisp white shirt. Those knife-creased slacks the man sported would get dirty. Not his problem.

"Let's go into the office."

The architect seemed to sense he wasn't happy, and he followed Carson into the hangar like a puppy after its mother.

"How long have you been in town?" Blaine stopped in the middle of the hangar and did a three sixty. "Whoa!"

"What?"

"The place is totally different from the last time I saw it."

He strode back to the architect and glanced around the cavernous building. "What do you mean?"

"I almost broke a leg the last time I was here. You couldn't even see the floor. It was covered with cr–" He cleared his throat. "That's why you got the dumpster."

He raised an eyebrow and waved his arm at the office. "Got it in one. Let's go."

"I'd forgotten there was an office in the hangar."

He stopped mid-stride and his eyes drifted shut. Blaine hadn't remembered his uncle's hangar office? Where in the world had Uncle Patrick found the man? How was he supposed to renovate the place?

When Carson stepped through the door, the portable AC unit he bought hummed in the background. The cool air chilled him, and he needed it.

Blaine went straight to the desk and pulled a roll of paper from the cardboard cylinder he carried. "Your uncle commis-

Lily's MECHANIC

sioned me to draw a set of plans for the terminal building offices, the hangar, and wanted to renovate the house, but these are only for the two airport buildings." His voice took on a professional edge.

Carson stepped closer to the desk and eyed the professional drawing. "Show me what my uncle planned."

Seth designed the terminal in such a way that, with potential growth, Uncle Patrick could easily add to it with little or no disruption of business. The plans were quite good, and he really liked what the man had in mind for both buildings. Maybe Blaine had redeemed himself.

He read his uncle's name at the bottom of the plans. "I looked for the cost estimate and couldn't find it or a timeline. Where are those?"

Blaine scrunched his nose, and a hand flew to his hip. "We never discussed a budget or schedule."

Despite feeling cooler earlier, heat traveled from Carson's arms to his face. "What? Why?" While his voice remained calm and his tone soft, his body betrayed him.

"Your uncle called and told me he wanted to put the project on hold until he got the hangar cleaned. I told him I'd wait for his call. When it didn't come, I started other projects."

He gritted his teeth. "Do you have a cost for it?"

To give the man his due, he looked chagrined for once. "I assumed your uncle had found the treasure, and we'd discuss the budget when he was ready." His voice trailed.

Carson's head swung so fast a doctor's appointment would be needed for the whiplash. *That darn treasure.* "There is no treasure." The pad of his thumb and forefinger stroked the intense throbbing at his temple. The headache that had threatened all morning blasted into the stratosphere. He drew a deep breath and continued. "How soon can you give me a quote?

54

SERALYNN LEWIS

Red inched up his neck to his face like an all-day sunburn. "Here's the thing. I didn't know the project was moving forward, and certainly not this quickly. Unfortunately, I can't commit to anything until the middle of next year."

"Next year?" His voice had risen, and his head shook so quickly the dizziness rattled him. The taste of defeat churned in his gut.

"I have an out-of-town family situation that will consume the rest of this year and part of the next. The few projects I had wrapped up and will be the last until I get my personal crisis sorted. I'm so sorry."

Sorry? The guy hadn't returned his calls and had wasted almost a week he didn't have. *Easy Carson. Remember your training.*

"And the plans?"

"They belong to your uncle. He'd already paid for them and told me to hang on to them until the project was a go."

"Can you at least recommend another builder I can contact?"

Blaine clenched his jaw and gazed at the plans. "Any good commercial contractor will already be working on multiple projects this time of year. They schedule out at least three months to a year in advance."

He leaned his head back, blinked, and gave the contractor a hard glare. "I'm dead in the water." His back straightened. "What about a residential builder?"

"I suppose you could use a residential builder, but they'd have to research commercial regulations… specifically those for an airport. They'd be busy now, too, but you can try a few local guys."

Desperation seized him and he grasped for any solution the guy offered. "Who?"

55

Lily's MECHANIC

"My office is in city, so I'm not familiar with any of the local contractors, but I'll email you the ones I know of in the Columbus area."

"Fine."

"I apologize about the way this played out."

He sighed and extended his hand. "It's not your fault. Thanks for bringing the plans. At least it's one thing that's done."

When Blaine drove away, Carson went back to the office and called his uncle's attorney, but he was out of town for a week and couldn't be reached.

He slumped in the new office chair and stared at his phone. Finishing the project he'd started was out of the question. He'd get back to the B&B and do some research. Rolling up the plans, he put them in the office closet, locked up, and left.

It was almost eleven o'clock by the time he showered and stepped into the dining room.

Amy had begun to remove the breakfast service. "You're back. Coffee?"

"I could use some, thanks."

He glanced into the living room as he sat in his usual spot in the dining room. "Are you by yourself?"

"I am, but I'm prepping for tomorrow." She cocked her head as she poured him a cup and handed it to him. "Didn't you say you'd be at the airport all day?"

She made herself a mug and sat at the table.

"I planned to, but got a bit of bad news."

Amy's forehead crinkled. "Anything I can do?"

He gazed at her and gave a slight nod. "Maybe you can."

She scooted her chair closer, and her head tilted toward him. "What?"

"Do you know of any building contractors who might

SERALYNN LEWIS

have time for a meeting?"

"Rob Marino," Bryan said as he stepped into the room.

Amy's hand flew to her chest. "Geez, give a girl a heart attack, why don't you?"

Her brother raised his arm and waved to the kitchen. "Didn't you hear the kitchen door slam?"

"I did not."

The last thing he wanted was for the siblings to start an all-out war when he needed information. "Who is Rob Marino?"

She gave her brother a hard glare and turned to him, softening her features. "He did my kitchen renovation and revamped the carriage house a few years ago. He's the best."

"My contractor bailed, and I need to find a builder who can follow plans the architect designed."

Bryan stepped to the registration desk, rummaged through the drawers, and handed him a card. "Call him. Tell him we referred you."

"Think I can call him now?"

Amy got up and went to the swinging door between the kitchen and dining room. "I think you two can work it out on your own."

Her brother grabbed a pastry and made a shooing motion.

"Thanks." He lifted himself out of the fancy blue chair and took his coffee with him.

As he quick-stepped to his room, the siblings bantered good-naturedly.

If he could schedule a meeting with the builder ASAP, he might still have a chance.

Lily shifted in the office chair, lowered her head, and grabbed clumps of hair. "What is going on? I'll never dig out from under the debt."

She dumped every overdue bill into a folder and shoved the office chair back from the desk. After dinner, when the boys were out of earshot, she'd have a candid talk with her dad about the farm's finances.

Lucas popped his head around the door. "What's for dinner?" But he stopped, then made his way into the room with slow steps. A myriad of emotions passed over his face. "What's wrong, Mom?"

Her gaze shifted, and she straightened. "Oh, just farm business. I have hamburger casserole waiting to go in the oven."

Lucas's tousled hair reminded her he needed a haircut, but as she gazed at her son, she'd have to buy new clothes soon too.

He dropped into the chair opposite the desk. "Are we going to move again?"

The last thing her son needed was to be burdened with anything related to finances. He'd already seen his fair share of the lack. She'd have to ensure neither of her boys suffered any further hardship.

Her mouth dropped open. "Whatever gave you that idea?"

He looked away and shoved his hands under his thighs, a boyish habit he developed as a small child. The material of his too small shirt pulled against his arms. "This place needs new everything. It's worse than the last place we lived."

She moved to the front of his chair, placed her palms on the arms of the chair, and leaned in. "Look at me."

When he looked up, she frowned at the fear in his eyes. "I know this place isn't as nice as our last apartment, but the farm is huge, and you can go anywhere and not be afraid.

We're going to paint the place to make it nicer for all of us. Grandad…" She swallowed and looked away. "He needs us."

He lifted his hands and wrapped them around her forearms. "I… I just don't want to move again."

She squeezed his shoulders and her voice wobbled. "We're not moving. This is our home now. I have to get a job soon, so you'll have to help with Evan." Her brow furrowed, her throat constricting with the sense of disappointment. It was wrong to burden her older son with responsibilities greater than he should have, but what choice did she have? "Where is he anyway?"

"He went down to the pond. Grandad gave him some grain to feed the ducklings." He pulled her wrists away from him and pushed his way to his feet. "I'll go check on him."

"Dinner won't be for another few hours. Take your time."

Dad and Evan came around the corner and into the room.

"There you are, Lucas." Her father glanced from her to her eldest and a concerned look flew over his face. "I'm taking the ATV over to the south pasture to check on the cows. You boys want to take a ride before dinner?"

Lucas nodded to her dad and glanced at her. "Mom, can I have an apple to tie me over until dinner?"

"I want one too," Evan said.

"OK." She smiled and dug in the fridge for the fruit. "Apples all around."

She handed Pink Ladies to the boys, but her father refused. "Go on out to the barn, boys. Grandad will be there in a few minutes."

The boys chomped on the sweet treats. Dad's garden looked pretty dismal. She'd try to resurrect it, but she'd need help from her dad and sons. Fred, the farm manager, and the few farmhands her dad kept could only do so much. The or-

Lily's MECHANIC

chards still produced crop, but not nearly as much as it once had. She'd have to see about what could be done about that too. Another task on the ever-increasing list of things to do.

"After the boys go to bed, we need to talk, Dad."

A grim look planted on his face, he turned on his heel. "I need to go check on the cows."

She followed him and watched as her dad and the boys took off for the south pasture. While she finished preparing dinner and folded a load of clothes, her mind turned to looking for a new job. Mentally, she ticked off the things she'd need to do to find one that paid well and allowed her some flexibility. An almost impossible hope.

Before dinner, she called Mia and scheduled to meet her for lunch. She couldn't wait. Maybe her friend would know what jobs were available. Tonight she'd get on the laptop and research.

Her sons bounded through the kitchen door. When her dad followed, she handed him a basket with his clothing. "Get washed up, we'll be eating in a few minutes."

While they ate, the boys regaled her with the trip to the south pasture and how much fun it was going on the ATV. Her dad was quiet, but his keen eyes took in every interaction.

A sigh of relief moved through her. The boys no longer quizzed her dad about the treasure. Her father had given her his word and his word was gold.

"Can we watch television, Mom?" Evan said before he stuffed his mouth with the last bite of apple pie.

"When you're done eating and load your dishes in the dishwasher, you can go watch your favorites in my room."

The boys scrambled to do her bidding as her dad's piercing eyes watched them.

When the upstairs door slammed, she placed her elbow

on the table and cupped her chin. "What happened with the farm's finances, Dad?"

He scratched the back of his head. "I don't rightly know. Things just… got away from me, I guess." He shrugged, then his face brightened. "But you're here now. You'll take care of all that."

She sighed and leaned back in her chair. "You keep paying Fred and the other farmhands, but you're behind in all the other bills. I'll catch up the utilities, so they aren't turned off. Why did you close the farm store?"

His body stiffened, discomfort etched on his chin. "No one wanted to work in the store, and I couldn't take care of it and oversee Fred and the other guys."

"It was profitable when I left for college. It looks like you closed it about four years ago." Keeping the note of disapproval out of her voice was all but impossible. "Why didn't you keep the store open when you weren't doing farm chores, Dad?"

"I kept it open, but it got to be too much."

The breeze from the kitchen window blew the delicate lace curtains that had turned yellow with age. Those needed to be replaced along with a host of other household items. She'd been home for less than two weeks and hadn't put a dent into the things that needed to be handled. "I see. Well, we can reopen it. I haven't gone over there to see what condition it's in, but it'll need a power washing. Do you think you can help when you're not dealing with the cows?"

His hands dropped under the table, and she guessed he was rubbing his arthritic fingers. "I guess. When did you want to do that?"

"Friday. Remember Mia my friend from high school? I'm having lunch with her on Thursday. Do you think you can keep the boys busy while I go? I'll be about an hour and a half."

Lily's MECHANIC

"Why are you meeting with her?"

She cocked her head and gripped the table. "Because I need a break and I haven't talked to her in years."

He held his hands palms up. "I didn't mean anything by it."

The calming breath left her lungs slow and steady. "I'll need to find a job to help with the bills. I've arranged to pay installments on the back taxes. We can't afford to lose the farm, Dad."

He frowned. "I wish Patrick would have found the treasure."

Shaking her head, she closed her eyes. "Not that again."

Lines creased his brow as he glared at her. "Well, it sure would have helped right about now and then you wouldn't have to go to work. I hate that you have to get a job to handle the farm's bills."

She snaked her hand across the table, her voice soft and comforting. "I know, Dad, but it has to be done."

He straightened and leaned forward. "Wait... Carson might need someone with your talents. Ask *him* for a job."

Her eyes widened, and she struggled to utter the words. "I can't."

"Why not? You two were tight back in the day and you have the smarts."

"I can't and let's leave it at that."

After what she'd found out about her father's interference in her life back then, she hadn't understood his change of heart. Why? And now wasn't the time to bring it up. If she ever would.

"I also want to see if I can resurrect the garden and the orchards need a lot of work too." She stilled and waited for her father to respond.

"I'll have to make sure the tiller works." His face con-

torted, and he looked away. "That garden is... a mess."

"Yes, it is. But having our own vegetables will give us produce we won't have to buy. It'll be good for the boys to learn how to grow their own food."

"I still think you should ask Carson for a job. Do you want me to talk to him?"

"No." The word burst from her lips with a force that staggered her. She flew out of the chair and cleared the table. "Let it go, Dad."

"Suit yourself. I'm going to watch some television." He got up with measured movements. When he got to the door, he turned and placed a hand on his hip. "Come to church with us on Sunday."

She grabbed the remaining items on the table without looking at him. "Fine."

What could she do? She'd have to face the gossips at some point. Better to have it done with sooner rather than later.

Chapter 6

Carson dragged more junk out of the hangar checking his watch every few minutes. Stone cold dread washed through him, and the scent of grime and dirt filled his nostrils. Not even the ridiculous amount of outdated and unusable parts his uncle kept lying around kept his mind off the time.

Just as he threw the last box over the side of the dumpster, a late model pickup truck pulled in next to his tricked-out vehicle.

A burly guy stepped out and thumbed his hand to Carson's truck. "Nice wheels."

"Sweet, huh? You must be Rob Marino. Thanks for being on time."

He introduced himself and they shook hands. The man looked around the airport and frowned. "Somewhere we can talk?"

A hint of enthusiasm hadn't crossed the man's face, but it could be he was just a sober kind of guy. He prayed it was the latter.

"Hangar office."

They made their way around the dumpster into the cavernous building.

Rob stopped next to the Cessna, a glimpse of admiration

on his face. "Yours?"

He gave a clipped nod.

"It's a beaut."

A lightbulb flickered in Carson's brain as he led the man into the office. He might use the plane to sweeten the pot. He grabbed the tube that held the plans and pulled them out. "I explained the situation on the phone last night. It's crucial the place is functional in the next three months."

He'd reduced the original timeline in the will in case there were setbacks he'd be covered.

Rob smoothed his hand across the plans for the terminal and then lifted the page to stare at the hangar's plans. "May I ask why?"

"If I can't get it operational in the next several months, I'll be forced to take a mechanics job at a larger airport, and I don't want to do that if I don't have to."

The builder frowned and scratched his cheek. "That's a super quick turnaround. I'm uncertain it can be done that quickly." Rob glanced at him then at the planes behind him. "But... it seems to me, the hangar is serviceable as it is so we could concentrate on the terminal, then move to the hangar once the terminal is operational. Would that work?"

Relief eased his tense shoulders. At least Rob considered the project. "Maybe. I'm not sure."

Rob's head jerked, and he narrowed his gaze. "What do you mean?"

He lowered his chin and took a moment to consider what he'd tell the contractor since gossip seemed to be rampant in Worthy. Amy's delicious breakfast churned in his stomach. "There are certain stipulations to the renovation, and I'll have to check with the attorney."

The contractor smirked and tapped the plans. "Old man

McClellan calling the shots from beyond the grave, huh?"

When he frowned, the man halted.

Rob held his hand up. "Sorry. I meant no disrespect. My sense of humor sometimes leaves a lot to be desired. At least that's what my wife says."

"It's OK. But I'd appreciate it if you kept this conversation confidential."

"No problem. Let's look at the terminal. Are there lights in the offices?"

"The power is on, but I haven't replaced the fluorescents."

"Don't bother. Just grab a couple of flashlights and we'll check it out."

After they went through the entire building while looking at the plans, they returned to the hangar office. They discussed what Carson's vision was for the terminal while Rob took copious notes.

The contractor pulled on his ear lobe. "It might be doable."

"Might?" He pounced on that one word.

"Yeah…" The filthy office chair squeaked as Rob moved forward and nodded at the plans. "I can probably get the terminal completed and ready for tenants if and these are *big* ifs… One, we agree on a price. And two, you provide a project manager to oversee the details and research needed for airport requirements. I have other projects I'm working on, and I wouldn't be able to manage it and oversee the actual work in the time frame allotted."

He leaned his head to the side and bit his lip. "I have questions."

"Shoot."

"How soon can you get me a quote? Where can I find a project manager and how much would one cost?"

His brain zoomed to Lily. She was in construction but

in what capacity, he didn't know. Maybe she'd be a wonderful resource? No. He had to distance himself. He couldn't afford to have her figure out she and her father could gain the land back if he failed. It was crucial for expansion at a later date.

Rob rubbed his hand along his cheek and fingered his chin. "All good questions. I can have a quote for you on Friday and I'll do some research on project managers. Finding one will be the toughest part of the entire project. The cost is usually a percentage of the project, sometimes with bonuses if the project comes in under budget and under the time frame."

His shoulders slumped. "I guess I'll have to wait and see what the cost will be. Is there anything I can do before you give me the quote and we sign a contract?"

The corners of Rob's mouth lifted and his eyes gleamed. "You already have the dumpster, start pulling anything out of the terminal you think is garbage. Anything you think we might use later, put it to one side. It will save considerable time during the demo."

"They'll drop off another one tomorrow and dump the one that's out there."

"It looks like you put a dent in the hangar's trash."

"As you saw, the terminal is in a sad state, but I'll get to it. First things first. Thanks for making time in your day to meet up."

Rob stood and held out his hand. "Give me a set of plans to prepare the quote. I appreciate the opportunity to do a commercial project."

"Sure hope we can get it done in the time frame allotted."

"Me too."

As they stepped into the June sunshine, Carson pointed to the old farmhouse. "If we can get the terminal and airport... running, we'll talk about that renovation as well."

Lily's MECHANIC

His uncle's house would have to be done piecemeal as funds were available, but he didn't care. If he pulled this off, he'd get it done in his own time.

"We might work it in our schedule sometime late in the fall when the cold forces us inside."

"Let's take it one step at a time, shall we?"

Rob got in his truck and drove away. He couldn't wait to have workers swarming around the airport. Now all he had to do was call Bottleson to see if the stipulation allowed for a staggered renovation and wait for the quote.

"Lily Sandburg, is that you?" A voice chirped from across the room.

The Countryside Diner was the same as Lily remembered it. She welcomed the distraction of lunch with an old friend in familiar surroundings, inhaling the aroma of all the great comfort food. Georgia, the owner of the quaint eatery, bustled over, and enveloped her in a hug so tight air whooshed out of her lungs.

She grinned and pointed to herself. "It's me. A little older and hopefully a little wiser." People dotted the old oak dining tables, and they made note of her, but went back to their conversations and meals. "I'm meeting someone for lunch."

With a brisk nod, Georgia guided her to a table in the back. "Who are you meeting?"

Mia sidled up behind the older woman and bumped her arm. "Me."

The diner's owner must have slowed down because Mia snuck up on her. Something that would not have happened back in high school. She had eagle eyes.

68

Georgia whipped around and put a hand to her heart. "Mia McDermott. How in the world did I not hear another bell?"

Mia grasped the woman's forearm and smirked. "Old age, maybe?" Her friend took the seat across from her and leaned her head toward the door. "I snuck in behind some other folks."

"That explains it." Georgia huffed as her pen hovered above the pad. "What can I get you?"

They both ordered a cold drink as Lily perused the menu. "The food hasn't changed much. You must have it memorized."

Mia smiled and shrugged. "I've tried everything, and I get one of my two favorites."

After they placed their order, Lily leaned her head to the side. "Catch me up on how you ended up back in Worthy with a husband and two kids."

Her friend's smile faltered for a split second. "I left New York to care for Steve's two daughters."

When Mia explained her brother's wife had passed away and she'd come home to help, Lily's hand reached over, touched hers and expressed her condolences.

Her head moved from side to side. "I was so upset when your brother married that girl. He was so hot in high school."

"Your only interest was for Carson back then." Her friend grinned, then her face took on a look of complete serenity. "Steve remarried and is the happiest I've ever seen him. But we're here to talk about you. Tell me about your life in Texas and what brought you home."

She took a sip of the refreshing cold tea Georgia placed on the table moments ago. "But you haven't told me how you met your husband."

Lily's MECHANIC

Mia explained how she had lost her memory in a car accident and how Sean cared for her. The sparkle in her eyes grew as she spoke of her two sons.

"That was succinct. I'm sure there's more to the story than that," she scoffed and played with the napkin.

Her best friend narrowed her gaze. "You're stalling, Lil, and you know it."

Mia had zeroed in with a compelling stare, and Lily wouldn't get away with surfacy explanations. When her friend's compassionate eyes met hers, it was all she could do not to blurt every detail from the time she left Worthy to now.

"I came home because living in Austin after my husband died was too hard," she whispered.

"How did he die?" Her friend's quiet voice comforted her.

She drew her gaze to the window and stiffened her back. "He died by suicide… in prison."

To Mia's credit, she never blinked. "I'm so sorry for your loss."

An enormous sigh escaped her lungs. "I didn't love him, Mia. I married him—"

Georgia appeared with two plates that smelled heavenly. She'd forgotten how good the food was here. The owner eyed them, opened her mouth, but snapped it shut.

"Smells delicious. You still have those cinnamon rolls?"

The woman smiled. "Sure do. Back in the day, Amy's grandmother made them. Now, Amy makes them and they're even better, but don't tell her I said so." She winked. "I'll bring you one in a bit. Enjoy."

"You were saying…" Mia snatched the oversized burger and bit into it.

She dropped her hands under the table and wrung them. "I married him because I hadn't wanted to be alone. He al-

ways wanted more, so he embezzled and was sent to prison. The court case took a few years. I don't think he could handle being incarcerated so, he checked out."

The burger in her friend's hand stopped mid-way to her mouth, and she placed it back on the plate. She leaned forward and her face was full of regret. "I didn't know you were going through such a hard time. I wish we would have remained in contact. You needed friends who supported you."

Lily blinked, willing herself not to cry and make a spectacle of herself. "My colleagues looked at me with scorn although I had nothing to do with the embezzlement. I couldn't take any more. Worthy had been an awesome place to grow up, and I wanted that for my boys." She faltered at first, but the words came out in a rush.

Pain seized her all over again. Would it ever go away? All at once, her hunger evaporated, but she forced herself to pick up the burger and eat.

Mia took a sip of her tea and with careful precision placed it next to her plate. "So, what's next for you?"

She lowered her hand to her lap and squeezed her fingers. "That's part of the reason I wanted to have lunch with you away from the farm and kids."

"OK." Mia drew out the last letter to nothingness.

"Two things. Something's not right with my dad. On occasion, I see him staring off into space. And he forgets things… things he should remember. He repeats himself and I'm worried about him."

"I've never noticed his behavior being any different. He's in church every Sunday… but then our conversation is minimal. I'll have to pay more attention in the future. Maybe you should talk to his doctor."

"Dad says everything is fine. I doubt he'll be keen on

me talking to his doctor. Besides, doctor patient laws prevent me from asking anyway." She fingered her napkin and tucked her chin to her chest. "All I can do right now is keep watching him."

"And commit everything to the Lord. What's number two?"

She adjusted herself in the booth, the reference to God pulled at her, but she dismissed it. "I think that's it in relation to my father's issues, but the farm's in trouble and I need a job. The big companies in Columbus require more education than I have. The experience is there, but I'm not sure it's enough. Do you know anyone in town who might need a construction project manager?"

"I can give my brother-in-law a call. I can't guarantee anything, he's in construction and might know."

She took a bite of the cinnamon roll Georgia dropped off. "Your husband's brother?"

Mia's head shook. "Sean's sister's husband."

"Well, I'd appreciate anything you can do."

Georgia stopped by, refilled their tea glasses, and eyed them with curiosity.

When she left, her friend put her elbow on the table and cupped her chin. "Now let's talk about Carson."

She gulped her drink and spluttered. "There's nothing to talk about."

Mia's eyebrows rose as she shook her head. "Don't give me that. He stopped by your house."

"Yeah, because the boys had gone to the airport to look for that stupid treasure."

Mia laughed and winked. "Steve's girls and I went out to the farm years ago to look for it."

She exhaled and frowned. "Not you too."

"Yup. Just once, though. Go on. This is getting good."

72

Her friend wiggled in her seat and took a bite of her scone.

Lily told Mia about the encounter, then told her about the meeting with him on Wednesday. "I was an idiot. I point blank asked him why he never came back."

Mia's eyes widened, and she swallowed her food. "You did?"

She leaned her head back and stared at the ceiling. "Blurted is more like it."

"What did he say?"

Her gaze went to the remaining half of the sweet roll on her plate and her stomach roiled. "Dad told him to stay away, so he did."

"Oh, my gosh. I can't believe your sweet dad would do such a thing. Did you ask him about it?"

She exhaled and pushed the plate away. "No. I... I haven't found the time. But I'm guessing he won't remember, so why bother? It's over and done with."

Her friend shifted in her seat and leaned her forearms against the edge of the table. "Don't give up. Maybe you can rekindle your relationship."

"I can't, Mia. The farm, my dad, and my boys need me. I can't entertain a relationship." She held her hand up. "Please let it go, OK?"

Mia took a deep breath and gave her a slow single nod.

Georgia stepped to the table and handed them their checks. "Lily, how's your dad doing?

She hadn't expected the woman to ask about her father, and with the fresh memories of his betrayal and health issues, she almost blabbed the entire story.

Grabbing her wallet out of her purse, she forced a smile. "He's doing well, thanks for asking."

"It was good to see you. Come in again."

"Of course."

They paid their bills and walked out arm in arm into the warm sunshine. Bees buzzing around the square clay pots of pink and red flowers made her happy she'd come home.

Mia stopped at a late model SUV. With a gentle prod, she tapped Lily's forearm. "I've seen the boys and your dad at church, but I haven't seen you. It would be great if you could come. This Sunday we're studying Jeremiah 29:11 about the plans God has for us. You should come. It might help with everything going on. No pressure, OK?"

A forced smile covered her lips. "I'll be there."

After a brief hug, Lily turned and walked to her car.

Not her best friend too? First Carson, then her father, and now Mia. *Lord, you're working overtime to get me in church.*

Chapter 7

Carson paced across the hangar with his hands on his hips. The cost estimate uncertainty made him antsy, and he prayed Rob would give him a decent price. But... he still needed a project manager.

And work on the planes stalled as he waited on parts. He needed a new dumpster for the terminal trash, and they couldn't replace it until Monday.

He'd wasted days waiting, and it was unacceptable. He had to make things happen.

He jogged to his truck, grabbed his backpack with his laptop and planning notebook, then headed back to the hangar office. The recent rains of late spring made the grass green again, and the trees had already budded. The aroma was as he'd remembered.

Pulling out his phone, he called his close friend and Navy buddy, Ben Garrison, who had been a godsend through his breakup. They'd commiserated about the women in their lives on many occasions.

His good friend answered on the first ring. "It's about time you called. I was wondering how things were going. I still can't believe you and my former commanding officer live in the same area. It's a small world."

Lily's MECHANIC

His face screwed up as he rose and strode to the wall with the alarm system, and opened the panel. "My uncle left me his airport and home."

"That's great. Congrats."

"Save the congratulations until I actually inherit it."

"What do you mean?"

The hesitation in his friend's voice came through the phone line and he could almost see his questioning blue gaze.

"I'll tell you all about it, but first, are you still interested in starting your own charter service?"

"Matter of fact, been thinking about it a lot lately. I'm sick of the rat race and kowtowing to arrogant, insufferable men... and women." Ben's voice gritted.

"Remember when I told you about the proximities of Worthy to major metropolitan areas like Columbus, Cincinnati, Louisville, and Pittsburgh?

"I'm listening." The eagerness in Ben's voice was all he needed to generate excitement for the endeavor.

He held his breath for a moment, determined to have a taste of success. "How about a two-year discount on an office and a parking space for your helicopter?"

He told Ben about the terminal and hangar, the state they were in, his plans for renovation and the time frame he had to inherit.

"What happens if you fail?"

"Not going to. I can't lose it. My uncle loved the airport and so do I, regardless of the condition everything is in right now. It'll cost me time and money." He was certain his sigh reached across the phone line to his friend.

"I'll need to check out the place before I make a commitment, but I'll give it serious consideration. I haven't forgotten how you kept me afloat after the fiasco with Jenna."

"That's what friends are for."

"Exactly." His voice became quiet and thoughtful. "But I wasn't much help when you and Tanya split. I dodged a bullet, but you, my friend, took a full hit."

"Doesn't matter. I want to forget it... and her. Women are just trouble."

Ben gave a deep grunt. "No kidding."

He closed the panel with a soft click. "The airport is all I care about right now."

A little voice nagged him about the woman next door. Lily, his first love, the woman he'd lost, and yet, she tormented him on a daily basis. He had to stop thinking about her in those terms. It was dangerous to his mental state, especially now that he had so much on his plate.

"Hang on, let me check something." Ben shuffled through pages and mumbled. "I'm back. I have a trip scheduled to Columbus late next week. If I can arrange it so I have a few hours to swing by to check things out, will that work?"

"Fantastic. Maybe I can pluck two birds at the same time. I'm waiting for parts for my uncle's planes. They weren't in the best of shape from having sat so long."

"Are you planning to offer mechanical services as well?"

"You bet. It's what I love to do. I'm not sure how the whole thing will work. I'm not a businessperson, but my uncle's attorney will be a valuable resource for a manager if I need one."

"Good deal. Have you seen any of your childhood friends?"

"Some. I ran into Lily and her two sons." As soon as the words popped out of his mouth, he wanted to pull them back and rip his own tongue out. Why had he even mentioned her? Both he and Ben had committed to women and had suffered at their hands. He hadn't needed to dump on his best friend.

The creak of his friend's chair came through the phone line, and he could almost see Ben's frustrated face leaning toward him.

"You're kidding, right?" The disdain in Ben's voice came through loud and clear.

Sweat pooled on the back of his shirt and he lowered the temperature on the AC unit. "No."

"Start talking." His friend growled. Ben would never let it go.

He slumped in the still-broken chair and told his good friend about his encounters with the boys and Lily–except for his renewed attraction to her. He'd keep that tidbit to himself. The girl he remembered had turned into a beautiful woman and he couldn't stop thinking about her, but the silence that greeted him made him uneasy. "Are you going to say something?"

"Yes." His friend hissed across the line. "Be careful. You don't need another Tanya in your life right now."

"Not happening, Ben. Her father hadn't wanted me to pursue her back then and I'm certainly not going to now with the airport's success hanging over my head. Call me when you get in. I'll pick you up."

He needed his friend to back off.

The phone chimed with another call.

"I gotta go. It's the contractor," he said.

"I'll text you my schedule."

They disconnected, and he picked up the call from Rob. "You got some news for me?"

"What's with the attitude? Did you spill hot coffee on yourself?" Rob let out a half chuckle.

"Sorry, man. Nerves are getting the best of me."

"Quit stressing. I think I found you a project manager. I

have her resume and researched her. She has great commercial experience and she's available."

Excitement pulsed through his veins. Could it be this easy?

"What about the cost of the renovation?"

"Let's meet on Monday. I'll text you the link, but you need to nail down a contract with the project manager. I won't do the work without one."

"What time?"

"Seven good for you?"

"I'm used to early hours."

"Great. See you then."

He pulled his laptop out of his bag and powered it up, then read the message Rob had just sent him.

Excitement took a steep dive when he read the name and his heart sank. Lily? She's the hotshot project manager?

He leaned his head back, and his mind flew in every direction possible, zigzagging through every plausible scenario.

When he logged on, he keyed in the link and scowled the entire time. Before he could check out the company she came from and her work, he got an email from Rob with her resume and clicked on it.

Lily's extensive and impressive resume made his eyes pop open. She'd been a busy gal in Texas. Why wouldn't she look for work at a big company in Columbus?

What had Rob said? *She wants a job close to home.*

The website loaded, and he saw her work. Could he hire her? It wasn't what he wanted, though. He wanted a professional relationship.

It would mean a daily interaction and trusting her with the airport and with almost every penny of savings he had. He could lose it all.

He wasn't sure he could ever trust another woman again. He'd trusted Tanya with his future, but the marriage had crashed and burned.

It was time to go to the Lord in prayer. He should have been on his knees ever since the terms of the inheritance came to light. What was wrong with him? When he had life's challenges and he hadn't sought the Lord, nothing good came of it.

And Lily wasn't in church last week. Her spiritual life was between her and God. Who was he to judge anyway? Tanya hadn't wanted to attend church, and yet he went full steam ahead and chose to marry her anyway. He'd take ownership of that disaster.

What was he thinking? It didn't matter if Lily went to church. It only mattered that she was professional and did her job.

Still, he wasn't sure. Their relationship, professional or otherwise, was a cause for concern.

Lily dressed carefully. She'd washed her breakfast down with a large cup of coffee, but now it gurgled in her stomach and threatened to rise.

Church.

The last time she remembered attending was right before she left for college. She walked away from her faith when Carson walked away from her. *Forget about him.* She had more desperate things to worry about.

Her boys sat on the porch and her father strode from one end of it to the other as she opened the door.

"'Bout time you got ready."

She glanced at her phone. "We'll make it in plenty of time, Dad."

He mumbled to himself and got into the front seat as the boys jumped in the back of her old SUV.

She'd forgotten how long it took to get to church. Her dad kept looking at his watch and frowning. The boys chattered, excited to see their new friends.

When she parked the car, it seemed everyone was already inside.

"Let's go," her father said. His tone was furious at being what he considered late.

The old white clapboard church had gotten a fresh coat of paint and a blood red door. Honeysuckle climbed the pergola in the peaceful garden on the side of the church and gave off a wonderful aroma. When she stepped inside, the pews had gotten a facelift with a darker stain and had an appealing glossy sheen. There were more people than when she left for college, and most of them were strangers.

People looked their way, but since the service was just starting, she hadn't had to deal with questions. Her dad found his favorite seat and the boys eagerly had gone to their classrooms.

As she looked around, she saw Carson. He sat on the other side of her father a few seats away. Great.

She forced herself to concentrate on the worship music, all the while she wished she were back at the farm tackling every project that needed to be done.

The pastor was new too. He was young, but he had a caring face and eyes that reached into one's soul and pulled out every errant belief.

Her father gave her a strange look and handed her a Bible from the pew. She squeezed her fingers around it and

Lily's MECHANIC

found the 2 Corinthians 6:14 passage. The pastor talked about being unequally yoked, and she squirmed.

It described her relationship with her husband. She'd learned the same Biblical lesson years ago, but had dismissed it, and look where it had gotten her. A husband she hadn't really loved. If God was trying to woo her back to church, why did he choose that morning to throw her biggest mistake back in her face? She knew what she had done. Still, her poor choice of a husband had given her only two things that mattered. Her sons.

What would it have been like if Carson had returned? As her mind wandered, so did her eyes.

She noticed the grim look on Carson's face. Had he had the same issue as well? It would seem so, judging by the way he fingered the page of his Bible. She squinted at the book in his hand. Was it the one she gave him for his sixteenth birthday?

She shook her head when her father sent her a questioning look. But her focus shifted to the beautiful stained-glass window. So many things had changed, but thank goodness the calming scene remained.

While gazing at the brilliant kaleidoscope of color where Jesus seemed to be alive, she missed the end of the service and jerked when her father poked her.

"What?"

"The service is over, Lily."

She pointed to the glass depiction of Jesus in the garden. "Sorry. I was admiring it." Childhood Bible stories flooded her mind. She remembered who she was before she'd left for college, and she pondered the return to her faith.

He gave her a troubled look.

When she got up, she saw Carson had exited out of the other side and rushed out the back door.

By the time she and her father left the church, the boys had headed to the car with Mia's son, Drew.

Her friend strode to her. "Lily, I wanted you to meet my brother-in-law, but he didn't make it to church today. His daughter was sick."

"I hope she's OK."

"Probably just a stomach bug. Anyway, I passed along your resume to Rob. He seems to think he may have something for you."

"That's awesome." She beamed at her friend, breathless from the exchange. "I look forward to meeting him and appreciate the help, Mia. More than you know."

Lucas came over and hugged her arm. "Mom, we're hungry for the cornbread you made. It's better than the stuff in Texas."

She ruffled his head as he shrugged. "When aren't you hungry?"

Mia called to her older son as her husband brought the baby to her. "I'll call you next week, Lily."

When they got in the car, she looked around but hadn't seen Carson. *Why didn't he talk to her?* After their heated meeting, what had she expected? She hadn't exactly been friendly. He probably had too much work to do at his uncle's place to bother with her anyway.

The only thing she should think about now was funding the farm's coffers. Her entire body throbbed with excitement. Would Mia's brother-in-law have a job for her?

Chapter 8

Carson stood by his truck as Rob drove up the lane while a new dumpster was dropped in front of the terminal.

He shook the driver's hand and headed to Rob's truck. "I didn't get much done removing the debris from the offices, but I'll work on it today."

Rob got out and grabbed his bag. "No problem. It'll be at least a few days before I can get permits lined up."

They walked into the hangar and stepped into the office. He'd started the AC unit, and the room had cooled to a comfortable temperature.

"I hope you have a great deal for me."

Rob laid out the contract with the pricing.

His lips compressed and his heart pounded. "That's a little more than I expected, but I think I can make it work."

Almost all his and his uncle's savings would not cover the entire renovation. His only hope was to take on inspection services to cover the shortfall. He had connections, so it was doable. He'd have to get on that. His financial advisor recommended taking a loan out against the 401k since penalties were so steep on withdrawal before retirement. He opted to leave it alone and not risk his entire life's savings. He had his Navy pension to live on until he had planes to

work on and others parked, but he'd need to do inspections until that income stream was available.

"Did you call Lily Bennett?"

The question jarred him. On Friday, he'd called every construction management firm within an hour's drive of him and struck out. Every single time.

"Uh. No, not yet."

"I told you, we can't come to an agreement unless you hire a dedicated project manager."

He drew his hand through his hair and scrunched his lips, keeping his frustration to himself. "I know."

The meeting reminded him of the times he'd spent at attention to answer for an aircraft's mechanical failure to his superiors rather than him hiring a contractor.

Rob drummed his fingers on the desk, his jaw clenched. "Why haven't you called her? It should have been a piece of cake to get her. And bonus, she's right next door and will be available when needed."

Time was up. She'd been his last resort.

"I'll go over there after we sign the contract."

Rob pushed the contract to him. "Good. Based on her experience and her completed projects, she's top notch. We'll be lucky to have her. With her on the team, we'll get it done so the airport can open."

After he read the terms of the three-page contract, they signed two copies. One for him and one for Rob.

His new contractor stuffed the documents into his bag and shook Carson's hand.

"I'm not pulling those permits until I hear from Lily and determine the next steps." The contractor handed him another business card. "Give this to her when you talk to her."

Even though Rob hadn't said it, he made it clear he

Lily's MECHANIC

wouldn't begin the project until he was certain Lily was on board.

Rob meeting with her bothered him. The man was happily married, and Carson was being a jerk about it. He had no reason to even be thinking along those lines.

Maybe it was because he hadn't wanted to think of himself as groveling to Lily to work for him.

Everything hinged on her saying yes.

Carson drove up to Sandburg's farmhouse real slow. He told himself he hadn't wanted the gravel to damage his paint job, but the knot in his stomach and his clammy hands told him otherwise.

The boys played catch in the side yard, but when they saw him, the youngest boy shoved the mitt under his arm and ran to the truck.

He slammed the door while Evan skidded to a stop right in front of him and caused a plume of dust to rise around them.

"Mr. Carson, are the airplanes ready for us?"

"Not yet. I'm waiting for parts so I can fix them. The engines are dismantled, so it's not fun to see them that way."

An incredulous look passed over his little face. "You fix planes too?"

He chuckled and ruffled the boy's head. "Sure do."

The older boy came forward, throwing the ball in the air. "Then why are you here?"

"I need to speak to your mother."

Suspicion drew Lucas's brows together. "About what?"

This wouldn't be easy. Not only was he worried about Lily accepting the position, but he had to win over the boys

86

as well. The cow stench filled his lungs and almost choked him.

"Business." He heard the clipped tone come out of his mouth as he stared at the boy who tried to be a man for Lily. He remembered being that boy and how he would have been angered if a strange guy had sniffed around his mother.

"I'll go get her," Evan said over his shoulder as he raced inside.

Lily came out, wiping her delicate fingers on a dishrag sporting the same apron she'd had on when he stopped by the first day. He cocked his head and just couldn't reconcile the highly accomplished woman on the website with the woman in front of him. They were total opposites.

He strode to the steps. "I need to speak to you."

Her father stepped out of the house behind her, and his gaze flicked between him and Lily. He asked the boys if they were ready for a ride to the south pasture to check on the cows.

They whooped and put their mitts on the porch and ran to the barn.

"Now you can talk in peace." Her father scaled the steps, then turned back to them. "You two should go out and have fun, like when you were in high school. It would be perfect."

Her father was none too subtle, and the last thing he needed was a woman gumming up his plans. He needed a project manager, not a date.

He swallowed, and Lily turned a delightful shade of pink. "Sorry," she muttered as she waved to the males in her life as they zoomed past. Then she turned to him. "Can I get you a drink?"

"That'd be great."

"Have a seat. I'll be right back."

Anything to put off the inevitable.

When she returned, the apron was gone, and she carried

Lily's MECHANIC

a tray with glasses of lemonade, something he hadn't had since he left Worthy.

He took a long gulp and puckered his lips, tart and refreshing. Sort of like Lily. *Stop it. You are here for one reason only, and that's to hire Lily.*

"Why are you here?"

"I need your help."

That wasn't what he wanted to say. But that's what came out.

She raised her arched brow and frowned. "How so?"

"I need an ace project manager for the terminal and hangar renovation. Rob Marino can't get the work done in the time period without one."

Her arms came around her waist and she slumped in the chair. "Do you remember Mia? My best friend from high school?"

The change of subject confused him, but he'd go along with it if it meant she'd accept his proposal.

"Yeah, I see her at church all the time. By the way... it was good to see you there."

"She told me Rob might have a job for me."

"Wait. How does Mia know Rob?"

"He's Mia's brother-in-law."

He scratched his head. "OK. Why do you need a job? I'm guessing there's more than enough to do around here." He waved his hand to encompass the farm.

Her face colored. "Dad is behind in his bills. I need to help him get caught up."

"OK." Air expanded in his lungs. The whole thing could blow up in his face.

"Is the airport the job Rob had in mind for me?"

"Probably. Are you interested?"

88

She shook her head and sighed. "I'm not sure. I'd have to see what the market rate is for the Columbus area. The bigger question is… can we work together?"

He rose to his feet. "I don't think we'll have that much interaction since I'll be in the hangar most of the time and you'll be working more closely with Rob and not me."

"I see. Well, in that case, let me do some research and I'll get back to you."

"How soon can you let me know?" He wanted to kick his own butt for not coming sooner. "Rob wants to get started and I'm under a time crunch."

Why had he told her about that now, before she agreed? What a knucklehead.

"What's the rush?" She eyed him from the comfort of the chair, took a sip of her lemonade as if she had all the time in the world, and waited.

He couldn't very well tell her he'd lose the property if he didn't get the work done in a timely fashion. Or if he didn't find a project manager, he was dead in the water. And she certainly didn't know there wasn't enough money to fund the project in the first place.

"I need to generate an income. I can't do that if the airport is closed."

"Fair enough."

"Call me when you have a price and a contract. I'll be at the airport all week hauling out trash from the terminal so Rob can get the demo done quickly."

His top priority was to get their contract nailed down tight despite his reservations.

He got up to leave and turned toward her. When she rose from the chair, he almost drew her into his arms, but backed away.

Lily's MECHANIC

She grabbed his arm. "Careful. The steps are behind you."

He looked over his shoulder and sure enough, if he'd stepped a little farther, he'd have taken a tumble. Wouldn't *that* have been a sight?

"Thanks. I'll let you go." He turned when he reached the end of the walkway. "Call me."

Working with Lily would be a terrific challenge, and he needed his good friend to keep him grounded and focused on the bigger picture.

Ben, where are you?

Lily stared at her father after she'd told him about the job offer from Carson. He'd grunted and said he was hungry, then ate everything on his plate. He must have forgotten he didn't like Mexican.

The boys loved tacos and Dad hadn't complained or refused when she promised her sons a once-a-week taco night.

And he was doing it again. He had a far off look on his face. Could he have dementia? She had to confront him or his doctor… and soon.

Evan wiggled out of his chair and hugged her. "Mom, those were the best tacos ever."

"Thanks."

"Can we have them again tomorrow night?"

"Once a week, remember?"

Lucas placed his hand on her father's forearm. "Farfar… tell us more about the treasure."

She rose to take the fixings off the table. "There is no treasure, Lucas. Don't you remember what Carson told us?"

Just then, her father looked up. "Of course there's a trea-

sure. Why would Patrick tell me there was if there wasn't?"

"I'd prefer it if we didn't discuss the treasure anymore."

"Are you taking the job with Carson?"

"I'm not sure."

"Why not? He needs the help and with the airport open, it might be good for the farm store."

Another item on her list she'd forgotten about. She'd have to work that project in while she was feeding her family, doing chores, and working for Carson. She was tired just thinking about all the tasks that had to be done. She wasn't twenty-five anymore.

"I need to research what I can charge. That's tonight's project."

"But Mom… if we found the treasure, you wouldn't have to go to work." Evan's pleading eyes made her want to cry.

She grabbed her son's hand. "Listen to me. The treasure doesn't exist, and even if it did… if you found it, it belongs to Carson. So, let's stop talking about it."

Her father straightened and slammed his fist on the table. "It exists. Patrick said it was there and I believe him."

The boys stilled at the violent action and became quiet.

"Boys… Go upstairs," she whispered. "I'll bring milk and cookies in a while."

The boys got up and moved far away from their grandfather and cast worried glances over their shoulder.

"Go on." She kept a soft smile on her face until the sound of their footsteps on the stairs drifted to silence.

"Dad?"

He seemed to come out of it and his fist opened and his eyes roamed the room. "Your mother loved this kitchen."

"I remember." She dropped into her chair. "Why did you sell the west pasture to Patrick?"

Lily's MECHANIC

The confused look on her father's face cleared for a moment.

"Patrick wanted to expand the airport with new runways, and I needed the money to upgrade the milking machines. He wasn't going to expand right away anyway, and Carson has a lot of work to do, so he won't be using the land right now, either."

She moved to a chair closer to her father and leaned in. "But, Dad, that land could have been leased to another farm for crops. It would have helped on a continual basis."

Her father's chin rose. "I know that, but it would have taken five seasons to get the kind of money I needed for the upgrade. Patrick did me a favor. I'm done talking about it."

He moved his chair back, but stopped when she gripped the edge of the table.

"Dad, is there something else you want to tell me?"

"Like what?"

"How are you feeling?"

"I'm fine. Why do you keep asking?"

"You sometimes talk to me as if I were still in high school."

His mouth opened, then he clamped it shut and lifted himself off the chair. "I'm going out to the barn for a minute."

When he reached the door, he turned and stared at a spot above her head. "It's because the last time you lived here, you *were* in high school."

In the quiet of the evening, Lily loaded the dishwasher and cleaned the kitchen. The boys ran down the stairs and eased into the room.

Evan's gaze darted around the room. "Where's Farfar?"

"Out in the barn. You don't have to be afraid of him. He'd never hurt you. Not in a million years."

Lucas slid into his chair. "But he—"

SERALYNN LEWIS

"Was upset. Everyone gets upset. It doesn't mean he'll hurt you."

Evan's eyes were troubled. "Are you sure?"

She stiffened, then sat next to her youngest. "Why would you think that?"

Her son stared at the table, his body rigid. "Remember my friend, Carlos, in Texas? His dad hit him. He didn't like it."

"Farfar will never hit you. I'll admit he's not himself, but he'd never hurt you. Think about how he treats the cows."

Lucas stilled. "He's really kind to them and talks to them like they're human." His quiet voice warmed her heart.

She smiled. "That's right. You haven't seen it yet, but when one of them gets sick, he tries to make the cow feel better. He was angry because I don't believe there's treasure next door and I don't want you asking about it again and upsetting him." She gave them her stern motherly stare. "Understood?"

"Yes, Mom," Lucas said.

Evan jumped out of his chair. "Can we have cookies and milk now?"

After she gave her sons their snack, she told them to clean their plates and cups while she stepped to the office to research rates and get the contract ready for Carson.

It wasn't the job she wanted, but it was one she needed. If she had to work with and for him, she prayed her heart would remain intact.

Somehow, she doubted it.

Chapter 9

It had only been two days since Carson offered Lily the job, but waiting made his neck tighten and he'd have to find a chiropractor if he didn't stop cracking it. He'd call her after lunch.

Sweat poured from Carson's face as he pulled more debris from the terminal.

His nerves eased now that he had signed the contract with Rob, but he was at a standstill until Lily got back to him. Time was not on his side.

At that moment his stomach growled. He hadn't eaten since Amy's continental breakfast early that morning.

He'd stopped by the deli on his way to the airport and had a sandwich in a cooler in the truck, but he had to wash up first.

As he rounded the hangar door, he spotted Lily's sons as they rubbed the plane's underbelly. Parts were organized on old, faded tarps his uncle had used for decades. He could tell the boys had walked around on the sheets because there were dusty footprints.

He hadn't wanted to startle them and possibly have them get hurt when they saw him.

Lucas smoothed a palm over the plane's fuselage with appreciation. "We better get out of here."

94

Evan tilted his head to the side and stared at the cockpit. "Think we can climb up there and sit in it?"

"Don't even think about it," he growled. "You boys were told the hangar was dangerous, and I'd call you when it wasn't."

He gritted his teeth, and his muscles tightened. He hadn't padlocked the hangar like he should have. He was a boy once and remembered how exciting planes could be, evoking a memory of how angry his uncle had been when he sliced his leg on one of the parts scattered around the hangar. Now he understood his uncle's need to protect. He felt it himself.

When the boys turned and saw him, they raced around the plane, nearly upsetting the precise order of the parts laid out on the tarp. He stepped to the tarp and surveyed it to make sure every part was in its place, then ran after Lucas and Evan. But the boys were already at the tree line when he got to the hangar door.

Now he'd have to tackle not only Lily working for him, but her sons' disobedience. He expected Lily would handle it. If not, he'd have to be more diligent to lock the hangar… and that was inconvenient.

With the entire inheritance at risk, he couldn't upset Lily. Not when he desperately needed her expertise. He could have called her, but the situation required an in-person visit so he could gauge Lily's reaction.

Lunch would have to wait. He padlocked the hangar and the terminal and headed over to the Sandburg farm. The drive would allow him to cool his anger.

When he got there, the place looked deserted.

But when he slipped out of the truck, he spotted the boys by the corner of the barn peeking their heads out now and again watching him.

Veins on his forehead throbbed and popped. His feet

covered the distance from the truck to the walkway with resounding thuds.

The screen door slammed, and Lily appeared on the porch with her ever present apron. Paint smudges smeared on her face and hands. "I planned to call you."

He strode to her and stood at the bottom of the stairs. "Yeah, well… that's not why I'm here, but we can talk about that later."

She wiped her hands on the apron. Her eyes traveled over his face, but her features remained neutral.

He scaled the steps and stood in front of her. "We have a problem."

"You found someone else to do the project."

The look on her face was fear and relief at the same time—if that was even possible.

"Not even close." He wiped his grimy and sweaty hands on his worn jeans.

She looked him up and down. "You look like you've gone ten rounds with a plane and lost."

"I caught the boys in the hangar without permission." He sighed and the pent up frustration fled from his body. "I had taken apart the engine and had the parts laid out in a precise manner. Thankfully, they hadn't disturbed anything. But there were some sharp edges, Lily. They could have gotten hurt."

Her jaw clenched, and she wrung her hands, but stopped when she caught his eyes glance at them. "They were supposed to go with my dad out to the pasture." She stepped forward and clasped his arm. "You're mad, aren't you?"

He shivered from her nearness. "I'm furious at myself for not guessing the boys would desperately want to see the planes. I'm angry I hadn't locked the hangar. I was in the terminal hauling out trash."

At that moment, his stomach rumbled, and a scowl appeared, but he quickly hid it. "And I was going to get a bite to eat, otherwise I'd never have known they were there unless they had gotten hurt."

Her face fell, and she pulled her hand away. "Instead, you had to stop and come here to tell me about it."

"Listen, Lily. I can lock the hangar when I'm in the terminal. I'd prefer it if I didn't have to, but I will, just to make sure they're safe."

"You're being awfully nice about their disobedience."

"Well, I was a boy once too. Before I met you, I went into the hangar when I was told not to and got a deep cut on my leg. My uncle was livid. I don't want your boys injured. They seem to be good kids." He leaned in. "Don't look now, but they're hiding by the corner of the barn watching us."

Her eyebrows rose and her eyes rounded. "They are?"

"Yep. And I'm going to do something that will probably get them to come running. Maybe even anger you."

A perfectly arched brow raised. "What's that?"

"This." And he leaned forward, grasped her arms, and hauled her to him for a tight hug. "Because I never got a chance to welcome you home. The boys will not like it, I'm sure." He pulled back and leaned his forehead against hers and stared straight into her eyes. Her shiver moved through him and settled into his heart.

Every situation he had faced in the past month coalesced into a giant ball of emotion when his skin brushed hers. All the dormant feelings rose and flattened him in the gut like a steamroller.

The look on her face probably mirrored his, but they couldn't talk about it because the boys raced to the steps and stopped, their tennis shoes squeaking on the walkway.

Lily's MECHANIC

"What are you doing?" Lucas screamed, his face was hot with perspiration and red with fury.

He narrowed his eyes at one boy then the other. "Getting you to come out of hiding."

Evan crossed his arms, his face a mask of rebuke. "You can't hug my mom."

He glanced at Lily who seemed to be poleaxed and gave the little boy a hint of a smile. "I just did."

The little boy's mouth worked, and he moved toward his mother. "Well, I don't like it."

He turned to their mother. "Lily, we need to talk about our agreement."

Lucas stepped up to him, chest expanded. "What agreement."

With a snap of her head, Lily busted out of her stupor. "Boys." Her voice sounded strangled. "Get washed, and go to your rooms and stay there. You went into the hangar without permission when you were expressly told not to. You disobeyed. Now go."

Her last words were a bit more forceful than he would have liked, but she was their mother, and he'd stay out of it.

His lips flattened, and he kept silent.

After casting angry looks at him and their mother, the boys mumbled but went inside.

She moved to the door with her feet dragging. "Come on in. I'll get you a drink and we can talk."

He followed her into the living room. None of the furnishings had changed, but it looked like it was freshly scrubbed and painted. *That's what she's been doing all this time.*

Hopefully, the morning's fiasco wouldn't deter her from being his project manager.

And what about the hug?

98

The electricity arcing between them and staring deep into his eyes flustered Lily to the point she hadn't even seen her sons race up to Carson and call him out.

A tiny grin pushed its way on her face. Her sons were troopers. Her lips curved down, and she inhaled. How would she negotiate bringing them with her on occasion if they had disobeyed Carson?

Now she had no leverage. Nothing. What's the worst he could do? Say no? She'd still have to find a sitter for the boys anyway. Dad was unreliable, and she couldn't trust the boys on their own while she worked. Not after that stunt. Her life just got more tangled.

She gave him a glass of lemonade and motioned for him to follow her into the office. "I apologize for the mess in here. I can only tackle one project at a time. Have a seat."

He sat and looked around the room, eyeing the stacks of folders on the desk and the layers of dust on the bookcases. "How are you going to manage my project, the boys, and the farm?"

The serious look on his face bothered her. What was he thinking?

She stiffened her back and projected an air of confidence. She hadn't wanted him to see her desperation. "I lived for quite a number of years on my own with just me and the boys and had a full-time job managing multiple multi-million dollar projects, so I think I can handle one small airport reno."

He took a sip of the tart lemonade and cleared his throat. "I saw your project portfolio online. You're exceptional, but

there's a lot of stress around here. And it doesn't even include what's going on with your father's health." He propped his forearms on his knees.

"You're right. There is a lot of stress. But I can handle it. Besides, I don't have a choice. Won't you give me a chance?"

She hadn't wanted to beg, but that's what it sounded like, and she needed to get an upper hand. Her sons just made it almost impossible for her. She'd never spanked them, but right now they should have their behinds reddened for their rebellious act. Unfortunately, they were too old for spankings, and she'd find another way to punish them.

"I prepared a contract last night after I verified what the going rate was for project managers in the Columbus area. A lot of work can be done from here, but my plan is to be available at the airport only when needed and to not exceed forty hours in any given week, billing you every two weeks. Payment will be expected within two weeks."

When she quoted him the rate, he never blinked.

"Sounds reasonable," he said. "Where's the contract? I'll sign it right now."

"There are one or two more things."

He sat up straight. "What?"

"I plan on hiring Bobby, a high school kid from church, for when I must be at the airport. But that may not always work out. I'll need to bring the boys with me on those occasions."

Her hands moved to below the desk so she wouldn't give away her nervousness.

"As long as we are clear they don't go anywhere near the hangar on their own, I can live with that."

An enormous sigh of relief moved through her body, but she simply nodded once and pulled the paperwork from the

drawer and pushed it to him.

"Here's the contract, but there's one more thing."

He picked up the document and scanned the two pages.

"Yeah?" He glanced at her and then returned his attention to the contract.

"No more hugging me."

His head shot up. "What?"

She gritted her teeth. "No. More. Hugging."

A slow grin pushed its way to his lips. "Why? Did it bother you?"

Leaning forward, she gripped the desk, and her fingers tightened until they turned white. "We *will* be professional. Our former personal relationship is over. Period."

His brows creased, and a frown replaced his grin, and he grabbed the pen. "Then we are agreed."

She waited for him to sign both sets and handed him a copy. "Good. I'll put the fear of God into my sons to keep them from heading to your place."

He gave her a long look and lifted himself from the chair. He pulled a business card from his pocket. "Rob is expecting your call. Keep me in the loop. Text is fine."

"Of course." She rose and followed him out to the front door.

When he passed her, she got a whiff of rank motor oil, and she crinkled her nose as he loped to his truck.

The past flittered through her brain with visions of times spent picking blackberries and using the rope swing to jump into the pond on hot summer days. Longing swept through her.

How in the world was she going to keep her promise of a professional relationship when a welcoming hug practically scorched her and reminded her of their past?

Chapter 10

Carson couldn't stop thinking about a casual hug that set off a whole slew of need. It was only meant to mobilize the boys. But the warmth of her in his arms meant more to him than he could have imagined, and it ticked him off.

Hot and sweaty, he'd taken off his t-shirt hours ago and his shorts stuck to his thighs. He used his forearm to wipe the sweat from his brow, then carted the last of the junk from the terminal to the dumpster, which was full... again.

He kept himself in shape with calisthenics and hefting heavy equipment and aircraft parts, but the daily grind of clearing out junk kicked his butt.

A plume of dust rose from the lane, and he spotted Lily's old SUV lumbering toward him.

He hadn't seen her since he signed the contract three days ago, but his brain short-circuited, and his mind traveled to her almost every hour.

What was wrong with him? He had to get a handle on his wayward thoughts. Jeopardizing his inheritance wasn't an option. Besides, what would she think if she discovered that if he failed, he'd lose his inheritance and she'd get her father's land back? She could sell it to a developer and make a tidy sum. Would she torpedo the entire project?

He had to stop thinking the worst. Uncle Patrick paid her father for the land. And that was that.

After Lily parked and got out of the car, her sunny yellow sundress billowed out as a gust of wind hit her. His mouth went dry, and he swallowed. Grit, like the shavings of his favorite mill file, rasped against his throat.

She had a brilliant smile on her lightly made-up face as she turned and came toward him.

It was the first time he'd seen her dressed up. Sunday church clothes didn't count. She was a vision, and he couldn't move if his life depended on it.

"Carson? What's wrong?" Her soft voice came to him as if in a fog.

He shook his head to clear the rambling notions as she stared at him with her beautiful blue eyes. "Zoned out for a minute."

She pushed a huge plastic cup at him. "I brought you a cold drink."

He caught sight of her red roughened hands and his heart sank. She'd worked her fingers raw to care for her father, the farm, her boys, and now the airport.

"Thanks."

He took the icy cold cup and gulped her signature lemonade.

"Hey there, slow down. You'll get brain freeze."

He breathed deep. "Too late."

"I wanted to stop by and talk to you about the project and see if you had an extra set of plans I could keep."

The golf ball that took residence in his chest wouldn't move, no matter how many times he tried to force it down.

"Sure thing. They're in the hangar office." He thumbed his hand to the padlocked door. "Before we go, do you want

Lily's MECHANIC

to look at the stuff I saved to see if there's anything worth saving?"

"Actually, it'd be better if I had the plans before I see the space. I'd like to get a feel for what the architect had envisioned."

He did an about face and headed to the hangar door. When he passed her, he could smell her sweet scent. The light floral smell wouldn't go away soon, and he scrunched his nose.

When he held the door open for her, he glimpsed her painted toes. "Maybe we should wait. The terminal isn't safe for your feet in those shoes."

She waved her arm in a wide arc. "Nonsense. They're fine. I'll have my steel-toed work boots and jeans on tomorrow, but I'll be safe enough for today."

He led the way to the office, but halted when the tapping of her heels stopped.

"What's wrong?"

She turned in a full circle. "I'd forgotten how cavernous the hangar was." She stopped in front of the Cessna. "Your uncle's planes look terrific."

He walked back and stood next to her, immersed in the past. "Remember when we hid in there during that terrible storm and fell asleep? Your dad was livid, and Uncle Patrick wanted to kill me. We both paid the price for that stunt."

The narrowed eyes and frown made him stop talking.

Her nose and lips scrunched in displeasure. "Carson…" Her voice took on a cutting edge.

He could feel the heat as it rushed to his chest. "Sorry. Forget it. No more talk about our former relationship," he mumbled and turned away. *What was I thinking?*

The click-clacking of her heels followed him to the office, and it annoyed him.

The door shut behind her with a quiet snick. "I'm sorry,

104

Carson. I shouldn't have used that tone. If we stray from a professional relationship, it could affect the work and... I need this job."

He kept his back to her, grabbed his t-shirt and pulled it on, and gave himself time to corral his foolish mind. "It's fine. You were right. I'll get the plans and we can walk through the terminal so you can see what's been done so far."

She moved further into the tiny office. "At least it's cool in here."

After he'd grabbed the plans from the closet, he turned, and she looked ready to drop into one of the filthy chairs. "Don't sit. The grease will stain your pretty dress." His voice lowered and thinned out.

She gave him a slight smile, held out her hand and wiggled her fingers. "Give me."

He handed her the rolled-up plan.

She spread it out on the desk and flipped through the pages, then scanned the tiny notes at the bottom and on the far side of the document. "Let's go look at the terminal."

Moving through the door, she stopped and opened the plans to the third page and sent her trained eye around the cavernous room, hesitating at the Cessna's nose.

For months, that one night spent with her troubled him. Nothing happened except a few kisses and her in his arms all night long, but that night had stayed with him. It had branded him. Had it only been a teenage crush? Now that he looked back, he realized she'd never left him. She'd always been the measuring stick with anyone he dated. Even his ex-wife recognized it long before they parted ways.

She moved to the door, and he followed her into the terminal. He turned on the flashlight and adjusted to where he thought she was looking.

Lily's MECHANIC

He couldn't think of her as anything other than his project manager, and he had to remain professional.

Easier to say it than to do it. If only there weren't so many memories.

Lily's arms shook, and she gripped the plans in her hands. She nearly swallowed her tongue when she saw him shirtless.

Thank goodness he put his shirt back on when they went into the office. Carson had filled out and was quite a man. She could barely make out the Navy tattoo on his beefy bicep. Normally tats weren't her thing, but his were hot and she pondered if he had any others. *Stop it. Stay professional, Lily. You need this job.*

Dust and dirt filtered into her lungs, but there weren't any chemical smells, so she'd not have to worry about remediation of any sort. She'd make note to check it.

Carson pointed to a darkened corner of the main area. "I put the items we could reuse in the corner over there."

"We'll need more light."

"Rob is bringing industrial lighting in the morning. Based on the plans, all the interior walls except for load-bearing ones will be removed."

Did he think she didn't know how to read an architectural plan? It was her job.

"I see that."

Her face must have shown her scorn.

"Sorry. You probably know how to read those plans better than I do."

She moved to the other side of the building. "Probably."

He sidled next to her and peered over her shoulder at the

106

plans. "Do you think we can have the place operational in the time frame allotted?"

"It'll be tight. You'll have subs, that's sub-contractors, working on top of one another to get it done. I still don't understand what the rush is."

He drew an agitated hand through his hair and stepped away from her. "I told you, I need an income. Without tenants, parked planes, and mechanic work, I'll have to find another job and it would take me away from here."

She stepped away from him and walked to the exterior door. "I'll study the plans and be back in the morning."

"Will your boys be with you?"

"No. Bobby from church will stay with them for part of the day. My father, Fred, and the farmhands have started teaching the boys how to move the cows to the milking barn and hook them up to be milked. But that's only part of the day. Most of what I have to do, I can do from home."

When they stepped out into the sun's brightness, she squinted and shaded her face. The cows lowing in the distance reminded her of her responsibilities next door.

He stepped closer to her. "Why was your husband in jail?"

She stiffened as she turned and glared at him. "Bet you had that question locked and loaded and have been waiting for just the right moment to trot it out. We're supposed to be professional."

When he asked her about her husband, a knee jerk reaction gave her a start. *Focus on why you're doing this.* All the bills on her father's desk needed to be paid.

"We are. We're also childhood friends and I want to know what your life was like." He hadn't blinked, but he shoved his hands in his back pockets and waited.

She stilled and stared him straight in the eye. "If you

must know, my husband embezzled from his clients. My sons… we lost everything. I kept my job and my 401k, but it became more difficult to go to work every day. Especially after he died." The ball of bitterness wedged in her throat.

He reached out, but she pulled back. The kindness on his face nearly gutted her.

"I'm so sorry, Lily. I had no idea. Is that why you came home?"

She could never lie to Carson. "Yes and no."

His face registered confusion. "I don't understand."

She crossed her arms around her waist. The plans dangled at her hip. "Your uncle called me about three weeks before he died. He made it clear my dad was lonely and insisted I should come home. I had already thought about it, but I hadn't called my father. Patrick hinted there was something wrong with dad but wouldn't say what. By the time I worked my notice, sold what little I had and drove here, your uncle was dead, and I couldn't ask him."

His eyes bulged and his head shot forward. "Uncle Patrick called you?"

She nodded. "I'm so sorry for your loss, Carson. I know how much your uncle meant to you. And I will do my very best work to honor him."

The sadness in his eyes went straight to her heart.

"Thank you." His quiet voice pained her.

After talking about her husband, her mouth formed the first words that popped into her mind. "Tell me why you got divorced."

"She traded up."

She glimpsed pain on his face before it disappeared. "Excuse me?"

He lowered his eyes to the ground, embarrassed by his

stupidity. "My wife had an agenda. Tanya married me so she could go on base when I was out at sea. She wanted to be an officer's wife, and I was the stepping stone. Her plan panned out."

She stepped closer to him and gulped. "I'm so sorry. No one deserves that kind of betrayal."

"You had betrayal as well."

Her head cocked slightly. "Let's just say we were both betrayed, but in different ways."

"True."

The SUV's handle burned as she grabbed it. "I'll see you in the morning. We'll talk more then."

She stepped into her car and started it, hoping they'd gotten the personal conversation out of the way. But she doubted it.

Chapter 11

Since the start of the terminal renovation project over six weeks ago, Carson had seen Lily's boys often and had gotten closer to them. At her request, he had kept her at arm's length, which had become more difficult each day that passed.

He hadn't wanted to get involved. No way. But he had. Two small boys had captured his heart when they watched him work on the planes and asked questions.

Whenever the boys came with Lily, he'd taken them into the hangar and explained aerodynamics in a way the little guys could understand. Like him, so many years ago, the planes and flying enthralled them.

Occasionally, he'd even allowed them to help him, particularly when they had talked to him about the treasure. The myth was on constant replay, and they couldn't seem to get it out of their little brains.

Trusting his first love had been a challenge. Slight twinges of unease surfaced when he least expected. The betrayal he'd suffered at the hands of his ex-wife created confusion in his already muddled mind.

Lily, though, deserved his trust. He should have remembered she'd never hurt him, and it had been him who had hurt her. Her attention to every detail kept the terminal's

renovation going. And working with Rob had been the joy Amy and Bryan told him it would be.

But Carson perceived Lily would balk if he broached the subject of their relationship. When the project was completed, his hope was he could convince her to give their relationship another try. After all, her dad had hinted on more than one occasion she needed him in her life.

With the great progress on the terminal, all the workers took the Independence Day weekend off.

The day was perfect for the holiday. Not a hint of humidity in the air. White puffy clouds ambled along pristine blue skies. The scent of the mock orange flowers Lily had encouraged him to plant in big tubs on each side of his uncle's front door flooded the still air, and he breathed deep of their heady aroma.

He'd asked Lily about taking her and the boys to see the Fourth of July fireworks in town, but she'd refused. Instead, he'd move into his uncle's farmhouse.

Amy gave him a great send off that morning with a box of his favorite pastries. His mouth watered every time he thought of the bag sitting on the kitchen counter. A treat for later. It was time he began work on the old farmhouse, and he'd have more time to do it if he were living there.

With the last of his stuff stashed in his old room upstairs, he stepped to the hall closet to get linens for his old double bed. After the breakneck speed of the past month, he had a simple plan for the day. He'd get his room and belongings organized, then inventory what he needed to make the house more habitable and pitch the junk.

He hadn't even made the bed when the phone in his pocket blared with Lily's ringtone. He chuckled every time he'd heard it. The boys insisted he needed to have a specific

Lily's MECHANIC

one, so he'd know it was her calling.

But when he heard her stilted and choked voice saying his name, his stomach lurched. "Lily?"

"I won't be at the airport tomorrow. Crucial things are happening this week and I... I can't be there. But I'll text what needs to be done and I'll make myself available by text, email, or phone to guide you along." Her voice cracked. "I'm sorry, Carson."

Her car door slammed, and he heard it rumble to a start.

His heart dropped. "What's wrong?"

She heaved a long breath. "It's Dad. I had to call an ambulance."

A siren had pierced the morning's silence at least twenty minutes ago, but he dismissed it.

"What happened and which hospital?"

"Dad took a fall in the barn. He's headed to Columbus General."

"Are the boys with you?"

No response.

"Lily. Are the boys with you?" His voice rose.

"Yes. I don't—"

"I'm on my way. I'll see to the boys, you take care of your dad."

"Thank you, Carson."

He threw the phone on the bed and jumped in the shower, thankful the plumber had replaced the hot water tank and all the faucets before he moved in. He was in his truck in less than ten minutes, but it would take over twenty to get to the hospital.

In the time it took him to get there, anything could happen. She had been shaken up. He observed her enough to know she was the coolest cucumber of the bunch. It seemed nothing rattled her, but this had.

112

He worried about her state of mind and desperately wanted to call her, but she was driving, and with the boys in the car, distracting her was out of the question.

So much had been placed on her shoulders since she'd been home. She'd planted a small garden and managed to re-open the Sandburg Farm Store where locals could buy milk, butter, ice cream, and fruit from their farm. She planned to add crafts from local artisans. What an amazing woman.

As he drove, he prayed. For Nils, for the boys, but mostly for Lily.

What would he find when he got there?

Lily held tightly to her son's hands and dragged them through the emergency entrance. Her throat convulsed at the hospital's antiseptic smell.

When she hit the registration desk, the clerk took her name, but Lily could not supply the insurance information since she had no idea what kind of coverage, if any, her father had.

"Can I see him?"

There wasn't one compassionate bone in the woman's body. She saw distraught family members day in and day out, blinded to the suffering of others.

"A nurse will be out shortly to take you back."

Clacking keys resumed, and the woman's intense stare at her screen told Lily she had been dismissed.

She let go of her son's hands and wrapped her arms around her waist, unwilling to allow her sons to see her break down, but she was having a tough time. If something happened to her father... Now that she had returned to Worthy, she wanted more time with him.

Lily's MECHANIC

"Do you know when I'll be called?"

The clerk's startled look told her the woman had forgotten she was there. "I have no idea. Have a seat in the waiting room to the left."

Releasing her clenched fingers, she wrapped her arms around her son's shoulders and led them to the waiting room.

"Mom, I have to go to the bathroom." Evan moved from foot to foot with a look of discomfort on his face.

Lucas pointed to the hallway. "It's down there. I'll take him."

She turned toward the restrooms. "We'll all go."

"But you have to be in there when the nurse comes to get you." Her older son's reasonable tone almost did her in.

"I can see it from the hallway, and it won't take long."

Her eldest stared at the floor as they walked down the corridor, then turned to her before they went into the restroom. "Will Farfar be OK?"

What had happened? How had her father fallen? Her mind had covered those questions and more on the trip to the hospital.

"I don't know. Take your brother so we can get back to the waiting room."

The boys slipped into the men's room as she leaned against the gray wall on the other side of the corridor. A chill filled her heart, and she pulled out her phone. Her hands shook as she left a message for Mia and texted the sitter.

She'd just finished when her sons stepped through the door. They hurried to the waiting room and sat.

Another twenty minutes went by, and she became antsy. She jumped up and approached the clerk.

The woman barely glanced her way. "The nurse will be out shortly."

If she could have reached over and put her hands around the clerk's throat, she would have, but it wouldn't solve anything except to make her look like a mad woman and she'd be thrown out of the hospital.

When she turned to the boys, Carson had arrived and sat between them, talking. Why had she been so adamant that she keep her distance? To just be professional? Had she feared she couldn't do her job? Or was it because she hadn't wanted her heart to be in jeopardy? Too late for that.

He rose, as did the boys, when she walked over. "How is he?"

She couldn't look him in the eye because she suspected she'd cry. "I don't know. They haven't called us in yet."

A voice came from behind them. "Sandburg family?"

She stiffened, and he clasped her frozen hand.

"That's you. I'll stay with the boys." His low voice comforted her, and he motioned his head to the doors.

Squeezing his hand, she turned and walked with the nurse through the locked doors.

"How is he?" Her voice cracked, and she cleared her throat.

When they reached the room at the end, the nurse opened the door and motioned for her to go in. "Doctor Kirk is with him. He'll give you the details."

"How is it my dad's family doctor is here right now?" She squinted at the nurse.

"Dr. Kirk was making his rounds, when he heard your father was in the ER, he stopped in to check him."

The nurse's gentle words did nothing to help with her uneasiness.

She inhaled and plastered a smile on her face, but she hadn't needed to because her father's eyes were closed.

The doctor looked up as he checked her father's heart.

Lily's MECHANIC

"How's he doing?" she whispered and moved closer to the hospital bed.

"He suffered a fractured arm, but I'm concerned about a concussion."

"I'm fine." Her dad's eyes popped open, and he slurred his words. His face whitened with pain.

"Dad, do you remember what happened?"

The doctor lowered his chin and her father glared at him. Dad shifted his gaze to her. Something was going on and she'd figure it out if it was the last thing she did.

A grimace covered her father's face, and he moved his agitated legs under the covers. "I was in the hayloft and lost my footing and fell."

Her eyes bugged out, and she rushed to the bed. "You fell from the hay loft? You're lucky you didn't break your neck." She hadn't wanted to say that last part in such a sarcastic tone.

He gritted his teeth. "I was halfway down the ladder when I fell."

She pulled back and turned to the doctor. "What's the prognosis?"

When the swelling goes down, we'll put a soft cast on his arm. He's got a hairline fracture which will heal on its own with care. His ankle is bruised and swollen, but not broken. Because he was knocked out, I want him admitted for observation for a few days.

Her father's scowl was one she'd seen only when he was frustrated. "Aww, Doc."

She moved her fingers over his good hand and squeezed. "He's right, Dad."

"Where are the boys? You need to go home and take care of them."

"Carson is with them in the waiting room. You didn't

116

think I'd leave them alone at the farm, right?"

"Oh, right." He sighed and his eyes drifted shut. "I'm really tired and want to sleep."

The doctor straightened and tapped into his tablet. "We gave him something for pain, so he'll sleep, and we'll move him to a room later." He turned to her. "You should go home. There's nothing you can do for him. He'll rest all night and be ornery in the morning."

She gave him a half grin. "No doubt. I want to talk to you."

The doctor stepped to the door, and she followed him into the hallway, then stopped a little way from her father's room.

"Your dad should be OK and can go home pretty quickly once we determine he's not concussed. But he'll need a physical therapist to help him deal with mobility issues."

"What else is going on, Doc? I saw the glances between the two of you."

Doctor Kirk tilted his head, clicked the pen in his hand, and shoved it into the pocket of his lab coat. "I can't discuss your father's medical issues other than his current injuries."

"What do you mean? What medical issues?" She could hear the harshness in her voice, but refused to back down.

The doctor's face tightened. "Without his permission, I can't speak to you, and he hasn't given it. I'm sorry."

"But—"

He removed her hand from his arm. "Get him to sign the forms, and I'll be happy to talk to you."

She stiffened as she watched the doctor walk swiftly down the hallway. A nurse bumped into her, and she backed up against the wall and tried to breathe normally. She fast footed back to her father's room and slowed her pace as she entered until she stood over him. "What haven't you told me?" she whispered to her snoring dad. "You need to tell me everything."

Hot tears threatened, and she blinked them back. He'd aged so much in the last dozen years. She'd seen it when they'd first come back to Worthy, but she'd been so focused on making her childhood home more comfortable, then the farm's degradation and making it profitable, she hadn't wanted to think about his condition, even though the signs had been there from the first week. He was sick. She suspected he'd hidden it from her.

Her flip flops slapped on the tiled floors as she strode through the corridors as if in a trance. Carson joked with the boys and played cards with them.

She forced a smile on her lips. "Hey, guys. Where'd you get the cards?"

Evan jumped and wrapped his little arms around her. "Carson brought them. Is Farfar going to be alright?"

How could she answer his trusting face when she honestly couldn't say what would happen long term?

She sat on a chair next to Lucas. "He's got a hairline fracture in his arm and his ankle is swollen, but it's not broken."

Carson glanced at her and his face was a mask of concern. It was all she could do not to throw herself into his arms and let him take over. She was tired of being strong. She was tired of all the problems she faced. When would it ever get better? The weight of her problems dragged her to exhaustion.

She had reached the end of herself. God had been chasing her to this moment. To a place in her life where she had to admit to herself, she needed him to lead and guide her.

Lucas gathered the cards. "Will he come home today?"

She clenched her hands under the table. "No. The doctor wants to keep him for a few days since he hit his head. They want to make sure he's OK."

Evan looked at her and then at Carson. "Can we go

home and eat?" He rubbed his tummy in wide circles. "I'm real hungry."

She smiled and massaged his shoulder blades.

Carson took the cards and gave her a hard stare. "Your mom is exhausted. How about I treat you three to some great burgers and milkshakes? And the boys should see the fireworks."

He had been her friend and had always been there for her until he left for the military. Why had she rejected a more personal relationship? Her brain could only focus on her father.

What had her dad told Carson years ago? She'd been so busy with the farm and her work, when her head hit the old, uncomfortable pillow, she fell into a dreamless sleep. There'd been no time to confront her father about it. He might not even remember the conversation from years ago.

She mustered enough strength to stand. "You don't have to do that." Her token words lacked force.

He stood and came around the table to stand next to her and took her hand. "It's after five. The boys and I are hungry, and you need a break. Let's go."

A heavy stone the size of a dump truck lodged in her throat, and she could only give him a slight nod. It was easier to just let him take over... at least for tonight.

His sweet smile dazzled her. "I'll follow you back to the farm and we'll go in my truck. The boys can't miss the fireworks."

Suddenly, she was so exhausted all she wanted to do was send the boys with Carson so she could go to bed, but she couldn't do it. The boys would never go with him without her.

Evan stepped to Carson and hugged his legs.

By Sunday, Worthy's rumor mill would be alive and kicking and she couldn't summon the strength to worry about it.

Chapter 12

With Nils out of commission since the fourth of July, Carson had offered to give Lily a hand, but she refused, of course.

Fred, Nils's long-time farmhand, had been willing to work extra hours. With a pregnant wife, he could use the extra money.

Was the farm making enough money to cover the cost of the farmhands? Had Carson been paying her enough to supplement the expenses?

If he brought it up, she'd probably tell him to take a hike on a short pier and keep walking when he reached the end.

And she'd be upset about him depositing funds into her account for doing her job for the last week while she handled her father's affairs.

Wasn't that what friends were for? He'd deal with her displeasure when the time came.

A solid rap on the front door brought him down the steps from the bedroom. Through the wavy glass, his friend Ben stood grinning like the fool he was.

When he opened the door, they clapped one another on the back as if they hadn't seen each other for years. But he'd seen Ben less than three months ago, and Carson was glad to see him.

"What are you doing here? Why didn't you call?"

Ben stepped into the living room. "I'm sorry I had to bail on you last month. Work has been a nightmare. I refused to be on call another weekend and told my boss I needed time off."

His friend looked around the room and zeroed in on his uncle's framed detailed pencil drawings of various aircraft.

"No problem. Maybe it was better you hadn't seen the terminal before the work began, but it's coming right along."

"When do you think the place will be operational?" Ben glanced at him, then pointed to the black frames. "These are amazing."

A wistful smile lit his face. "Uncle Patrick started collecting them when I was in grade school. My hope is the terminal will be ready for tenants by the end of August. Lily suggested we use the photos to decorate the terminal and I'm considering it."

Ben made himself at home and dropped onto the sofa and stretched his arm over the back. "Sounds perfect."

Carson sat in his uncle's old recliner and shook his head. "You hadn't said a word when we spoke two weeks ago.

"I hadn't decided then, but I've had enough. I'm making the move to Worthy. Last month put me over the edge." Ben scrubbed his hand over his chin. "Between the stress of the job, my old commander calling me, and your great offer, I had to ask myself why was I hesitating." His grin was infectious, and he pulled his shoulders up. "So here I am."

"That's terrific. When will it be permanent?"

"My contract says I have to stay for another month. I've started the process, but I'll need your help."

He wasn't sure he could help since Lily had been dealing with her dad's health issues and he had been filling in for her. "I'll do my best, but I'm kind of in a bind for a while."

"I won't need your help until I'm ready to make the move at the end of August."

Lily's MECHANIC

"What do you need?"

"I need you to come to Virginia, check out the mechanics of the helicopter, then fly it here. It shouldn't take you more than a day. I think it's in pretty good shape, but I don't want to risk flying it unless it's checked out."

"Why not have your mechanic take care of it?"

Ben ran a hand through his hair and rested his forearms on his knees. "Because they'd done sloppy work, and I almost lost the engine."

"That's not something you want to have happen when you're twelve-hundred feet in the air. At least in a plane, you can glide in for a rough landing."

"Exactly."

"If it's next month and only one day, it shouldn't be a problem. Right now, I'm in a tough spot."

"What's going on?"

"Lily's dad fell, and I've been doing her job and mine."

His friend's brow furrowed, and he moved his head real slow from side to side. "You hired your long-lost love to project manage a renovation that if not completed and be profitable would cause you to lose everything?"

He ignored the reference to him having been in love with Lily. "I couldn't get anyone else and she's qualified, over-qualified, actually."

Ben lifted his chin. "You're doing her job *and* paying her? You've got it bad, man."

He stood and strode from the recliner to the kitchen entryway and back, his body tense. "At first, I hadn't wanted to hire her. I did everything I could to find someone else, but no one was available, so I resigned myself to hire her. I'm glad I did. She works hard and is incredibly detailed."

"Is the relationship headed back to where it was?"

He plopped onto the recliner, causing a puff of dust to fly in the air. Decades of old dirt filled his nostrils. "We agreed to not pursue anything... or rather she told me she wanted it strictly professional, and I was fine with it. The last thing I needed was a female entanglement."

"And now?" Ben's voice was quiet and thoughtful.

He hadn't wanted to say what was in his heart when he wasn't even sure of it himself.

"I don't know. All I know is that I need to help her as much as I can while her dad is laid up. Where are your bags? I have a guest room, but I'll warn you, it's not super comfortable."

His friend looked a little chagrined. "No need. After your description of Amy's B&B, I had to stay there once. I'm looking forward to her pastries."

"Good choice." He glanced around the dated living area, and his face screwed into a frown. "I don't blame you for wanting to stay there. I loved it, but I needed to be here."

Ben followed his gaze with a more critical eye. "We've lived in less than desirable places and this place isn't so bad. A coat of paint and some modern furniture and you'll be in good shape, but you didn't answer my question about Lily."

He cocked his head and smirked. "Maybe I didn't want to answer it."

"Why?"

"Because I just don't know how I feel about it. I vacillate between wanting her and running away as fast as I can."

His friend stood and gestured. "I get it, and I don't blame you after all you've been through."

It was time to leave Tanya behind, put Lily out of his mind, and nail down his first contract. "Thanks. Why don't I show you the terminal and hangar and then I'll take you to the diner for lunch and we can talk? Best full breakfast and

Lily's MECHANIC

lunch in town."

Ben slapped him on the back. "Sounds good. And the stuff with Lily? It'll all work out the way it's supposed to."

He wasn't sure it ever would, but he'd never voice it.

Lily's sons bounced in the back seat and leaned their heads out the window, pointing to all the horses and barns. Mia's ranch was everything Lily dreamed it would be and then some.

When the car came to a stop in front of the stately farmhouse, the boys jumped out of the car with their stuffed backpacks and dropped them on the porch.

Drew hopped down the stairs. "Let's go in the barn. We'll get Gingerbell saddled and take him for a ride around the paddock." He turned to look at Mia. "That's OK, isn't it?"

Her best friend nodded as she lifted the sleeping baby into her arms. "If it's OK with their mother, I'm fine with it. I need to put this little guy to bed."

The boys raced to the barn, and she cast a glance at her friend. "They'll be OK on their own, won't they?"

"Sean's in the barn, he'll keep an eye on them."

She gazed at the gorgeous wraparound porch and a twinge of guilt assailed her. She couldn't begrudge her best friend her happiness. "Your home is beautiful, Mia."

Her friend chuckled. "It's not mine, it's my brother-in-law Shannon's home. That's my house." She turned and pointed to an incredible contemporary log cabin in the distance. "Sean had started to build it for himself and Drew before we got together."

"Why are you here?"

"Sean and I are staying here while Shannon, Wendy, and

124

little Wyatt, take a much-needed vacation."

Lily followed her into the house and stopped in the middle of the living room. She stared wide-eyed at the cozy living space. The neutral colors and comfortable furniture were expensive, but casual. "This is gorgeous."

"It is. Give me a few minutes and we'll grab a cup of coffee."

In five minutes, Mia was back and led her to the homiest farm kitchen Lily had ever been in. "I so appreciate you taking the boys for the weekend. I'm completely overwhelmed."

"It's not a problem. Drew has been hyper all morning waiting for the boys. It'll be good for all three of them." Mia popped a pod into the coffee machine.

Lily turned to her with worried eyes. "You sure you don't mind?"

"No. Now what's going on?"

"Dad is being difficult. He won't go to rehab, and he won't tell me what other health issues he has, and I know he has them."

Mia strode to her and gave her the best hug. The warmth and comfort of the tight embrace drifted throughout her entire body. "What else can I do to help?"

"Not having the boys underfoot is a huge relief while I get dad situated at home and take care of farm business. He needs someone to help with his arm, and I need to figure it out."

Mia cocked her head and cast her a questioning gaze. "You mean like a physical therapist?"

At her nod, her friend pulled a phone out of her back pocket. "I know just the person. She's terrific. I'll send you her contact information. Sean got slammed by a horse and had trouble with his back. Pam just finished working with him. Make sure you drop my name."

"Is Sean OK?"

125

She blew a raspberry and rolled her eyes. "He's fine. Whined for days his back hurt but would not call Pam. Men can be so stubborn." Mia shrugged and brought the cups to the table. "So, I forced the issue. She helped me when I broke my wrists. We're good friends."

The instant the coffee's hazelnut aroma hit her nostrils, Lily revived, and the taste rippled across her tongue.

"I have to be back at work on Monday, and I need to check on the insurance for his PT."

Her friend waved her arm. "Pam will guide you through all of that. What else is going on?"

She took another sip of the delicious brew. "We're headed into a crucial stage of the renovation, and I need to be there. Carson has been terrific and very understanding, but he has inspections scheduled in Columbus and has to find tenants for the terminal."

"How's your relationship with him?"

"It's fine."

"I meant your personal relationship."

"There isn't one. I only want our interaction to be professional." *Lord, forgive me for lying to my best friend.*

"Uh-huh. Tell it to the judge." Mia's mouth pulled to one side.

"What?"

Her head tilted, and Mia gave her the I-know-what-you're-doing look. "You think the entire town hadn't seen you and Carson and the boys at the Fourth of July fireworks? I even saw you at Dale's Burgers acting like the perfect family."

She straightened and her back got stiff. "Where were you? I didn't see you."

After Mia had taken a sip of her coffee, she lifted her gaze and gave her one of those secret smiles she always

pulled out when her mind worked overtime. "Of course you didn't. I hadn't wanted you to see me when I ran in to use the restroom. I left the boys in the car."

Her best friend's laughter was infectious and there was no way Lily could be angry with her.

"OK." She gave her a tiny grin, but her face sobered, and she looked away. "It was the day my father fell. I was so tired by the time the evening rolled around that I just went along with it." The rim of the cup held her attention. "I've never had a better time and their antics kept me from worrying. And the boys… They seem to get along great with Carson, but I don't know if my heart could take another rejection. I don't want to disappoint my sons. Carson and I both have so much baggage, the entire situation scares me."

"The solution is simple. May not be easy, but it's simple."

She quirked a brow and took her cup to the sink. "What's that?"

"Work on the baggage together. You two were always an amazing couple and I think you could be again."

She hadn't wanted to think about the future much less a future with Carson. It was all she could do to keep her head above water with the bills and now her dad's injuries.

"I need to get going. I promised I'd be there by two for Dad's release. I'll pick the boys up after church on Sunday."

Her best friend threw her arm across her shoulders and gave her a side hug. "Don't worry about the boys. They'll have a great time. We're grilling dogs and burgers tonight and they'll love the horses."

"You're the best, Mia."

"Go on. Take care of your dad."

If only she knew what was wrong with her father and what to make of her relationship with Carson.

Chapter 13

A car door slammed and brought Carson out of the open hangar.

He'd waited for a load of supplies to arrive, but Rob jumped out of his truck and strode to him. "We have a problem."

Everything had come together, and he had been praying he'd complete the details of the open house he'd planned.

He straightened, shoved his hands in his pockets, and trudged to the contractor. "Is there a supply issue?"

"No. That's still scheduled for today. The inspector should be here this morning to inspect the terminal's electrical and plumbing."

"So, what's the problem?"

With a grim face, Rob pointed to the five-hundred-gallon fuel tank that sat next to the hangar. "We need it inspected, and I think it'll need to be buried, which will push our timeline."

His hand flew out of his pocket, and he ran it through his hair. "How do I find out? I figured I'd have to buy at least two more tanks if I plan to offer fuel to my tenants."

The contractor pulled his cap off and put it back on, then looked around the area. "And that's why I wanted a project manager for this renovation. I think Lily dropped the ball on this one."

He cast his gaze away to avoid Rob's frustration. "She's been out for a few days to care for her father after he suffered a nasty fall. I don't think she missed it." He heaved a huge breath. "But I can't afford a pushback on the timeline."

The last thing he'd admit to his contractor was that he'd done Lily's job for almost a week. It was more his fault than hers, wasn't it? He should have told her weeks ago he intended to buy two more tanks, and he was certain it would have triggered a question about the EPA and inspections.

"I don't know what to tell you, man." Rob leaned against the front bumper of his truck and waited.

Cow dung odor filled the morning air. He'd gotten used to it, but the smell that morning was particularly unpleasant.

"How much of a delay are we talking here? Will it affect the open house at the end of the month? And will I be able to use the current tank?"

"I can't answer any of those questions. No new storage tanks were on the plans. As far as the open house... It depends on the new tanks' proposed location—and the EPA."

He rubbed his forehead with his fingertips. "Right. I don't think my uncle considered the project's scope. Buying new tanks now makes more sense to avoid a disruption in business later. The current tank isn't rusted, but it may not pass inspection either."

"It looks good to me, too, but what do I know about fuel storage tanks?" He lifted one shoulder and moved away from the truck. "Lily needs to order the tanks and schedule an inspector as soon as possible. And you need to determine where you want them to go. The EPA is a stickler."

"Can you hang around for a few minutes while I call her?"

"Sure."

He put Lily on speaker, and from the raucous noise, the

Lily's MECHANIC

boys were in rare form. He stole a glance at Rob and the man all but scowled.

After she got to a quiet place, they discussed what had to happen, and she fell all over herself to apologize to him and to his contractor

When he hung up, Rob cocked his head. "You're just going to let the oversight go, even though it may mean the timeline is compromised?"

He widened his arms. "What can I do now? We're too far into the process to look for another project manager, even if there was one available." He'd never do that to Lily or her sons anyway. "And what benefit would it be to lose my temper?"

Rob's chin lifted and he scrunched his lips to one side. "You're right, of course. It would make you—and me—feel better if you blew a gasket, but it wouldn't help matters much. It might even make it worse."

"That's for sure," he muttered when the roar of a rumbling engine broke the silence. He stared at the lumbering truck crawling up the lane.

The long-haired driver jumped to the ground and thumbed to the back of the flat bed. "Where you want the drywall?"

"I'll show you." Rob stepped to the terminal as the other guy grabbed the cart to take a load into the building.

He kept pace with the contractor. "Anything I can do to help?"

"Watch for the other truck and the inspector."

A distracted look came over Rob's face, and it told him the man's concentration had shifted to construction related issues.

Outside the terminal, a few well-placed pieces of wood kept the door open for the guys as they made multiple trips back and forth from the truck.

130

When they were done and leaving, another nondescript utilitarian vehicle drove up the lane.

The contractor strode to the vehicle as the man got out. A pleasant smile lit Rob's face, and he shook the man's hand. They strolled toward him, and his contractor introduced the man as the building inspector.

Rob motioned to the terminal. "We'll head in. Can you wait for the other scheduled truck and let me know when they're here so I can direct them to where I want the supplies? They tend to drop the load right inside the door and that's not where I want it."

Antsy, he would have liked to follow behind the two men, but Rob's directive prevented any eavesdropping on the building inspection process. "Sure thing."

"Lord," he prayed to himself. "Let Lily solve the fuel tank issue without compromising the timeline."

Another burst of dust was preceded by the rumble of a different engine, but it wasn't the supply truck.

As the car drew nearer, he groaned. "Bottleson."

The portly man parked the car off to the side, drew himself out of the vehicle, and ambled toward him. "Carson." He extended his hand for a brief shake. "I wanted to stop by and see what progress you've made in the renovation."

He stretched his neck and rolled his shoulders. "Actually, I'm waiting on a delivery and the contractor is in the terminal with the county inspector."

"Good. Sounds like you're moving right along. Do you have any tenants yet? That will show the airport's profitability more quickly."

"The first tenant will park his helicopter here at the end of the month and he'll take a terminal office as soon as it's completed."

He wasn't about to tell Bottleson about the fuel tank issue or that Ben, his potential first tenant, was an old friend or that he'd given him a discount on rent.

The attorney stood next to his car and mopped his brow with a towel he grabbed off the seat. "That's wonderful. I think you're doing an outstanding job and your uncle would be pleased." Then he made a full circle, taking in all the buildings and zeroed in on the farmhouse and frowned. "Will you renovate the farmhouse? It looks rather run down compared to the terminal and the hangar."

"My first priority is the terminal, then the hangar. I'll tackle the farmhouse last."

"At a minimum, to make a good impression on prospective tenants, slap a coat of paint on the old place and repair the porch."

He ground his teeth. His uncle's requirements never mentioned the farmhouse, and he couldn't think of that right now with the fuel tank issue looming over him.

"I need to get this place operational before I work on the farmhouse."

The older man shrugged and stared at Carson's grungy old overalls. "I dropped by to give you some leads on potential tenants. I was at a Columbus chamber meeting the other night... and collected business cards. When I mentioned your airport, there seemed to be quite a bit of interest, and I wanted to give them to you. A few seemed to remember your uncle and the airport."

His brows had to have risen to his hairline. He'd never expected the attorney to help him. "Thank you. That was quite generous."

Bottleson placed his finger under his collar and his face flushed. "I think your uncle would have wanted me to help

you as much as I could, and it was a simple thing I could do. Consider joining the local and the Columbus chambers. You never know where business could come from."

The attorney pulled a stack of rubber-banded business cards out of his suit pocket and handed them to him.

"Great idea. I've planned an open house as soon as the terminal is completed. Hopefully, by then, we'll have the hangar completed as well."

A smile lit the man's face. "Wonderful. An invitation to every contact in that stack would help you expand your sphere of influence."

Carson was desperate to ask if he'd make the deadline, but fear choked him. "Right. There's still a lot of work to be done. Now that I live on site, I can work later and start earlier."

Bottleson swung his head around to the farmhouse and chuckled. "I guess you're more like your uncle than you know. He always worried more about the state of the hangar and terminal than he did for his home."

The man was pretentious as all get out, but his uncle liked him, so he'd tolerate the backhanded compliment... or was it a put down?

"I plan to renovate the farmhouse as soon as the rest of the place has demonstrated its profitability and I'm assured of my inheritance. As it is, if I fail, I lose a lot more than the property. I'll lose my savings."

Bottleson's face fell, and his shoulders slumped. He clasped Carson's forearm. "I'm so sorry your uncle forced those mandatory requirements for you to inherit. I wish there had been some way to keep you from having to spend your own money to do it, but before I could talk to Patrick about that aspect of the estate, he was dead."

A small smile covered his face and tilted his head. "I have

faith, and I don't plan to fail."

"Good. God is with you, and I'm rooting for you."

At the sound of low voices, he gave the attorney a brief nod and turned to see Rob and the inspector step out of the building. His contractor chuckled at something the inspector said. He guessed it meant the terminal passed.

Rob jogged back to them once the inspector left and shook the attorney's hand. "The terminal passed the preliminary building inspection. I'll have my crew here in the next hour to start dry walling. That is, if the rest of the supplies ever get here."

They all heard the distinct sound of a clutch being engaged before they saw the huge truck.

Carson chuckled and shook his head. "Like clockwork, the supplies are here. I want to show the attorney the progress we've made."

As he and Bottleson walked into the terminal, Rob directed the truck near the entrance and told the workers where to put the supplies.

"I'm stunned at how much has been done in such a short time period. I'm thrilled you were able to get Rob to do the work after the architect bailed on you. He's brilliant at what he does."

"Me too. The project manager has helped to make sure everything happens when it should."

The attorney put his hand out when they were back in the parking lot. "I don't want to sound condescending, but I'm proud of you, Carson. I think you'll be quite successful."

Bottleson's attitude eased his mind, but the anxiety caused by the fuel tanks and the EPA inspection troubled him.

134

SERALYNN LEWIS

"I can't believe I missed that aspect of the project," Lily mumbled as she slammed drawers in the farm office. "I know better than that. I've had to deal with these types of issues before." Frustration edged her voice.

A text buzzed from Carson with the size of the two tanks he wanted.

While she placed the order for the tanks, she plowed through websites researching EPA standards. After she verified the tanks' delivery date, she placed a call and had an inspection appointment to have the fuel tanks inspected next Wednesday when a sharp rap came to the front door.

"Someone's at the door, Lily. It's probably that *person* you hired," her father called out from the living room, his voice filled with disdain.

She rolled her eyes and charged through to the front door, opening it to a lady with laughing brown eyes. "I'm Pam, the physical therapist."

"Come on in. He's… been waiting."

The woman chuckled and winked. "I heard him yell for you, and from his tone, I can tell he's going to be a pistol."

Lily's face got hot, and she was sure she had turned red. "I'm sorry you heard that."

Pam's smile was one of encouragement. "No one wants me to work with them, but I don't care. It's my job to make sure they get back their prior mobility." She grinned bigger. "Besides, Betty and Bertha won't allow anyone to keep them down."

She was certain a look of confusion passed over her face as she trained her gaze past Pam for the other two people, worrying how much it would cost for three therapists.

Pam let out a heartfelt giggle. "Let me introduce you to Betty & Bertha…"

135

With that, the physical therapist turned around and shook her booty.

No. She hadn't actually named her...

Pam looked over her shoulder, arched her brow, and grinned. "You guessed it. They are my frenemies."

Lily bent, grabbed her thighs, and burst into laughter. "Sorry. That was just about the funniest thing I've ever heard, and it made my day."

"I'm glad. Now—"

"You going to stand in the hallway and chit-chat?" Her dad's voice cut through the laughter. "Or are you going to put me out of my misery?"

When the introductions were made, Lily excused herself to go to the kitchen to check on dinner. She could hear Pam cajoling her father to do one more rep and making him laugh. The spicy tomato sauce bubbled in the pan as she tasted it for salt. What a wonderful woman. Her father had had little to laugh about in the past week. Probably ever since Patrick died.

He groused and complained, but he forced himself to do the exercises.

When she was done in the kitchen, she plopped herself in the chair and watched the exercises and their exchanges. "Dad, the farm needs you to get better quick."

Her father narrowed his gaze at Pam while he groaned in pain. "Who have you tortured recently?"

The therapist stopped, tilted her head, and gave him a serene smile. "Sean McDermott. His back went out when a horse slammed him. You're ornery, but not nearly as much as he was, and he's doing great. You will too."

He wheezed as he did one more rep. "Lily is best friends with Mia."

Pam's eyes got wide. "I didn't know that. Mia and I have

been good friends ever since I helped her with her wrists several years ago." Pam sighed and grunted her way through the PT exercises with her dad. "I met Brett through her and Sean."

She leaned in, interest in the therapist's story. "Brett is your boyfriend?"

Pam's face twisted, and she looked away. "Was. We parted ways a while ago. He moved to the west coast, and I stayed here."

She frowned. "I'm sorry."

The physical therapist stood and put her torture devices back into a sack. "Don't be. That's it for today."

Sensing the woman hadn't wanted to speak about her relationship, she couldn't figure out why she'd mentioned it in the first place. Perhaps it was because she'd talked about Mia and Sean. It appeared memories of her former boyfriend were painful, and ones it seemed she'd rather forget.

"Thank goodness." Her father's face was weary and registered pain.

Pam leaned over and got her father's attention. "The first session is always the hardest. Sleep for a few hours and do the exercises tomorrow, and I'll see you again in two days." Pam straightened, grabbed her bag, and headed to the front door.

Lily followed her, handed her a check, and saw her out to her car. "I have a question. Have you noticed anything about Dad's overall health?"

Pam opened her purse and dropped it in. Her solemn face gave nothing away and gone was the playful woman of earlier. "I'm not a doctor, so I can't speak to your dad's mental or physical health other than what pertains to the work I do. It'd be best if you consult with his physician."

Not even the smell of freshly cut grass took her mind off her father's illness.

That was it. Pam knew something and she wouldn't say... or probably couldn't.

"Thanks. Dad and I will see you in a few days."

The woman drove off and Lily went inside. Her father was fast asleep on the recliner, and he looked at peace.

She'd have to tackle him on his health... and soon.

Chapter 14

"I can't do anything until those blasted fuel tanks are inspected, and the drywall cured." No one answered him, of course, and Carson's arms stretched out and his voice echoed in the empty hangar as he strode from the plane to the work bench. He left the hangar and passed the dumpster as he jogged to the house. It would be taken away next week, and he'd decided to clear out his uncle's junk from all the closets and the second-floor bedrooms before it was picked up.

He worked steadily through the day, and the last room to be done before he called it quits was his uncle's room. A sense of loss washed over him. All this time, he'd hesitated because it pained him to throw away things dear to his uncle. His room was private. It always had been. But Carson couldn't live in a house full of stuff that didn't work or was outdated.

After all the drawers in the bedroom were emptied, he packed away the good clothing, which wasn't much, to give to the homeless shelter in town. The rest he tossed.

He opened the closet door and took hanging clothes to add to the others when he noticed something covered with several towels in the back corner of the closet.

When he pulled the hangers aside and lifted the bath

blankets, a gasp left his mouth and the sight astounded him as he took in what had been hidden.

A metal detector.

Why had his uncle bought it? And why was it covered and hidden away in his bedroom closet? It hadn't made a bit of sense.

Could there have been a treasure? And if so, where was it?

If it existed, he could really use the influx of cash so he wouldn't completely deplete his savings.

He figured Nils might know about the device and it would give him an excuse to get an update on the fuel tanks from Lily.

On the way to the Sandburg farm, he considered the enormity of his uncle's mysterious *treasure*.

What if his uncle bought the Sandburg land knowing there was treasure there? That would mean his uncle had exploited his best bud. Uncle Patrick would never do anything to jeopardize his relationship with Nils, would he? Carson couldn't believe it of his uncle.

He hadn't been by the farm in weeks. Vehicles dotted the parking area of the small farm store that was off to the side of the barn. People came out with baskets of fruit and gallons of milk.

Lily had told him she'd had her father's farmhands make butter and bottle milk. She'd even taught the boys to make ice cream with the old ice cream maker. They loved sampling the different recipes she had.

She had taken her hard-earned income and funneled it into the farm store. The farmhouse still hadn't been painted, but at least the porch was clean and there were flowers planted next to the walkway.

Before he could raise a hand to knock, the boys raced

up the steps and shoved past him through the screen door. "Mom," Lucas yelled. "Carson is here."

She came to the door, flustered, and dressed in a paint-splattered pair of shorts and t-shirt. "Is there an issue at the airport?"

"No." He took in her appearance from head to toe. "You're painting?"

A tired smile and weary eyes met his. "Brilliant deduction."

He swallowed. Even in her exhaustion, she was, hands down, the most gorgeous woman he'd ever seen. Her loving heart made her even more beautiful. "I wanted to ask you about the fuel tank inspection and to check on Nils. Is he around?"

She tilted her head back to look him in the eye. "It's federal law that all fuel tanks must be buried and we're at a standstill. New tanks were delivered yesterday, and the holes have been dug, but until the EPA inspector shows up on Wednesday, we won't know whether the original tank or the placement of the new ones will work. I'm praying it all goes according to plan." She crossed her arms and frowned. "Why do you want to see Dad?"

"I've been praying non-stop about the tank inspection. We can only wait on God. I want to talk to Nils about my uncle."

"Dad is doing better, but not as well as I'd have expected—"

"Is that Carson?" Her father's voice boomed from the living room. "Come on in, son. I haven't seen you since you came to the hospital to visit."

He gave her a quick grin as he passed her. "Sounds like his lungs are in good shape."

She blew a raspberry and followed him through the door. "I'll leave you two to chat while I finish painting. I'll be back in a bit."

141

Lily hadn't wanted him to visit, but that was too bad. He needed answers and prayed Nils could supply them.

As he dropped to the sofa next to the old man's chair, the boys flew back out the door toward the farm store.

He reached over and shook the man's veiny hand. "How you doing, Nils?"

"Fair to middling. What's on your mind?"

Right to the point. Today his uncle's friend seemed lucid. Perhaps he'd get to the bottom of the treasure thing.

Best to get it out there since he blew it off when he was told about it. "I found Uncle Patrick's metal detector. You know anything about that?"

Nils chuckled and slapped his thigh. "Patrick was fixated with that thing. I think he covered every inch of his property. He was determined to find the treasure."

"Why hadn't you told me he'd been using a metal detector to search for it?"

The old man's face and body drooped and made him look much older than his years. "I forgot." He moved his hands to his lap and rubbed his fingers.

"Do you think he found it?" Carson whispered, his body tense at what it could mean.

Nils cocked his head, stopped rubbing his fingers, and gave him a sly smirk. "He put in a security system, didn't he? Why'd he do that if he hadn't found it?"

He sat back on the sofa and stared at the freshly painted cream-colored walls. The new paint smell still permeated the room.

"I don't know." Carson forced the words out of his mouth.

The old man gripped his arm. "Patrick didn't do anything without a reason. He wouldn't have put the security system in if he hadn't found the treasure. Never had a need for it

before, you know? Question is, where is the treasure now?"

Good question. For which he had no answer.

They became silent, each lost in their own thoughts, until Lily floated down the stairs. She had changed and looked beautiful in a pink sundress. Still barefoot, she offered him a drink.

As much as he wanted to spend the afternoon sitting and chatting with Lily and her dad, he had to figure out where the treasure was.

"What's taking you two so long?" Her father's voice broke his stare, and it registered disgust.

"Excuse me?" he said and turned a confused look at the older man.

Nils lifted his chin and gestured to Lily. "I see the way you look at her and the way she looks at you. Why don't you two go out and see if what you had back in the day, you still have? I'm sure Bobby can watch the boys so you can have an evening out."

Lily turned redder than the fire engine at the Memorial Day parade. "Dad." His name sounded strangled on her lips as she drew out her father's name.

"What? It's time you found a good man, Lily, and there's none better than Carson. Besides…"

He got up because Nils words moved something in his chest. Something that hadn't been there in many years and his brain warred between wanting to grab her and kiss her hard and—escape.

With her father's blessing, and the terminal renovation almost completed, they could see if their relationship had a chance. They had always gotten along, and now they worked well together, but did he want to pick up where he left off all those years ago? The darn treasure floated around in the back of his mind and disturbed him.

143

She strode to her father and placed her hands on her hips. "Enough, Dad." She had that no-nonsense look on her face, telling him she wouldn't back down.

"Fine." Her dad huffed and crossed his arms.

Lily gripped his forearm and dragged him to the door. "Let me walk you to your car."

He looked over his shoulder at her dad and winked. Nils put a hand to his mouth to stifle a chuckle.

At his truck, she stopped and swallowed. "I'm so sorry. I don't know what's gotten into him."

A small smile covered his face. "Newsflash. I think we're at a point in the renovation where it's almost smooth sailing ahead. It's time for us to explore what we have."

"But…"

He shook his head. "No buts. It's time. We're going to dinner on Friday night to celebrate the tanks passing the EPA inspection."

Her shoulders drooped, and she stared at the soft dirt beneath their feet. "You don't know if the setup and tanks will pass inspection, and I don't know that going out is a good idea."

His finger lifted her chin, and her blue eyes were enormous. "I have faith God will answer my prayers. And you know your father is right."

"I don't want you to hurt me again, Carson." Defeat colored her words.

He frowned, and with a gentle caress, stroked her cheek with his forefinger. "You could hurt me too. I remembered what we had, and I missed it. With both of us free and in one place, it makes sense to see where it could go." He couldn't let a pause give her the ability to refuse. "I'll pick you up at six."

At her slow, reluctant nod, he got in his truck. His ex-

citement for a date with Lily was overshadowed by the mysterious treasure and he needed to figure it out, if only to disprove the myth.

Lily dragged her feet into the house. Years ago, her father had put her in a place where her heart had been crushed, and now he hurled her toward another potentially painful situation.

When she stepped into the room, her father had a framed photo of her mother in his hand, and he traced her profile and hair. A sense of calm came over his face and he sighed and placed the photo with a loving caress on the side table.

Since he stayed in the house and had not even ventured to the barn, Lily placed the picture where her dad could gaze at it. She planned to make her father sit on the porch after lunch, but that last stunt meant it got pushed to right now.

"Dad."

He looked up and swiped a hand across his cheek, and cleared his throat. "What?"

Was he crying?

Any mention of tears would embarrass him, so she ignored the telltale weakness and sat next to him.

"Let's sit on the porch and talk."

With no expression on his face, he sighed and got to his feet. "Will you make some lemonade?"

When he ambled to the porch, she went to the kitchen and pondered the approach she'd take with her father.

She set the tray with two tall glasses of lemonade on the table next to her dad's rocker and dropped into the white wicker chair. "Why did you tell Carson to stay away from me when he left for the military?"

Her father had the grace to look ashamed, with a hint of red on his cheeks. "I wondered when Carson would tell you about that. You both were just kids. I wanted you to have the same kind of marriage your mom and I had. That wasn't going to happen with a husband out at sea all the time."

"Why are you pushing me to date Carson now?"

He took a sip of the tangy drink and stared with unseeing eyes at the barn. "I admit I made a mistake back then. And now that he's back for good, I want to make sure you're taken care of and settled." His voice softened. "I'm not going to be around forever."

It was the first time he'd spoken about death, and the shock of it made her heart almost stop.

"Are you sick, Dad? You wouldn't give me permission to speak to the doctor about your health. Why?"

"I didn't want you to worry with the farm's finances the way they are."

She gave him a sad smile and patted his hand. "Since I've been working for Carson, and the farm store opened, the financial situation has eased. Now tell me what's going on."

He stared intently at Fred loading crates of fruit in the truck. "The doctor has been after me to tell you, and it's time."

She stiffened and stilled. "Time?" she whispered in a choked voice.

"I have Huntington's Disease. I'm on medication, but I get confused. The doctor insisted I tell you because it's hereditary and you have a right to know." The words came out slow and measured as if he'd recited them in his mind over and over again, preparing for the moment he had to say them.

"Is it fatal?"

"Eventually. It's progressive and I'll die at some point. But I'm on medication and it helped a lot in the beginning,

146

but the confusion is getting worse." His lips quirked in a semblance of a smile. "Patrick figured out something was wrong and forced me to go to the doctor. He wouldn't take no for an answer, stubborn man that he was. Came by every day while I waited for test results."

"That's why you didn't want me in your room. You were afraid I'd see the medication." She lowered her chin.

His face beamed with pride. "You always were inquisitive and smart. I knew you'd figure it out." His hand shot out, and he grabbed her arm with a tight squeeze. "You need to get tested. The boys too."

The idea of getting tested for a disease she'd never heard of made her break out in a cold sweat. "I need to call the doctor."

"Go ahead." His face contorted with what looked like regret. He focused his gaze on the garden she'd planted. "He's been waiting for your call for weeks now."

"You'll be OK here?"

"Yes."

She shut herself in the farmhouse's small office and stabbed the doctor's number on her phone.

While she waited, she logged on to her computer, but her finger hovered on the enter key, the disease already keyed into the search box. *It's probably not a good idea anyway.*

Doctor Kirk's voice startled her, and she dropped her hand to the desk.

"Your father told you about his illness?" Without preamble, his voice was a matter of fact.

"He told me he would die eventually. I never heard of Huntington's Disease. Educate me."

"Your father was diagnosed about six years ago. It has progressed. There's a myriad of things that could take his life,

Lily's MECHANIC

which is why I kept him at the hospital for all those days after he fell. It was an opportunity for me to get much needed follow up MRIs and other tests related to his disease. It was important to him that he be the one to discuss it with you."

Her shoulders had stiffened with extreme nerves to the point they ached. "He told me. But what does that mean exactly? Do I have it, too?"

"Not necessarily. You have a fifty-fifty chance of not having the gene that causes the disease. We don't think your mother had it, which lowers your risk. But you'll need a test, and it's an expensive test. Since it's a rare condition, the co-pay could be high, or they may not pay for it at all. It depends on your insurance."

The last thing she wanted to do was to tell her father's doctor she didn't have the money for an extremely expensive test. It was all she could do to keep her current insurance and her father's physical therapy co-pays paid.

"Dad told me the boys need to be tested too."

She gazed around the freshly painted office. Between the faint fumes and the devastating news, her belly cramped.

"If you test negative, the likelihood of your sons having the gene diminishes. We can't test them until they're much older anyway. I know your husband is deceased, so testing him is out."

"That's right."

"Get tested. If we catch it early—earlier than we caught your dad's—there are drugs to prolong the onset of the effects of the disease."

"I understand, and I'll make the appointment as soon as I can."

"It's a simple blood test, Lily, but we won't get the results for four to six weeks."

"That's a long time."

"Yes, it is, but it could be the shorter end of that time frame. Don't wait too long. I promised your father as soon as he told you, I'd push to get you tested."

"I understand. I'm just not in a position to do it right now."

Certain her words made Doctor Kirk understand she didn't have that kind of money right now, she pulled her lips in and waited.

"Very well. Call me as soon as you're ready."

Shell shocked, she dropped the phone on the desk.

One blow after another all day. First with her father pushing her to date Carson, then Carson agreeing with her dad and forcing her to commit to a date, and now this. She placed her elbows on the desk and covered her head with her hands.

How can I date Carson with a potential disease hanging over my head?

Chapter 15

The August sun beamed stifling heat as Carson moved to the holes where fuel tanks waited to be inspected.

Panic had seized his chest when the EPA inspector, a quiet unnerving man, arrived. His white pickup truck with the EPA logo blazoned on it made his stomach clench. *Lord, please direct the situation the way it's supposed to go.*

Lily showed up late. Distracted, she lost track of the conversation several times. Rob jumped in and asked basic engineering questions and clarified his role. He'd been none too happy to have to do Lily's job for her, and Carson couldn't blame him.

But both he and Rob walked away from the inspector while he performed the inspection with Lily at his side. The man took notes on a clipboard.

The contractor grasped his forearm when they reached the other side of the tanks. "What's with Lily? She was out of it." His voice was low and measured.

With the equipment blaring in the background, no one had heard their conversation. He'd been more concerned about the inspection. The man's demeanor had not given him confidence.

He drew his gaze to the inspector and wouldn't look at

his contractor. "I don't know, but now is not the time, Rob."

After what seemed like hours, the EPA guy looked up, a barely there smile covered his lips. He gave them a thumbs up on the tanks and their location. He motioned they could cover the holes. When he first arrived, he had told them he would stay to oversee the entire process and do a final check once the holes were covered since they were under a time crunch. His OK was crucial to the timeline.

Lily stood next to the inspector on the other side of the holes and received the documents for the airport's file. She hadn't spoken to him or Rob, but she seemed to have charmed the EPA guy. Once she had the papers in hand, she thanked the inspector, waved to him and Rob, and left.

She was not herself. Something was wrong. Had she questioned their date on Friday? He pulled out his phone, ready to text her while Rob went into the terminal to get the three of them water.

"Excuse me." The excavator boomed from the other side of the gigantic hole where the tanks were placed.

He jerked his head toward the tanks' installation crew. "Yes?"

"The crew wants to show you how the fuel tanks work alone and in tandem." The man walked back to the backhoe and hoisted himself into the cab.

Carson had spaced out over Lily, and he had to remain focused. His goal was just within reach.

After the men showed him how to connect the three tanks using the valves, Carson stepped back when the inspector nodded his approval once dirt covered the tanks. The man took the cold bottle and left.

Rob guzzled the water and turned to him while the excavator expertly maneuvered the big piece of equipment onto the waiting flatbed. "With the tank issue, the timeline

Lily's MECHANIC

has been pushed back a week."

A sigh of relief rushed through his body. "And it won't interfere with the planned open house."

"Nope," Rob said. "I'm headed out and I'll be in touch."

His phone vibrated in his pocket, and he pulled it out while he jogged to the hangar's interior for some quiet. He'd expected Ben's call.

Calls to all the leads Bottleson had given him yielded a dozen prospects. Half were interested in becoming tenants and half had small planes they wanted to park at the airport.

Almost every one of the business card contacts wanted an invitation to the open house.

"I'm ready to make the move to Worthy. Can you fly out sometime in the next two weeks to service and fly the helicopter back to Worthy?"

"The situation has gotten a little sticky, but let me check the schedule and I'll get back to you."

"What's the problem?" The concern in Ben's voice had nothing to do with whether he could do the job, but more for Carson.

"We had a situation with the fuel tanks, which has been resolved, but the project manager has been... a bit rattled recently, and I'm concerned." He rubbed the back of his neck.

"Rightfully so. You have your life's savings tied up in that airport. Is the situation with Lily personal, or does it have to do with your professional relationship?"

"I don't know. I'm trying to figure it out."

"Ask her. Bite the bullet and get your work and personal stuff squared away."

"I know. I've got to go. I'll call you later with the schedule."

Worry furrowed his brow and made his belly knot. He hadn't wanted to go back outside. Had he made the right

152

decision and invested in the airport's renovation? Or should he have walked away from his childhood home?

No. He'd decided, and he'd see it through.

Carson had one brief text from Lily the day before, then radio silence. He hesitated to call or text her because he was worried she'd bail on the date that night.

Rob strode over and drew a hand through his disheveled hair. "Yesterday was a nightmare. I'm glad it all worked out."

"Yeah, me, too." He stuffed the phone in his back pocket after he checked texts, confused by Lily and what issues she had.

"We're almost ready for the security system to go live in the terminal. I contacted Eric Winters and he'll be out this afternoon. Where's Lily?"

"She had doctor's appointments."

Rob crossed his arms and tilted his head. "You don't really know what's going on with her, do you?"

He jerked his head. "No. Do you?"

A crease appeared between his contractor's brows. "Yesterday was not cool, Carson. I like Lily and I think she's a straight shooter. But something has put her in a tailspin. We passed the crucial juncture, but there is still a lot more to accomplish to keep the timeline. Frankly, I'm worried."

Carson rubbed a hand over his smooth face. "We're at the tail end of the terminal renovation. The office and airport furniture are scheduled to arrive next week, and the interior designer will bring in a crew to set everything up."

Rob took steps to the back of the hangar, looked around, and paced back to him. "Right, but we still need the terminal's occupancy inspection, and we haven't even started on

the hangar. My other crew finished the project they were on and both crews are ready to start in here. With a double crew, we just might keep the original timeline, but we need to discuss next steps."

His shoulders dropped in relief. "Great."

Thinking of Lily and her problems made him shaky, so he stuffed his hands in his pockets as they stepped into the hangar office and went over what would happen in the next two weeks.

"I suggest you order a couple of temporary storage units to store everything from the hangar. If you order them today, they can be here tomorrow. It's Lily's job, but I guess you're it now." He glanced at the storage bins and parts. "Can you have the hangar cleared out by Monday?"

He stared at the plans on the desk and his body sagged at how much work it would be to pack the hangar by Monday. He'd call in reinforcements. "It'll be a stretch. Moving the planes is not a problem. They'll have to sit in the field next to the house because the paving company will be here on Monday to begin the plane parking areas and work on the runway."

Rob waved his hand around the office and to the hangar behind them. "What about everything else?"

He straightened and lifted his head. "I'll figure it out."

With a succinct nod, his contractor got up. "With the incredible time crunch, call a landscaper for the terminal and around the fuel tanks to disguise them. Especially since you have an open house scheduled."

It had vaguely crossed his mind, but he felt scattered between Lily, the renovation and finding the blasted treasure. He was not good at multi-tasking. Give him an engine to work on and he'd be methodical and efficient. The project was way out of his wheelhouse. "Any suggestions?"

"I'll send you a few contacts, and they can give you a design and quote." Pulling out his phone, Rob pursed his lips. "This should have been in the works weeks ago."

How many phone calls and orchestration Lily had actually done since the renovation began boggled his mind, and he was hard-pressed to keep everything straight. Rob had been a lifeline even now with Lily's issues.

He couldn't go on like this with the open house looming and all the details for that. He had to talk to her about her continued role as project manager.

"Lily and I talked about landscaping at the beginning of the project. I know she had it on her project list, but I'm not sure where in the process it should have been done. It completely slipped my mind. We didn't have the dates of the open house nailed down at the time, but I'll talk to her about the schedule."

Running the airport himself would kill his concentration on repairs to the planes, and he couldn't risk doing sub-par work. He had to hire someone, even if it was just part-time.

The date tonight with Lily made him uneasy, and he still hadn't figured out whether there was a treasure. He'd have to tackle her situation, but also theirs.

They stepped out of the hangar where not even a breeze cooled them and the smell of freshly turned dirt assailed his nostrils. It was better than cow dung, though.

Rob pointed to the small mounds where the tanks had been buried. "The ground has settled some. Get a landscaper before the dirt turns to unmanageable weeds."

One more item on his never-ending list of things to do. Even after he'd forgotten to tell her he wanted to buy new fuel tanks, she'd managed the impossible in an incredibly short time. Her focus on making it happen despite her fa-

Lily's MECHANIC

ther's health astounded him. It could have spelled disaster for the entire project. But something else bothered her. He had to figure out what else was going on because he wanted her for his airport manager. No two ways about it.

The date would either make or break their relationship. Could he stand the loss?

The doctor's office was sterile and unappealing to Lily, and she cringed at being ill. She had always been as strong as one of her dad's rented bulls.

With the boys out at the McDermott ranch and the terminal just about completed, she took the morning to take her father to his doctor's appointment. While in the waiting room, she texted Carson, and made phone calls keeping her finger on the pulse of the remaining tasks at the airport.

She hadn't smiled since she learned of her father's illness. Her sons noticed, too, but she'd convinced them she'd been focused on work. No doubt Carson noticed she hadn't cracked a joke since she dropped the ball on the fuel tanks.

She'd redeemed herself when she managed to take care of it in record time, despite the initial shock that additional fuel tanks were required. Technically, it wasn't her fault, but she'd take responsibility for it. She hadn't been proactive enough, and it was crucial in her line of work.

The schedule for the week along with notes and documents had been uploaded to the project folder for approval. Her contract stipulated she'd do most of her work from home, and she'd covered everything except those darn fuel tanks. She prided herself on her professionalism and that one bungled issue rankled.

156

"Why haven't you been out to the airport, Lily?"

Her father's words stung as he pulled her out of her own little world.

"I've been working remotely." She hadn't wanted to admit to herself she'd dropped the ball on a crucial airport element, much less to her father.

He gave her a side stare, then opened his mouth to say something just as the nurse called him.

"Do you want me to go with you, Dad?"

"You know the truth, so it doesn't matter." He shrugged his bony shoulders.

He'd lost weight, and she hadn't noticed. His shirt hung on him. She'd have to make sure he had lots of high calorie nutritious food in his diet to keep him healthy—as if she had nothing else to do than monitor her dad's food.

As they trudged through the office, they followed a stern-looking nurse. The hideous brown carpeting muffled their steps, and the corridor closed in on her.

With her father sitting on the exam table, she took a seat next to him. He stared at the artwork opposite him and was silent.

Her focus was shot. She'd dumped various work responsibilities onto her employer and her stomach lurched at not having a job. She needed to get her act together... pronto, and promised to lay it all out to Carson on their date that night.

"You need to get back to work. You can't babysit me every day." Her father's voice penetrated the silence.

"What?"

"You heard me."

The door opened and Doctor Kirk stepped in with a somber face and fiddled with the tablet as he sat on the rolling stool. "The results from your tests have come back. I

Lily's MECHANIC

waited because I wanted to give them to you in person."

Goose bumps rose on her arms and neck. The air-conditioning must have been set to an almost too low temperature.

She stole a glance at her father, who looked resigned. "What are those results?"

The doctor hadn't spared a look at her, but at her father. "By not regularly taking your meds, your condition has deteriorated." Then he turned to her. "And that's why you should be tested as soon as possible."

Her body shrunk in the chair. She hadn't wanted to face what might happen, but the disease was real. Too real.

"I'll make sure she gets tested, Doc." Her father and the doctor made eye contact and communicated in that way men seem to do without saying a word.

"Good," the doctor said as he monitored the screen. "In the meantime, we need to increase the dose, but not until you're consistent with the current medication. How much of your prescription do you have left?"

She fumbled in her purse and withdrew two small bottles and handed them to the doctor.

"These are almost full." Doctor Kirk eyeballed the refill information and gave a more than stern look at her father whose face registered sadness and a hint of remorse.

"According to my records, you should have had another refill this month. How long have you not been taking them?

Her father's face flushed, and he cleared his throat. "Off and on for about a month."

The doctor pursed his lips. "I'd say it was longer than that. I warned you it was crucial to take your medication, Nils."

Dad kicked his feet out and stared at them. "I kept forgetting, and when I remembered the time wasn't right."

She placed a hand on her father's arm and stared into

eyes so much like her own. "I'll make sure you take your medication." Lily turned to the doctor and put her hand out for the drugs. "Do I just follow the instructions on the bottle?"

"Yes. When he has a five-day supply left, call the office and I'll order the increased dosage."

She cleared her throat and got up. "What did you mean when you said it was crucial he take his medication?"

The doctor stopped at the door, turned, and a sadness filled his eyes. "It means the disease progresses at a faster pace when the medication isn't taken as prescribed." He shut the door with the soft click.

She swallowed, the doctor's words tasted like doom. It was all she could do to stand.

What could she say to her father? She couldn't yell at him because he'd been forgetful. Her heart ached. Thank goodness Patrick had called her to come home. Her father's best friend guessed her dad wasn't taking his medication like he was supposed to and needed her.

"I'm sorry, Lily. I should have been taking my meds." Her father's feet slipped to the floor, and he stared at his one and only pair of good shoes.

She hugged his side. "It's OK, Dad. I'll be right with you and will force those pills into you if I have to."

"Can we go home now?"

Giving him a soft smile, she led him to the car.

She'd have to buckle down, do her job, take care of her father and sons, and the farm. But right now, all she wanted to do was go home and have a good cry. Life just got harder and more complex.

What about Carson? They had a date tonight, and she wasn't sure pursuing a relationship right now was the best thing for her... or was it?

Chapter 16

"I see her every single day. Well, almost every day," Carson muttered to himself. "A date with her shouldn't be so hard. You'd think I was sixteen all over again."

Disgust with the war in his brain over how he felt about Lily, he splashed aftershave on his freshly shaven face and tightened his neck at the sting. He adjusted his collar and stared into the mirror, glancing at the age lines, and then went in search of his good cowboy boots.

After he checked his wallet and grabbed his keys, he jumped into the truck and glanced at the terminal building and hangar. *What am I doing? I should try to find that stupid treasure. It wouldn't be stupid if you found it, knucklehead.*

Not even the crickets chirping, or dusk's pink sky, held his attention.

He'd almost talked himself out of the date a half dozen times all day, but Lily won in his mind's final battle. He'd never bail on her again. Not after the suffering he and her father had put her through years ago. In his defense, it wasn't all his fault. But he should have gone after her.

She was the other half of his soul, and he was determined to take care of her.

When he pulled into the drive, the boys met him at the

160

truck and stood by the door with their arms crossed, with no expression. They surprised him all the time and were far from boring.

As much time as he'd spent with them, he couldn't figure out what they wanted. Then he stilled. They weren't really going to ask him his intentions, were they? Carson cast a glance at the boys' sitter, Bobby, who stood near the porch.

He got out of the truck and grabbed the box of candy he'd bought for Lily. He wanted to buy her flowers, too, but he dismissed the idea because she had more beautiful flowers growing in her yard than whatever he could buy.

Lucas stepped right in front of Carson and pointed at his chest. "Mom told us you're going out on a date. Don't hurt her. She's been sad for a long time, and we want her happy."

Evan scooted next to his brother and mimicked his brother's stance. "That's right. Be nice to her."

It was all he could do to not chuckle, but he pressed his lips together and plastered on his serious military face. "Your mom has worked hard on the farm and at the airport. I wanted to treat her and have no intention of hurting her. I like her too much to do that."

"She likes you too," Evan whispered loudly.

Lucas pointed to the box of candy with the wide red ribbon. "Is that for Mom?"

"Your mom's favorite."

Evan turned and raced up the porch stairs and slammed open the screen. "Mooommmm," he yelled. "Carson brought you candy. Can we have some?"

Carson called Bobby over and gave the boy his cell phone number in case of an emergency.

Lucas climbed the steps at his side. "Are the planes ready to fly yet?"

Lily's MECHANIC

"Just about. I'll let you know when they're airworthy."

The boy gave him a thoughtful stare. "I've never been on a plane. Is it scary?"

He ruffled the boy's hair. "You know when you go on a rollercoaster, and it tickles your stomach on the inside?"

Lucas nodded and opened the door for him.

"It's like that until the plane evens out, then the view is amazing. I remember the first time I flew. It was incredible. My uncle took me."

"You mean Farfar's best friend?"

"Yes."

Lily descended the stairs, a vision of loveliness in a simple blue dress that matched her eyes. His mouth turned down when he noticed she had camouflaged her exhaustion with a bit more makeup than she usually wore.

They stood and stared at one another until Lucas's voice pierced the silence and he grabbed his brother's shoulder. "Evan and I are going outside to play catch with Bobby. Save us some candy."

The boys raced out the door and he could hear them bantering with their babysitter, their whoops of joy filtering into the house.

"I'm sorry Evan spoiled the surprise." She frowned as she took the box and admired the ribbon.

He grinned and stared at her. "It's OK. I'd have to be a moron to expect anything less."

She chortled and her eyes lit when she noticed what was in the box. "I can't believe you remembered my favorite. Turtles." Her smile warmed his heart. "Come on in. Dad wanted to say hello. Do you mind if I share?"

He chuckled. "It's a two-pound box, Lily. It was made for sharing."

162

Her father raised his chin when they came into the room. "Carson, my boy. Did you find the treasure?"

She closed her eyes and shook her head. "Not now, Dad." He could almost hear her counting to ten in her head. "Have you taken your medication?"

Her father smirked, then frowned.

She stopped near her dad and checked the pill pack on the side table, then handed it to him. "You didn't. Take them now and I'll give you some candy."

Nils grabbed the medication and downed them with a swig of lemonade. She removed the ribbon and placed two pieces next to his pill box.

She leaned in and glared. "No. More. Talk. Of. Treasure. Got it?"

"Spoilsport," her dad mumbled, and grabbed a turtle.

Lily held the box and fingered the ribbon. "Let me put the candy away or it will be gone before I taste it."

"What was that all about?" He whispered to Nils when she stepped into the kitchen, and slammed cupboard doors.

"The boys get amped about the treasure, and it gets Lily riled. She reminds me of her mother when she gets like that." The man sighed. "I miss my wife."

As far as he knew, Lily's mother had been dead for over twenty years.

He blinked, frowned, and he thrust his neck out. "You've been goading her?"

The twinkle in the old man's eyes made him laugh.

"Stop it." His lips twitched and he couldn't quite keep the slight grin from his face.

"Stop what?" Lily appeared at his side with a confused look on her face.

Her father cleared his throat. "Men talk. Now get on

with you."

She cocked her head and gave her father a look he couldn't quite decipher.

"Do you have a sweater or something? It might be chilly later." He guided her to the front hall.

"No. I'll be fine."

It hadn't mattered. He had a hoodie in his truck if she got cold.

"Let's go, then."

"Where are we going?"

"Dinner in Columbus. Rob recommended a great steak place, and we have reservations in less than thirty minutes. It's not far. We can get back quickly if necessary, and I gave Bobby my cell phone number just in case."

At her sense of relief, his chest tightened that he'd had the foresight to do that. He wanted her to relax and enjoy the evening.

After he opened the door and she hopped into the cab, he went around and waved at the boys.

"Why did Dad ask you about the treasure?"

"You do know your dad is goading you, right?"

At her look of shock, he grinned and held out his hand, and she hesitated before she took it.

"When you get riled, it reminds him of your mom. That's why he does it."

Her mouth dropped open, then she clamped it shut.

"Don't be mad at him." He squeezed her fingers.

She sighed and wiggled into the seat. "I'm not. I never knew. He's been giving me grief since the day I got back."

"What happened with work last week, Lily?"

Now why had he mentioned her performance? He mentally berated himself. He should have waited to confront her.

164

Her body stiffened right before his eyes, and she pressed her shoulders back in defiance. "I was distracted, and it affected my professionalism. I'm sorry to have dumped my responsibilities in your lap. It won't happen again."

"Forget it, Lily. Let's just relax and enjoy dinner. I should have kept my big mouth shut."

Lily pulled her dress over her knees and turned to him. "No, we're having a discussion about my lack of responsibility. We both know I blew the issue with the tanks. I was too worried about... doesn't matter. It won't happen again."

He gave her a quick glance, the light from the waning sun casting beautiful shadows on her face. "The tanks don't matter, Lily. What I want to know is what rattled you."

"We need to talk about it, but can we save it until after dinner? I'd like to have dinner like a sane person."

Talk? That didn't sound good. He bit his tongue to keep himself from blurting what was on his mind and in his heart.

He sat up straight. The realization hit him square between the eyes. He loved her and he'd do whatever he could to help her. Heck, he'd been doing it since he first saw her on the farm's saggy porch. Even if it meant he'd lose the airport and his savings. He'd take a job at the Columbus airport, if things didn't work out. She had become more important than the airport and his beloved planes.

The quiet by her side overjoyed him, and he prayed for wisdom and discernment as they traveled to the eatery.

When she got out of the truck, her face was awestruck, like a teenager on her first prom date. "This place is gorgeous."

The scene looked like something out of a magazine with the pristine flower beds. Deep purple hydrangeas bloomed and livened up the pale blue Victorian mansion which had been turned into a restaurant. Their flowery aroma was in-

Lily's MECHANIC

toxicating. Rob hadn't told him how romantic it was. The photos online hadn't prepared him for what it would look like with the twinkle lights and the comfortable seating on the wraparound porch.

"They have a small man-made lake and more gardens in the back."

She turned wide eyes at him. "You've been here before?"

"I saw photos on their website and peeked at their menu."

Grinning, she placed her hand in the crook of his arm. "Of course you did."

It seemed what they'd talked about in the truck had been relegated to the back of their minds. And that was fine with him.

When they were seated and had ordered, they talked about their mutual friends and reminisced about their youth. She laughed to the point of crying over some things they had done when they were in high school. By silent mutual consent, they avoided work-related topics.

He'd enjoy her company and being with her in the present. "Remember when we went blackberry picking, and you fell into the patch because you were laughing so hard?"

She cocked her head and her lips quirked with a tiny grin. "If I recall, you made smacking noises with your mouth as you ate the blackberries and then you showed me your black tongue. The scratches I got upset my father."

There'd be time later to talk about matters of the heart... after they talked about what bothered her.

The server brought the check, and he gave him a credit card.

She sat back and wiped her mouth on the pristine napkin, leaving a telltale sliver of pink lipstick. "Living in Austin, we had some pretty fine steak, but that was the best steak I've had in a long, long time."

He stashed the card in his wallet and smiled. "I'm glad."

"Shall we go find a quiet place to talk?"

Her face was a kaleidoscope of emotions, with none of them overpowering the other. The slab of beef he'd just eaten sat like a capsized boat in his stomach.

The forthcoming talk could be really good or really bad.

Lily had to tell him the truth. Carson had become the man she'd always dreamed he'd be. She just couldn't keep her father's disease from him. She loved him too much to lie.

The refreshing night air gave her a much-needed boost of courage as they strolled along the waterway. They found a secluded spot with a stone bench under twin oak trees. The soft path lighting made the spot ideal and the distant voices from the restaurant stilled her uneasiness.

Laying her heart bare could cause a heartache much greater than her disastrous marriage, greater than her father's diagnosis, and even much greater than her own diagnosis, if it came to that.

She loved him and she had to tell him.

He had taken her hand as they walked along the stamped concrete pathway and had not let go. His hand was warm and comforting, just like him. Things had been so much easier with him in her life. Even with the farm's financial difficulties and her father's illness, she could cope with all of it when Carson stood at her side. But was it him? Or was she seeing the Lord through Carson? He'd been in church every Sunday and prayed. He'd grown into the type of man she'd always wanted. Someone who would put his relationship with God at the forefront of his life.

The silence lengthened after they sat, her hand still in his, until she cleared her throat and they spoke in unison.

Lily's MECHANIC

She squeezed his hand. "Sorry, go ahead."

He half turned and rubbed the top of her hand with his thumb. "I've been worried about you ever since your dad came home from the hospital. You haven't been yourself. Even before then, you've kept me at arm's length."

She couldn't see his eyes in the darkness, but the cautious note in his voice made her feel cared for like she hadn't been since before she left Worthy.

"We agr–"

"I know we agreed to keep everything professional, but the renovation has come a long way in a very short time, and I have a list of potential tenants. Once I get them under contract, the airport will be on its way. The path to secure my future... our future will be set."

"Are you saying—?" She choked the words out.

"Yes. I should have followed my gut when I left for the military. I should have fought for you. Neither of us would have had the heartache we've had if I had. I love you, Lily. Your sons are fun and will keep me on my toes. I want a life with you and a family." He inhaled and begged her with his eyes. "Tell me you feel the same." She could hear the note of desperation in his voice.

Terror filled her heart. She couldn't tell him she loved him. She could only tell him the truth of what her life looked like right now.

"Oh, Carson, I care about you too." Turning, she clasped his arm with her other hand. "You've been a lifeline... and not just with the project. I've not been this happy since we were in high school." Her head shook, and she gave a heart-felt sigh. "We both have so much baggage, and it's more than the distraction you've seen these past two weeks."

"But..." His voice was soft, softer than she'd ever heard

168

him speak.

"First, it was the farm's finances, and I tackled them because you gave me a dream job. But I worried about my dad's health, and I was right. He's sicker than I thought." The last words trailed.

Carson moved closer and wrapped an arm around her shoulders. "I figured something was wrong. Is it Alzheimers or dementia?"

She shook her head, her spine strengthening like steel rebar pressed into wet concrete. "No. He has Huntington's Disease."

"What's that?"

"It's… a progressive disease. He has not been taking his medication, so the doctor wants to increase the dose, but won't do it until he's regulated with the current dose." She stumbled with words she hadn't wanted to utter. "And it's hereditary."

He pulled back. "You have it too?"

She was glad she couldn't gauge his facial expression, but the lurch in his body made her cringe and squeezed all the air out of her lungs.

"I'm not sure."

"Wait." He paused, obviously trying to understand. "You mean it skips generations?"

"No. It means there's a fifty-fifty chance I have the gene that causes the disease."

"How will you know?"

"A blood test will determine if I have the gene."

"Then get it, Lily. You owe it to yourself to know." He squeezed her shoulder and tucked her closer to him.

She leaned her head back and stared at the starry sky. "I know I do. I'm just… not ready to take that step yet.

He pulled away from her and stood up, pacing away from her and rubbing the back of his neck. "Why?" The word

shot out of his mouth like a missile.

"Part of me is afraid. Another part is the test takes four to six weeks for the results. The wait will be awful."

"The sooner you get the test, the sooner you'll know." He crouched in front of her and took her hands again. "You need to know what you're facing. *We* need to know."

The hesitation had morphed from fear to practicality. She couldn't tell him why she put it off. It was such a simple thing to do and yet...

She stood and glared at him as he rose to his full height, forcing herself to take the no nonsense professional demeanor for which she'd been known. "I'm not ready."

With that, she turned and walked away.

"Wait." He stepped to her and grasped her arm, his hand like an eagle's talons. He stood in an area where the moon shone on his face, lighting his distressed features. "Does your reluctance have to do with the cost?"

Her fingers pulled his hand from her arm and her body tensed. "My reasons are my own and I'm not scheduling it right now. I'd like to go home now."

She couldn't bear to look at him as they walked in silence back to his truck. All she could think about was how much he'd suffer if she were as sick as her father. She could *not* do that to him.

When they got in the truck, he switched on the map light and turned to face her. "I won't let the blood test go, Lily. I'll pester you just as you hounded me about airport things. You need to know, and so do I."

Her head told her it would make a difference in the way he felt about her, but her heart wanted to believe it wouldn't.

She just wasn't ready to face him not being a part of her life.

Chapter 17

Carson vaulted up the church steps and into the sanctuary. His mind went over every excruciating detail of his conversation with Lily on Friday night. He hadn't wanted to come to church, but knew it was the best place for his tormented brain. The service had yet to begin as he scanned the rows, looking for her and Nils.

He hadn't seen Lily since their date, but had spoken to her on the phone about the open house. He had asked to speak to her so they could review the scheduling. Her professionalism was in place again and she'd agreed to meet him later in the afternoon so they could plan.

When he spotted Lily and her dad, he made his way around and came into their row from the other side and sat just as a rousing chorus began.

Nils nodded at him, and Lily acknowledged his presence but avoided glancing his way. Her father looked at him and then at Lily and sighed deeply.

What was that about?

Time spent with Lily bubbled in his brain and kept him from concentrating on the service. What had happened on their date on Friday kept him from the deeper message from Genesis 16 about the mess Abraham made of God's plan

171

and promise.

The final song rang out and Nils turned to him. "Why don't you come over for Sunday dinner? We'd love to have you." He glanced back at his daughter. "Right, Lily?"

When he looked over Nils's shoulder, her eyes bulged, and she had a sickly smile on her face. "Certainly."

"I don't know…"

Her father's hand clutched at his arm. "You're alone over there at Patrick's and you have to eat. Lily made her mother's pot roast. You don't want to miss that, do you?"

"OK. I'll be there."

Nils beamed and shook his hand. "Follow us home. We'll eat as soon as we get there, right Lily?"

Scattered thoughts about the invitation and Lily's coolness filled the drive to the Sandburg farm. He and Lily had to work together, and he still wanted her and her sons for his family. How far he'd come since he'd determined he hadn't wanted to be near her.

He shook his head at himself, at the changes in his life as he pulled in behind Lily's old SUV.

The boys jumped out of the car and raced to the farmhouse and went inside before their mother. The six windows across the porch sparkled, and the screen had been replaced. Lily tackled one task at a time and made the place more of a home than it had been the first day he'd seen her. Even the porch furniture had a new lease on life, with cushions and fresh paint.

Nils stood on the porch and waited for him.

As he approached Lily's father, she popped back through the screen door. The ever-present apron tightened around her waist. "Dinner will be in a few minutes."

He glanced at her father, then at her. "Can I help with anything?"

"No. Sit with dad. The boys will set the table and bring drinks out in a minute or two."

The screen door shut with a quiet click, and he could no longer see her, but heard the boys bantering in the dining room.

"Have a seat, Carson."

Nils tapped the chair arm next to him.

"Thanks."

Lucas brought two glasses of Lily's lemonade and set them on the table. "Mom said dinner will be ready in ten minutes."

Discomfort welled within him. What was he doing here? Lily could have come over to the airport yesterday to review the schedule and she hadn't. She had only texted. This was a bad idea.

Nils grabbed his arm with a force he hadn't believed the man capable of. "If something happens to me, I want your promise you'll take care of Lily and the boys."

His gaze swung to her father, and he had the look of a man possessed.

He was almost breathless. "What?"

"You heard me."

"Nothing is going—"

The pressure on his arm increased, and he was certain Nils would leave bruises.

"I'm dying, and I need to be sure she'll be taken care of. Promise me."

He patted Nils's hand and barely whispered the words, "I will."

Relief came out as a long-heaved puff of air from the older man. "I know Lily told you about my disease. I want her tested, and I need your help to convince her."

"I'm on it, don't worry."

With an exaggerated nod, the farmer leaned his head

Lily's MECHANIC

back, and closed his eyes as if all was right with the world.

Lily's voice called out from the hallway. "Dinner's ready. Come on in and bring your drinks."

The boys took turns grilling him about the planes and the airport, but thankfully, her father never mentioned the treasure and neither did he.

When Lily came back to work tomorrow, he'd tear through his uncle's house in search of the treasure. It had to be there. At least he wanted it to be.

After a dinner of a tender pot roast and the best apple pie he'd ever tasted, he stood to help with the dishes.

Lily took the plates from his hands. "You don't have to do that."

"You cooked, so it's only courteous to help clean up. It was delicious, by the way." He followed her to the kitchen, where the aroma from their dinner continued to waft throughout the rooms and made the old house a home.

Lily side-eyed him and put the leftovers in the fridge, then donned rubber gloves and filled the sink with soapy water.

He stood shoulder to shoulder next to her as the boys brought in flatware and glasses. "You have a dishwasher. It should go quick, then we can talk about the airport and next week's tasks."

"It's full and there's no room. We'll have to do these by hand. You can dry."

Her smirk told him it was a test to see if he would stay the course.

He rolled his shoulders and grabbed the dish towel, drying every plate, glass, and pan she handed to him.

She barely spoke except to direct the boys to go play and tell her father to take his pills. It was as if Friday night had never happened. And yet, he felt more at ease, happier than

174

he'd ever been on his own or even when he lived with his ex when he wasn't out at sea.

When she removed her apron and hung it on the hook next to the door, she turned and led him to the office down the hallway on the other side of the kitchen. "I need to check on my father and get my laptop. Have a seat. I'll be back in a few minutes."

Her face softened. But was it for him or for her father? He'd take it no matter what.

As he waited, he glanced around the farm office. She had cleared out all the clutter and painted the walls a soft blue and the woodwork a bright white. She'd even hung framed photos of her parents, and the antique desk glimmered with a fresh coat of wax. A faint scent of lemon filled the air. He imagined her as she sat at the desk, and bit her lip, thinking.

The door clicked shut, and he turned to watch her glide in. She had changed her clothes and pressed the laptop to her chest. As she sat, she placed it on the desk, turned it on, and got her phone out. "What's on the agenda next week?"

After they discussed the plans, he told her he had to remove everything left in the hangar so Rob's two crews could start that phase of the renovation.

She gave him a worried glance. "How much is left to do?"

He kept his expression neutral. "Thankfully, I hired a few high school kids from church to help all day yesterday, but I left the more crucial pieces of equipment for myself."

"How long, Carson?"

He gave her a slight shrug. "A couple of hours, max."

"So, you'll rest tonight?"

"I will. But we need to talk… about us."

She lifted her chin and closed her eyes, then slowly opened them. "I think our discussion on Friday said it all."

175

Lily's MECHANIC

"No. You shut me down. I want to know why you think it can't work between us. We loved one another back then. Our ease working on the renovation these past months in conditions that would sever any good relationship only made ours stronger." He held his hand up. "And don't tell me it's our baggage or the disease."

"It's true we've gotten close again." She got up and paced to the door and back. "But I'm afraid, OK?"

He rose to go to her and touched her cheek, then cupped her chin. "Of what?" he whispered.

Raising her eyes to his, her worried gaze troubled him.

"Everything. What if what we had isn't there anymore? It would ruin me." Her voice trembled and the last part trailed off into nothingness.

"Listen to me. It's true we've both been hurt and we're both cautious, me even more than you, if you can believe it. But, working with you these past months and spending time with you raised old feelings I truly hadn't wanted to have and yet, I can't deny they're there." With his other hand, he cupped her neck. "I love you, Lily. I'm not going away ever again, and my feelings won't change either." He drew her in for the sweetest kiss he'd ever had.

When he pulled away, her face was flushed, and her eyes slowly opened. A soft smile graced her lips. "I'd forgotten what a good kisser you are."

He grinned and smoothed a thumb across her cheek. "Thanks. If that's any indication, I'll make even better on my promises. So, what do you think? Do we try to make our relationship work?"

She inhaled, then her breath whooshed out. "I don't know if I can judge based on the quality of the kiss. I'm not convinced we are a good idea. Let's take it one day at a time, agreed?"

Nodding, he stared into her eyes. "I can live with that. But right now, I have work to do. Walk me out."

"Let me know if you need any help. I can call Bobby. He's always on the lookout for extra work."

He held her hand as they strolled to his vehicle and stood by the truck's door. "No need. I'll get it done." Before he got in his truck, he softly kissed her. "I'll see you in the morning."

On the road to the airport, the blasted treasure popped into his brain again. A part of him yearned to find it, and a part of him expected he wouldn't. If Lily ever learned of the terms of the inheritance and that maybe his uncle somehow might have duped her father, she'd never forgive him.

"Uncle Patrick, what have you done?"

Chaos reigned at the airport as Lily got out of her car on Monday morning. The day hadn't even started. She inhaled and let it out, knowing it would be a long day.

Juggling her kids, her father, and job kept her awake at nights wondering how she'd do everything.

With Bobby, Fred, and the other farmhands' help, her family and the farm were in good hands, but it didn't mean she could check out to do this job.

Carson stepped to her car and knocked on the window just as she finished setting the alarms that would ensure she'd text everyone at the farm. "What are you doing?"

She got out of the car and raised her hand against the sun. "Personal stuff."

He took a step back and opened his mouth, but Rob's voice stopped him from commenting. "Can you both come into the hangar? I need clarification."

Lily's MECHANIC

As they quick-stepped into the enormous building, she side-glanced at Carson's closed profile. What was up with him?

After yesterday, she assumed they were on the same page. Obviously not.

The sounds of crowbars hitting wood and plasterboard reverberated and echoed in the cavernous structure making it sound louder than it was. The crew knocked walls down causing dust to fly everywhere as she and Carson made their way around debris piles to the other end of the hangar where they could talk and not shout. The heat in the hangar staggered her.

Rob rolled out the plans on a saw table and placed tools on the corners so they could review the drawing. "I got to thinking over the weekend about the layout and the timeline."

She glanced at Carson who pulled on his ear, but kept his mouth shut and waited for the contractor to make a point.

"Is there a problem?" Her voice held concern.

"No problem. Rather, a change suggestion. But I needed both of your input as to the viability of what I'm proposing." Rob clamped his mouth shut and waited with a hand casually laid on the table.

The man had learned the fine art of negotiating. Say what had to be said, then shut up. It worked every time.

Carson glanced at the plan, then stared at the contractor. "Are the changes the result of a design flaw?"

"Not exactly, but I reviewed the plans, and it occurred to me the architect's design..." He took another sheet, folded it, and placed it next to the revision. "It shows the bathroom in a totally different location, which means breaking a huge swath of concrete floor and plumbing it somewhere else. It will push our timeline back and then some to where it was before, even with two crews working."

"I wonder why such a drastic change was made." She

178

fingered the new plan. "It's at a completely different place."

Rob tapped the page. "The notes I received from the architect said Patrick wanted the bathroom closer to the entrance for visitors to use without going farther into the hangar."

"That was a good call on my uncle's part. The last thing we need is for people traipsing through the hangar and getting hurt. Insurance would skyrocket."

She should have seen how problematic the design was and it infuriated her she missed it when she initially went over the plans. Her preoccupation with her father's health, the farm, and the boys got in the way of her usual perfectionism. "What are you suggesting?"

"If we leave the bathroom where it is—make it bigger, increase the number of stalls and sinks, cut out an exterior door and make the bathroom accessible from the outside— then no one would have to go through the hangar to use it." His finger followed the path of what he wanted to do. "We put a motion mercury light above the door and a walkway between the tanks and the building. That way, pilots and mechanics have access to the bathroom without going into the terminal or the hangar."

Carson lifted his chin and tilted his head. "It would also give everyone a secondary access to the hangar, and we'd have to adjust the security system. Access would be a problem too."

"It's brilliant, Rob." She motioned to the plans. "We could put a coded panel for both accesses, and they'd have access depending on their security level. Both doors would be inaccessible from the other direction."

The contractor beamed and became animated. "That's exactly what I was thinking. We'd still have to break the concrete for the additional stalls, but it would be far cheaper and less disruptive than the original plans."

179

Lily's MECHANIC

Carson narrowed his eyes. "Will the new plan increase the price? How will it affect the rest of the design?"

"Let me show you the plan I drew over the weekend. It will give you a good indication of my vision." He pulled another page from the bottom of the plans and smoothed it out.

Her alarm went off, and she had to text the farm. Rob and Carson could easily discuss the changes while she made the call. "Excuse me for a minute, I'll be right back."

She stepped away and out of the corner of her eye, Carson and Rob's faces registered concern, but they turned their attention to the drawing.

When she returned, both men rose to their full height, and she prepared herself for backlash for leaving the meeting, but checking in with the farmhand, babysitter, and her father gave her peace of mind to do her work.

She drew her hand over the revisions. "Can I see the original design? I'd like to see how different the two are."

Rob clenched his jaw and glanced at Carson who shrugged. The contractor moved his design next to the original design.

She studied both designs while Rob crossed his arms and frowned, and Carson clasped his hands behind his back. "Actually, the new design is better and much more efficient. It doesn't look like it will affect the rest of the hangar."

A slow smile slid over Rob's face, and he shifted closer.

Her gaze slid from the old plan to the new one, then stopped. "I have one additional suggestion."

"What's that?" Rob's earlier smile faded.

When she outlined her thoughts, and why, the contractor nodded. "Yeah, that might be a good idea. What do you think, Carson?"

He pulled his hands out of his pocket and flattened them on the table. "If we can save time, and it's the same price, the

180

new design makes sense and with Lily's suggestion, I think it'll be terrific. Will we be able to open sooner?"

"I think we can have it done before your open house in two weeks." Rob's voice held no hint of hesitation.

"Great. Let's do it." Carson put out his hand and Rob shook it.

The contractor outlined what he needed her to do this week to move forward. She told him she'd contacted the landscaper with the changes to their original design.

When they were done, she and Carson exited the building while Rob took charge of the crew. The heat in the hangar and the warm sun caused perspiration to seep from her pores.

Carson turned and tilted his head. "I need to check on the planes. Walk with me?"

"Sure."

"What was all the texting about?"

"I set alarms so I could check in with Fred, the boys, and my dad periodically today."

She stumbled, and he wrapped his arm around her waist for a few minutes.

"Good idea. Is everything OK?" He smiled and his eyes twinkled. "I questioned if there were issues, but I'm glad you're here… with me."

She chuckled. "You're incorrigible."

"I am." He beamed.

When they reached the planes, Carson walked around each one and smoothed his hand over the sides as he moved his head from side to side making sure everything was OK, then shot her a wide smile.

At the sound of engines, trucks spewed dust on the lane and they both craned their necks to see what came their way. The overwhelming smell of tar made her nose wrinkle.

Carson rubbed his hands together and a smile spread across his face. "Looks like the blacktop guys are here."

He reminded her of her boys when their exuberance bubbled and got the best of them.

She strode toward the graveled parking lot with him at her side. "We should probably get out of their way. How long will they work on the runway?"

He glanced in her direction. "All week. It means we can work on the open house stuff, but I need to talk to the paving contractor. I'll see you in the terminal in ten minutes. I have a proposition for you."

Her stomach churned like the butter her father used to make in the old-fashioned device glancing his way as she walked to the renovated building.

What could he want from her now?

Chapter 18

A niggling doubt cast a pall on Carson's week. Everything seemed to be falling into place and it was only Wednesday.

Though a distinct uneasiness filled him. Was it the treasure, the open house, or Lily? He wasn't sure why he had this sense of discomfort. Was the Holy Spirit trying to tell him something?

The open house was in two weeks. Invitations had been sent out to a myriad of people, including the local newspaper, television reporters, and town officials. He'd gotten a lot of positive responses.

Lily came to work, the boys were happy, Nils was relatively healthy for a diseased man without a cure, and the airport was taking shape faster than he imagined. But he hadn't been able to work on finding the blasted treasure.

His phone vibrated in his pocket, and he pulled it out. Ben.

He frowned at the rickety chair in his uncle's den, upset with himself he hadn't bought a new one. This one was worse than the one in the hangar office, but at least he'd replaced that one. "You ready for the move?"

"Sure am. Can you come on Friday to inspect the helicopter and fly it in? If you can fly in before eight, we can meet, discuss the plan, and I can get on the road directly afterward. It's a long drive from Norfolk to Worthy."

183

Lily's MECHANIC

"I think I can do that. Airport permits are all in order, and it can be used even if we're not officially open. The runway and helipad will be ready by then too. Let me make reservations and you can pick me up at the airport."

"Make it as early as possible."

"Will do."

He swiped his phone and searched for and bought a cheap flight, then texted Ben. That shot his intention of searching for the treasure this weekend. It couldn't be helped. His tenant took precedence over a treasure that may or may not even be there.

He texted Lily he'd be out of town on Friday and would let her know if he'd be staying the night before he flew Ben's helicopter to Worthy.

Excitement ran through his veins, and he pumped his fist for the first of what he believed would be many new tenants.

Rob's crew had pulled out all the stops and the landscaper would be there in the morning to start the planting. The airport was quiet, and its tranquility comforted him, so the sound of a vehicle driving up the lane before sunset startled him.

He stepped to the living room window to see two men get out of a late model Hummer and do a one-eighty taking in the terminal, the hangar, and the runway.

Opening the front door, he quick-stepped to the stairs and stood before them. "Gentlemen. What can I do for you?"

When they had introduced themselves as the officers of the Ohio Training Association, a breathlessness gripped him. He'd sent them a letter a month ago about the airport renovation.

The men were about his age, but the older man introduced himself as Richard Gilbert, the president, and gestured to the other man as their Secretary-Treasurer, Mark Peterson.

184

Gilbert moved to shake his hand. "You invited us to the open house, but we chanced visiting before the event. Would it be possible to look around?"

"Sure. I'll give you a tour. Someone from the association sent back the RSVP. Will you not attend the open house?"

Peterson gave him a brief smile. "We wouldn't miss it. But if we like what we see today, we want to get the ball rolling and discuss our association's and our personal needs before then."

His heart did a two-step as he showed the men the terminal, all the offices, the hangar, the runway, and helipad.

They peppered him with pertinent questions about the facility and potential new runways and hangars. He explained he planned on building with the extra land the airport had, but cautioned it wouldn't be right away. He hadn't memorized any of the rates, so he avoided them.

The president lifted his heels and did a tiny bounce. "I landed at this airport years ago but hadn't seen its potential. I do now. We did a bit of research on you. I was quite impressed with your credentials. We're all veterans, so we wanted to work with guys who understood our need for precision maintenance and timeliness."

"Understood."

Carson led them back to the terminal where he could talk to them in depth about their needs and give them the printed rates.

Mark kept step with him. "When will the airport be open for business?"

The new carpet and furniture smell hadn't dissipated when Carson unlocked the terminal's airport office door and ushered the men in. "The open house is in a little less than two weeks. Our official opening day won't be for a week or two after that."

Lily's MECHANIC

He gave them the printed mechanic rates and sample parking and office contracts, then offered them something to drink. They accepted, and he walked to the other side of the terminal to get bottles of water. The few minutes away would allow them a little privacy to discuss without him hovering.

Richard accepted the water but leaned forward in the chair. "Personally, I'm ready to make the move. The mechanics where I'm located now are young and do sloppy work. I want someone I can trust. The parking and office contract rates are reasonable. I, personally, don't need an office."

Mark nodded and wanted a parking contract as well.

He wanted to burst at the seams. Two contracts, and Ben hadn't even signed his yet. The open house would surely bring in more contracts.

The president gulped a swig of the ice cold water. "You have any helicopters interested in parking here?"

Carson beamed. "Actually, I'm headed to Norfolk on Friday to do maintenance on a buddy's aircraft and will fly it back on Saturday."

Mark sat up. "Good deal. We want to expand. Perhaps your guy would like to farm out his aircraft for training."

"I can't speak for him, but he'll be at the open house, and I'll introduce you." Carson sat opposite the two men and folded his hands on the desk.

Richard lowered his chin and gave Mark a hard glare. "We won't decide to move our business until we speak to the entire group. Would it be possible to invite our membership to the open house?"

Carson wanted to high five someone, but maintained his cool. "How many would there be?"

A sheepish look came over the president's face. "Aside from the two of us, there are between forty and fifty for-

186

mer-military from all branches."

He'd have to call the caterer, but what a great problem to have and he smiled wide. "The more the merrier."

The president clapped him on the back. "Great. Let's sign our contracts and give you the deposits."

He agreed to send soft copies of the invitation to them both to send out to their group.

When they had left, his chest expanded with a sense of accomplishment. With the contracts in hand, he raced into the house and called Lily.

He wanted to share with her how much he appreciated her hard work and how it had all paid off with two contracts, fifty new guests for the open house, and a potential contract for a pilot training facility.

Placing a call to Bottleson, he left a message for the man to call him.

Lily's excitement fueled his own, but as he went back into his uncle's office, the shabbiness of the room along, with his worry over the treasure cast a pall on the past few hours' excitement.

He vowed to get the room ship-shape and find the treasure before the open house.

A frown marred Lily's forehead. Carson's offer to keep her on permanently on an ad hoc basis to run the airport, was a grand gesture on his part and was probably the best thing she could do, but something held her back.

She'd requested he wait until after the open house for her to decide. He hadn't been upset but seemed disappointed.

Uncertainty kept her from jumping at accepting. He'd be

Lily's MECHANIC

more inclined to give her grace if a situation came up with the boys or her father... or even her. It reminded her she needed to get the blood test done, and she still wasn't ready.

Weekends spent harvesting her small garden, checking on the farm store, and keeping her father and boys in line exhausted her and she fell into bed at night. But it was a good exhaustion, her mind filled with productivity and the tasks that lay ahead.

She'd contented herself that the interior of the house was freshly painted and sparkled. Every room had the scent of lemon oil, and her father commented on how much nicer it was to come inside at night. She'd have liked to paint the house's exterior, but it would have to wait until next year when the farm was in a better place financially.

Everything had been going so well, she worried the proverbial shoe would kick her in the shins.

With the last push to ready the airport for the open house, Carson had not bugged her about the blood test, and she was thankful for his understanding. She smiled wide as she hung up the phone. His exhilaration over the two new parking contracts and a potential contract for a training facility was contagious.

She made her way to the living room where her father dozed in his recliner. While he had a good two weeks left on his current dosage, her father seemed perkier, and he'd been cleared to go back to work. He had spent the day with the farmhands and the boys, putting them to work so when they came in, washed up, and had dinner, they almost fell asleep eating.

Farfar chuckled and teased them the entire time. How much happier her father was these days despite the prospect of an incurable disease. She thanked God every night for the many blessings since finding her faith again. A comfort she

188

hadn't known possible rushed through her despite the Huntington's Disease looming in their lives.

Since she left Worthy, she had run from God when things were tough, but during these difficult weeks she came to understand she had needed God in her life every day. And depending on Him had become second nature in the weeks since she'd given her heart to him again. The Bible verse from Sunday's sermon on Matthew 11:28-30 invaded her spirit, and settled in with a peace she hadn't known in years. *My yoke is easy, and my burden is light.*

The gossip mills she'd worried about never happened. She went to church every week and rekindled friendships even if it was just on Sundays. She expected things would even out and she could join a church group.

Quietly, she dropped to her corner of the sofa and watched the program as her dad dozed in his recliner.

Her father blinked and turned his head toward her. "How long have you been sitting there?"

"Just a few minutes. Carson called. He has two contracts already for the airport and he wants to take the boys flying next weekend before school starts. I'm not sure I want them to go."

"You don't trust he'll keep them safe?"

"I trust him. It's just…" Even she couldn't figure out why she felt the way she did. Her sons were growing up, and having Carson around as a role model was how she'd dreamed it could be for her boys.

"Aw… Let them go. It'll be fun for them and a treat after they've worked so hard on the farm."

"I suppose you're right."

He gave her a hard stare. "And you need to get the blood test."

She inhaled and let it out slowly. "I plan to, Dad. The

Lily's MECHANIC

timing is bad right now."

"Why?"

"There's a lot going on, but I promise I'll get it done the first chance I get."

"Have you told Carson? What does he have to say about it?" He squinted at her with disapproval.

Her head jerked in his direction. "He doesn't have any say over what I do or don't do, Dad." She wanted to roll her eyes at him, but it would be disrespectful. "But yes, I told him about it."

Dad's face screwed up. "You're dating him, and he deserves to know what he's facing."

"He does, and he'll support me whenever I choose to get it done." Her words were spoken matter-of-factly.

When her father harrumphed, she wanted to chuckle but pressed her lips together instead. Her dad was from another generation where a man had more input. *Not happening, Dad.*

She rose and fetched her father a drink. "Take your pills, Dad."

He swallowed them without question or giving her a hard time. He grabbed her arm and the pleading look in his eyes made her heart ache. "I need to know you're free of this dreadful disease."

She crouched beside his chair and touched his hand. "I want to know too. I just need another week to get everything settled, including getting the boys back in school."

"Alright." He rose from the recliner and his bones creaked. "I'm going to bed. Sunrise comes quick on a farm."

"That it does."

She clicked the remote, and she climbed the stairs to her room. The sound of her dad moving around downstairs comforted her. But, she heard him coughing off and on, then

it stopped. She'd have to ask him about the cough. How long had he had it?

Her heart heavy as she tossed and turned all night worrying about her dad and her health. What would it mean for her relationship with Carson?

She loved him, but could she saddle him with the prospect of a debilitating incurable disease? And what if her sons had the gene too?

Chapter 19

The wind whipped through Carson's hair as he made his way to the Norfolk hangar, where he agreed to meet his friend. Ben had been unable to pick him up at the airport like they agreed.

He stepped into the hangar, the unmistakable clattering of tools filled his ears, and he glanced around. "Nice setup."

Ben strode to him and shook his hand. "I guess. How is the renovation going?"

"Great. We'll have almost everything completed by the time we have the open house."

He hadn't wanted to tell Ben about the other planes, or the potential work that could be headed his way. The pilot's association could speak for themselves.

When they stood in the hangar near his friend's helicopter, Carson smoothed his hand over the door of the aircraft. "Do you have the last inspection documents?"

Ben pulled papers from his bag and handed them over. "I arranged a stall so you can inspect it and make sure everything is in order."

He flipped through the inspection, took a pen, and checked areas that might be problematic. With him flying the helicopter, he wanted to make doubly sure the aircraft was flight worthy. "I'll review the inspector's work and if I

192

get done early enough, I'll fly it back before sunset. Otherwise, it'll be the crack of dawn tomorrow."

"Take your time."

"I have to get back, Ben."

His friend lowered his aviators and stared at him over the top. A frown pinched his forehead. "Is it the airport, or is it Lily you have to get back to?"

His lips scrunched, and he looked away. "Both."

"Take it easy, my friend."

"We're taking it one step at a time right now." His chin dropped, and he rubbed the back of his neck. No way would he admit to falling in love with the girl next door to Ben. "She's got some personal issues and right now, the airport takes precedence. My inheritance depends—"

"I get it. Your livelihood hinges on its success."

His smile faded. "I sunk almost every penny of my savings on this project, plus the house still needs a boatload of work and I promised Lily's boys a ride in the Cessna. It got inspected last week, and I want to surprise them before school starts."

Ben's gaze hardened, and he crossed his arms. "You're spending time with her sons too?"

"A little. They come to the airport on occasion, and they're interested in the planes."

His friend hitched his gray pants as he sat on the corner of the worktable and shook his head. "I'm not sure it's a good idea. It—"

"Why don't you come with us and be my co-pilot? We'll fly them around Columbus."

"Is Lily going too?" The disdain in Ben's voice was clear.

"I can ask her, but I'm sure she has things to do on the farm. Her father isn't well."

The hangar boss interrupted their conversation with facility instructions. His friend took a last walk around the helicopter and crossed his arms and waited.

When they were alone, Carson turned to his friend. "Let me get started right away. I'll text you my progress and whether I'll fly back today or tomorrow. Either way, I'll see you after church around three at the airport, unless you come out sooner."

They shook hands, and Ben left.

He hadn't expected he'd have to wait in line for tools. Didn't they have multiple sets?

Because of that, it took him three times as long to review the inspection docs. When he finally finished, he was outside the window to make the flight, so he'd leave in the morning. He hadn't made a hotel reservation and hadn't wanted to waste transport time, so he opted to sleep in the helicopter. He'd done it before, but it was years ago. He cringed because his body would take a beating.

Thankfully, one of the other mechanics had brought him dinner from a fast-food place. How he missed the taste of Lily's cooking.

He'd texted Ben and set his alarm. He'd be up and out of Norfolk when the sun rose. He made those arrangements before he stretched out as well as he could in the back seat.

Besides, he needed to get back to the farmhouse to look for the blasted treasure. He'd made a mental list of all the places to look right before his eyes drifted shut.

The alarm jerked him awake, and he squinted blurry eyes at his phone.

He'd gotten out of Norfolk in time to avoid the storm coming up from the south, landed at the airport, and secured Ben's helicopter just before the deluge hit.

Racing to the farmhouse, he jumped on the porch, and

went inside. He texted Ben and checked in with Lily, noting Bottleson had called, but hadn't left a message.

He took a hot shower and brushed his teeth. The minty flavor revived him. A sandwich and a glass of iced tea and he was ready to tackle what he set out to do and hadn't done yet.

The blustery rain wasn't expected to last, but it was a perfect day to scour his uncle's home, looking for the treasure. He'd start in his uncle's den down the hall from the kitchen.

Before he tackled the search, he dialed Bottleson, who picked up on the first ring. "I saw you called but hadn't left a message. Something wrong?"

"Not at all. I wanted to check in with you because I stopped by the airport yesterday. It looks terrific, and I'm looking forward to the open house next week."

"I'm glad you called. I had visitors last Thursday and have contracts with two private owners, plus they're coming to the open house and may need a facility for their pilot training company."

"That's fantastic. Didn't you say you already had one tenant for the terminal?"

"Yes. I just flew Ben's helicopter in from Norfolk and he'll be in tomorrow to sign the contract."

"How will you handle the terminal's management and do the mechanical work on the planes?" A hint of worry drifted into the attorney's voice.

"I've offered Lily, the construction project manager, the position."

"Oh? Is she experienced in managing an airport? What about the financial end of things?"

The rapid-fire questions made him tweak the bridge of his nose. He hadn't even asked her about accounting.

"I imagine she'd have some sort of experience. It won't

Lily's MECHANIC

be a lot. The airport will have minimal expenses, but there'll be a lot of deposits."

"What about your mechanical work? Don't you order parts and have to bill clients?"

Now his stomach churned. He hated paperwork and would need someone for that too. Maybe Lily could take on both.

"For now, I'll do it myself, but I'll find someone."

The attorney heaved a long sigh. "These are good problems. By the way, I like what you've done to the hangar. I spoke to your contractor, and he seems to think you'll be able to open on time."

His hand went to his neck, and he rolled his shoulders. Rob shouldn't have spoken to the attorney. "I hadn't wanted to say anything until everything was done."

"No need. I think you'll be fine. Come around the office next week with the signed contracts so I can look at them and we'll discuss the next steps."

Excitement throbbed throughout his body. "Does that mean the airport is mine?"

"It means I reserve judgment until I examine the signed contracts."

The wind just knocked out of him like a jet blast, and his prior elation disappeared in a nanosecond.

"What exactly does that mean? If I have signed contracts, it should be—"

"I want to see you succeed, but I have to follow the terms of the will." Bottleson huffed out a puff of air. "Instead of next week, why don't we wait until after the open house when you might have more contracts signed, then we can meet."

His shoulders slumped. If he badgered the attorney, the man would clam up and it would be worse.

"Great. See you then."

After he hung up, he threw the phone on the desk. Bottleson hit every one of his last nerves.

It was time to tackle the den and sort through the hundreds of books his uncle kept on the three built in floor-to-ceiling bookshelves. He grabbed the four-step ladder he spotted in the living room closet and dragged it to the office.

One by one, he painstakingly opened each book and determined if he'd keep, pitch, or donate it. Dust flew as he pulled each one from its spot. The particles made him sneeze. How long it had been since anyone had moved the books to clean was anyone's guess.

Rather than move the ladder, he stretched to reach the last highest shelf closest to the doorway when his hand slipped, and the book hit the ladder and sailed across the room.

A key and piece of paper flew out of the book.

He tensed and held his breath as he watched the paper flutter to the floor and the key bounce away from it. His heart pumped faster as he jumped off the ladder and grabbed the two items.

Opening the folded paper, his hands shook as he read his uncle's precise handwriting.

Carson.

I knew you'd go through the books first, so if you're reading this, it means I'm no longer with the living but spending eternity with my Jesus. The key is important and unlocks the trail to the treasure.
Go find it, my boy.

Uncle Patrick

Great. Not only was he searching for a treasure, but now it had become a scavenger hunt.

When his phone blared, he jerked and placed a hand on his chest.

"Carson Brown." His voice shook. Why was he so jumpy? He had no reason to be except the letter proved there actually was a treasure. Or was his uncle playing the ultimate prank?

Ben chuckled. "What's up with you, man?"

"You caught me coming off a ladder."

"What are you doing?"

"I'm clearing out old books from my uncle's den so I can clean and paint it. What's up with you?"

"I'd offer to help, but I'm at my former commanding officer's home. I was supposed to stay at Amy's place again, but he insisted I stay here. I wanted to let you know I'll be at Worthy church with him and his family in the morning."

"That's across town from my church, but no problem. Come over after lunch tomorrow and we can go over the paperwork and take the kids flying."

"Excellent. Let's get it done before the boys show up at three."

He slumped into his uncle's worn chair and stared at the tiny key in the palm of his hand, then glanced at the multitude of books and the rest of the shelves he had to clear.

No way could he leave the room in such a disarray. Carefully placing the key and note back in the book, he carried it upstairs, and put it in his nightstand drawer before he went back downstairs. The rest of the books held no other clues.

As he took the last of the cartons to the guest room across the hall, looking for a keyhole somewhere in the house overwhelmed him, and the daunting undertaking would take a considerable amount of time. The idea of an opening that small being anywhere in the house made his nerves jangle.

He made himself some dinner. The darn key took up res-

198

idence and rattled around in his brain like a flag flapping in the wind. What in the world could the treasure be? More importantly, where was it? He still wasn't sure he wasn't wasting his time. Instead of working in the hangar or catching a game and chilling out, he stressed over a key and a treasure. Exhaustion overtook him, and he wanted nothing more than to shower and go to bed.

Fear curdled in his stomach. His uncle had been called a nut job, so he couldn't tell anyone about the note and key.

He slapped his head in frustration at something he should have been doing all along. Pray.

Tomorrow was a bust. With the joy ride with the boys, the treasure would have to wait.

Lily's father sipped his coffee and eyed her over the rim. "Have you made an appointment yet?"

She glanced at her sons and shook her head.

"What appointment, Mom?" Lucas bit into his toast.

Her sons were not only curious, they were protective. Something she had not shared with her father, but by now he should at least know they were inquisitive.

Pursing her lips, she released them and smiled at her son. "I need my annual checkup. I didn't get one before we left Austin." She glared at her father. "Farfar gave me a reminder."

Evan's wary eyes shifted from her to her father. "Are you sick, Mom?" His lower lip trembled and the last thing she needed right now was her sons to be worried she'd leave them too.

She cocked her head and quirked one side of her face. "Do I look sick? It's a checkup and bloodwork." She wanted

Lily's MECHANIC

to promise him she was fine, but she couldn't. She just didn't know if she was.

It definitely was time.

Her father cleared his throat. "We need to get ready for church. You boys through?" When they nodded, he motioned to the sink. "Put your plates in the dishwasher and get dressed."

The boys dragged their feet but did as they were told and left the room.

When she heard them upstairs, she leaned forward and crossed her arms. "I'd appreciate it if you didn't talk about my potential health issues in front of them. They are still reeling from their father's abandonment and death. They don't need to worry about me too."

His face was a mask of contrition. "It just popped out. Get the blood test and I won't mention it again."

She rose from the table. "Well, make more of an effort. If not for me, but for them. I plan to make the appointment tomorrow. I can't hold off any longer."

"Good." He got up and went to the door and turned. His eyes had a sadness about them she hadn't ever seen. "I truly am sorry."

She stepped to him to give him a hug and a smile of encouragement. "I know you are. Just try, OK?"

He gave her a hurried nod and went to his room to change.

The drive to church was silent, with everyone focused on their own thoughts. She calculated how much room she had on her credit card now and figured she could charge the test. Lucas and Evan glanced back at her as they made their way to kids' church.

Her father leaned in. "I see what you mean."

200

She squeezed his hand. "Just don't mention it again."

They were early, and she sought Mia in the back of the church as she changed her toddler's diaper. "What's your schedule this week?"

Her friend looked up. "It's funny. It's either feast or famine with my work. This week it's famine so I'm free." Mia lifted the baby in her arms and her brow puckered. "What's up?"

She moved closer so she could be discreet. "I need to make the appointment to get the blood test done. Will you go with me?" she whispered. "I'm a big baby about needles."

Her friend had been upset and saddened when she had told her about her father's illness and her need to have a blood test to find out if the gene was present. Lily had asked her to keep the situation confidential.

Mia glanced at the women who stood nearby and frowned. "Do it and text me the details."

They understood one another and went in different directions, Mia to the toddler room and her into the sanctuary, just in time for the first song.

She glanced at her father and then back at the entrance, but Carson wasn't there. He said he'd be in church.

Just as the pastor went to the podium, Carson slipped into their row at the far side.

Worry lines framed his face and his eyes looked puffy, as if he hadn't gotten enough sleep. The trip to Norfolk and the renovation seemed to have taken a toll on him.

She'd have to encourage him. How, she didn't know. She couldn't even take care of her own health issues. Prayer was the answer for them both, but she hadn't prayed with him since before he left for the military.

When church was over, people came by to chat with her and her father. Carson stepped over to the pastor and spoke

Lily's MECHANIC

to him for a few minutes.

They met up in the parking lot. She mentally coached her father not to invite Carson to lunch.

He walked to them and extended his hand to her father. "Nils. How are you doing today?"

"I'm just–" A coughing fit took over, and he wheezed.

Alarm rang through her body and her concern spiked. "Dad. What's going on? You've had that cough for a while."

"I'm fine, Lily. I cough now and again, that's all."

Carson glanced at her, and she shivered though it was near ninety degrees. "I think we need to talk to the doctor."

"No doctor. I'm fine. And that's final."

She stepped back. Her dad was in one of his moods and she could use someone in her corner. As much as she hadn't wanted to invite Carson, she turned to him. "Want to come for lunch? I made a big pan of lasagna."

His smile widened even as he glanced at her father. "I'd love to. I wanted to ask if we're still on with taking the boys flying."

Her father lifted his eyes and smiled. "It sure is. Right, Lily?"

"Sure." Her eyes narrowed. "You've renewed your license to fly, right?"

He laughed and took her hand. "Of course. I wouldn't have offered if I didn't have my credentials up to date. If it makes you feel any better, my good friend Ben, will co-pilot. He was in the Navy and has been flying for years."

Nils beamed. "That's terrific and will make Lily feel even more comfortable."

"We'll tell them after lunch," she said.

Her worry over the blood test had her questioning things she normally wouldn't. She had to get a grip.

Lord, help me.

202

Chapter 20

Carson tried to be cool and professional, but his chest puffed out in pride as he watched Lucas and Evan. They went to every person at the open house, telling them how awesome flying was and how he was the best pilot ever.

Now that the tour was over, his nerves settled, and he enjoyed the crisp blue and cream décor. It made the terminal and its offices comfortable and inviting.

The decorator had been wild about his uncle's black and white airplane art collection. The guests loved them. He'd spent time researching the background on each plane and the drawings. The description had been placed beneath each frame. Two of his favorites hung in his office in the terminal.

The local news fell all over themselves for an exclusive, in-depth interview. He deferred because he wanted to corner Lily about being the new manager so she could handle the press for him.

All he wanted to do was work on the planes—and find the treasure.

Lily quick-stepped to him and her breath whooshed out. "I'm so sorry. I called Bobby. He'll be here in fifteen minutes to keep the boys busy, so they don't bother the guests. I should have brought him along in the first place."

203

Lily's MECHANIC

She looked around in dismay, as if she were ready to wring her hands. Her sons' attendance at a work function was out of her comfort zone, but her discomfort was cute.

He leaned in and winked. "They're having a good time. They're the best advertising. Chill out, Lily."

Her eyebrows rose and her mouth dropped open. "You're not mad?"

Rubbing his thumb on the back of her hand, he frowned. "Why would I? They're boys. Boys who loved going high in the sky." He lifted his arms as if he were ready to take off.

She pulled her hand from his and jerked around and scanned the clumps of people for her sons. "I still think they're a little too exuberant."

"It's not a big deal. They just dragged my attorney, Mr. Bottleson, outside."

Her brows rose. "They did?"

"Yeah. My guess is they wanted to show him the planes and he'll ask them questions to keep them busy until Bobby gets here."

People mingled, ate the scrumptious food from the Countryside Diner and munched on Amy's pastries. They wove in and out of the terminal offices. He pulled her into the administrative office and locked the door.

Her arms flailed and her voice rose. "What are you doing? We need to get back out there and schmooze."

"We will, but I need to talk to you for five minutes." He chuckled and went to the desk and pulled out paperwork. "We got another dozen pilots who want to park their planes and the president of the Pilot Training Association told me their membership was unanimous to have their school here. They'll sign a two-year contract for six offices." He laughed. "The airport will be very busy."

"Oh, my goodness. That's terrific. You already have more than half the offices rented." She walked into his arms and gave him a robust hug.

He held her to his chest and the scent of her coconut shampoo gave him courage. "Have you decided on the airport manager's position? I desperately need your help."

She pulled back and drew her hand through her hair, looking away. "I thought I'd be able to tell you now, but I can't. Not yet."

He frowned and his heart pitched. "Why?"

She stepped out of the circle of his arms and placed her hand on her heart. "I went to get the blood test yesterday. Until I'm sure of my health issues, I don't want to commit to anything."

"Great. Now, what am I going to do?" He shoved his hands in his pockets and frowned. He shook his head. "Sorry, Lil. I should be thinking about your health. You've had more than enough on your plate. Forget I asked. I'll figure something out."

Stepping over to him, she tapped his chest. "I'll help you get through this phase of the process because, honestly, I don't think you need a full-time manager." She smiled and nodded. "I truly think you can do it on your own. You just need a process in place."

"I guess that answers the question about us, too, doesn't it?" Every nerve in his body screamed he should have seen it coming, but he had been too wound up by seeing her again. He should have known better.

Her back stiffened. "You're jumping to conclusions, Carson. The job has nothing to do with our relationship. I still want to explore that. I just can't commit to a full-time job right now. I have to know if I'm destined to have my father's

disease." She practically choked on the last words.

He forced a slight smile and drew a forefinger down her cheek. "Fine," he whispered. "We need to go back to our guests."

She grabbed his arm and smiled. "We'll work to set up everything next week while Rob finishes the hangar. OK?"

A ghost of the past filled his spirit, and he worried this was a turning point. *A turning point for what, though?*

They left the office and saw Bobby kept the boys occupied with food and treats.

Lily would have a tough time tonight with sugared-up boys. Unless, of course, they crashed because of the excitement.

He mingled with guests who wanted more information, which he supplied. Lily fielded questions like a pro and worked the room, but exhaustion etched her features, and he was certain his face mirrored the same weariness.

When the last of the guests had left, the boys came in from outside, bumping into the sitter as they walked.

"You can take off now, Bobby." Lily grabbed Evan's hand and Lucas's shoulder with the other. "I'll take over now."

"No problem, Mrs. Bennett," Bobby said.

"Let me just pay you."

"Mr. Brown already took care of it."

"He did?" She turned narrowed eyes his way. "Go get in the car, boys. I'll be right there."

When her sons left, he cleared his throat and gave her a tentative smile. "Don't worry about it, Lily. Consider it a work-related expense."

She harrumphed and got her things together. "You *will* take the payment off my next paycheck."

"Come on, Lily. Don't be like that."

Her glare caused him to take a step back. "I mean it,

Carson." Her shoulders slumped, and she placed a hand on his chest. "You don't understand how it was in Austin."

He put his hand over hers. "OK. I'll take what I paid him from your next paycheck."

"Thank you. I have to go."

He walked her out of the terminal and waited until he could no longer see the taillights on her car.

He leaned back and looked at the dark sky. Despite it having been an extraordinarily long day... and night, the beauty of the twinkling stars held his attention for a few minutes before he locked up.

He headed into the house, but the lock for the key was uppermost in his mind. He'd renew his efforts next week after he spoke to the attorney.

The boys, despite their overindulgence with sampling every dessert at the open house, were about to crash, and Lily needed to get them in bed before she had to carry Evan up the stairs. He was too big now, and forget carrying Lucas.

She glanced in the living room and saw her dad had already gone to bed. Good. He needed his sleep too.

By the time she got the boys ready for bed, her limbs dragged, and she longed for sleep.

When she finally dropped into bed, she fell asleep before the covers were drawn up to her neck.

She awoke groggy but washed her face, dressed, and went to the kitchen to fix breakfast. Her sons were already there, dressed for church and prepping for their usual Sunday morning breakfast.

"We're hungry, Mom." Lucas measured out the ingredi-

ents for pancakes. There was more flour on the counter than in the bowl, so she took over.

As they sat down, she frowned. "Did you see Farfar go out to the barn?"

"No," they chorused, then stuffed their mouths with the crisp cut up melon.

Before she put the pancakes on the griddle, she went to her father's door and knocked. "Dad. It's late. We have church this morning."

Silence met her, so she twisted the knob and the door creaked as she looked in.

The bed hadn't been slept in.

She flicked the light and ran into the bathroom. He wasn't there.

She raced into the living room and looked around. He wasn't on the floor anywhere.

The barn.

As she ran out the door, she saw her sons jog after her as she glanced over her shoulder. "Go back in the house. Call Carson."

"But, Mom," Lucas said.

"Do it, Lucas," she screamed as she made a beeline to the barn and opened the old door. It stuck, and she pounded on it.

She switched on the light. The truck was parked in its normal spot, as was the ATV. Then she saw his feet. Gulping air as if she had been under water too long, she made her way around the haystack to the back corner of the barn.

Tears fell on her cheeks as she dropped to her knees and grabbed his hand. He was cold and breathing unnaturally. She checked his pulse, and it was fast. At least it seemed fast.

Lucas rushed in and his chest heaved. "Carson is on his way."

"Give me the phone, Lucas."

"I left it in the house."

Evan came in slowly. "I have it."

Her hand shook as she reached for the phone. "Bring it to me." She could barely get the words out.

She tapped in 911 and turned to see her sons holding one another as they backed away from her and her father. A strange calmness came over her. As if the Holy Spirit had come alongside her and girded her up. She told the operator her father was unconscious but breathing and to send an ambulance. Despite her inner peace, the address came out choppy and stilted.

"Go watch for Carson," she whispered and nodded to them.

They turned and raced out of the barn.

"Dad, wake up." She patted his hand and face until Carson trotted over to her.

"What happened?"

She glanced back at her sons and lowered her voice. "I don't know, but his hands are cold. In fact, he's cold all over."

He turned to the boys. "Can you get some blankets for your grandfather?"

They ran out of the barn.

"What do you think happened?

A tear fell, and she shook her head. She couldn't get another word out.

"I don't think we should move him in case he's injured."

"I should call Bobby to come and take care of the boys." Her voice wobbled and her hands still shook.

Carson cocked his head. "Wouldn't he be on his way to church?"

"You're right, he would be. The boys are terrified." Her stomach cramped with nausea.

Lily's MECHANIC

"I know. I'll take care of them. We'll follow the ambulance to the hospital. You can ride with your dad."

Sirens split the morning quiet, and the flashing lights reflected on the truck in the barn.

Carson escorted the boys to his truck and told them to get in.

One of the EMTs jogged over to her dad and crouched down. "I'm Kate. Can you tell me what happened?"

The woman took his vitals while Lily stood and watched. She wrapped her arms around her waist. "I don't know. My boys and I came home last night around ten. I thought..." Choking, she swallowed. "I thought he'd gone to bed. When he didn't come to breakfast, I went to check on him. He wasn't there and... and I panicked."

Kate looked up at her as she listened to her father's heartbeat. "It's OK. You did the right thing. We'll take good care of him."

She glanced at the boys. Their faces pressed to the windows inside Carson's truck. "You don't understand. He has Huntington's Disease."

Kate's brows rose and her eyes widened. "We need to move. Now."

Both EMTs loaded her dear father into the ambulance, and they sped off to the hospital with Carson following as best as he could.

She vaguely heard Kate tell the hospital the patient had Huntington's Disease, then asked her who her father's physician was. The EMT administered oxygen and kept checking his vitals. A grim look on her face.

The reality of her father's disease slammed into her, and it could very well be her life as well. It was too much... for her... and for Carson.

She loved him with the depth of love of a woman who had suffered an intense hurt, but she wouldn't give him such a devastating future. He had been a sweet boy who had turned into a caring, loving man. She'd walk away to protect him from the anguish.

"Dad." She rocked back and forth and held her father's hand and kissed it. "Please wake up. Don't leave me."

Pain writhed throughout her entire body. She hadn't prayed in all the time she was in Austin, not even when she'd been at her lowest point. Not even when it was the best thing for her. She had only recently started praying for everything in her life.

Would God answer her prayer?

Chapter 21

For the second time in a matter of weeks, Carson sped to the hospital, but this time he had Lily's boys with him.

Words eluded him, so he kept quiet and maintained a comforting presence. It would be worse if he told them their grandfather would be OK, and he wasn't.

Both boys were subdued and silent, and it pained him. He couldn't imagine Lily's state of mind right now dividing her worry between her father and her sons.

The heavy guilt weighed on him and compounded the situation. If he hadn't had the open house last night, Lily would have been at home and would have known her father hadn't returned from the barn. How would he ever apologize to her?

When they arrived at the hospital, Lucas took Evan's hand and walked ahead of him into the emergency room.

Lily wasn't in the waiting room. The hospital must have put her closer to her father's room.

Lucas pulled on his arm. "Where's Mom?"

A frown pinched his brow, and he blinked. "She's probably with your grandfather in the ER."

Evan stepped closer to him. "Can we go too?"

His heart cracked with a longing to comfort Lily's sons. "We need to let the doctors do their job and take care of your

212

grandad. Your mom will come out when she can. I texted her. She knows we're here."

With heads hung, they shuffled to a bank of chairs opposite the two doors to the ER and sat close to one another.

While he kept the boys busy the last time, he wasn't certain he could keep them occupied like he had then.

Just as he had planned some sort of conversation in his head, Lily burst through the doors with red-rimmed eyes. She quick-stepped across the room as they stood and waited. The boys squeezed his forearms and moved closer to him.

His heartbeat thumped so fast he thought he'd hyperventilate, and he surreptitiously took long, even breaths to keep calm.

She squatted before the boys. "Farfar..." her voice choked, and he could tell she struggled with every word. "He's very sick..."

When he chanced a glance at the boys, they held their tears in check.

Lucas stepped over to her. "Is he going to die?" he whispered.

Tear tracks dampened her cheeks as she gazed at her two sons. "I don't know. It doesn't look good."

"Can we see him?" Evan's voice was tiny and heartfelt. His slight hand tightened around his mother's wrist.

The need on her face gave her away, and Carson gave her one vigorous nod. He could have taken the boys home and stayed with them, but she needed him more.

She swallowed and her body stilled. "I called Mia to come and get you."

Lucas hugged his mother and stood tall and stiff. "Mom. We want to say goodbye."

The boy had the makings of a good, no, great man.

213

Lily's MECHANIC

He cleared his throat. "I'll wait for Mia and have the nurse come get them if they aren't back by the time she gets here."

"He won't be able to speak to you, Lucas. He's... He has a lot of equipment attached to him." Her voice was barely above a whisper, and he could see the struggle etched on her face.

"Doesn't matter. We want to say goodbye. We didn't get a lot of time with him, but he was good to us, and we want to do the right thing." Lucas stood stock still and waited in silence for his mother's decision.

Evan took his cues from his older brother, but his lips trembled from the effort to not cry.

She rose from her position and squeezed both boys' arms and gave them a tiny sad smile. "Let's go."

They slowly crossed the room, and she turned her head toward him and blinked right before they went through the doors.

He paced back and forth in the room, rubbing the back of his neck glaring at those double doors as he passed them. Determined to stay with her until the doctors gave them an update... or until the end. A hand on his forearm startled him.

Mia pulled her hand away. "I'm so sorry, Carson. I can't believe it. Where are the boys?"

He swallowed, the stench of hospital smell filtered into him. "They wanted to say goodbye to their grandfather."

"Lily and her boys have had it rough these past years, and now this." The woman shook her head, stepped to a chair, and sat.

Mia told him how Drew could be a comfort to the boys because he had lost his grandmother.

"Let me see if I can—"

The doors swung open, and Lily made her way to Mia. Lily's best friend comforted her the best way she could with

214

a hearty embrace.

Lucas and Evan's red-rimmed eyes told their own story as they stared at the floor and dragged their feet to the two women who whispered to one another.

He couldn't tell what was being said, so he hugged the boys to himself, and they stretched and tucked themselves to his side and tightened their hold around his waist. He couldn't have spoken if his life depended on it. The boulder-sized lump in his throat wouldn't move, and his heart shattered for the woman he loved and the boys who had become like sons to him.

How would he comfort them? This was new territory. He hadn't needed to comfort anyone in a long time, especially not children. He shifted his head and held on to the boys.

Lily turned pain-streaked eyes to him and forced her lips to a slight curve. "Thank you for waiting, Carson. Mia will take the boys home and I need to get back to dad's room."

"I'm staying." The gravel in his voice scared him and he couldn't imagine how it sounded to them.

Mia crouched in front of the boys. "Drew is waiting for you, but he'll understand if you don't want to play or talk."

Lucas stood straight and pulled his shoulders back. "We're ready." Then he turned to his mother. "Will you call us?"

She gathered her sons in her arms. "I'll call you later to check on you. It's best if you stay with Mia…" Her voice trailed off and tears seeped out of her eyes and down her cheeks.

Carson stood next to her as the boys walked away. Mia tried to engage them, but they seemed to be too wrapped up thinking about their grandfather to pay attention until they got to the door and turned. Both boys gave her a chin nod.

It amazed him how observant the boys had been. They must have seen him do that when they'd been with him.

Lily's MECHANIC

After they went out the door, he took Lily's hand and sat with her. "Tell me what's going on."

She could barely talk but just leaned into him. "The doctor told me he probably won't live through the night. The disease exasperated the double pneumonia. He hasn't woken up. I should have paid more attention to that cough, but he blew me off."

"He wouldn't have wanted you to fuss over him. All the times I've seen him, he forced himself to be the man he'd always been. There wouldn't have been anything you could do. He and Uncle Patrick were from a different generation. They did what they had to do for their families and for themselves."

"There wasn't enough time. I never got to tell him how much I loved him."

Her sniffles killed him. "He knew how much you loved him, Lily. You came home. You got the bills paid and turned the old farmhouse back into a home with love and care."

"It wasn't enough," she mumbled into his shirt.

He pulled away. "Listen to me. Everything you did for him, for the farm, for your boys, you did out of love. They know it even if they don't tell you."

"Why didn't God answer my prayer, Carson? I've been on my knees asking God to intervene."

"How do you know he hasn't?"

At her shocked look, he rubbed her back. "Think about it. Nils is a proud man. He wouldn't want to be a ghost of himself. Like my uncle, I think he had a sense of how much time he had left. It might not be what you want to hear, but he told me a few times he wanted to pass before he became an invalid." He drew a deep breath and hugged her to him. No way would he tell her all the things her father made him promise. The timing was terrible. It had to wait. "Let's go sit

with your father. You can still tell him how much you love him, Lily. Even if he's unconscious, the mind can hear."

He got up and offered his hand to her, and they walked hand-in-hand through the ER to get to her father's room.

It was at the end of the corridor, away from all the hustle and bustle of a typical ER.

He stood behind her as she sat and took her father's hand. She told him how much she loved him and how happy she was they had returned to Worthy. His throat dried up as he rubbed her shoulders.

Heart monitors beeped and slowed as the ventilator forced oxygen into the old man's lungs. Aside from Lily's frequent murmurs, those were the only sounds in the room.

Lily glanced up at the man who'd left her all those years ago. "You don't have to stay. You've been here for hours."

Carson squeezed her shoulders. "Yeah, I do. He was… is my uncle's best friend. I want to honor their friendship, but I'm staying to support you."

At the stalwart look in his eyes, she nodded and turned to her father when the alarms on the machines went off, and the nurses rushed in. "Step outside."

The roar around her and in her head threatened to level her when Carson grabbed her under the arms and pulled her out of the chair. It happened in a matter of seconds, but it seemed to go in slow motion.

Down the hall, she melted into Carson's arms, and he hugged her tightly. It was just what she needed. She'd already said her goodbyes earlier when the boys had been with her.

Carson stiffened and she looked up at him and followed

his gaze to the doctor coming out of the room, and she knew.

Her father was gone.

"I'm very sorry for your loss." The doctor's words scarcely registered. "We'll give you a few minutes with him and the nurse will be in to talk to you."

"Thank you."

She wrapped her arms around Carson's waist and melted into him as they walked back to her father's room.

The silence in the room startled her after the hum the equipment made. The ventilator had been taken out, and her father had a peaceful look on his face.

"He's in the arms of Jesus, now," Carson whispered. "No more pain, no more sorrow."

No words passed her lips, they stuck in her throat. The scripture verse 2 Corinthians 5:8 pounded in her brain and embedded itself in her heart. *Absent from the body, present with the Lord.*

She kissed her father on the cheek and turned when the most compassionate nurse she'd ever met gave her a hug and a card and told her to call with the name of the funeral home.

A final touch of her lips to her father's cheek, and she left the hospital with Carson at her side.

In silence, they walked to his truck and got in. Thankfully, Carson hadn't pressured her to talk. Her throat closed, and she couldn't have formed a word, let alone a cohesive sentence.

Her mind went in a thousand directions at once, but what was foremost in her brain disgusted her. Was the disease her father suffered in her future as well?

She should have gotten the blood test weeks ago like her father wanted, but she shook her head and focused on the next practical things she had to do. Her father's funeral, her sons, and the farm took precedence over her own health.

"Lily?" Carson's voice came from faraway and had a strange quality about it.

The trip back to the farm went unnoticed, but she turned to look at him as they stopped in front of the farmhouse.

"I can't talk about anything right now, Carson. I need to call Mia and see about the boys."

He placed a hand on her arm. "I'm worried about you."

She squeezed his hand and her heart shattered as she moved to get out of the truck without a word.

Carson's hand on her arm stopped her. "I don't want to leave you here alone. I'll stay and sleep on the couch."

She inhaled and stared at his neck, not wanting to see the love in his eyes. "You've been my rock, but I just need to be alone."

"Please, Lily."

Pulling away, she straightened, and got out of the truck. "I appreciate the offer more than you know. I'll call if I need you."

She mentally cataloged everything she had to do as she opened the door to the farmhouse. But in the end, with the horrible disease hanging over her head, there was no way she'd entertain a relationship with Carson. She couldn't put him through it. She loved him too much to give him that kind of heartache. And what about her boys?

Chapter 22

The sun shone brightly, a direct contrast to the cool, dreary day yesterday when the last shovel of dirt was thrown on Lily's father's grave. The smell of the fresh earth would stay with her for a long time. With a splintered heart, she had stood with her arms around her sons' shoulders and had willed herself not to cry. She had to be strong for them.

Carson paid his respects and came to the house after the funeral, but he kept his distance. She'd told him she'd talk to him when she was ready. Minimal interactions with him had made it easier to walk away, but her heart ached at what could have been.

Her boys had been more than helpful in the past week with so many callers and the tremendous outpouring of love from their church and her friends.

It grieved her she hadn't been able to share her father had been ill all along. She hadn't wanted her children to know, nor could she stand anyone's pity.

A meeting had been scheduled with William Bottleson this morning after she took the boys to school. She hadn't known Patrick McClellan's attorney was her father's too. Nor had she known her father had a will. They'd never talked about it.

What would become of the farm? Of her? Of her children?

It kept her awake last night as she tossed and turned. She'd done everything she could think of to keep the farm going since she returned. The farm store and the cows were tended to as her father would have wanted. She even manned the store for a few hours every day, kept her farmhands busy, and managed her children's activities at school while remotely overseeing the last of the airport renovation tasks.

When the doorbell rang, she wiped her wet hands on a dishtowel and made her way to the front door to greet the attorney.

The man extended his hand, and she shook it.

"I'm sorry for your loss, Lily. Your father wanted me to talk to you as soon as possible after his death."

"Come in."

She led him through the old house to the office.

He surveyed the interior of the house with a keen eye. "You've done wonders with the farmhouse since you returned. Your dad was happy and grateful to have you home."

She was thankful he hadn't mentioned the outside should be painted like he'd told Carson about Patrick's house. She wasn't in the mood to discuss the farm's shortcomings or needed repairs.

"I know." The words poured out as if by rote, but his words settled within her spirit like a warm blanket on a chilly morning. "Have a seat."

She sat behind the antique oak desk and leaned in. "Dad's finances weren't the best, but I've done what I could."

The attorney pulled a folder out of his brown case, set it on the desk, pulled his bifocals out of his pocket, and perched them on his nose. "Your father bought a life insurance policy when your mother passed away. It's not a lot, but I'm sure it'll cover the hospital bills and final expenses."

Lily's MECHANIC

She stiffened and laid her hands flat on the desk. "I didn't know."

Bottleson's face hadn't given anything away, but his eyes overflowed with sympathy. "Your father hadn't wanted you to know he was sick, either."

"You knew?"

He lifted his chin and tightened his grip on the folder. "Yes. I'm not speaking out of turn since both men are deceased, but when your mother passed, Patrick McClellan was instrumental in ensuring Nils bought life insurance. Your dad was heartbroken. I don't think he ever got over the loss. Patrick also encouraged him to get his affairs in order when he was diagnosed."

Good thing she was sitting, or she'd have fallen on the floor. She didn't know Carson's uncle had helped with her father's affairs or that her dad had even arranged anything. Her concern was more for his health than any plan he might have had. The policy wasn't in the farm office. But she hadn't gone into his room since she'd returned.

Bottleson cleared his throat. "I'll read the will now."

As the attorney read, her mind drifted to Carson and his uncle and wove back and forth while Bottleson read the legalese.

"I know it's overwhelming right now." His gaze softened. "I'll file the forms to transfer the farm into your name once the death certificate becomes available. I have the policy and agency contact information in the folder. Perhaps, if you're judicious, it will go a little further in making any necessary farm repairs."

He pushed paperwork to her, and she read through them and signed the highlighted sections.

She handed him the documents, and he gave her the

policy. Her eyes widened as she glanced at the amount. "This is a lot of money. Did Patrick help fund the policy?"

His lips tightened, and from his stance, she had offended him. "We were all good friends, Lily. Nils was inconsolable, and we helped as much as we could, but ultimately, it was his decision. As far as I know, your father made the payments. We made sure he could mentally decide. I assure you neither Patrick nor I had anything to do with the money."

"So, you didn't know the property taxes hadn't been paid in some years?"

The attorney's eyes widened, a sure sign he'd been kept in the dark. Her mind pondered if Patrick was aware of the farm's financial status. Carson wouldn't have known either. He hadn't been around when it all went down, so she couldn't ask him.

With the proceeds, she'd be able to pay off her father's medical and funeral expenses and she might even pay off the back taxes. But she'd rather have her father goading her about the stupid treasure than the money.

And it would mean she wouldn't have to work for Carson. She could concentrate on making the farm viable for her sons and their future.

Bottleson had given Carson a thumbs up when he perused the airport contracts. He had fulfilled all the will's requirements, and he'd signed all the paperwork for the transfer. The airport was his. The taste of success excited him and gave him a bounce in his step.

But it was time to move onto other things. His living space had to be organized before the airport opened and he

Lily's MECHANIC

was inundated with work.

Planes had landed and parked on the new tarmac. The smell of the tar overshadowed the manure next door. He'd been meeting with the pilot training group all week to prepare for them to open their offices at the terminal, but he hadn't seen Lily except when he went to the funeral. As much as it pained him, she'd made it clear she needed time, but she popped into his brain several times a day and he missed her presence.

Other than to express his condolences, he hadn't spoken to her much after the funeral. The boys had seemed OK, and he chatted with them for a bit. They'd been enthusiastic about the planes flying overhead and wanted to see all of them.

There had been too many people flowing in and out of her house and he had other things on his mind... like how he'd find the treasure and manage the terminal.

Lily's offer to help him set up the processes to run the airport would have to wait since she was dealing with her father's death. He understood, but he still had a job to do. He'd keep manual records until he could hire someone.

The rain and the rolls of thunder kept him inside, away from the final things still happening in the hangar. Rob's two crews had made excellent progress, and they'd met the renovation's deadline with flying colors.

He'd be holed up in his uncle's house all day, cleaning out the den, pulling up the filthy carpeting, hoping there were hardwood floors underneath.

Ben had been by the day before and helped him move the furniture from the office out into the garage. He loved the desk, so he'd called a refinisher to pick it up.

He rolled the dirty carpet and padding from the window back to the far wall and was pleased with the condition of

the uncovered floors. They'd need to be sanded and refinished, but it didn't have to happen today.

He'd paint the bookcases a bright white and the walls a pale coffee, all the while hoping for inspiration on where to look for a keyhole that fit the key.

Tugging at the carpet, he hit a snag under the bookcase by the door. When he stopped and examined what kept the rug from moving, his fingers passed over something on the toe kick near the wall.

He laid on the filthy rug grimacing at the odor and then moved his hand over the baseboard. What was it? He popped to his feet, got a flashlight, and returned to the floor.

A keyhole.

Could it be?

He jumped up and went to his room and pulled the key from the book and raced back to the office.

A grin spread across his face. "Uncle Patrick, you sly dog. It was here all along."

His hand trembled as he put the key in the hole. It fit. He stilled, then turned the key, and the lock clicked.

Now what?

Further examination showed a small piece of the baseboard had no caulking where the keyhole was, so maybe it could be moved. But the area was too small for a treasure, wasn't it?

"What are you up to, Uncle Patrick?" he muttered to himself.

He moved his hand over the small toe kick piece, and it moved. He pulled and off it came, along with a plume of dust that made him sneeze. The filth in the den alone was enough to damage his lungs.

The flash of light in the tight space exposed a small narrow box. He wedged his fingers in and pulled it out. It was

the size of an old-fashioned pencil case.

He sat cross-legged on the floor and was just about to open it when someone pounded on the door and caused him to jerk. He hadn't expected anyone, and it was darn inconvenient.

Setting the box and key on an empty shelf, he went to the door.

Ben.

His friend brushed rain from his jacket. "You look like you've gone ten rounds with the heavy weight champ and lost. I just stopped by to check on the helicopter. Can you spare a cup of coffee?"

The last thing he needed was Ben there. *Or maybe his best friend could help.*

"Come on in."

"What are you doing?"

He led the way to the kitchen and poured his friend a cup of coffee from the pot he'd made a little while ago.

"I started to pull out the carpet in the den. It has fine hardwood floors under all that grunginess and needs to be refinished. Then I'll paint the bookcases and walls."

"You're doing all that today?"

He gave him a wide smile. "Probably not."

"Need some help? I'm waiting for a call from the pilot training group."

"Good. I hope it works out for your business." He scrubbed a hand through his hair. "Actually, I found something."

Ben straightened and his brows furrowed. "What?"

"It might be nothing, but it has to do with the buried treasure story my uncle told everyone."

"What about it? You told me it was bogus." A disbelieving smirk covered his friend's face.

226

SERALYNN LEWIS

"I found a key a while ago. And just a few minutes ago, I found the key hole."

His friend's eyes widened. "Is there a treasure?"

He lifted his shoulders at the same time he lifted his brows. "I don't know. You knocked on the door before I could open the box I found."

Ben's face fell. "Sorry."

With determination, he grabbed his friend's arm and dragged him from the room. "Come on. Let's go open the box. I bet there are more clues. I need to find the treasure, if it exists."

His friend grinned and followed him to the den. "What are best friends for except to barge in at the moment you find buried treasure on a rainy day?" Ben stopped and placed his hand on the door. "Whoa! You weren't kidding about working today. Where's the box?"

Carson pointed to the shelf and moved closer to it.

Ben's arm flew out. "Open it already."

He picked up the box and pushed the clasp over the hook, holding it away from him as dust flew in the air.

They stared at the two folded papers in the box.

Ben scratched his head and pointed. "That looks like a map." Then he chuckled. "X marks the spot."

"Brilliant deduction, for a former Navy commander. Just what I needed… a treasure map."

He unfolded it, and it was big, not unlike the size of the old travel maps you could buy at gas stations years ago. "Grab the box and let's go into the kitchen and spread it out."

"Maybe the note will shed some light on the map." Ben stepped into the hallway. "Prayer always helps too."

He grunted, closed his eyes, mouthed a quick prayer, and grabbed the papers out of the box.

Tensing, he whistled as he unfolded and read the note.

227

Lily's MECHANIC

"My uncle found part of the treasure. It's here, in the house. The map catalogs the treasure sites."

Ben stepped to the table and drew a finger over the map. "It looks like the airport. There are the buildings… the hangar, the terminal, the house, and the runway. It's crude, but from here you can see… wait, what are these red and green dots?"

He grabbed the paper again. "According to the note, the green dots have been excavated, the red ones have not… but the question is, what is the treasure?"

As he stared at the map, Patrick's land had mostly green and a few red dots, and Lily's land had red dots, but no dots were marked on the parcel his uncle purchased from Nils. He let out a huge breath.

"Is this all your land?"

He shook his head. "No." He motioned to the right side of the map. "Those trees form the border between my land and the Sandburg Farm."

Ben's nose scrunched. "It looks like there are quite a few red dots on Lily's farm. Not many are left on your land."

"We need to see just what the treasure is. It's in the basement. But I have to grab the key. The note says we'll need it."

"Has Eric been out to look at the security system?"

"He stopped by two weeks ago, and the system is operational. I blew it off before, but now I have to make doubly sure I secure the house when I'm not here."

The condition of the main living areas made the cellar and attic low priorities, so he hadn't bothered to go down the basement since he'd been back.

The cellar door opened with a creak, and he flicked the light on as he stepped on new steps. "This is different from when I was a boy."

Ben looked around the whitewashed cement block walls

and the low ceilings. "What is?"

"The walls, the steps, and the floor. My uncle did some work down here." The faint paint smell made his nose wrinkle. He looked around the cramped room filled with more stuff he'd have to pitch. It was like his uncle brought everything to the basement that he could and made it look cluttered and unkempt. His gaze swung to a wall of shelves, and he stepped over to it. "There used to be a door here to my aunt's fruit cellar."

Ben nudged the cupboard and stared at the crack against the wall. "It looks like it's been there forever."

"If I know my uncle, it's how he wanted it to look. He whitewashed the walls and painted the floors so he could store the paint on the shelves along with other stuff, so people wouldn't know there was a room behind it. I know because my uncle kept surplus canned goods and other stuff in there."

Ben pointed to Carson's hand. "How does it fit anywhere? That's a really small key."

Excitement flowed through his veins as he marveled at what he was about to uncover. "It is. Let's take the stuff off the shelves and look for a small keyhole."

They piled the paint cans and paraphernalia where they could since there was stuff everywhere and looked for the keyhole as they worked.

Ben grinned as he pointed to the back corner of the second shelf. "Here it is. A keyhole."

"Let's see what my uncle unearthed."

With shaking hands, he placed the key in the lock and turned. His heartbeat escalated as the shelving came away from the wall. They pulled it open to find a solitary item against the far wall in the tiny room.

He stepped over to it. "Well, I'll be. It's Uncle Patrick's

munitions chest. He had two. One he used for old tarps and stuff. It's in the hangar. And this one."

"Is it locked?"

He shook his head. "He padlocked it when I was a boy to keep me safe."

Grunting, he pulled the top open, and they both leaned in to take a look.

Ben stood beside him and whistled at the booty. "What's the story on it?"

"I don't know."

A corner of a cream-colored envelope peeped out at him under the gold coins filling the bottom of the chest.

His friend pointed to the envelope as he pulled it out from under the weight of the gold. "Maybe the envelope has more information."

He ripped it open and read the contents. "The letter said it had been buried in the early 1800s by John Baldwin, who ran an inn and only accepted gold coins. He hadn't believed in banks and buried it on his land for safekeeping. My guess is the guy forgot where he buried it."

"Anything else?"

"Yeah, Uncle Patrick had been reading in the library some years ago, when he came across the information about buried treasure in the area. His research showed the gold was somewhere on airport land. He searched and found it, but said he got tired of digging and thought he'd have folks come out. See if they could find anything under the remaining dots, if they dug anywhere near it. According to law, anything found on his land belonged to him."

"That is wild."

"It is and I'm super thankful he found it."

"There must be hundreds of coins in there. They could

be worth hundreds of thousands of dollars, maybe millions. What are you going to do?"

"Don't get ahead of yourself. I should get a safe deposit box at the bank."

"What for? Your uncle installed a state-of-the-art security system, and rightfully so. You need to get the stash appraised."

"I can't transport it all to an appraiser. Do you think I'm nuts?"

Ben rolled his eyes. "We'll count it. See if there are different type coins and you take *one* of each to the appraiser. Then you'll know how much it's worth."

"Good idea. Nils was right."

"About what?"

"He was sure Uncle Patrick had found a buried treasure, and he made me think... why would Uncle Patrick install such an expensive system if there wasn't anything to be secured? You saw what was upstairs. There was nothing of value in the house."

"Other than the gold." Ben smirked.

"Right."

The gold count yielded three different coin types. He marked how many of each on his uncle's note and took photos, then pocketed one of each.

"Let's go and research who can do the appraisal."

They replaced the gold, shut the chest, and locked the door, placing all the items back on the shelving.

"You won't be able to make an appointment until Monday. You need backup?"

He slapped his buddy on the back as they made their way upstairs. "That would be great. Thanks."

He climbed the stairs two at a time to grab his laptop from his room and went back to the kitchen.

231

Ben rubbed his chin and stared at the map, then looked up. "You need to tell Lily about it, buddy."

"Not today. She's dealing with her father's death, and I haven't talked to her since the funeral."

With a nod of understanding, Ben remained silent.

The proof of the treasure was in his pocket. What would Lily think if he showed her the coins he'd found and there could be more on her land? Could he tell her, and would she believe him? What if there weren't any buried on her land?

Chapter 23

With nerves stretched taut, Carson squeezed the phone to his ear and almost fell on the floor after hearing the appraiser tell him how much just one coin could bring at auction.

Thank you, Lord. His prayers for finding the treasure had been answered. The reputable company he procured to auction off the coins was God's bonus answer.

He dialed Ben, and without waiting for a greeting, his words came out in a rush. "You won't believe how much those coins are worth. My uncle was right all along, and I didn't believe it."

"How much?"

"That stash could bring in more than a million—maybe even two million—at auction."

Ben's whistle pierced the phone line. "So now what?"

"Want to fly to New York with me tomorrow? We'll take the Cessna."

He scanned the kitchen, and a deep sense of satisfaction went through him. He could afford to replace his savings, renovate the old farmhouse, and build additional hangars and runways. The airport could be as successful as his uncle intended. He winced. Uncle Patrick would have been ecstatic to see the airport's transformation and success.

Lily's MECHANIC

"Heck yeah. But what about Lily and the red dots on her land?"

Ben's words threw an ice-cold bucket of water over him, and he shivered.

"I need to tell her."

"Yeah, you do." The exasperation in his friend's voice drifted into his ears, loud and clear.

"But what if her farm doesn't yield anything?"

"Doesn't matter. You love her and you need to man up and be honest… about everything."

If indeed there was more treasure on the Sandburg farm, Lily would have what she needed to upgrade end-of-life farm equipment and take care of any medical issues that might arise, but it would also mean she wouldn't need the manager's job—or him. *Lord, I pray she doesn't have the gene.* He'd offered the prayer every day since she told him about her father's disease.

He narrowed his gaze out to the terminal. "What do you mean, everything?"

"The treasure, the terms of the will, and how you feel about her."

A sick feeling gathered in his stomach, and it wasn't because of the expiration date on the cream he used in his coffee this morning. "What if she hates me because I wasn't honest with her?"

Ben blew out a breath. "It's a chance you'll have to take. If she loves you, then she'll come around. I see the way she looks at you, even if you don't."

"You're right. Enough time has gone by since the funeral. I need to talk to her about the manager's position anyway. But if there's treasure on her property, then she won't need the position."

"So what? She becomes your woman without all the work-related issues hanging over either of your heads. You can afford to hire an army of managers. You don't need her at the airport."

After he hung up, Carson pulled the map from its case and made copies of the portions of the map that covered the Sandburg farm and placed them in a folder, then grabbed his jacket and jumped in his truck.

He glanced at his phone. Lily's farm store would close in fifteen minutes, which meant Lily would be free to talk to him. He should have texted, but he hadn't wanted her to refuse to see him. Why was he worried? He had news that might ease her financial situation.

People trickled out of the store. Lily had given it a down home feel with cornstalks and a scarecrow on a bale of hay to welcome customers. No doubt everyone in town wanted to support Lily and the boys. For that, he was glad.

Tension in his back threatened to give way as he strode to the farm store's entrance, and he took a deep breath.

The cowbell's low pitch clanged overhead as he stepped through the door. "We close in five minutes." Lily's tired voice rose above the two women chattering, who came toward him with bags in their hands.

Dairy and freezer cases stocked with milk, cream, butter, and ice cream lined one side of the small store. Wide aisles with shelves with homemade jams, fruit bins, and crafts led the way to the counter in the back.

When he came around the corner, Lily's head was bowed, and she was staring at her phone.

He cleared his throat, and she looked up. Wariness replaced the look of concentration on her face.

"Hello, Lily. I haven't seen you since the funeral. How

are you holding up?" He shoved the folder under his arm and stuffed his shaking hands in his jacket pockets.

"I'm doing alright, actually."

Did her body seem to relax?

"The store looks good."

"Thanks."

He shifted his weight to his other foot. "We need to talk."

Her sigh was heartfelt, and it didn't bode well for the conversation he had in mind.

She turned, grabbed her jacket, and laid it on the counter. "We'll go over to the house after I close out the register and lock up."

Neither spoke during their short walk to the house, not wanting to upset the fragile bond that had forged between them.

She eyed the folder he held to his chest. "Let me get you a cup of coffee."

"That would be great."

He sat at the table like he'd done when he was a teenager and again in the more recent past, and waited. A spicy chili aroma wafted from the crock pot to surround him. The folder sat conspicuously in front of him.

She plopped into the chair opposite him and shook her head. "I can't be your manager, Carson."

"What?" His heart plummeted and his breathing sped up.

"I can't even help you beyond what we contracted for the renovation. The farm is all I can think about right now."

What if she never wanted to see him again?

"I understand, but that wasn't the only reason I stopped by." He choked out the words.

"You're not angry?"

"No. You have responsibilities at the farm. More now

than ever. Doesn't mean I'm not disappointed." *I'm still desperately in love with you.*

"I'm sorry."

And what if she had her father's disease? Eventually she'd need help and he was in a position to help even if she didn't want it. "Did you get the results of the blood test?"

She squirmed in her seat, took a sip of her coffee, and wouldn't look him in the eye. "Not yet."

"When will you know?"

"I'm not sure. What else did you want to talk about?"

He leaned back and fiddled with the handle of his coffee cup. Her change of subject told him she hadn't wanted to talk about her potential illness and for good reason. "I found the treasure." He'd blurted the words and wanted to kick himself.

Her body shot straight up, and her eyes widened. "What? You mean there actually *was* a treasure? I can't believe it." Her voice trailed in confusion. "Dad was right all along."

He kept his face bland and lifted the cup to his lips. "I'd appreciate it if you kept it confidential between you and me."

"No problem. What is it and where is it?" Excitement laced Lily's words.

"It'll stay hidden until I deal with it. I don't want everybody and their brother coming out of the woodwork to look for more. We're poised for the airport's grand opening, and I can't have that kind of chaos."

The sadness in her eyes caught him off guard. "You don't trust me."

"In the beginning, I didn't because of my past and how my uncle left his will. But it changed when your project management skills became apparent, and you hustled to make the airport renovation happen."

Lily's MECHANIC

"What about your uncle's will?"

He swallowed, then cringed. "Don't think poorly of me, Lil. I had to do what I had to do to fulfill the conditions of the inheritance."

The crease between her brows deepened. "What conditions?"

He twisted his neck as far as he could until it cracked. "I sunk almost everything I had in savings to renovate the terminal and hangar, The will stipulated I had to do that and demonstrate the airport's profitability, or it would be auctioned. And my savings weren't enough. I had to take inspection jobs and use credit cards just to take care of the shortfall."

"What does that have to do with me other than my project management skills?"

"If I failed and the property went to auction, the land your dad sold Patrick would revert back to Nils or his heirs."

She slumped back in her chair and her jaw clenched. After a moment, her gaze narrowed. "And you assumed I'd torpedo the renovation, so you'd lose the airport, and we'd get the land back?"

"The land was crucial to the airport's future and I didn't know who you'd become, Lil. It sounds awful, I know. I intended to tell you everything, but... Then your father died, and you haven't been around."

Her lips pursed as she rose and took her cup to the sink and turned to face him, her arms wrapped around her waist. "You need to leave."

"But..."

The expression she wore was her professional persona.

"The renovation will be one hundred percent complete in a few days. Anything left to do will be done via email or text, then it's over. I don't want to see you again. I can't be

238

around someone who doesn't trust me." Stilted and choppy, her words hung in the air.

When he got up, the chair skidded and clattered to the floor.

"Lily, I…"

She held her hand up and closed her eyes. "Just leave."

"I guess this is it, then."

Her eyes popped open, but the mutinous expression on her face told him everything between them was over. It was nothing like when he'd left her, when he went into the military. It was ten thousand times worse. At least then, he hadn't had to see her every Sunday in church. The visit crushed his soul.

And it was all his fault.

He grabbed the folder off the table and stumbled out the door. He had to get out of there or embarrass himself by begging. The pain consumed him, and he hadn't even shown her the maps.

As soon as the truck rumbled out of the drive, she raced upstairs and threw herself on the bed. She curled herself into a ball and sobbed. She'd kicked the love of her life out of her home.

Every time she'd asked him what the rush was on the renovation, he hadn't been truthful with her. She couldn't trust him, and it hurt. The agony was much worse than when her deceased husband deceived her.

He'd given her the perfect out to allow her to protect him from her illness and the potential illnesses of her children. It hurt worse than Christopher's thievery and what she'd endured afterward. The blood test didn't matter. Nothing did. The pain obliterated her. She loved Carson not only

as a woman loves a man, but with an agape love—an unconditional boundless love.

The months of financial stress culminated in the loss of her father, and the wait for her blood test results had taken its toll. But the loss of the only man she'd ever loved flattened her and her eyes drifted shut.

Distant musical tones forced her puffy eyes open. Was that her phone? It was downstairs. How long had she been asleep?

She lifted herself off the bed with a groan and made her way to the kitchen. Mia had called and left a message.

Rubbing the bridge of her nose, she returned Mia's call without checking voicemail.

"Are you OK?" Her friend's voice sounded frantic.

"Yeah. What's up?" She hadn't wanted to tell her friend she'd cried herself to sleep. Her foggy head couldn't understand why Mia called her.

"Did you forget to pick up the boys after the bowling birthday party after school?" There was censure in the words.

Her gaze flew to the clock and to the darkness outside. "Oh my gosh. I fell asleep. I'm so sorry, Mia."

A heartfelt sigh came over the line. "I'll drop them off. Since we were supposed to visit while the kids bowled and you didn't show, you scared the heck out of me. I've been calling off and on for over an hour. I'm just glad you're OK."

"I'm so sorry."

"I'll be there in thirty minutes."

When Lily swiped the phone, she raced upstairs to wash her face and change her clothes. The last thing she needed was Mia or her boys to see she'd been crying.

She applied a liberal amount of makeup and flew down the stairs. The crockpot chili she'd put together before the boys went to school bubbled, and the aroma filled the kitch-

en. She shoved a tray of cornbread in the oven when Mia's car rolled to a stop in the drive.

The boys trotted into the house and up to their rooms. She admonished them to clean up and come downstairs for dinner as she went through the door and strode to Mia's car.

She leaned on the open window. "I'm so sorry, Mia. Thanks for bringing them home."

Mia stared at her face, then lifted her chin. "That's what friends are for. But I'm worried about you, Lily."

"Something—"

"Mom," Lucas's voice pierced the darkness. "We're hungry."

She rubbed her forehead. "I need to get them dinner and you need to go home to your family."

Her friend shook her head. "I'll come over tomorrow after the store closes and we'll have a chat."

At her nod, Mia put her car in gear and left.

Her boys hadn't noticed the extra makeup or how quiet she was as they ate dinner.

She cleared the dishes and helped the boys with their homework, praying the evening would go by quickly.

Exhaustion and sadness had taken its toll, and she longed to rest.

When the boys had gone to bed, she sat in her father's recliner. "What am I going to do now, Dad?"

With all the doors locked, she trudged upstairs, checked on her sons and after placing soft kisses on each of their foreheads, she fell into bed.

The last image in her head was of the hurt on Carson's face before she closed her eyes.

Lily's MECHANIC

The morning flew by as Lily stocked bins and coolers to keep from thinking about the test results that had not yet come in or the potential disappointing news. She'd kept an eye on the clock and when the store finally closed, she went back to the farmhouse. She arched her back and her body ached. Could it be the start of the disease? No. She couldn't... wouldn't think negatively. She had to trust the Lord had it all in his hands.

High school kids from church agreed to help with the last of the piddly orchard harvest and prepare the trees for winter. They'd be there on the weekend to start the project. As she strolled by her garden and pulled her sweater around her, she made a mental note to have the kids help harvest the last of her summer crops and ready the ground for next year.

She'd responded to Rob's text about questions on final details of the renovation, then straightened the house before Mia arrived.

Her task list kept her mind from the two things she'd have to address when Mia showed up.

A car door slammed. She glanced out the kitchen window and waved as Mia quick-stepped to the front door. "Fall is coming on with a vengeance. Colder than last year."

She hugged her friend and pulled her into the house. "Let me take your jacket. I made soup and sandwiches."

"You're the best. Smells great in here. You have coffee?"

Despite her best efforts to bring life to the kitchen, the shabbiness of the room hit her once again, but she shrugged it off. Mia hadn't ever looked at her place with disdain and she was grateful for it.

She pulled tasty hot ham and cheese sliders from the oven and ladled steaming vegetable soup into bowls. "Help yourself."

Mia pulled a chair out and sat at the square table covered

in one of her mother's vintage tablecloths. "You want to tell me what yesterday was all about?"

She placed the food on the table and dropped into the chair. "Carson stopped by yesterday."

"And?" Mia broke off one of the sliders and popped it in her mouth.

"He told me there was a caveat to his inheritance."

Her friend wiped her mouth and leaned in. "So? What does that have to do with you?"

She crossed her arms. "He didn't trust me enough to tell me the truth."

Mia blinked and dipped her spoon in the soup. "What truth?"

"If he hadn't demonstrated the airport's profitability, he would have lost the property and it would have been auctioned off. The land my dad sold to his uncle would revert back to us."

Her friend wiped her mouth on the matching cloth napkin. "I don't understand. Based on the open house and how great the place looked, I'd say he's fulfilled the criteria, right?"

"That's correct."

"How valuable is the land?"

She ground her teeth. "That's not the point. The point is as the project manager he assumed I'd do something, so he'd fail. I wouldn't do that to gain back a piece of land and I resented it."

"I see. Did he actually tell you he didn't trust you?"

"Yes."

Mia folded her arms on the table. "Put yourself in his shoes? What would you have done?"

"I get that he'd practically sunk his life's savings into the place, but…"

Lily's MECHANIC

Her friend's arm flew out, and she slapped the table. "What? His entire future was on the line, Lily. Surely you see he had to do what he had to do. You think acreage was worth more than his entire future? His life's savings?"

Her friend's words made her stop and think, but she couldn't reconcile his lack of trust. Christopher's deceit rose up and punched her in the gut. He'd lied to her about where all the money was coming from to afford the huge home they lived in with the in-ground pool and expensive vehicles in the garage.

Mia pointed her finger. "I know you. You love him. You always have. It was a way for you to distance yourself from him, wasn't it?"

She hung her head. Her friend pounded the nail of truth, and it stabbed her in the heart. She couldn't deny the truth of her friend's words.

"I can't saddle him with my health issues. A scythe swings back and forth over my head ready to strike and could take my life and my sons' lives." She sniffed and put her shaking hands under the table. "I just couldn't do it to him."

Mia rose and sat next to her and wrapped an arm around her shoulder. "Have you heard from the doctor?"

"No. They told me they'd call as soon as they got the results. The doctor said he'd call personally. Especially now."

Her friend gave her a side squeeze. "Do you think Carson is an honorable man?"

"Of course I do." She huffed out the words.

The comforting arm around her shoulder dropped and Mia gave her a hard glare. "Don't you think he should be able to make the decision whether he wants to be a part of your life despite the potential illness?"

She shook her head, first fast then slower.

Mia grabbed her hand, her eyes compassionate. "I saw the way he watched you, the way he looked at you at the open house. You are dynamite together. Even Sean commented on the two of you, and he doesn't talk comment on our friends' relationships. Think about how Carson has been with your sons. There's not another man who will love your boys like he does. They adore him. It's Carson this and Carson that."

"I can't do it to him."

"What you're doing is preventing you, your boys, and him from being happy... now. You may not even have the gene."

"I need to know I'm OK."

Mia blew out a breath and went back to her own chair. "Your stubbornness makes me sad because I remember when Sean and I... It doesn't matter. I disagree with you, but I will support your decision and will pray for discernment and direction."

Her friend had overcome such enormous hardships in her life, but it wasn't life or death like hers. Could she have some time with her one true love before the ax fell?

Chapter 24

"I'm glad the coins are not in my possession any longer. Uncle Patrick had done a tremendous amount of leg work to verify he was the rightful owner." Carson swiped a hand over his cheek. The crispness of the day washed over his face as he and Ben walked from the Cessna parked in its designated spot.

"It's a waiting game now," Ben said. "And I'm ready to take a nap."

Two days in the Big Apple nearly did Carson in. Nervous about the coins, he and Ben took turns sleeping to keep them safe until they'd delivered them to the auction house.

By tacit agreement, he and his friend would maintain radio silence to not disrupt the airport's grand opening.

Carson zipped his jacket against the cool October wind. At the airport, the temperature seemed to always be ten degrees cooler in the winter and ten degrees hotter in the summer than anywhere else in town.

He placed a hand on his friend's shoulder and squeezed. "Thanks for your support and taking time off to go with me. I can't wait for the auction at the end of the month."

"Not a problem. That's what friends are for." Then Ben stopped near his helicopter. "There's something that's been bothering me, though."

"What?"

"Why hadn't your uncle auctioned the coins off?"

He shrugged, then pursed his lips. "He'd probably wanted to wait for me to come to Worthy."

"Are you going to tell Lily?"

"I tried. She told me to leave and didn't want anything to do with me."

Ben reached over and grasped Carson's upper arm. "I'm really sorry, man. I'll pray for you."

He'd need every prayer he could get to get through the pain. "Let's go see if Rob is done."

They stepped through the service entrance and stopped. Ben let out a long whistle.

Carson walked over to Rob and slapped him on the shoulder. "It looks terrific."

Ben followed him and stood off to the side. "It's fantastic." Thumbing his hand toward the door. "I'm headed over to the terminal. My office furniture is scheduled to be delivered tomorrow."

Carson waved as his friend left.

Rob turned to him. "We're doing the final cleanup and we're out of here."

"Can I move the tools, parts, and planes back in?"

"Wait until tomorrow. By then the paint should be dry."

He rubbed his hands in glee. "Great. I have a few planes scheduled for service next week and I'm not doing it in the elements. Those days are over."

Rob chuckled and smirked. "Don't blame you. Looks like your tenants have started to move in."

"Yeah. Ben will be the first and the rest of the tenants will be in by the weekend, so the airport will officially open next Monday. The place will be hopping until the first snowfall."

247

Lily's MECHANIC

"Lily stopped in while you were gone."

"She did?"

Rob scratched his stubbled cheek. "I verified her job was completed. I'm guessing she'll send you her final bill shortly."

"No doubt." The last thing he wanted to talk about was Lily. He should have kept his mouth shut about the terms of the inheritance. But it was better to know now and have the bandage ripped off clean, even if he bled. "What's your schedule look like in the coming months?"

Rob pulled his cap off and ran a hand through his hair. "We have a few jobs scheduled, but can take on more work. You ready to work on the house?"

"I have a few phone calls to make, and I'll get back to you. Furniture has to be refinished, and I want to talk about making some major structural changes."

"Text me when you're ready."

"Will do." He made his way to the service entrance and jogged to his house.

After having a quick lunch, he checked email and returned work calls. Sure enough, Lily had sent him the final bill and the sign off for the work she'd done.

Professional and cordial, her email ticked all the boxes to finalize their association. His shoulders slumped, and he placed his head in his hands and prayed. He prayed for strength and guidance. He prayed for Lily to be healthy, and that he could move on.

With a few quick clicks, he paid Lily, and swallowed at the balance in his bank account. When Rob's final bill came in, he'd be lucky if he could buy a tank of gas.

Thankfully, work came in and would keep him flush until the auction.

He strode to the window and noticed all the vehicles in

the airport parking lot were gone.

After he moved the equipment back in, he'd tackle the few remaining red dots on his property, then he'd see about the Sandburg farm. If he found anything, he'd take it to Lily. Technically, he shouldn't dig on her land without permission, but he hadn't wanted to get her hopes up if he excavated, and it yielded nothing. Her boys would go bonkers if they were told. He stifled a grin, then pursed his lips at his duplicity.

Three days later, with warmer clothes and his hands stuffed in heavy winter gloves, he grabbed a shovel from his garage, the map, the metal detector, and went in search of more coins.

Wind whipped his face, and he pulled his fur lined hat low on his head. His fingers were numb even though the temperature outside hovered in the mid-forties. But being outside all afternoon digging on his property, chilled him to the bone.

The remaining red dots were a bust, and he replaced the dirt in the last hole just as the sun dipped in the sky. While he dragged his butt home, he admired the pink, blue, and magenta streaks as the day made its way to dusk. A run for takeout after a hot shower was the next order of business.

He ate another slice of the spicy meat lover's pizza, studied the maps of Lily's land, and made a plan for the next day.

His main challenge would be to avoid Fred and the farmhands while he traipsed across her fields and prayed Lily would understand his motivations when he told her about the map and what he'd done.

The brisk wind from the past three days died down, and the faded grass glistened with dew as Carson walked on the right side of the runway and headed to the back portion of his land crossing over onto the Sandburg farm.

He shifted the metal detector and shovel on his shoulder

Lily's MECHANIC

and made his way over the barbed wire fence, then checked the map.

As he made note of the less than easy to see landmarks his uncle scratched on the map, he found his first red dot and began the arduous process of using the metal detector and digging.

By eleven o'clock, moisture trickled down his back and he'd removed his jacket and flannel shirt, but hadn't found anything other than old bits of metal like he'd found on his property yesterday.

He shouldn't be there, but he couldn't disappoint Lily again. Better to keep quiet and risk her wrath than to cause her any pain.

The other dots were closer to her house, and with less than a dozen red dots to investigate, he'd tell Lily before he ventured closer to the barns and farmhouse.

After the much-needed infusion to her bank account from the insurance money and the final payment for her project management work, Lily had made headway with the bills, but her mind went to her sons. They'd groused when she'd nixed the idea of inviting Carson for dinner and wanted to know why. They pestered her to head over to the airport, and she put her foot down... hard.

How could she tell her sons she'd pushed Carson away for his sake and theirs? A deep sigh came from her belly and blew through her body.

As she sat in her home office, she tilted her head back as far as it could go and Mia's voice rambled through her brain. Carson deserved to have the opportunity to walk away if he

wanted, once he had all the information about her health. She hadn't heard from the doctor, but kept her mind busy with chores around the house and the farm store. Most afternoons she prioritized various farm projects, but all day she wallowed in her misery and just sat staring into space.

A loud knock at the door brought her back to the present, and a wrinkle formed on her forehead. She glanced at the antique clock on the bookshelf.

Occasionally, a customer came late and begged her to open the store, but it happened less and less as people memorized the farm's hours.

She rose and went to the front door. Fred stood there with a frown on his face. This was not good. He'd taken over as the farm manager and oversaw all the other farmhands, and she needed him.

When she unlocked and opened the storm door, she motioned for him to come in. "What's up?"

The man shifted his weight from one foot to the other, and he shoved his hands in his overalls and wouldn't look at her.

"I moved the cows to the north pasture, and we fixed the fences over on the east side." His voice wavered.

Why had he given her a rundown on his day? They'd agreed he would do what was best for the farm, just as her father had done before he died. She had complete confidence in Fred's ability. He'd worked on the farm long enough and with no complaints from her or her father. Something was off. She'd let him get to the point on his own.

A hand rested with nonchalant ease on her hip. "OK. Can I fix you a cup of coffee?"

"No. I'm ready to head home, but there's no easy way to say it."

She could not afford for Fred to quit and braced herself.

Lily's MECHANIC

None of the other farmhands had experience or the maturity to run the dairy.

"Is there a problem?"

The young man pulled his cap from his head and drew a hand through his rock-star long hair. "I spotted Carson in the northwest field just before I returned to the barn. He was digging around in the field."

"What?"

He looked sheepish, and she was sure her face registered shock.

"It looked like he had a couple of shovels with him. I didn't want to approach him without talking to you first. I think he was looking for old man McClellan's treasure."

She swallowed and her mind raced. "I don't think there's any treasure, Fred, and I'd appreciate it if you wouldn't talk about it to anyone, including your wife. I don't want a bunch of strangers prancing through my land and disturbing the cows. I'll handle Carson."

"Right. Will do."

Her mind zoomed in and out while her farmhand said his goodbyes and went to his truck.

As Fred turned his truck around and left, she glanced at the clock in the living room. She'd have enough time to race over there on the ATV and see what damage Carson had done before she had to be back to prepare dinner and pick up the boys from school.

Was it possible there was treasure on her land? Was it another lie from Carson?

While dressing in warmer clothes, she fumed. How dare he keep this from her.

She zipped over to the barn, got on the ATV, and high-tailed it to the northwest area of their farm with a watchful

eye out for Carson.

The ATV stopped behind some pine trees when she spotted him in the distance. He looked around him, but when the engine faded, he went back to shoveling and crouched on the ground.

She sprinted across the field until she was within yards of him and out of breath. "Just what do you think you're doing?"

Carson nearly fell in the hole he'd dug but caught himself, and rose to his full height and grimaced. "Lily. I…"

"Don't say it." Her nostrils flared, and she held her hand up. Acid had formed in her belly. She eyed the metal detector. "You're digging on my land? You're trespassing."

She barely held on to her temper.

"When I came by last week, I had the maps my uncle left, but you told me to leave, and I…" His face fell. "I was upset, so I left. I wasn't sure there was anything on your land, and I didn't want to disappoint you if it was a bust. I figured I'd suffer the cold and if I found anything I'd bring it over. No strings attached. It was a poor judgement call."

Her shoulders slumped. From the expression on his face, she'd hurt him. Something she'd never meant to do. He hadn't lied to her, he just hadn't told her his business. And now he tried to protect her from being disappointed. Over the past week, she remembered he'd been there for her in a million ways when she was dealing with her father's health, and shame engulfed her. "And have you?"

"Huh?"

"Have you found anything?"

He shook his head and bent to pull odd pieces of metal from a sack she hadn't noticed lying on the ground.

"Nothing of value, I don't think."

"You mentioned there was a map. Can I see it?"

253

Lily's MECHANIC

He frowned, but dug in the pocket of his jacket and pulled out a crumpled mass of papers and put them in order.

"Uncle Patrick placed red dots in areas where he hadn't had the time to dig before he died."

"Dad was right all along. But why hadn't he said there might be treasure on our land?"

"Good question. I don't know. It could be my uncle hadn't told your dad anything until he was sure there was something there."

Carson's manly smell of sweat and clean soap wafted over to her and mingled with the crisp air. "But these dots are close to the house and orchards. Dad or any one of the farmhands would have had to see him lurking around."

"True. Uncle Patrick would have known the farm's milking schedule. He could have timed his searches then."

"That old…"

Carson stiffened. "Watch it. That's my uncle you're talking about. He cared about your dad."

"Right… and he trespassed on my land. Just like his nephew."

His face colored, and he lifted his chin. "Everything my uncle had done, the phone call to you, preparing the map and note, he'd done out of love."

She remembered the insurance money and the will and how Patrick cared enough about her father—and her—to make sure her dad's affairs were in order. There was no malice there. Just love.

With a look of chagrin, his shoulders slumped. "You beat me to it, Lil. Even though you told me to stay away, I was coming over to see you this afternoon to tell you what I'd done."

"You should have told me beforehand." Her voice softened.

He put a hand on her forearm and all her anger dissipated like the morning fog. "I should have... But I didn't want to get the boys' hopes up or have them spread the word. Those boys talked about it too much to keep it quiet."

Her sons' preoccupation with treasure hunting and what a map would do made her cringe. "The last thing I need is for folks going out there searching for more treasure. Wait. Didn't you say you found treasure on your land?"

"I did."

"So why do you care if there's any on *my* land?"

"My uncle went to great pains to mark, in detail, where there might be more based on his research of the man who buried the treasure in the first place. I figured if there was more, you'd be set and wouldn't have to struggle as much."

She crossed her arms over her chest and squinted at him. "After I kicked you out, why are you doing this?"

He pulled his work gloves off and placed his hands on her upper arms. "Because I love you, Lily. And I care about your boys."

They stared at one another for what seemed like an eternity, and she'd made her decision. "How many more red dots are left?"

"I've already done a dozen, but there are another six."

"Do you have any planes to service this week?"

"We don't officially open until after the tenants move in next week."

"You think we have enough time to check out the rest of the locations tomorrow?" Excitement filtered through her veins. What if there was treasure on her land too?

"We?"

She lifted her chin and smirked. "Now that I know about it, you think I'll let you have all the fun?"

255

Lily's MECHANIC

His lips curved, but then flattened. "Don't you have to run the farm store?"

"I do. Can't we hunt after the store closes?"

He scratched his head. "What about the boys?"

"I'll have Mia pick them up after school and take them to her place so we can work until dark. Fred and the other farmhands leave around noon, then they return at dusk to milk the cows. Come over after the store closes."

"Let me fill this hole and I'll leave." He seemed to struggle for a minute. "Have you heard anything about the test?"

She hesitated, then thumbed in the direction of the farmhouse. "Not yet. I have to get back to pick up the boys."

He reached out in supplication. "You'll tell me when you find out, won't you?"

She gave him a slow nod and walked with a hurried pace to the ATV. She should have just told him to look for the treasure and keep her posted, but she'd missed him.

What was she thinking agreeing to go with him on a treasure hunt when she had to keep her heart detached?

256

Chapter 25

Carson had a spring in his step, and a smile covered his face on the walk back to his house. Maybe all wasn't lost with Lily. After all, she agreed to help him search for treasure on her farm. Right?

But when the sun rose the next morning, doubt rushed in like waves on a shore. A sense of dejection climbed into his soul. Was she only interested in his help to find the treasure and not in him?

It hadn't mattered. He would convince her to give him a chance despite all the health obstacles she faced. She'd helped him achieve his goal of renovating the airport. Contracts had been signed, and planes dotted the new parking spaces even though the airport had not officially opened.

Bottleson called and told him he'd made the transfer, and Carson would have the deed in a few days, when it had been recorded. The new and improved airfield would buzz with activity it hadn't seen in years and he couldn't wait.

No longer was the airport terminal a dilapidated mess. He had put one foot in front of the other, and with prayer and Lily's help, the airport was successful. Now it was his turn to make all her dreams come true, *if* there were more buried coins.

257

Lily's MECHANIC

He rose before the sun and sat in his uncle's recliner. Somehow, when he sat there, Uncle Patrick's comforting presence enveloped him. He hadn't understood it, but there it was. When he had read the day's passage, he closed his eyes. Lily's health, her boys, and wisdom had been in his prayers every day since he'd fallen in love with Lily again. His heart told him he'd never fallen out of love with her.

The morning passed as he talked to tenants and scheduled time for service and repairs.

A quick glance at his phone, and he scrambled to get home and change into warmer clothing. The metal detector and shovel were already in his pickup from yesterday, and he was ready to go. The day was bright and crisp, and the air cool. The scent of pine wafted in the open windows of his truck.

As he pulled into Lily's drive, he glanced at the barn and outbuildings. She sure could use an influx of cash to get the farm buildings spruced up to make it more appealing for customers.

He knocked on the door and prayed she hadn't changed her mind. He hadn't texted her for fear she'd call the whole thing off.

After a few minutes, she opened the door. "I have a couple of thermoses of coffee to keep us warm."

His smile widened, and he expressed his gratitude.

She pulled on her coat and slipped on her gloves. "We can use the ATV. It'll save time tramping around the farm. You have the map?"

The Lily who had been angry and upset was gone. It was as if the terrible scene that happened in her kitchen last week had never happened, but they had to talk about it. He could still see remnants of the strain she'd been under since she'd returned to Worthy, but the lines seemed to have smoothed out.

258

"Yep. Let's check the last one farther afield and then work our way back."

She nodded and tugged her knit cap further down on her head. "Come on. Let's go."

After he pulled the tools from his truck and deposited them into the ATV, they made their way to the farthest set of dots on the map.

The first four sites yielded more metal bits, and they took a break. He leaned against the vehicle and drank the strong coffee. Steam rose from the scalding drink and reminded him to talk to her about her anger, but he hadn't known how to broach the subject, so he remained quiet, staring into the plastic cup.

She shoved her free hand in her pocket and lowered her head, staring into her coffee. "I want to apologize for my behavior."

"You don't–"

"Yeah, I do." She lifted her chin and pulled a gloved hand out of her pocket, and placed it on her thigh. "I was shocked you believed I would compromise the renovation just to get the land back for the farm and lost my temper. I had a chance to think about what I would have done if I had been in your position with my life's savings on the line." Her deep sigh reached into his very soul. "I would have done the same thing."

"Thank you, but I don't care that you lost your temper. What I care about is our relationship and if we can move past my stupidity to ever think you'd jeopardize me. That requires forgiveness too."

Her smile warmed him more than the steaming coffee in his hand. "Let's just forgive one another. Deal?"

"Deal. What about us, Lily? I care about you, your health, and your sons."

The smile she beamed earlier fell to a flat line. "I've heard nothing from the doctor yet. I keep praying…" Her narrow shoulders lifted, and she stared at her booted feet.

"I've been praying since you told me."

"Thank you." Her tiny voice barely lifted above the slight wind.

"Tell me if it's none of my business, but now that the renovation is complete, how are you holding up financially?"

"Dad had a life insurance policy I didn't know about. Your uncle talked him into it after my mom died."

He shook his head. "Uncle Patrick always looked out for those he loved."

"It was enough to bury him, pay his medical bills, and maybe help with the farm store. I didn't have to dip into my retirement, and I'm not out of the woods yet, but things are looking brighter."

"That's wonderful. Let's hope we can find some treasure that will get you out of the forest once and for all." He grinned as he screwed the cap back on the Thermos. "Are you ready to search the rest of the sites?"

They chatted about the boys, the farm, and the airport. She planned a hayride in late October to bring more folks to the farm store, and they brainstormed what she could do next year.

It saddened him they had only found more of the same metal bits and pieces he'd found in other spots on her land. Two more dots remained to be checked.

"I think the hunt is a bust, Carson."

"My uncle painstakingly mapped these locations. I won't stop until every one of them is checked."

Lily leaned against the ATV while he dug the hole where the metal detector indicated. A weird thump sounded

260

when he put his foot on the shovel. He hit something hard. Different. *What was that?*

"There's something here."

She trotted over, and excitement flickered in her eyes. "What?"

"It looks like some sort of box. Old too."

"I brought the hand trowel in case we needed it." She raced back to the ATV. "Here, try this."

He scooped the damp earth from around the box until he could pry it loose.

Lifting it out of the hole, he set it on the back of the ATV and pulled out his pocketknife. The rusted nails squeaked as he removed them from the top, and he glanced at Lily, who stood stock still. "Breathe, Lily."

A whoosh came out of her mouth, and she bit her lower lip as she waited, her body stiff.

"You ready?"

They both leaned in as he lifted the cover. He reached in and swiped a finger over the discs, and they glistened in the sunlight.

He turned and lifted Lily into a tight embrace and twirled them in circles. The heat of their embrace staved off the cooler early fall air. Unable to resist, he leaned in and kissed her with all the love he had in his heart.

"I love you, Lily. No matter what happens, I'll always love you."

A soft smile covered her face, and she drew her palm down his cheek, then glanced at the box of coins. "How many are there?" Her fingers shook as it grazed the coin. "How much do you think they're worth?"

"We'll have to count them. But they look different from the ones my uncle found on his land. Hang on."

Lily's MECHANIC

He pulled out his phone and accessed photos of the coins he'd already taken to the auction house. "I don't know how much these are worth since they're not the same type of coins I took to New York."

She stepped back and her face paled. "How will I keep them safe and what do I do with them?"

"I took my uncle's stash to an auction house in New York last week."

Her eyes widened, and she pointed to the box. "You think I could sell those to the same place?"

"I'd have to check. But let's count them and see if they're all the same."

With the phone, he zoomed in and photographed the two different coins, five dozen in all.

Staring at them, she held one aloft. "If these are worth good money, I could put it away for the boys' education, maybe even expand the store and do some major farm repairs."

"That's wise."

She dropped the coin back into the box, covered it, and gingerly placed it on the floor of the ATV. "We still have one more dot. Do we skip it or check it?"

"Heck, yeah, we're going to check it. This site is really close to the farmhouse. My guess is there had been a house here. My uncle left a letter with historical information. He believed that the inn described in his research was around here at one time. Probably why the gold was buried where it was."

He filled the hole in and put the shovel back in the ATV.

Lily gave him a thoughtful stare. "You know... come to think of it, Dad once told me there was an old shack close to the farmhouse, and he tore it down because he feared I'd get hurt if I played near it. I was so little. I can't remember where it was, though."

262

"Let's go, then. There could be more."

They went to the last spot. After using the metal detector, he dug and unearthed a teardrop shaped pouch with more coins in it. The leather crackled when he held it.

Lily jumped up and down, her excitement contagious. She placed the pouch in the box with the rest of the coins while he filled in the hole and grinned the whole time. With all the treasure sites excavated, exhilaration washed over him as they headed back to the farmhouse.

Lily grabbed the coins and headed into the house while he dumped his tools in the back seat of his truck. He jogged to the door and went inside. The most amazing aroma greeted him, and he was certain the taste would hit the homey spot.

"I made crockpot soup. You want some?"

"I'd be a fool to pass on your great cooking."

Her face beamed, and she hurried to put steaming bowls of chicken noodle and vegetable soup on the table.

They prayed and thanked God for the food, the successful day of treasure hunting, and God's provision for their lives.

She glanced at the box on the counter. "Now what?"

"With your permission, I'll send photos of the different coins to my contact in New York."

"Thanks." She pointed to the box. "I can't keep them here. The boys will blab we found the treasure and we'll be inundated. You have a security system. Will you take the box until you can make arrangements?"

"You trust me, Lily?"

"With my life."

He slid his hand across the table. His need to hold and kiss her again staggered him, but he wouldn't push it. "I'll reach out to my contact right now. It's still early, so they may give us an idea on the value of the haul."

She covered his hand with hers.

The only cloud hanging over their heads was the blood test, but he would not let it deter him from the happiness that brimmed out of him.

Lily awoke to a much brighter day, and she jumped out of bed. In less than two days her entire financial picture went from a nose dive to soaring. Even the dreary day couldn't cast a pall on her joy and good fortune.

Carson had spent the evening on the phone with her and helped her to make plans after his contact's giddiness told him the coins were valuable. The man couldn't give a definitive quote even though he had received photos. He had to physically inspect them. He had been reprimanded by his manager for having given Carson a quote based on photographs.

While her mind whirred with the possibilities, the coins were a financial turning point for her after so many years of drought.

When Carson's ringtone sounded, she had just waved goodbye to Fred and went in the kitchen to make some lunch. "What's up?"

"Doug Weisen, my contact at the auction house, wants to place them in the same auction as mine. We need to take the coins to New York as soon as possible."

The tension in his voice reached out to wrap around her.

"Do we ship them?"

"Too risky. My friend Ben will fly us there in his helicopter."

"Why not take the Cessna?"

"I would have, but I rented it to the pilot training group

and I'm still waiting on parts for the prop plane. We'll deal with the auction house, deliver the coins, and fly back the next day."

With the phone on speaker, she shoved a thawed pan of lasagna in the oven for dinner and set the timer. "I can't leave the farm."

"Sure, you can. It's only one night, Lil. Between your friends and Fred and the farmhands, the farm and the boys are covered. I can't sign the paperwork for you, Lily."

She pulled her hands through her hair. "They'll want to know why I'm going to New York."

"Just say you have to go out of town on farm-related business. It's not a lie, you just won't supply all the details." His exasperation came through the phone line, loud and clear.

"When do we go?"

"Tomorrow?"

"I'll see what I can do and get back to you."

When she hung up, she blew out a long calming breath, and called her best friend.

"Hey there. Everything OK?" Mia's chipper voice came through like a fresh breeze.

"It's all great." She barely kept the excitement out of her voice, and she longed to tell Mia everything, but Carson cautioned her to keep it to herself until the coins were out of her hands or the auction had already occurred. "You've been an amazing friend and I know it's a lot to ask, but can you pick up the boys tomorrow, keep them overnight, and take them to school on Friday?"

"Sure. It's no hardship because your boys are so well-behaved." A creak came through the phone line as if her friend leaned in. "What's going on? Did you get the test results back?" A hint of hesitation and worry colored her friend's words.

265

Lily's MECHANIC

"Not yet."

"What happened?"

"Nothing's wrong. I made my peace with Carson."

She could almost see Mia beaming. "You did? That's great. Did you tell him?"

"Tell him what?" Her nose wrinkled, and confusion filtered through her brain.

"That you love him, Lil."

"No, I didn't. I'm still waiting for the test results."

"Then what's going on?" Frustration laced her tone, then she stuttered. "I mean, I'm happy to watch the boys. They're great kids and Drew is over the moon when they're here. He loves to spend time with them."

She picked at her fingernail. "I have some out-of-town farm business I need to take care of. It's important and will help with long term finances. Carson is going with me."

The sigh of relief on the other end of the phone made her smile. "Well, in that case, no problem. I'll stop by tomorrow before school to get them and their stuff."

She could almost see the glee on Mia's face that she was taking time to be with Carson while on a business trip.

"Awesome, thanks. I owe you. Big time. I'll buy dinner at the diner when I get back." She'd tell Mia everything and hoped she could give her friend a double portion of good news.

Thank you, Lord, for good friends and bringing Carson back into my life.

"You're on. See you tomorrow."

She swiped the phone and called Carson back. Things were moving so fast she found it hard to catch her breath. It gave her pause to forgo any worry about the lab test... at least for now.

Chapter 26

With the newest batch of coins stowed in Carson's overnight bag and his best friend checking the aircraft before the flight, there was nothing left to do but wait for Lily.

Her beat-up SUV rumbled toward him. She could afford a new car when the coins sold, and he made a mental note to add paving the lane from the country road into the airport parking lot. With the upcoming auction and his potential newfound wealth, he could afford it.

A smile graced her lips as she got out of the car, and he jogged over to her.

When she spotted Ben walking around the helicopter, her smile turned into a frown. "What's he doing?"

He cast a swift glance at his friend and grabbed the bag from her hand. "He's doing a pre-flight. Are you afraid?"

She swung her gaze to him, and a tiny quiver of fear appeared, then disappeared and a smile lit her face. "I've never been in a helicopter before."

His fingers stroked her cheek with his free hand. "Do you trust me?"

A brief but hearty nod reassured him.

"I've known Ben for over ten years and serviced the helicopter myself before I flew it in from Virginia."

267

Her eyes bugged out, and she pointed to the aircraft. "You flew that? I mean, I know you have a pilot's license, but isn't flying a helicopter... different?"

He chuckled and put his arm around her waist. "It is, and it requires a different skill set too. Ben flew helicopters in the Navy. Since his discharge, he has flown for television stations and other companies. It's his job. Come on, I'll introduce you."

As they approached the aircraft, Ben met them at the door and introductions were made.

His friend extended his hand. "Carson has told me all about you."

A stab of jealousy went through him when Lily turned smiling eyes toward Ben. "All good things, I hope."

"The best." Ben gave her one of his bad-boy winks, and Carson wanted to punch his best friend.

Her smiled wavered, and she glanced at the rotors and turned to him. "I'm nervous—and excited."

Carson squeezed her side. "You'll be able to see and hear everything in the cockpit. I'll be right there with you."

At her nod, he settled her in a seat behind Ben, buckled her in, and placed a headset on her head.

When he and his friend were seated and strapped in the front seat, she shifted her gaze from the back of Ben's head to him. "I was so excited and dealing with the boys, I forgot to ask how long of a helicopter flight it is."

He reached back and held her hand. "We'll stop in Pittsburgh and again in Philadelphia to refuel, then we'll land at La Guardia and take a cab to the hotel near Rockefeller Center and the auction house. After we deal with the coins and get them out of our hands, we'll go to dinner and do something fun before we return home in the morning."

Lily nodded and gestured to the back of Ben's head.

"Can he hear us?"

He chuckled and squeezed her hand. "He's on a different channel, listening for instructions from the Columbus flight tower. He'll switch to this one after we're on our way."

Ben cut in, flashed him a look, and smirked. "We ready?"

He glanced at Lily's tightly clasped hands, reached out and smoothed them under his. When he nodded, she squeezed her eyes shut and held the air in her lungs.

"Breathe, Lily. We're in the air," Carson said.

He struggled not to grin and pulled his lips in as she opened one eye and then the other.

"That was different." Her voice came out in a pant.

Ben chuckled, then sobered. "If you feel queasy, there's a b–"

"She's fine." He glared at his friend and then turned to smile at the love of his life. "Right, Lil?"

Lily gave Carson a forced smile, opened her mouth, but shut it again.

A corner of his mouth quirked. "Look out the window."

She turned her head to stare in amazement. "It's clear why you love planes, Carson."

"Sunsets are incredible in a helicopter," Ben said. "But the timing of our trips won't allow it. Still, there are great things to see. Especially in New York."

The look of delight on Lily's face as she took in the landscape and the fall trees filled him with warmth.

"Doesn't matter. This is… I don't even know how to describe it except… gorgeous." She leaned her face against the window and admired God's creation.

He grinned at Ben, who chuckled and shook his head. "I can see I'll be lending the helicopter to you on occasion."

Their three-way conversation filled the aircraft with laughter and musings. Ben and Lily had gotten along as if

Lily's MECHANIC

they'd been friends forever. It was just one more indicator he'd made the right decision and that he and Lily could make a go of their relationship.

The rest of the trip, including the two fuel stops, went by without a hitch. Lily gushed with excitement over the flight, and he was overjoyed at her enthusiasm.

When they landed at La Guardia, they grabbed a cab to the hotel and checked in. Since he returned to Worthy, the city smells crinkled his nose, and he wanted to chuckle. He *almost* preferred the cow dung.

A porter loaded their bags on a cart and led them to the suite he'd booked for the night.

As they entered the spacious living area, he motioned to Lily to check out the room with the king bed. He and Ben would share the other room.

"You booked a suite?" Lily leaned into him and whispered.

He gave her a long look. "I want to make sure you're safe. New York is a crazy place."

With a hand on her cocked hip, she looked cute. "I lived in Austin for over ten years and for the last five, I lived alone with my boys. Why are you giving me the master?"

"Because the other room has two beds. I'm not sleeping in the same bed with Ben, no matter how good a friend he is."

A giggle burst from her lips.

He turned just in time to see Ben give the porter a tip, then grabbed Lily's bag and took it to her room. "Freshen up and I'll put the coins in the safe, then we'll go to lunch."

After a too expensive hotel restaurant meal that wasn't nearly as delicious as Lily's cooking, her excitement grew as the three of them went back to the suite to get the coins.

While the auction house was less than a mile away, with the traffic, it would be a twenty-minute cab ride. When they

arrived, Ben got out and came to stand on his side where the backpack holding the pouch hung on his shoulder.

He could feel the tension in Lily's body as she tilted her head and gazed at the imposing structure. The mammoth auction house overwhelmed him the first time he saw it, so he could imagine her trepidation. "It should only take a couple of hours at most."

After they told the receptionist who they were meeting, she smiled, but her gaze traveled to Ben's face and totally dismissed him and Lily. "He's expecting you. He's on the fifth floor. Someone there will help you find his office."

Doug met them at the elevator with a huge smile and a firm handshake. "I didn't expect to see you again so soon, but I'm excited you're here."

After Carson introduced his contact to Lily, Doug led them to his office, which was a typically bland small room in contrast to the building's impressive size.

"We are eager to help you with the auction of this latest batch of coins." One eyebrow rose. "Will there be another lot coming soon?"

Carson grinned. "No. This is the last of it."

Doug pulled paperwork from a drawer. His eyes never left Carson's face. "You told me your uncle dug up the coins on his land before he passed away. But where did these come from?"

He glanced at Lily and she nodded. "Uncle Patrick left a map not only with the treasure he found, but he'd checked Nils's land—that's Lily's father—and had marked the map with potential sites where coins might be located."

Doug stopped preparing the documents. "I'll need the owner's signature on the forms."

Lily sat straighter and placed a hand on the desk. "I am the owner. My father passed away a few weeks ago and left

271

the property to me."

"My condolences, Ms. Bennett." Doug frowned as he glanced from him to Lily and back again. "You didn't tell me the owner of the land where the coins were found had passed, Carson."

"I didn't think it was an issue. You didn't ask me about ownership of my land when I was here less than two weeks ago."

"About that." Doug's chinned bobbed. "We'll need recorded copies of the property deeds from both of you. We don't need them right this minute, but we'll need it before the auction."

Relief ripped through him. "Not a problem. Can we send them via email?"

Doug grabbed two business cards and handed them out. "Sure. The sooner the better. The auction is in two weeks and my boss wants the file in order."

"It'll be a priority when we return to Worthy."

With the paperwork on his desk, Doug walked Lily through the terminology and how the auction worked. She asked pertinent questions, and his pride over her intelligence grew. Doug's face lit up as he explained the procedure.

"We need to photograph the coins, catalog and update the electronic file, then put them in the safe." Doug said.

Carson opened his backpack and pulled out the old leather sack and unraveled the drawstrings, dumping over six dozen coins on the desk.

Doug's eyes widened as he placed them in order and in one layer on the desk and pulled the camera over them, shot pictures, and placed them back in the sack. "The pouch lends authenticity to the buried treasure. Can we include it as part of the auction?"

He looked at Lily and she gave him a brisk nod. "What do you think these coins will get at auction?"

"Some of these are extremely rare and they are in unbelievably good condition for having been underground. No doubt the leather that held them helped. They're not as pristine as those that have never been handled, but amazing. We can only give a low-end estimate."

"And that is?"

Doug stared at the leather pouch. "I'd guess the low end is about a half million."

Lily fanned her face and began breathing so fast Carson worried she'd hyperventilate.

"Easy, Lily." He took her hand. "Could we get her a drink?"

The man's chair squeaked as he turned and pulled three bottles of water from a hidden fridge in the credenza behind him.

She uncapped it, took a deep gulp, and lifted her chin. "Sorry. I wasn't expecting that number."

"It's…"

He gave a warning glare at Doug, who took the hint and slammed his mouth shut. The number was quite low in his opinion based on Doug's exuberance, and he guessed the coins would fetch upwards to two million or more when the auction was over. Once taxes were calculated and the tithe taken out, it would be considerably less, but Lily would never have to struggle again, even if she had the terrible gene. He gave a silent prayer and vowed to talk to her tonight about it.

When the meeting ended, they took a cab to the hotel. Ben told them he'd get room service and have an early night so he'd be fresh for the flight in the morning.

What a friend. He made it easy for Carson to have an evening alone with Lily.

"There's not a lot of time to do any sightseeing, Lily, but why don't we go somewhere nice for dinner to celebrate?"

Her soft smile made his heart stutter in anticipation.

While Lily changed her clothes, he planned to have a horse drawn carriage take them for a ride around Central Park and had the concierge make reservations at a trendy bistro at Rockefeller Center.

He smirked at Ben, who grinned like a loon, got up from the sofa, and went into their room. "Enjoy your evening."

They walked the short distance to the eatery and passed people of all ethnicities and walks of life. With his arm around Lily, he was on top of the world.

When they arrived at the grille, they were shown to a semi-quiet little table in the back of the long, narrow establishment. It was dark and intimate with wooden walls he guessed were from the early twentieth century, but he only had eyes for the woman before him.

She examined the cloth covered table after they ordered, and their drinks came. "I can't believe this is happening." Her voice became quiet. "I struggled for so many years and imagined I'd be doing the same on the farm because of Dad's financial mismanagement. I wish I would have listened as he talked about..." She glanced around at the closely positioned tables. "You know what."

The server placed their food on the table with a flourish, and she giggled. The sound made his heart zing, and he wanted to hear it all the time. He'd do whatever he could to make it happen.

He nudged his arm across the table and squeezed her hand. "Don't think about it, Lil. Think about all the good that will come of it."

"You're right. I can put my boys through college now and have money to make technological improvements to the farm."

"I want the boys to know I'll be there for them no matter

what, Lil." He released her hand and picked up the utensils.

The fork with a bite of fish stopped mid-air to her mouth and her eyes watered. "You don't even know if I'm sick or not."

His gaze was intent as he focused on the pulse in her neck. "It doesn't matter. I'm there for both you and them. I said it before, and I'll continue to say it until you believe it. I'm not going anywhere and if any of you need me, I'll be there." He placed a hand on his heart. "I mean it, Lil."

She stuffed the flaky fish in her mouth, chewed, and swallowed. "Let's talk about the airport and what you're going to do with…" She stopped short of saying *treasure* in the packed place and he was grateful she hadn't mentioned it.

"I made a mental note to have the lane paved."

Her tinkling laugh reached into his soul and made him whole. "Surely you can think of more things."

He dipped a chunk of lobster into melted butter and enjoyed its delicate flavor.

"I'll definitely rehab the house. I'm waiting until next month when I know more and can call Rob to do the work. He might do the interior during the winter months."

"That's awesome. I'd like to renovate the farmhouse as well."

He worried once she had her house the way she wanted it, she wouldn't be interested in making them a family. It was too soon, but he couldn't let it go. "What all do you want to do?"

She stared at her plate and her mouth set into the widest smile he'd seen since he'd been back. "The first week I got home I made a list of all the things I wanted to do, then stopped because I was so overwhelmed by the magnitude of the work needed. I stuck the list in the desk drawer and refused to think about it."

His heart stalled, but he kept the half smile on his face to keep her from questioning what was on his mind.

Lily's MECHANIC

When dinner was over, he followed her out of the restaurant with a hand at the small of her back.

"I have another surprise for you," he whispered.

She put a hand to her chest. "I don't think I can take another one."

"This is a fun one." He guided her across the street. "A ride around Central Park in a horse drawn carriage."

She clapped her gloved hands, and he helped her into the open-air cab. The coachman handed him a blanket, and he tucked it in around them.

"This is awesome, Carson. Thank you for thinking of it."

Magic surrounded them. As they made their way through the streets of New York with the glow of old-fashioned streetlights, it almost felt as if they had been thrown into the past, but the cars honking dispelled that fanciful notion. Couples walked hand-in-hand, near and in the park, and they marveled at the families with tiny tots who enjoyed an evening stroll despite the cooler air.

When the coachman stopped, Carson guided Lily back to the hotel. Before he opened the suite door, he turned to Lily and took her in his arms. "Thank you for a wonderful evening. It was the best night of my life."

Her eyes lifted to his lips, and she leaned closer. The invitation was clear, and he took it and kissed her.

He'd told her he loved her twice, but she had not responded in kind. Was she waiting to see what happened when she got the test results? No way would he say anything and spoil the magical night they'd had.

No matter the outcome, she was his and at some point, he'd have her and the family he'd always wanted. Even though there might be health issues to work through, he didn't care. Not one bit.

276

Chapter 27

Wrapped in the bliss of the knowledge her financial worries would be a thing of the past, Lily returned from their whirlwind trip to New York. Her health drama would not influence her decision about Carson, and she'd take one day at a time. She pocketed her keys when the phone rang. She glanced at the screen, ice cold dread washed over her. The doctor's office.

"Mrs. Bennett?"

"This is she."

"Could you come into the office on Monday at two?"

She dropped into a kitchen chair and her eyes fluttered shut as she unzipped her coat. The thick jacket strangled her. "Why?"

"Doctor Kirk wants to see you."

"What's this about?"

"I'm sorry, you'll need to speak to the nurse. I only schedule the appointments."

Her hands trembled, her palms dampened, and she gripped the phone tighter. "Could you get the doctor on the line?"

"I can try, but I don't know if he's available."

Lily shot up, paced, and bit her fingertip while she waited. Dear Lord, please don't let it be bad news after the won-

277

derful days I spent with Carson. I'm scared, Lord, but it's all in your hands.

The appointment scheduler came on the line and her voice sounded odd. "I'll put you through to the doctor."

"Thank you," she stuttered, and her body rattled.

"Lily." Doctor Kirk sounded rushed. "I'm so sorry. The scheduler confused you with another patient."

"What does that mean, Doc? Did the test come in?"

The doctor sighed. "The test results came in and you were on my list to call tonight, but because of this mix up…" His tone was thoroughly put out and frustrated. "We can talk about it now. The test came back negative. You do not carry the gene."

Her whoop of joy must have deafened him. "Sorry, Doc."

"It's understandable, Lily… But I'd still like you to get a full physical. Can you do that?"

"Yes." She paused, then rushed on. "What about the boys?"

She could hear him move around and sit in his office chair. He heaved a long sigh. "I'd say they have less than a twenty-five percent chance of having the gene, but I think it'd be wise to have them tested when they are older."

"Absolutely."

"Don't forget to schedule the physical, Lily."

"I won't."

When she ended the call, she danced around the kitchen, then took her bag upstairs. She'd left her phone downstairs and raced to get it to call Carson when she thought better of it.

A quick glance at the microwave clock told her she had enough time before she had to be at the school.

She rushed back to her car and waved at Fred as she

stormed out of the drive.

Her left foot jiggled, and she stomped on the gas. Gravel flew every which way and pinged against her beat-up car, but she hadn't cared. She needed to get to Carson.

There was one other car in the lot, so in her exuberance, she laid on the horn and jerked to a stop by Carson's cool truck.

He flew out of the hangar and sprinted to her car with Ben on his heels.

She jumped out, plowed into him, and hid her face in the crook of his neck.

"Lily, what is it? What's wrong?" His voice quavered, and she could feel the tension in his body.

She leaned back and could barely hold it together. "The doctor's office just called."

He forced her head back to his chest and his chin brushed her hair. "It doesn't matter, Lily. I love you, and that's not going to change. We'll fight the disease together."

She pulled back against his tightening arms and gave him a huge smile as tears of happiness slid down her cheeks. "You don't understand. Test results showed I don't have the gene."

"What?"

"I'm healthy, Carson." She screamed her joy, then calmed. "He still wants me to have a physical, but he told me it was routine."

When his brain registered what she'd just told him, he lifted her in his arms, laughed, and swung her around in circles. She noticed his friend stood a little way off watching them with a weird expression on his face.

Ben stepped over. "Carson told me you had some health issues, but didn't say what, but based on what I witnessed,

Lily's MECHANIC

you're fine now."

"I am." She waltzed over to Ben and gave him a hug. "Thank you again for taking me to New York. You and Carson need to come over tomorrow night for dinner." She peeked at Carson. "That is if the two of you don't have plans."

Ben glanced at his friend. "I'd love to. What time?"

"Six?"

"Perfect. See you then." Carson's friend turned and made his way to the helicopter parked on the pad.

The love of her life turned to her and took her into his arms. "Let's go in the house. We need to talk and it's cold out here."

"Good or bad?" She blinked as he pulled her to his side.

"All good, babe."

"I don't have much time. I have to get the boys from school. I can't ask Mia to do more than she's already done, and I have to tell her everything."

He opened the front door and let her go ahead of him, then shut it and hugged her. "Course you do. I'm so happy for you and the boys. I want to spend more time with the three of you."

With his arms wrapped around her and the knowledge that her health was no longer an issue, her breath caught in her throat. This was the moment of truth. When she'd be completely honest with him.

"Carson, I—"

"I know it's really soon to think about spending more time together, but I love you Lily and those boys have flown into my heart and took residence. You've always been the love of my life and—"

She placed her fingertips over his lips. "You didn't let me finish." His body stiffened, and she needed to move it

280

along. "I love you, Carson. I never stopped loving you. I just wouldn't admit it because... the reasons don't matter anymore. I married my husband even though, deep down, I still loved you. While my dad did what he thought was best, he caused untold heartache for both of us."

He cocked his head. "That's true, but your dad recognized his mistake and tried to fix it. We're called to forgive, and I have forgiven him for the part he played to keep us separated. And if you hadn't married, you wouldn't have had those wonderful boys."

She gave him a thoughtful look. "That's true. But the heartache and sadness—"

"Is over... for both of us." He licked his lips and joy filled his face. "I don't want to waste any more time. We've already lost enough years being unhappy. I want to marry you, Lily, and I want us to be a family. I want to adopt those boys when they see me as a father figure."

She shook her head, and she choked with happiness. "They already see you that way. I hadn't paid much attention to it since it happened so naturally, but Mia reminded me the boys constantly say 'Carson this and Carson that'."

"There are so many things we need to talk about, and you have to leave to get the boys. Why don't I take you and the boys to dinner tonight and we can tell them?"

"I'm sure they'd love that."

He walked her out to her car and pulled her into his arms and kissed her with the promise of a bright and loving future. "I love you, Lily. I'll be at your place at six."

"To wait even another day will be torture, Carson. But I know we have to do what is best for the boys."

"You're right and we'll talk about our future tonight."

"Our future. It sounds so good. I can't wait."

With a final kiss, she slid into her car and waved as she glanced at Carson in the rearview mirror. With complete assurance, she knew he'd never leave her again. Her dream had finally come true.

The End... For Now.

Lily & Carson's Bonus future story!

Lily and Carson overcame challenges in both their lives to reunite once again after years apart.

They're happy for now, and plan to spend their lives together, but what exactly does their future hold?

To get the bonus story, sign up today for my semi-monthly newsletter and you'll receive Lily and Carson's future story at www.seralynnlewis.com/free-bonus-stories.

Every newsletter has something special... You can look forward to cut scenes, character profiles, blog posts, story prequels, contests, and sneak peaks of covers for upcoming books. You'll even have an opportunity to weigh in on future covers and stories.

Sign up today!

OTHER BOOKS BY SERALYNN LEWIS

Women of Worthy Series:

Rob Marino appears in Lily's Mechanic, but also appears as a supporting character here and in some of the other books listed.

Cassie's Secrets – Book 1

www.seralynnlewis.com/books/cassies-secrets

Mia Nardelli McDermott appears in Lily's Mechanic as Lily's childhood and high school best friend, but she has a story of her own.

Check it out here: Mia's Irishman – Book 2

www.seralynnlewis.com/books/mias-irishman

Kate Callahan Woodford briefly appears in Lily's Mechanic as an EMT, but she has a story of her own. Georgia Henry, the owner of the Countryside Diner also appears in Lily's Mechanic, but we first meet this lovely lady in Kate's Quest.

Check them out here: Kate's Quest – Book 3

www.seralynnlewis.com/books/kates-quest

Ben Garrison appears in Lily's Mechanic as Carson's best friend, but he has his own love story. **Check it out here: Sophia's Pilot – Book 4**
www.seralynnlewis.com/books/sophias-pilot

Amy and Bryan Dillon as well as Amy's B&B appear in Lily's Mechanic. **Check out Amy's love story here:**
Amy's Christmas Wish – Book 5

www.seralynnlewis.com/books/amys-christmas-wish

Although the books were written in the order they have been published, in Worthy, Ohio's timeline, Lily's Mechanic happens first, then Sophia's Pilot, then Amy's Christmas Wish. The first three stories are in order.

Available online at www.seralynnlewis.com/books

SCRIPTURE VERSES IN LILY'S MECHANIC

In all my books, there are scripture verse references and sometimes the verses are paraphrased by the characters or the references are stated. My go-to Bible is the New King James. The below scriptures are taken from that version.

The scripture verses in Lily's Mechanic are (in order of how they appear):

Chapter 5

For I know the thoughts that I think toward you, says the Lord, thoughts of peace and not of evil, to give you a future and a hope. *Jeremiah 29:11*

Chapter 7

Do not be unequally yoked together with unbelievers. For what fellowship has righteousness with lawlessness? *2 Corinthians 6:14*

Chapter 17

So Sarai said to Abram, "See now, the Lord has restrained me from bearing children. Please, go in to my maid; perhaps I shall obtain children by her." And Abram heeded the voice of Sarai. Then Sarai, Abram's wife, took Hagar her maid, the Egyptian, and gave her to her husband Abram to be his wife, after Abram had dwelt ten years in the land of Canaan. So he went in to Hagar, and she conceived. And when she saw that she had conceived, her mistress became despised in her eyes. *Genesis 16:2-4*

Chapter 18

Come to Me, all you who labor and are heavy laden, and I will give you rest. Take My yoke upon you and learn from Me, for I am gentle and lowly in heart, and you will find rest for your souls. For My yoke is easy and My burden is light." *Matthew 11:28-30*

Chapter 21

So we are always confident, knowing that while we are at home in the body we are absent from the Lord. For we walk by faith, not by sight. We are confident, yes, well pleased rather to be absent from the body and to be present with the Lord. *2 Corinthians 5:6-8*

THANK YOU!

Thank you so much for reading Lily's Mechanic.

While the small town of Worthy, Ohio, is fictional, it is located in Franklin County, about an hour southeast of Columbus, in the southern part of the state. After imagining a buried treasure, I researched the possibility of buried treasure somewhere in that vicinity. To my amazement and delight, the facts listed in the book are factual.

However, metal detecting in the state of Ohio is governed by each county and if the find is on government land, the finder forfeits the find to the federal government. But if the find is found on private property, then the finder may keep the treasure… unless, of course, there's some archeological significance to the find. So, if you are thinking about getting a metal detector to do your own treasure hunting, make sure you know the laws regarding any treasure you may find.

And I love to hear from readers—what and who they loved—and didn't love. And why. Feel free to contact me at info@seralynnlewis.com or at my website at www.seralynnlewis.com. While you're there, take a look at my blog *A Woman's Heart*.

Download the *free* book club and/or bible study questions located under *more* in the menu.

If you enjoyed Lily's Mechanic, I hope you'll consider leaving a review which would be most helpful to me as an author. I would so appreciate it.

You can also find and connect with me on:

FACEBOOK, TWITTER, AND INSTAGRAM: SeralynnAuthor
PINTEREST: seralynnlewis | **LINKED IN:** seralynn-lewis

And, thank you for your support.

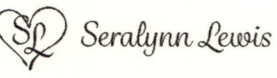 Seralynn Lewis

Dear Reader...

Within the pages of this book, you read about the character's spiritual life. If you were wondering how you could have the same confidence, it's as easy as A-B-C.

Admit that you are a sinner: **Lord, I am a sinner.**
Romans 3:23 For all have sinned and come up short of the glory of God.

Believe that Jesus is Lord, died for your sins and rose from the dead: **Lord, in my heart I believe you died for my sins and rose from the dead.**
Romans 6:23 For the wages of sin is death, but the gift of God is eternal life through Jesus Christ.

Call upon His name: **Lord, come into my life and be the Lord of my life.**
Romans 10:13 For whoever calls upon the name of the Lord Jesus Chris will be saved.

Your salvation does not depend on your good works, or how good of a person you are. You are saved by grace and grace alone!

No one is guaranteed another day. Please don't wait. Follow the ABCs and call upon the name of Jesus today and be saved. And please, contact me at info@seralynnlewis.com so I can pray for you and welcome you into the family of God!

Many blessings,

 Seralynn Lewis

ABOUT THE AUTHOR

Seralynn Lewis was born and raised in a small historical town in northern Ohio. After having lived in various parts of the United States and for a short time in Germany, she and her husband have found their forever home in the Raleigh-Durham area of North Carolina.

She has two grown daughters, two lovely grandchildren, and a husband who supports everything she does no matter what it is.

When she's not writing, thinking about writing, or plotting her next novel, she's busy preparing a telephone Bible Study that's she's been doing for years.

A long-time lover of romance novels, she'd like nothing more than to sit on a deserted beach somewhere sipping iced tea and reading to her heart's content. She and her husband travel to visit family and friends in her hometown where they browse and delight in their favorite library.

WRITING AWARDS:
2020 Serious Writer, Writer of the Year Finalist
2019 Tarheel Award for Contemporary Romance
2019 NaNoWriMo Winner

MEMBERSHIPS:
American Christian Fiction Writers (ACFW)
ACFW-NC Chapter (Treasurer)
Faith, Hope & Love Christian Writers (FHLCW)

Contact her at www.seralynnlewis.com or visit my blog at www.seralynnlewis.com/blog.
Check out her books at www.seralynnlewis.com/books.

Made in the USA
Columbia, SC
01 May 2023

15858567R00178

Sign up for the 1001 Dark Nights Newsletter
and be entered to win a Tiffany Key necklace.

There's a contest every month!

Go to www.1001DarkNights.com to subscribe.

**As a bonus, all subscribers can download
FIVE FREE exclusive books!**

One Thousand and One Dark Nights

Once upon a time, in the future…

I was a student fascinated with stories and learning. I studied philosophy, poetry, history, the occult, and the art and science of love and magic. I had a vast library at my father's home and collected thousands of volumes of fantastic tales.

I learned all about ancient races and bygone times. About myths and legends and dreams of all people through the millennium. And the more I read the stronger my imagination grew until I discovered that I was able to travel into the stories… to actually become part of them.

I wish I could say that I listened to my teacher and respected my gift, as I ought to have. If I had, I would not be telling you this tale now. But I was foolhardy and confused, showing off with bravery.

One afternoon, curious about the myth of the Arabian Nights, I traveled back to ancient Persia to see for myself if it was true that every day Shahryar (Persian: شهریار, "king") married a new virgin, and then sent yesterday's wife to be beheaded. It was written and I had read that by the time he met Scheherazade, the vizier's daughter, he'd killed one thousand women.

Something went wrong with my efforts. I arrived in the midst of the story and somehow exchanged places with Scheherazade — a phenomena that had never occurred before and that still to this day, I cannot explain.

Now I am trapped in that ancient past. I have taken on Scheherazade's life and the only way I can protect myself and stay alive is to do what she did to protect herself and stay alive.

Every night the King calls for me and listens as I spin tales. And when the evening ends and dawn breaks, I stop at a point that leaves him breathless and yearning for more. And so the King spares my life for one more day, so that he might hear the rest of my dark tale.

As soon as I finish a story... I begin a new one... like the one that you, dear reader, have before you now.

Prologue

For years, there was only him. The boy I'd loved with his shining blue eyes and a laugh that could brighten the darkest of days.

We were one, he and I. Two halves of a whole.

That's what he'd always said.

That's what I'd always believed.

Together, our childhood days had been marked with laughter and sunshine. Our teenage nights with heat and hunger, the days with plans and promises, caresses and kisses.

We'd shared our dreams. Our hopes. Our bodies.

We discovered passion in each other's arms. There was trust. There was love.

And there was betrayal.

That's when my world tilted without warning. He was gone, with only a scribbled note as proof he'd existed at all. His absence like a wound upon my soul.

I thought I'd never see him again. The boy who'd once been mine. The man who'd disappeared, taking my broken heart with him.

But now he's back, swathed in a cloud of danger and betrayal, tied up in a conspiracy that could destroy everything I hold dear. Cold where once he was warm. Hard where once he was soft.

Deceitful. Dangerous.

Desirable.

I want to hate him. I want to hurt him as he hurt me. And yet the bond we shared still tugs at my soul, and all I can do is hope that I have the strength to hold fast to my mission. To fight the man he has become...and not lose myself in the memories of the man I wish he was.

Chapter One

"No," I say, waving the dossier as I pace in front of my boss's desk. "This can't be right."

Behind the desk, Ryan Hunter leans back, watching me. With his chestnut hair and sky-blue eyes, he could almost be Maxim's twin. Honestly, that was the hardest thing about coming to work for Stark Security. Because every time I looked at my boss, it was as if someone had thrust a knife straight through my heart.

But time heals the pain from even the vilest betrayals. Within a few weeks, I could talk to Ryan without wanting to curl up into a ball of self-pity. Within a few months, we could carry on an entire conversation without me thinking of Maxim even once.

The day I realized that was the day I knew I was finally healed.

How wrong I was.

I draw a breath and stand even straighter in front of Ryan's desk. "You can't ask me to take this assignment."

For a moment he just sits like that, hands behind his head, his chair tilted as he studies me. I'm well above average at reading people. Their posture, their eyes, the subtle motions of their fingers. Even the smallest thing can help tell the story of a person's life. Their wants and desires. Their plans. Their secrets.

But I can't read Ryan Hunter. I've never been able to. Even so, I trust him with my life.

Right now, I wish I didn't respect him so much. Because that respect is the only thing keeping me from turning around, storming out of his office, and slamming the door behind me.

Instead, I slam the dossier down on his desk, so that the red-stamped *Confidential: PGU Clearance Only* is face up. "You can't possibly expect me to take this assignment."

"Actually, I can," he says. "Because you're the best person for the job, Cami, and you know it."

I do, of course. Ryan Hunter has one of the best tactical minds I've ever run across, so he's usually right about such things. But that doesn't

mean I have to like this particular reality.

With a grimace, I flop down onto one of his guest chairs. "When I joined Stark Security, I thought I'd be getting away from giant save-the-world missions."

He chuckles. "Did you remember to mention that to the bad guys?"

"Damn," I say, with a hard snap of my fingers. "I knew I forgot something."

Stark Security burst onto the private security scene several years ago, and has since grown into an organization with a worldwide reputation for excellence. I'm proud to work here, but one of the reasons I'd come on board was so that I could take smaller assignments and stick closer to my adopted home of Los Angeles. It's a nice change from my former job with the SOC—Sensitive Operations Command—which is a covert, off-the-books government organization with oversight from the NSC.

There, I'd been assigned to huge missions with worldwide repercussions. During my tenure, I helped bring down a hell of a lot of bad guys, and I'm proud of the work I did, but the lifestyle was a bitch. Basically, I'd been a real-life James Bond. Or Ethan Hunt. Or Sydney Bristow.

In other words, I'd had a job that was cool as shit and stressful as hell.

These days, my work is still fascinating and my private sector paycheck rocks. Plus, I have a house in Venice Beach right on the bike path, a chest of drawers instead of a suitcase, and an actual pet, albeit a hamster. I still don't feel quite settled enough to get a dog, but I'm working on that.

I've even joined a book club, and I go to yoga class twice a week.

Domesticity, thy name is Cami.

I'd grown up in the Bronx, and my memories from my childhood aren't exactly something you'd find on the Hallmark Channel. More like Shudder.

Needless to say, the thought of going back now doesn't sit well.

None of that, however, is the primary reason that I don't want this assignment. On the contrary, I don't want it for the exact reason that Ryan thinks I'm the perfect girl for it.

Maxim Wilder.

Just thinking his name makes me edgy, and I push up out of the chair and start to pace again.

"We're looking at the potential for mass genocide, Cami."

My eyes cut to the report I'd just finished reading. The confidential

one stamped PGU, which stands for Project Group Ultra.

Not long ago, Stark Security helped foil a major threat from Group Ultra, a terrorist organization with cells all over the globe. Unfortunately, the group itself hadn't been eradicated, and the leader—a vicious chameleon of a man named Killion Lambert—had crawled back into the sewer.

Current intel says he's behind a seemingly legit Manhattan-based non-profit organization that's developing an enhanced water processing and reclamation system for underdeveloped countries. Except that's not what they're developing at all. Chatter suggests that the water project is merely a cover for their work on a next-gen weapon with major destructive power. What it is and how it works is anyone's guess.

Which means the best way to find out is to infiltrate the organization and gather that intel.

That's where I come in. Because who has a better ticket into the inner circle than the woman who used to fuck Maxim Wilder, Lambert's right-hand man?

"It would be a mistake," I say. "Don't you get it? It would be too personal."

Ryan shakes his head. "On the contrary. I think it's just personal enough."

"And if I say no?"

He stands, then circles his desk in long strides before leaning against it right in front of me. "If you say no, it's likely that this weapon will go operational. You know that."

I do. I also know that I'm not going to turn down this mission. Ryan knows it, too.

With a frustrated sigh, I concede the point. "Mission parameters? Op tech? What about back-up?"

"Brax is your on-point here."

"Good." Braxton Reed is an amazing agent and one of my closest friends. For months, he and I were the only fully covert agents at Stark Security. As in, no one outside the office knows that we work for the organization. As far as the world is concerned, we're just ordinary citizens with ordinary jobs. Now there's three of us working in that covert capacity, with the third being his new wife, Sabrina.

They've only recently returned from their honeymoon, and I'm assuming that this is the first op Brax has worked since he got back.

"I'm going to head home to pack once we're done here," I tell Ryan. "I'll see if he and Brina want to come over for lunch. He can brief me

then."

"Fine," Ryan says. "As for on-site, Zane Parker will be your contact if anything goes sideways. Standard covert protocol for contact and extraction."

I nod as I run through a mental Rolodex, finally landing on Parker, who I recall is a relatively new research associate at Stark Security. As my extraction contact, he's only notified when I activate my emergency beacon. If I don't initiate contact, then he'll have no idea I'm even in the city. Another protocol to help ensure covert operatives remain covert.

"What's he doing in New York?" I ask.

"Research," Ryan says, without elaboration.

I raise a brow. "So I should start keeping an eye out for house-warming decorations? Or should I say office-warming?" I add with an innocent bat of my lashes.

"This is how rumors spread."

"And the truth. This is also how the truth is spread."

He just clears his throat, and I bite back a laugh. Everyone in the office has heard the rumors about a branch opening in New York. I may be the first to have actual, tangible evidence.

Ryan stares me down. "Moving on... We don't know how close the weapon is to deployment. Not a surprise since we still don't know what the weapon is."

"Which means time is of the essence."

"Exactly. Weapon specs. Timing. Anything you can gather. You know the drill."

"Get in, get the intel, get out," I say, understanding that the information I gather will determine when and how the tactical take-down will occur.

"I assume your cover will hold?"

"It will. You've seen my police record. I'm a dangerous little bitch."

He chuckles. "At least half of that record is one-hundred percent true."

I shrug. He's not wrong.

"It's your FBI file that worries me."

"Really? Why? My record there's buried deep. I was covert ops then, too. You know that."

"I do. But Killion Lambert's got resources."

I grimace. I've never crossed paths with Lambert and no one's seen a photograph, but just the thought of that man makes my flesh crawl. "You think someone from Stark Security's feeding him information?" I hate

even asking the question.

"No." Ryan's response is so firm that I'm certain he's not just trying to keep me in the dark.

"Then what—*oh!* You think Lambert's recruiting from the inside. FBI. CIA. Maybe even the SOC."

"We do. Which is why your employment file with the FBI has been updated to include a half-dozen more infractions. Serious ones. You've been a very bad girl, Cami."

"But I'm so very good at it," I say, making him laugh. "Have I been kicked out? Or am I still deep cover with the FBI?"

"Deep cover," he says. "Currently on leave because of all those infractions."

"And I don't appreciate the slap on the hand."

"You really don't."

"I get it. It's a shame, though," I add, kicking back in my chair. "This is going to be inconvenient."

He raises a brow. "What's that?"

"After you get through smearing my record, how the hell will I ever make employee of the year?"

"Stop Maxim. Dig out where Killion Lambert is holed up. Get us intel on that weapon. Sabotage it if you can. Most of all, don't get dead."

"I'll try to keep that last one in mind."

"Do that." He passes me the file, along with an envelope clipped to the cover. "Your flight and hotel info."

That's one of the downsides of being covert. I never fly on the company jets. But I have racked up a lot of airline miles. I'm about to rack up a few more.

A jittery feeling I haven't experienced since training takes me by surprise, and I have to admit that I'm a little undone by the very real possibility that I'll be seeing the only man I ever loved in less than twenty-four hours.

And the only man I truly hate.

Too bad they're one and the same.

"Guess I should pack," I say, impressed that my voice sounds normal. I am, after all, a professional.

"And Cami," he adds, "if you see an opportunity to turn Maxim, take it. You're the only one who might be able to pull that off."

"I can't," I say firmly. Once upon a time, I'd believed in Maxim Wilder. But those days are long gone. "I'll convince him that I'm on his side, though. That much, I guarantee."

Chapter Two

"You know you jinxed yourself," Brax says as he puts a mug of coffee in front of both Sabrina and me. "Telling him you'll get in close with Maxim? Now you've kicked that totally out of the realm of possibility."

"You're such an ass." I shift to face Brina, who's sitting beside me at my round kitchen table. "Your husband is an ass."

She takes a sip of coffee, then shrugs. "I think you meant to say, *Your husband has a great ass.* Because he really does."

Brax just rolls his eyes. He's back at the coffee machine filling his own mug, so that fine, denim-clad ass is facing both of us. "True," I say. "I'd definitely give it an eight."

"Eight?" Brax scowls at me with mock offense, then turns to his wife. "Are you going to stand for that?"

She shrugs. "We both know I'm the pretty one."

She and I share a laugh as Brax murmurs something about putting up with women. Brina and I just let it slide. We both know he loves us. In decidedly different ways, of course. Brina with the fiery passion of star-crossed lovers for whom the gods finally decided to cut a break. Me with all the love of best friends who'd bonded under the pressure of training for the covert work that we still do.

We'd been in our early twenties when we'd met the way so many young people do—tossed into the back of a police van, then thrust into covert government work for the ultra-secret SOC with the FBI as a cover.

I'd been mourning the loss of my first—and only—love, Maxim Wilder. He'd been my refuge in a life full of pain in the form of a brilliant but abusive father and a junkie mother. Brax had been mourning as well, and we'd bonded over the loss of the people we most desperately loved.

That was more than fifteen years ago, and Brax and I have been tighter than tight ever since. Never romantic, although there had been a

period when we'd slid into a friends-with-benefits arrangement. It had worked for us, then petered out, leaving a deeper friendship behind, albeit a non-orgasmic one.

That ended ages ago, and Brina knows the score, so there's no jealousy of me from her end. And my only jealousy about their relationship is that they actually *have* a relationship.

Me? I have a hamster.

Not exactly the same thing.

Once upon a time, I'd thought I had with Maxim what Brax and Sabrina have. A Great Love. The kind that plays out in epic movies and inspires incredible scores from the likes of Hans Zimmer or John Williams.

I thought I'd been a part of something bigger than myself. It wasn't just me and Maxim. It was MeAndMaxim. A unit. A couple.

He'd been my best friend, my confidante, my partner, my lover. He'd turned my life upside down, erasing the horror of the only life I'd known before, and leaving sunshine, chirping birds and blankets of rose petals.

Then he'd disappeared.

At first, I'd thought he was dead. He had to be. There was no other reason he'd leave me like that, and for weeks, I was despondent, moving through the world in a fog. Then I got a letter.

I had to.

That's all it said. And those three little words just about killed me.

It was my recruitment into the SOC that saved me. There's nothing like being pulled into a secret government agency to kick a girl out of her funk. Not that the longing had ever truly gone away. It was always there. Always under the surface. The desperate craving for him. The fear that something horrible had happened to him.

And the desperate hope that one day I would see him again.

What's that saying? *Be careful what you wish for...*

About the time I was undertaking my early SOC assignments, intel began coming in about Group Ultra. About its leader, Killion Lambert, and about the underworld talent he was recruiting.

For the most part, the participants in Group Ultra were unknown, especially the higher ups. A few names leaked out—undoubtedly aliases—but no descriptions at all. For all intents and purposes, nobody knew anything about Group Ultra except the name of its leader and the fact that it existed.

But then an undercover MI6 agent who'd been trying to infiltrate the organization had managed to capture a single image on a micro-camera

embedded in a ring. He hadn't made it out alive, but the ring was still on the body when it was found floating in the Thames.

British intelligence recovered the ring along with the image, then shared it with allies, one of whom got it to the SOC. The image was blurry, but I recognized him. And MI6 confirmed that the man was Maxim Wilder, an agent whom they'd recruited years ago.

An agent who had gone rogue, then aligned himself with Killion Lambert.

That was how I'd learned that Maxim not only had dual citizenship, but that he'd left me because he'd been recruited by British intelligence.

And that was also how I'd learned that Maxim had joined Group Ultra, betraying his country, mine, and me along with it.

The intelligence community may not know a lot about Group Ultra, but a few things are certain: First, that Killion Lambert is the group's leader. Second, that Maxim Wilder stands at Lambert's right hand. Third, that Group Ultra is plotting massive genocide with the ultimate goal of a worldwide dictatorship ruling over the significantly reduced population. And, finally, that the group is dangerously close to finalizing a weapon that could make all of that happen.

Scary shit.

And one hell of a lot of pressure on my relatively thin shoulders.

Chapter Three

"I still don't think you should be going on a mission like this alone," Brax says, pacing my kitchen. "I'm going to talk to Ryan again."

"That's bullshit, and you know it." I toe out the chair that Sabrina abandoned and put my feet up. Ostensibly, she left to run errands. In reality, she left to give Brax and me time to talk. "How many times has a team tried to get close to Group Ultra? It never works. But this...I can get in. I may be the only one who can get anywhere close to Maxim."

"You don't know that for sure."

I shrug. "True. But we have to try. You know it as well as I do."

"I don't like it," he says.

"Oh, well, if Braxton Reed doesn't *like* it..."

I can tell from the tightness in his jaw as he comes toward me that he's fighting back a snappy retort. He stops only inches away, his hazel eyes trapping me as he scowls his familiar scowl. The one he pulls out when he's in big brother mode, even though we're only four months apart.

"I don't like it," he repeats, then reaches to take the plait of hair from my hand. "And you don't like it either."

I'm caught out, and we both know it. It's a habit of mine; when I'm nervous or thinking, I pull a hank of hair over my shoulder and braid it. Stupid, but when I was a little girl and my dad put me in the closet for punishment, there wasn't much else to do. Not many options in the dark, after all.

Of course, by the time I was eight, he took away even that bit of self-soothing with the simple expediency of buzz-cutting my hair. Which, according to my various shrinks over the years, is another reason I like my hair long.

Yup. The day I ran away with Maxim was the best day of my life.

And the possibility that he's now at the center of something so vile absolutely breaks my heart.

"Fine." I sigh, then aim a grimace at Brax. "You're right. I don't like it much either. So why don't you trot on over to the phone and call Ryan to outline your better plan?"

"Yeah, well, that's the kicker." He grabs two bottles of beer from the fridge, then sits in the chair his wife abandoned. He opens them both with a pop against the edge of my table, then passes one to me. It's barely noon, but I take it.

"Ryan and I went round and round with this," Brax says. "We're fresh out of better plans." He takes a long slug, swallows, then rubs his hands over his face, looking both miserable and exhausted. "It's just that this is dangerous shit."

"That's what we signed up for. I'm pretty sure that's what the paperwork said way back when we were recruited. The Dangerous Shit Squad."

He chuckles. "God, I love you."

"Back at you. But don't let Brina know. Let her go on believing she's your one, true love."

He manages to keep a stoic expression. "I'll do my best."

An awkward silence hangs between us, and I know we're both thinking the same thing. Finally, when I can't stand it anymore, I say, "I'll be fine. It will work. He won't hurt me."

"*Don't.*" The word seems yanked out of him, and its ferocity startles me. "Do not think like that. Do not think you've got the magic pixie dust that will keep you safe. This is not the boy you loved. This man is Lambert's right hand. The Maxim Wilder you loved is dead, and you know it."

I open my mouth to protest, then close it again and simply nod. Because what can I say? He's right.

He takes another sip of beer as he studies me, as if looking for cracks in my resolve.

"You said Zane Parker's your in-city contact? What do you know about him?"

"Just that he's scouting real estate. He primarily works in research. Not a field agent. Have you worked with him?"

"Nope," he says, and I hear what he's left unsaid: *And I don't trust anyone I don't know.*

"He's former SOC, too," I say. "I checked his credentials after I met with Ryan."

"I know," Brax says. But of course he's still going to worry. It's the job. We've been doing it for years, but there's still always that twist in your gut. A twist that comes with a hefty dose of eagerness, too. Because if we weren't all adrenaline junkies at some level, we would have crashed and burned long ago.

"Weapons?"

"Minimal," he says. "You have to look like you're reaching out to Maxim because you want to join his party. Not because you want to blow away his research team."

"It's not my first time to ride this pony."

"I know." He lets out a long breath. "But you're going in alone. Even your in-town contact doesn't know you're there unless something goes askew. And—never mind."

"And it's Maxim. We've already been down this road."

He catches my eyes and holds my gaze. "Do you think I don't remember how broken you were when we first met? It had been, what? A year since he'd disappeared, and you were still among the walking wounded."

"I'm not anymore," I assure him. "If anything, I've grown a coat of armor."

"I don't think you can actually grow armor."

"Armadillos do," I say, officially ending the portion of our program where he worries needlessly about me. "I can handle myself," I remind him, just to drive the point home.

"Fine. You win. Memorize this," he adds, then rattles off a phone number. "Got it?"

"Got it," I confirm. "Wanna tell me why I have it?"

"One of my burners. I'll keep it on me until you're back safely. Actually, go ahead and program that into your phone. Lucky number seven on speed dial."

"Brax…" I never had a big brother. For that matter, I never had a real mother or a father. Just Gerald and Martha, my egg and sperm providers. So, yeah, as much as I want to tell him to back off, the truth is it's nice to have someone who worries about me. And, yeah, I program the number into my phone.

"If you get in trouble," he continues in a no-nonsense voice, "you contact Zane per protocol. But you text me, too. One question mark. I'll trace your coordinates. Deal?"

"Then you have to do something for me."

His eyes narrow, and I know he's expecting me to tell him to back

off, to chill, to just stop worrying about me because I know how to do my job.

All of that is true, of course, but there's no need to say it. He already knows, and he's going to worry anyway. Just like I worry about him.

So instead, I stand up and move into the living room. I lift Gimble's cage and set it on the breakfast bar. My sweet little hamster starts to scurry, his nose twitching in anticipation of adventure. "Take care of him, okay? And tell him I'll be back soon."

Chapter Four

Brax offered to drive me to the airport, but since navigating LAX's drop-off zones is the kind of favor that requires handing over one's first-born child, I told him I'd grab an Uber. And because I'm not a stereotypical female, I know how to travel light—just a computer backpack and a small rolling suitcase. (The secret is remembering that you're a grownup and can buy anything you forgot). Which is why I now have over an hour before my ride arrives, and I decide to use the time to do a closer review of the file.

And then I'll call Maxim.

I take a gulp of lukewarm coffee. I need it. My mouth's gone dry merely from the thought of talking to him. I'm going to need a gallon-sized water bottle when I'm actually undertaking the real deal.

As soon as Brax left, I'd stripped down to my typical at-home attire, which consists of a tank top and girl-style boxer briefs. In pink, of course. Now, I turn on the TV for company, then settle on the couch with my iPad to review the PDF that the research team put together.

As *Barbie* streams in the background, I scroll through the twenty-five single-spaced pages. The first page is a summary of the key points followed by a table of contents. An appendix at the end includes various relevant illustrations and photographs. Even from my quick scan, I can grok the major takeaway—we know there's a weapon; we have no clue what it is.

Armed with that rather obvious bit of information, I start a more comprehensive review. I skim the summary first, just to get the lay of the land. Then use my stylus to make notations as I read through the rest of the document. It's dense, but well-organized and very informative.

It also reinforces the fact that we don't know nearly enough. And that Maxim Wilder is our best chance for learning more.

Which means I need to find a way to contact Maxim.

My first thought was to simply try his old cell phone number, but

Research had the same thought, and the file makes clear that the number has been reassigned, and the assignee is a ninety-three-year-old nursing home resident who lives in Portland.

Research opined that he is not likely involved. I'll go out on a limb and say that's a pretty good bet.

Fortunately, there's another possibility. My mission stems from the fact that we know about the non-profit water project. Whether we believe it's legit or not is beside the point as far as locating Maxim is concerned. The bottom line is that corporations have addresses. Or they should.

In the case of the water project, the address turned out to be the business office of the agent of record. Who happens to be an attorney who pretty much makes a living by allowing the corporations he forms to use his physical address.

Annoying and dicey, but not technically illegal.

Thankfully, tracing that thread was Research's problem, not mine. And I only skim the paragraphs that describe how they used the New York State corporate records database to search for businesses incorporated by that lawyer, then narrowed those responses based on various factors, then narrowed again and again until they finally landed on a corporate entity that seemed to hit all the right buttons.

But corporations can have multiple names by filing even more papers, which meant that in order to hone in on the actual address, the research folks had to do a bit of digging and blah, blah, blah.

In other words, I pretty much skipped to the bottom line, which is that the team managed to peg the location of a second building owned by Group Ultra.

Specifically, a corporation called Foundational Tech Services both owns and is housed in a ten-story building called the Squire, which is located in the Flatiron District, an area that has become very tech-heavy over the last few years.

Presumably, the personality of the area is one of the reasons Group Ultra chose it for a location. Especially since, in addition to secretly working on next-gen weapons, we suspect that Group Ultra generates additional capital by creating and selling equally sinister—though not deadly—software through one of its many legitimate arms.

Well, legitimate on paper, anyway.

The building itself was erected in the thirties, originally as a bank, and has been completely remodeled. Now it includes office space, the original bank vaults, several massive server rooms, a theater for presentations, a classroom that one of the local universities rents for community education

programs, and a full-fledged, completely tricked out lab that would put both NASA and the CDC to shame.

In addition, a video game company, a documentary producer, and a company that develops cruelty-free cosmetics all rent space on site. All check out as legit businesses and add that air of respectability to everything going on at the Squire.

In other words, the building and the businesses all feel and smell legit.

Which, of course, is exactly what Group Ultra was going for.

"Killion Lambert is an evil genius," I tell Brax when I call him only minutes after reviewing the file.

"Which is why we're trying to stop him."

"Oh, right," I say. "I thought maybe he had too many traffic tickets."

"You called me to state the obvious and tell bad jokes? Because, gotta say, *newlywed*."

"Yeah, yeah. That one's going to start getting old, you know."

"Yes, but not before we get past our first month anniversary." He pauses, and when he speaks again, the humor is gone from his voice. "You think he'll be there. On site."

"Foundational Tech," I say. "It's the primary tenant. Once the research team got that far, all they had to do was use Google to find the phone number." I make a scoffing sound. "A criminal organization intent on genocide, and it's phone number is right there on the Internet."

"Dickens was wrong. *This* is the best of times. And the worst of times."

I sigh. He has a point.

"Have you called yet?" Brax asks.

"No." I don't say that despite my bad ass job, my stellar skills, and my passion for taking down bad guys, I haven't yet worked up the courage to simply dial up my ex.

"You didn't screw up." His voice is as soft as a blanket, and I wish I could simply curl up into it.

"I don't know what you're talking about," I lie.

"Yeah, you do. I'm talking about before. When you met him."

"You mean when I loved him." There's a hard edge in my voice. Hate, but not for Maxim. For me. For being such a goddamn fool.

"Whoever he is now, that isn't who he was then."

"Maybe not. Or maybe I fell in love with a monster, just like my mother did." I close my eyes, wondering how I could have been so wrong. And the only consolation I can allow myself is that I won't make that mistake again.

Chapter Five

Twenty-six years ago

"Goddammit, you stupid whore! You think you don't have a job, too? I bring home the fucking money. You cook the goddamn food!" *Crack!*

I hear my mother's sharp yelp, and force myself not to cry. I wish I didn't have to breathe, because my father has magical powers. He can wake Mommy up or put her to sleep. He can make fireworks from stuff in the kitchen. He always knows when I try to sneak out of the house.

Most of all, I know he's magic because he can always, always find me. He says he will.

Then he does.

Then he hurts me just like he hurts my mom.

Except he never lets me have the candy afterwards.

"*Idiot woman.* Now I either have to be late or not eat at all. Do you know how much thought and concentration it takes to teach molecular biology to a bunch of stars-in-their-eyes grad students suffering under the illusion that someday they'll make something of themselves?"

His voice echoes through our house, making me tremble.

"Maybe one in a hundred that comes through my classes has any potential at all. Yet I have to hold constant vigil for that talent despite the prattle of *Dr. Green explain this*, and *Dr. Green, I don't understand that.* And I can't fucking search out the cream while babysitting the chaff if I'm lightheaded with hunger, can I, woman?"

I hear a small noise coming from the kitchen. I can't hear words, but I know there aren't any. She's making her begging noises. Her hand is out, silently begging for her candy. The candy I'm not allowed.

Once, two years ago, she didn't swallow her candy, and I took it from the table. It was orange and shaped like a squashed jelly bean. I was eight,

and I loved jelly beans. I knew I wasn't supposed to have Mommy's candy, but she hadn't made any food all day, and my stomach was rumbly with hunger.

I'd just put the candy in my mouth when something hard smacked against my back, and I tumbled forward, spitting it out.

"Not *ever* again," my father said, lifting me up by my hair. "I made that candy special for mommy. It's good for her. It will make her better. You want her to be better?"

"Yes." My voice was a scrawny, little whisper.

"I'll buy you jelly beans if you're good. And if you're bad…" He still held my hair, and he tugged on it. Reminding me of the last time I was bad. When he'd cut it all off and I'd cried and had to lie and tell everyone at school how I'd been stupid enough to play with a bucket of tar and my dad had to shave my head.

"You understand me, Camilla?"

I'd nodded again, and then he'd pulled me to him so that I was sitting in his lap, my back pressed against him. He held me by the waist, and I could feel his breath when he bent forward to whisper, "You're my good girl, Camilla. One day," he added, sliding his hands over my chest, "I'll thank you properly for being Daddy's good little girl."

Now, flat on my tummy under the chaise, I tremble with the memory. I'm ten now, and a lot smarter than I was then. I know my father's a bad man. I know that's not really candy. And I know that I don't ever, *ever* want to be thanked for being his good little girl.

Except I still have to be good. Because being bad is worse. If I'm bad, he'll hurt me. Or he'll make me eat the candy, too. And I don't want to be like Mommy.

"Camilla! Get your little butt in here and make me eggs."

I squeeze my eyes shut, trying to make myself small. I hear the pounding of his steps as he walks by the chaise. It's low to the ground with fringe. I used to be able to slide under from the long side, but I don't fit that way anymore. This time I did what Maxim said, and I wriggled under from the short side with the back rest.

It's a good hiding place. But he'll find me. Daddy's magic, after all.

Except he doesn't. I see his feet go past me four times, and he never bends down to look. Then he says more bad words, mutters something about having to eat fast food crap for breakfast, and slams out the front door.

I close my eyes, silently thanking Maxim. He'd said the chaise would be my new magical place, and he was right.

I force myself to count to fifty, then I wriggle out from my hiding spot. I creep into the kitchen to check on my mother. She's on the floor, her eyes barely open. She looks at me, then sneers, then tells me I'm an arrogant little bitch.

I don't know exactly what that means except that it's bad.

Maxim once asked me if my mom was always like that, and I'd said I didn't know. He says that he heard his father talking on the phone one day, and he paid attention when he realized that Mr. Wilder was talking about a neighbor, and that the neighbor was my dad. He said my mom was once one of my daddy's most promising students. He'd taken an interest and tried to develop her talents, but he must have pushed too hard, because she started taking drugs, and now she's an addict, and all that talent has gone to waste.

I told Maxim that I already knew my Daddy was a bad man, and he told me I didn't have to worry. That we were best friends, and he would never, ever let anyone hurt me.

And because it was Maxim, I believed him.

* * * *

My carry-on and my computer bag are waiting by the open front door when my ride arrives, and I still haven't called Maxim. Annoyed with myself for procrastinating like an anxious teen, I hold up a finger to signal the driver to wait. Then I pull my phone from my back pocket and dial the number I've already memorized for Foundational Tech Services.

I half-expect the number to turn out to be a fake, but when I dial, I get an official-sounding recording with a crisp and professional voice. Not that I'd been expecting an evil-sounding drone, but there's still something about the normality of it all that unsettles me.

Or maybe there's something about the man for whom I'm about to leave a message...

Get a fucking grip.

With that stern command in my head, I force myself to follow the voice's after-hours instructions, then press the pound key to access the dial-by-name option.

I dutifully tap out W - I - L, and am a bit agog that I'm immediately transferred to his voicemail.

"You've reached Maxim Wilder," the familiar voice says as my heart does a little flip. "I'm not available to take your call, but please leave a message, and I'll get back to you as soon as possible. If you need

immediate assistance during working hours, please press the star key to be transferred to the front desk."

Weirdly, strangely, totally normal...

A second later—long before I'm ready to speak—the sharp beep explodes in my ear. I open my mouth, shut it again, then hang up the phone.

Apparently, I'm still a little girl and not a hardened and professional intelligence officer.

Fuck. My. Life.

I dial again, hoping that the second time's a charm. This time when the message begins, I stand up straighter. I'm confident. I'm in control. I'm—

Beeeeep!

—flustered as shit, but here goes.

"Maxim. Hey. So, you may not remember me, but this is Cami Green." I wince. Of course he remembers me. "I, um, well, I was going through some of my old things, and I thought of you. So I Googled you, which sounds perverted now that I think about it—*Seriously, what is wrong with me?*—and I ran across an article about the place where you're working."

I pause, forcing myself to take a breath. "Bottom line, I'm heading to New York for a few days on vacation, so I thought I'd succumb to curiosity and sentimentality and call you. I'm getting in tonight, and I should be at my hotel by around eight your time. I'm staying in the Flatiron District, and I'd love to have a drink and catch up. I swear I'm not mad about the way you ghosted me. I mean, I was, but I'm over it. Anyway, call or text me back," I add, then rattle off my number, end the call, and sag against the door frame.

I sounded like a neurotic, hormone-addled teen. But maybe that's the way all women sound calling their ex who also happens to have been their first fuck. And first love. And who is now an international criminal with terrorist intent.

Yeah, I think. *Perfectly normal.*

And all I can do now is hope that he really is in New York. And that he calls me back.

Chapter Six

Maxim Wilder stood by the window in his eighth-floor office in the Squire as the message played over the phone's speaker, that familiar voice seeming to move through the room like an aural caress. He tried to focus on her words, but his mind wasn't making the leap. Instead, his body was taking the reins.

Tightening.

Longing.

Even after all this time, he was still like a well-trained dog. She whistled. He came.

He wanted to spit out a curse as a wave of disgust crashed over him. Not for her—though she deserved it—but for himself and his traitorous body.

He ran his thumb across his fingertips, remembering the feel of her skin against his. The weight of her on him. The way his cock felt inside her.

Damned if he wasn't hard already.

But he didn't want to be hard for that conniving bitch, and those sweet memories he'd held onto for far too long dissolved the moment he let himself remember her duplicity.

Even now, with the clarity of all the years behind him, he couldn't believe he'd been so wrong about her. But actions spoke louder than words. He knew what she'd done. How she'd betrayed not only him but everything she purported to believe in. And that had been one hell of a brutal pill to swallow.

When he'd learned about her true loyalty, he'd been disgusted. More than that, he'd wanted revenge so badly he thought he would surely die if she was allowed to live even one more day.

Back then, there'd been practical reasons to allow her to continue to

walk the Earth. Reasons that no longer existed. Or, at least, not to the same extent. And at any rate, no one else need know.

What was it they said? Revenge was a dish best served cold? Well, his dish of revenge had been left sitting out for years. The time had come to make her eat it.

Because here she was, back in his life all over again. And once again, Killion Lambert was between them.

He'd truly loved her once upon a time, but that didn't matter. That old and dusty affection wouldn't buy her time. All it did, in fact, was ensure that the punishment was that much easier to mete out.

Bitch.

She'd ripped his heart in two. Made him question his own judgment. Made him mourn a girl who hadn't deserved his tears and regrets.

But he was over her now. And he saw the world a hell of a lot more clearly.

This time he wouldn't lose track of his purpose.

This time, he was coming out on top.

* * * *

Twenty-eight years ago

"Maxim, you little devil. Get out from under that porch this instant!"

Maxim peered out through the broken whitewashed board, just one of many that hid the muddy, cobweb-filled underside of Auntie Jean's porch from view. But Maxim had found a loose one near the rose bush. Every day, he pushed it aside, crawled under the porch, then put the loose board back in place.

Once he was under the long, wide porch, he'd crawl to the front and look through the gap left from where the rotted end of one board had fallen off. His father kept telling Aunt Jean that he'd get around to fixing that board, but so far he hadn't.

Now, it looked like he never would.

On most days, Maxim liked to sit under the porch and peek out at the world through that broken place. Except that wasn't why he was under the porch today.

Today, he was hiding.

Bang, bang, bang.

Dust and dirt and a few bugs fell onto his head as someone stomped on the porch above him.

"Get up here, Maxim." His father's voice was calm, and unlike anyone else's on the street. It sounded like Mr. Little from the *Stuart Little* movies.

"That's because I was raised in London. Hugh Laurie—the actor who plays Stuart's dad—is British, too. You are as well, my boy. But you grew up here, so you speak like an American."

Maxim had frowned at that. He liked where he lived just fine. But he wanted to be like his dad.

Now, he hurried out from under the porch, then scrambled up the steps. He frowned when he saw the suitcase at his father's side. "Are we leaving?"

"Just me, son." His father crouched down to look him in the eye, then put a soft hand on Maxim's shoulder. "You'll be good for auntie, yes? Daddy might be gone a while."

"Where are you going?"

"I have to work. You know that Daddy sometimes has to go away for work."

Maxim nodded, hugging himself. He hated when Daddy had to go away. Mommy had gone away when he was just a little boy, and he'd never seen her again.

"How long?"

"I don't know. But you be good for your aunt. Do you promise?"

Maxim nodded then threw his arms around his father.

"None of that. You're a man, Maxim. You remember that."

"I don't want you to leave." He didn't know why, but this time the leaving felt different.

"You'll have to do things you don't want all your life. Best to get used to it now." And with that, his father patted the top of his head, then picked up the suitcase, and walked down the steps to the sidewalk. As he did, a taxi drew up, and Maxim's father got into the yellow cab.

He looked back only once, then waved at Maxim before pulling the door shut. The cab took off, and his father was gone.

For a moment, Maxim stared at the space where the taxi used to be, overcome by a strange sense of dread. Like he would never see his father again, just like he'd never seen his mother after the last time she'd left.

He told himself that he shouldn't worry. His father had gone away before. And he'd always come back.

With a frown, he turned to look over his shoulder, hoping that his aunt would give him some assurance, but the front door was closed and she was nowhere to be seen.

With a sigh, he turned back to look at the street, imagining his father was still there. He wasn't, of course. But now there was a girl. She looked younger than he was, maybe eight, whereas he was ten now. Practically a teenager.

She had really short blond hair, cut close to the scalp like a soldier. He might have thought she was a boy if she hadn't been wearing a jumper-style dress over a pink T-shirt. Her feet were bare, and she was squatting on the sidewalk across the street drawing on the cement with colored chalk. And every few seconds, she looked up at him through lowered lashes.

He smiled, just the once, and she looked quickly away.

He was still watching her draw when the door behind her opened and a man stepped out. Burly, unlike Maxim's lean and tall father. The man scowled, and called a name. "*Camilla.*"

The girl kept playing with the chalk.

"Camilla," the man called again, this time with an edge to his voice. "Dammit young lady, you listen when I talk."

Maxim stepped to the side, so that he was halfway behind one of the posts that supported the roof over the patio. He didn't like the way the man sounded, and he didn't want the man to see him. He wondered why the girl wasn't answering, then realized that she was wearing a Walkman and probably couldn't hear the man.

He saw the fury build on the man's face, then he actually jumped when the man suddenly stormed down the sidewalk and grabbed the girl—Camilla, he remembered—by the arm. He dragged her backward, ignoring the girl's sharp scream and then her protests of, "Daddy! Daddy! You're hurting me!"

As Maxim watched, they disappeared into the house. Maxim's stomach twisted the way it did when he was going to be sick.

That poor little girl.

He wished he was older. If he was older, he'd punch the mean man in the stomach. He'd make the man apologize. And he'd keep the girl safe.

But he wasn't older, and all he could do was stay on the porch and hope he saw her again. He wanted—no, he *needed*—to know she was okay.

He stayed there for the rest of the afternoon and well past dinner time. It was summer, so it was past his bedtime by the time it got dark, but he'd begged his aunt to let him stay out, and she'd agreed. But the girl hadn't shown up again.

He'd finally gone inside about midnight, but he barely slept for worrying about her. He didn't understand why it was bugging him so

much. He'd never even seen her before.

He knew the family had moved into the house only recently, but unlike the chatty and friendly families in their little neighborhood, the people in the house across the street never talked to anyone. Maxim didn't even know their names. Except for her.

Camilla. He smiled, then whispered it to himself. He liked the sound of it.

The next morning, he was on the porch before dawn. He waited, hoping to see the girl, but weirdly afraid that she'd been taken away. From the porch, he could see the driveway that ran along the side of her house, but not the garage. He heard when the car started, though, and he watched it pull out, then disappear down their street with Camilla's father behind the wheel.

For a moment he feared that she'd been in the car, too, and he just hadn't seen her. Then he saw the front door open, and the girl stepped out. She looked down the street, as if making sure the car was gone. Then she moved back to the sidewalk, picked up the chalk she'd left the night before, and continued with her drawing.

On his porch, Maxim rocked from foot to foot, not sure what he should do. Finally, he scrambled down the steps, looked both ways, then crossed the street.

She looked up at him, her brown eyes wide. "I don't know you," she said. "I'm not supposed to talk to strangers."

"I'm Maxim. I live across the street. That's my aunt's house. And you're Camilla. See? We know each other"

"I'm Cami," she said. "Only Daddy calls me Camilla."

He nodded. "Okay. I like that. Can you play? Do you have to ask your mom?"

Cami shook her head. "She's on the couch. Daddy says she's resting, and I'm not supposed to disturb her."

"Can you come to my house? It's just across the street." He pointed. "I can show you my castle."

Her eyes went wide. "You have a castle?"

He grinned, then held out his hand to help her up. He didn't know why he wanted to play with this girl. She was younger than him, and he usually played with the older boys. But there was something about her. Something sad and a little lost that made him want to make her smile.

"Of course, I have a castle. Don't you?"

She giggled and shook her head.

"Then you can share mine. You can be the princess."

"Really?" There was something in her tone that made him feel like the best boy in the world for making her happy. He was pretty sure this girl wasn't happy very often.

He held out his hand, and when she took it, he led her across the street to his castle under the porch. As soon as they got there, he started to worry. What if she thought make-believe was stupid?

But all he had to do was look at her face to know that she saw it, too. "It's amazing. It has towers and everything. And I can really be the princess?"

"Sure. Why not?"

She shrugged. "Where's your daddy?"

"He had to go. "

"I saw him leave in a taxi. When is he coming back?"

Maxim just shrugged again.

"Do you have brothers or sisters?"

He shook his head. "Do you?"

"No."

"You can be my sister."

Her eyes widened as she shook her head. "Then you'd have to have my daddy. And no one should have my daddy."

He nodded slowly, her words, making him feel icky inside. "Then you'll be my best friend."

"But I'm a girl."

He shrugged. "Can you read?"

"Pretty good."

"Can you climb a tree?"

"Sure!"

"Do you like comic books?"

She tilted her head to the side. "Duh."

"Well, see? We're friends."

"Really?"

"Gosh, yeah." He held out a pinkie, then gestured for her to do the same. He hooked his around hers, gratified when she caught on and did the same. "Friends forever," he said. "Now your turn."

"Friends forever."

And they were, too. At least until they weren't.

Chapter Seven

"There you are," Killion Lambert said hours later, as the doors to the elevator Maxim had just summoned opened wide. He stepped out, his dark brown eyes looking Maxim up and down before he slipped a friendly arm around Maxim's shoulders. "I was just looking for you on three. I didn't realize you were up here."

"Just catching up on some paperwork before I head out." He thought of her voice. Their unfinished business. And the invitation he fully intended to accept. "I've got somewhere I need to be."

"I hope you can take a second," Killion said, expertly steering Maxim toward the conference room. "We have a bit of celebrating to do."

Maxim paused mid-stride, breaking the connection between him and his boss. Killion turned to face him, a question etched in the lines of his face.

"What celebration?" Maxim asked, fearing he knew the answer.

Killion only smiled, then continued toward the conference room. Maxim hurried to catch up. He was supposed to be the man's second-in-command, dammit. How could he do his job if the arrogant SOB continually sidestepped protocol?

His gut twisted and he forced himself to push the worry down. The celebration could just as easily be about finally closing on the office space in Dubai.

He entered the room as Killion turned on the wall-sized television. He resisted the urge to check his watch, knowing that would only irritate his boss, but he needed to get going. Things were in motion that he was looking forward to attending to.

"You know I'm always available for you," he told Killion as he settled into his seat at one end of the long table. "But I'm expected somewhere. I thought you were out this evening. Sasha mentioned cocktails."

The corners of Killion's mouth curved down as his eyes narrowed. "Sasha needs to better understand her job parameters..."

"Only to me," Maxim said. "She only mentioned it to me."

Killion looked somewhat mollified, and since he didn't lash out with suggestions that the girl should be fired or demoted to file clerk, Maxim considered that a victory. Which, of course, made Maxim wonder what had happened today to brighten his boss's mood.

"A cocktail party," Killion said, apparently unable to let that faux pas go. "Maxim, my boy, I thought you knew me better. This close to D-Day? Do you really think I'd spend any amount of time away from here? For that matter, do you think I'd be that ironic?"

Ironic? "Sir? I'm sorry, I don't—"

Killion waved away Maxim's words. "Later. Right now, we have a different focus."

"Do you wish me to cancel my plans?"

"No, no. I only want to share this one tidbit with you, then you can go enjoy your evening. Tomorrow we will approach the project with renewed gusto. Tonight, I'll be working on plans for carrying out Phase Two. We must move forward with a plan that achieves the most impact."

"Tonight?" That was something he wanted to stay for, but he wasn't about to miss the meeting with Cami. That was pressing, too.

Very pressing.

He cleared his throat. "You've been working around the clock. Don't you think you should rest tonight? Celebrate at home, then get some sleep?" He still had no idea what the celebration was for, but he knew Killion's moods well enough to know the man was very, very pleased. That alone was enough to worry Maxim. If Killion moved too fast...

"Sleep," Killion repeated, then chuckled. "For now. Perhaps that will be our next project. Imagine how high we could rise if it wasn't necessary to waste those hours. It's something to think about."

Maxim nodded. Yes, the boss was in a remarkably good mood, and he couldn't help but wonder why. Surely it was more than the upcoming completion of Phase One, which Killion liked to refer to as Delivery Day, or "D-Day" for short.

As for Phase Two...

Killion still hadn't shared the details. Only that it would be the final test and proof of the weapon. Small scale, yes. But large enough for world leaders to understand how scalable—and deadly—it was. And to fall in line accordingly.

As for the weapon itself, it was scalable tech, able to wipe out an

individual or a population. Maxim wasn't a scientist, but he understood the basics well enough, and there was no denying that the tech was impressive.

It required the delivery of a modified bacteriophage—which could be set loose in a population through the water supply or in an individual via a drink or an injection. Once in the host/victim, the bacteriophage—a type of virus that infects bacteria—would attach to the human host's gut microbiome, or any other targeted cell. There, thanks to genetic engineering, the bacteriophage would remain dormant until activated by a specific RF signal. Once that happened, the engineered bacteriophage would edit the DNA of the host bacteria to cause it to produce toxins.

Those toxins, of course, would cause death. Immediate, painful, bloody death.

Despite being Killion's second, all Maxim knew was that it would take place in the city...and in less than one hundred hours. It was frustrating as hell not to be in that inner circle, but Killion was his own damn circle. And the only control that Maxim had was to keep doing his job in the hopes that Killion would trust him enough to share the details of Phase One's implementation.

"Anything I need to know about?" Killion demanded, his tone turning businesslike.

Maxim stood up straighter. "Not a thing, sir." He didn't mention the possible blond complication who'd just arrived in town. *That* he would take care of himself. "Everything's on target," he added.

"It certainly is," Killion said, his smile growing wider in the kind of way that made Maxim very, very nervous. Killion was rash and unpredictable. And rash and unpredictable people tended to abandon vetted plans in favor of foolish, unpredictable actions.

The television snapped on, the screen displaying CNN. Killion made no move to change the channel.

"What are we waiting for?" Maxim asked.

"No scroll bar. No breaking news." The smile widened. "They don't realize yet. Good."

"What don't they realize?"

"The cause of Senator Alice Crowley's death."

Maxim worked to keep the fury off his face. "We talked about this. I thought you were going to wait until our full demonstration. We agreed that this kind of personalized targeting could put the entire project at risk."

Killion spread his hands. "What can I say? I got antsy."

"Sir…" *Dammit, dammit, dammit.*

"Just one woman. Just one little gnat in a world full of little gnats. And no one other than you and I have even the slightest clue that her demise wasn't entirely the result of a truly nasty bacteria she was exposed to during one of her humanitarian missions." He shrugged. "These things happen, you know. The water in underdeveloped nations can present all sorts of health concerns."

Maxim forced a smile. "Yes. It certainly can."

"There now, you see. No need for the two of us to be at odds. You're my good right hand, Maxim. You know that."

"Apparently, you used your left hand to work that stunt." He said the words mildly, and as he expected, Killion chuckled.

"*Touché.* But we both know the bitch deserved it. She was growing far too powerful. But I shall refrain from smiting any more enemies. You have my word. After all, as you said, time grows short and there's still much to do."

He cocked his head, looking at Maxim with a slow smile of pure delight. "You must admit that a nod to Senator Crowley could be useful when we make our demands. What better way to truly emphasize that the threat is serious? That we can reach anyone at all. But we can discuss that some other time. You do know how much I'm counting on you, Maxim."

"I know," Maxim assured him. "And I'm counting on the hundred million you'll be paying me for my exceptional service and loyalty."

"And that's why I love capitalism," Killion said. "What's a better motivator than cash?"

Maxim looked straight into his boss's eyes. "I really can't think of a thing."

Chapter Eight

I've always loved Manhattan. The architecture. The crowds. The parks and stores and museums. The hidden alleys and secret basements. There are worlds upon worlds upon worlds hidden on this one small island. Most people have no idea.

But I do.

Long before my slide into the world of espionage opened my eyes even wider, I'd seen the secret hovels. The fecal-smelling sub-basements where people like my mother went to get their fix. The towering corporate buildings where ideas, not back-breaking work, make money flow. The schools where men like my father worked. Where he'd hid his true self as he'd worked countless hours in research labs and lectured to eager young minds. Some who would turn out to be lions. Some who would be crushed as lambs.

That's how my father divided people. The lions who ruled, seeking glory and power. The lambs, always focused on the inevitable slaughter to come, living one moment from the next and looking only for instant gratification. And both groups, he thought, were parasites that should be eradicated. *Kill the Lions. Slay the Lambs.* I heard it over and over and over.

He was a brilliant man, but not smart enough to know how to act around people. "So much potential in the world," he would say, "but we will never reach it. Not while the lambs exist to drag us down. And false lions block the way."

It was a lesson he wanted me to learn, and his favorite teaching technique was to beat it into me.

"Tomorrow," Maxim said one night when I was fifteen. My back was bruised from the beating I'd just taken, and my mother had laughed through it all. After my father had walked away, she'd told me I deserved it. That I was a parasite. One of my father's hated lambs. That I'd

destroyed her body. And that the only one who'd ever helped her was my father, because he made the medicine for her, and the medicine was all that made her feel better.

I hated her, but I felt horribly sorry for her, too.

Him, I just hated.

"Tomorrow," I repeated, the word tasting as sweet as chocolate. "Really?"

Maxim just tilted his head. Of course he meant it. We'd sworn an oath to protect each other and never lie. And that oath was the strongest bond I knew.

That was the night I'd run away from my home in the Bronx and into a basement with Maxim. He'd been living there already for the past three months, ever since his father had disappeared.

We'd taken the 2-line to Times Square, then walked the short distance to the shitty building in a shitty neighborhood. My new home was literally a cage. Extra storage for one of the apartments above the little bodega. But I didn't care because I was with Maxim, and it was our shitty cage.

"We have to be careful that the tenants don't notice us," Maxim warned. "But I'll find us another place soon."

"How? We can't pay for it." I knew he had a job unpacking crates and restocking the shelves at the bodega, but that was hardly going to get us an apartment. What it did get us was running water and a bathroom, because Maxim had copied the owner's key, and at night we'd sneak up to wash in the sink. The store owner didn't have a clue. Not that we were living in the basement. And certainly not that we were using the employee bathroom to wash up.

"We'll manage," he'd said. "I'll teach you what to do." And because I'd trusted Maxim since the day I'd met him, I believed him.

I never saw my parents again.

I doubt either of them even knew I was gone.

* * * *

I lean back in the cab and watch the city go by. I'd landed at JFK, and we've been fighting traffic ever since entering the tunnel. Now, we're passing Madison Square Park, and I can see the iconic Flatiron building as we continue toward The Clover, a cute little boutique hotel on East 23rd that Ryan booked for me.

On a sigh, I pull out my phone, check that I have a good signal, then

open my phone and messaging apps. No texts. No voicemails. No missed calls.

Just like the last five times I checked. I tell myself I'm annoyed only because of the mission; it will be a lot harder if I have to track him down.

But that's not the truth at all.

I want to say there's nothing personal. That everything in the past is just water under the bridge. But it is personal, and the fact that he hasn't called or texted not only irritates me, it actually tweaks my feelings.

Not *hurts* my feelings, because I refuse to let a son-of-a-bitch like Maxim hurt me. But I'll cop to a little tweak. We have history, after all. A history that apparently means nothing to him.

And that, sadly, means my job here will be that much harder.

Well, fuck.

On all counts, just...*fuck*.

For the rest of the ride, I concentrate on watching the city go by. With flight delays, the flight time, and a three-hour time difference between California and New York, it was already dusk by the time I got in the cab. Now, it's technically dark, but this is the City that Doesn't Sleep, and there's plenty of light for me to watch the streets as the driver weaves through traffic to arrive at the bellman's stand for my adorable little hotel.

Since I'd flown commercial, I'm not armed when I arrive at my perfectly appointed room, but Stark Security has a small network of semi-active operatives all around the globe. As soon as I'm settled and have locked the door, I follow the instructions that Leah, another LA operative, had texted to me while I was waiting at LAX. Sure enough, there's a small lockbox concealed under a loose tile behind the pedestal-style sink in the bathroom.

I remove both the gun and the magazine from the lockbox, slap the magazine in, then rack the slide to chamber a round. The only other thing in the box is a small knife and holster. I pull up the leg of my jeans and strap the holster to my calf before sliding the knife into place. The gun's a tiny KelTec with a clip, so I attach it to my waistband, counting on my comfy tee to cover it up. Then I put my iPad in the lockbox and tuck it all away beneath the tile.

After that, I grab my key and phone, then head out of the room to scope out the area and grab some dinner.

The hotel has a charming indoor cafe that looks like an outdoor patio, with trees lit with string lights and dainty tables and chairs. It's so lovely that I consider grabbing a sandwich there. But, again, this is a city that's wide awake at night, and I'd rather grab something I can eat while

walking because I'm anxious to get my bearings.

I consider heading to the theater district for a slice at Sbarro's, but the building I need to see is on 23rd near Second Avenue. In other words, almost the exact opposite direction from the iconic pizza place.

I head that way, gratified to find a stand selling gyros just a few blocks from my hotel. I grab one, and rather than maneuver with a gyro and soda, I sit at an outdoor table and try to get a feel for the area.

This isn't a part of the city in which I've spent much time, and even if it had been my regular stomping grounds when I lived here with Maxim, Manhattan has changed a lot over the years.

It's July, so the air is warm and muggy, a far cry from the cool nights in LA, especially near the beach. And despite bumping up against the Pacific Ocean, *muggy* is the last word I'd used to describe the area where I now live.

It describes my current location to a T, though, and I pluck at my shirt to cool down as I stand up, ditching my trash, but keeping my soda as I continue to walk the sidewalk with my fellow pedestrians.

Despite the humidity, it's a nice walk. Even this late, the city feels alive. Vibrant. Purposeful. Everyone who walks toward me or passes me looks like they have a destination, which is so unlike the majority of people I see around my small house, most of whom come bearing skateboards or beach towels and have no purpose more formal than getting chill.

I cross the street as I approach the Squire so that I can see the entire building. Its windows are mostly dark now, with illumination coming from only a few on the third and fourth floors. Offices, I assume.

On the top floor, I see a few strips of faint light that form a series of connected rectangles. It doesn't take a genius to realize that there are blinds on those windows, but light is sneaking out around the edges. Which tells me that whoever is up there doesn't care if the world knows he's working…but he doesn't want anyone to see what he's working on. And he's paranoid enough that he needs blinds on the tenth floor.

Interesting.

Or not. Even if this was a legitimate tech/science operation, they would still want to protect themselves from corporate espionage. In other words, I won't know what's on that floor—and whether or not it's benign or dangerous—until I make contact with Maxim and get myself in that inner circle.

I'd hoped that would have happened by now, and once again, I check my phone.

Once again, I'm disappointed.

Irritated, I turn around, telling myself I should go back to the hotel, get a good night's sleep, and start fresh tomorrow.

I tell myself that, but I know that's not what I'm going to do. There are places I want to see. Memories I need to confront. Lost hopes and dreams that I need to exorcise.

None of those things are in that hotel. But they are in this city. They are, in fact, reasonably close by.

I came to New York to get back in tight with Maxim. To maneuver myself back into his world. To regain his trust.

That's all well and good.

But there's one other thing I need to do about Maxim. I need to exorcise him, once and for all. And to really do that, there's one place in particular I need to go see.

Determined, I turn to face the opposite direction. As I do, I see a quick *swish* of movement. Nothing I can identify. Just a shadow moving a bit too quickly, as if something behind me hadn't expected me to turn on a dime.

I'm immediately on my guard, my hand ready to draw my weapon if need be. At the same time, I'm not overly concerned. There are quite a few people out. Someone could have been waving for a taxi. A dog could have sprung his leash. A cat might have been chasing a rat into a sewer.

It might have been my imagination.

All plausible explanations.

But my gut says it was Maxim.

Normally, I'd trust my gut. But I know my past has colored this mission more than it should, and I probably should have fought harder against Ryan's assessment that I was the perfect person for this job.

But I didn't, and now I'm here. And if Maxim really is stalking me... Well, I guess I'll just have to hope that he doesn't kill me before giving me the chance to tell him that I want in.

And that my skill at deception is honed enough that he believes me.

* * * *

Maxim eased back into the shadows as she turned, confident she wouldn't see him. From the research he'd done, he knew about her career with the FBI. And he knew that her skills were sharp.

His, he was certain, were sharper.

The better to punish her with.

Slowly, he drew in a breath then fisted his hands at his sides, tighter and tighter, forcing himself back to calm. Back to canny and careful. After a moment, she continued walking, and he fell in step behind her, taking more care to stay further back as he moved through the shadows.

When she'd first started moving, he hadn't realized where she was heading. First along 23rd, then right on Seventh until she reached Times Square. Only then was he certain that she was walking for more than the pleasure of taking an evening stroll. She had a purpose.

And he knew exactly where she was going.

He considered going ahead—how better to ensure she didn't clock that he was following? But on the off chance his conclusion was wrong, he continued to tail her. As he'd suspected, she hadn't come to scope out the shops or listen to theater patrons discussing the show they'd just seen while sharing cheesecake and coffee.

No, she all but ignored the hustle and bustle of the iconic area, turning instead to the west, then winding through familiar streets and alleys until she stopped in front of a well-tended brick building with potted plants lining the steps up to the entrance, and a polished brass plate with ten buzzers to ring each of the apartments.

Without thinking, he took a step forward as he recognized the place that had changed so much. He caught himself, then immediately slipped back into the shadows, shocked that he'd come so close to exposure. And even more shocked at the reason. *He'd seen the way she was hugging herself, and he'd wanted to comfort her.*

He'd actually wanted to comfort the bitch. The girl who'd betrayed everything they'd believed in. Who'd all but erased everything he'd done and sacrificed in order to keep them both alive.

Comfort? Not hardly.

Confront. Now, *that* he intended to do.

And maybe when he did, he could finally exorcise the memory of the sweet little girl who'd melted his heart the first time he'd seen her. And then he could act on the reality of the bitch who'd taken her place.

Chapter Nine

Twenty Years Ago

"Three quarters, two dimes, and a nickel," I say, pulling myself up so I'm halfway on the checkout counter and can see into the open cash register till. I push my dollar bill toward the clerk. "Thanks so much for breaking it. "I really need the—"

"*Oh, shit! Help!*"

The words come from behind me and are accompanied by a metallic clatter. On the other side of the counter, the clerk jumps back, then circles the counter and hurries to where an entire metal shelving unit has fallen.

As soon as he goes, I reach into the till and pull out all the bills. I shove them down my shirt into my bra, then hop down and hightail it for the door as I hear the clerk say, "Good god. What the hell happened?"

I'm well onto the sidewalk and sprinting away before that same clerk bursts onto the sidewalk behind me, yelling for me to stop.

I don't. Instead, I make a sharp left into an alley, sprint another two blocks, then meet up with Maxim at the McDonald's we'd picked as our rendezvous point.

"You okay?" He looks me up and down.

I cross my arms and give him an eye roll. "Hello? I'm not the one who pulled a shelf down on myself."

"Missed me by a mile. And I was out the back just like we'd planned before that cashier even got to me."

I lift my hand for a high five, but he ignores it. Instead, he puts his palms on my cheeks, then kisses my forehead. When he releases me, I don't quite meet his eyes. I'm too afraid that if I do, he'll see the truth. And I'm terrified that the truth will mess everything up.

We've been best friends since that day he took me to his castle, and I think I would die without him in my life. But I don't want to be besties anymore.

I want to be his everything. Because he's already mine.

But I can't say that. How can I say that knowing it just might ruin everything?

"Hey, you okay?"

I realize we've reached the counter. "Sorry. Large fries and a Big Mac." He orders, too, then pays, and we take our food to one of the round booths, and I slide in next to him.

There's nobody else around, and I start pulling bills out of my bra and flattening them on the table. The score's over five hundred dollars, which is seriously spectacular. And totally justifies taking the rest of the day off.

"Wanna hit the museum?" We're outside again, the money sorted and our bellies full.

He shakes his head, and I sag a little.

"Then what? Just head back to the basement?" Not that I hate the basement storage area that's become our home. I don't. How could I with Maxim with me and no Professor Gerald Green to make my life miserable? But it's not exactly a cozy place. And it's better to stay away during the day, anyway, since that's when folks needing stuff from their storage areas will head down into what's essentially our back yard.

"We're not going back to the basement," he says. "Not ever."

"Very funny." But when I look at his eyes, I can tell he's not joking.

"I have a birthday present for you."

I laugh. "I have a whole week to go before I'm seventeen."

"Then call it an early present. Or a really late Sweet Sixteen. Does it matter? Unless you don't want it," he adds with a tease in his voice.

"Are you kidding?" I throw myself at him, and he catches me in a tight hug. "I totally want it."

For a moment, he holds me tight, our eyes locked on each other. I feel my heart pick up tempo, and I wait, craving more. But then he lets go, stepping back before I can work up the nerve to take what I want.

"Then we should go." I think I hear an edge in his voice. The kind of edge I want to hear. To feel.

But it's probably just my imagination.

I lecture myself about getting over this growing crush during the entire walk. And even though it's at least three miles, we barely talk at all.

Then he stops in front of a gray brick building in a neighborhood that's only slightly dodgy. I hold my breath, certain this can't be what I think it is.

Except it is.

It's an apartment. It's *our* apartment. A tiny seventh-floor walkup already occupied by a zillion roaches who scurry when Maxim opens the door. It's a studio with barely a kitchen and a bathroom that rivals the worst public toilets in the city. There are five locks on the door, one window, and one very saggy looking bed.

And all our stuff sits in a pile in one corner.

"This is ours?"

He nods, and I know him well enough to read his expression—he's nervous as hell about whether I like it.

I do.

"This is amazing," I whisper. "How—"

A grin lights up his handsome face. "We make a hell of a team. I've been saving for the deposit, but with as much cash as we have stockpiled and how much we've been scoring weekly..." He trails off with a shrug. "We can afford it."

"Wow."

He glances toward the bed. "I know there's just one. But I figure we shove a foam mattress under the bed, and at night I'll just pull it out. Easy-peasy."

I don't look at him. I keep my eyes on the bed. "We have to be even more careful now," I tell him. "If they catch us, they'll separate us."

"Never." He moves to my side, then takes my hands. "Best friends for life, remember?"

I swallow. "I remember." But I'm speaking to the floor.

"Hey." His voice is heavy with worry. "What's wrong? You do like it, right?"

"I love it." I can barely say the words through the tears that are clogging my throat. "I just..." I trail off, terrified of saying the words.

"Cami?" He squeezes my hands. "Hey, you can tell me. What's wrong?"

I tell myself not to be a coward. I basically flip the bird to the cops every day, and I'm worried about a few words?

But I am. I really am.

"You're starting to—"

I lift my head and blurt it out: "What if I don't want to be friends anymore?"

Pain—something close to terror—clouds his eyes.

"No, no," I say, frantic now. "No, I don't mean like that. I mean that I want—"

I cut myself off, terrified he doesn't want it, too.

"What?" His voice is the most gentle I've ever heard. Even more gentle than the day we met.

I lift my shoulders, but say nothing.

"Hey" he says, tilting my chin so that I have to look at him. "I want it, too."

At first, I can't process what he's said. Then I try to form words so that I can ask him if he means what I hope he means. But I don't have to ask, because now his mouth is on mine, and he's kissing me, and it's the most wonderful feeling ever. I don't want to stop, but my knees are weak, and I pull gently away, my heart pounding as I whisper. "We need a couch."

It's only when he laughs that I recognize the worried expression that now fades. He must realize, too, because he shrugs, looking more shy than I've ever seen him. "I thought you'd changed your mind."

"Never." I squeeze his hand. "But my legs don't work when you kiss me like that."

The corner of his mouth twitches. "That makes me sound pretty awesome."

I bite my lower lip and lift a shoulder. "You already know you are. To me, anyway."

He cups my cheek with his hand, and I close my eyes, soaking up the pleasure of his touch. When I open them again, I can't help but gasp at the intense heat I see in his eyes.

"Cami, I—"

"Yes," I say. Then I move forward and hook my arms around his neck. "Kiss me again."

He doesn't hesitate, but the first brush of his lips against mine is sweet, almost hesitant. I make a needy sort of sound in my throat, and he pulls away long enough to grin at me. Then he takes my hand and tugs me to the bed. "Your legs," he says. "'Cause we don't have a couch."

He releases my hand, then climbs onto the bed, then slides up so he's sitting on a pillow and his back is against the wall. I'm nervous. But I'm more afraid of letting this moment pass, and so I scramble onto the bed. I crawl forward, as if I'm going to sit beside him, but I change my mind and straddle his outstretched legs instead.

He looks at me, the heat in his eyes now raw and needy. I'm on his thighs, my knees on the mattress, and when I look down, I realize I'm only inches from the bulge in his jeans. Without asking, I reach out and press my palm over it. He closes his eyes and groans, and as he does, a wash of feminine power floods my body, making my core ache with need.

My whole body goes tingly, and I cry out with delight when he

pushes me backwards until I'm flat on my back and he's the one straddling me. He bends over, his mouth claiming me. His body caging me. His kisses are slow and deep, and his hands on my breasts are making me crazy, as is the way his hips are moving over mine, the way I can feel how hard he is through the denim of his jeans.

I have no idea if we're doing this right, but it feels so good I don't care if we're missing every one of the important steps. We'll get to them eventually, and there's something about kissing him that makes me never want to stop. Because his kisses are magical. They don't just make my mouth tingle, but my whole body.

My breasts. My thighs. My pussy.

"*Maxim!*" I arch up, realizing that he's unbuttoned my jeans and is kissing his way down the button fly.

"Lift your hips," he orders, and I do what he says, far too turned on to be even slightly embarrassed when he tugs off my jeans and panties.

"You, too," I beg, and he stops kissing my lower belly long enough to strip. I watch, feeling a wild kind of hunger as he gets naked. As I see his cock and think about what he's going to do with it.

I feel like I should be nervous, but I'm not. On the contrary, my entire body is humming, as if this is what I've been waiting for my entire life. "Please," I beg. "I need you. I want to feel you. I want to feel you inside me."

"Are you sure?"

I almost scream. "Do you want me to beg?"

He laughs, then kisses me, long and deep. But when he breaks the kiss, I see both passion and tenderness on his face. "If it hurts…"

"Stop teasing me," I beg. "Dammit, Maxim, please, please fuck me."

A fire seems to flash in his eyes, and I want to cry out with relief.

I can't, though, because his mouth is on mine, taking what he wants just as his hands on my breasts are doing. And when he slips a hand between my legs…

Oh. My. God.

It's magical. His touch. His fingers. His cock. And then that pleasure that presses up against pain, but never quite reaches it.

"Yes," I cry.

"Yes," I moan.

"Please," I beg.

But it's only when he whispers, "I love you," that I truly shatter. And there, in that filthy apartment with rats squeaking along with the rusty bed springs, I have the most magical night of my life.

Chapter Ten

We shared three more apartments, each more fabulous that the one before, the square footage and luxury increasing with our skills. And the truth was, we'd been an amazing team.

By the time I was nineteen, we were living in a two-thousand-square-foot townhouse near the park with a full kitchen, two bathrooms, a huge primary bedroom, and even a guest suite that we used as a rec room for our various consoles, games, and the projection television.

For most of that year, it had felt as if there was nothing we couldn't accomplish. Every dream was ours for the taking. Dancing. The theater. Long walks in the park. Travel.

And sex.

Lots and lots of sex.

We were living in a paradise of our own making. The Dynamic Duo. The Dream Team. We even bought a small souvenir store, which, despite existing primarily to launder our ill-gotten gains, actually turned a reasonable profit.

Life was glorious, and though we understood that our world could be shattered at any time if we were to get caught, we were both arrogant enough to believe that would never happen. We were young. We were clever. We were rich.

We were untouchable.

With a sigh, I let my gaze skim once more over the building I'd come to see. Maxim and I may have fallen and decayed, but this building has blossomed. Whereas before it looked ready to tumble, now it's strong and beautiful. The way I'd always believed Maxim and I would be, too.

I'd been so damn naive. Believing that we'd always be a team. Maybe even with kids. We'd have real jobs and be respectable. We'd live like the people we saw in all those old TV shows we used to watch. And whatever

problem entered our life would be over and solved by the end of the episode.

And when we were old and gray, we'd still be together and disgustingly happy.

So much for hopes and dreams…

I blink, tears filling my eyes as I take a seat on the stoop near a potted fern.

It had happened on a Thursday. I'd gone to a yoga class and had come home to find the apartment empty. I'd assumed Maxim had gone out to run errands. Usually, he left me a note or sent a text, but I wasn't overly concerned.

But when I still hadn't heard from him an hour later, I texted him.

No response.

I called.

Nada.

That was when I checked the bedroom. His clothes were gone. His books, his wallet, the notebook where he scribbled random things he didn't want to forget.

Even the I

into my job, and I squeezed Maxim out of my pores like squeezing a sponge.

Then I got a note in the mail with no return address, and I realized just how hard it is to wring away everything caught in a sponge.

I had to. I'm sorry.

I stared at the note, feeling sick. Wondering at the extent of his cruelty in sending it. And hating him all the more.

Even now, years later, I wish he'd never sent it, because by then he was dead to me, and I didn't need that tiny spark of life popping up again. The bastard had destroyed me, and for what? So that now he could come back into my life as a genocidal asshole I never saw coming?

The kind little boy who'd taught me to survive—who'd made me return money when we stole from people who couldn't afford it—who had been the only person I'd trusted at my side. Now he was in the upper echelon of Group Ultra and standing at the side of Killion Lambert?

Well, maybe he'd done me a favor by leaving. Because that Maxim Wilder wasn't a man I wanted in my life.

But here he is again, and I am *so* going to take him down. Not just for his crimes. But for betraying me, too.

For making me love him, and then walking away.

For ripping my heart in two.

Oh, yes. I'm going to fry the bastard.

And that, I think, will be a goddamn pleasure.

I draw a breath, then take one more look at the building where I'd first given myself to him. Where we'd shared our first *I love you.*

Except it hadn't been real. None of it had been.

Bastard.

With I sigh, I close my eyes, steeling myself against the inevitable. Then I turn around, and speak to the darkness. "Did you decide to join me on this trip down Memory Lane?"

For a moment, I see nothing. Just the shadows dancing as a few cars pass by. I'm almost convinced that I'd only imagined him when he emerges like a sorcerer from a shadow cast by a delivery truck.

Maxim.

The man I'd once loved. He's older now, of course, but the years have only enhanced his exceptional looks. That face I'd loved so much has lost some of the roundness of youth. Now it looks to have been chiseled from stone, brought forth by an artist of exceptional ability. His body is still long and lean, but he holds himself now with the bearing of a man and, damn me, I feel myself tighten with a longing I have no desire

to feel. But my traitorous body has other plans, and I give in to temptation and let my gaze roam over him, soaking in what used to be mine, and what I no longer want to crave.

I'd only seen him in a suit a few times, but before it had almost been as a child playing dress-up. Now, it seems like a part of him. A man who believes in his own value, and who would look just as powerful and put together in nothing more formal than jeans and a T-shirt.

But it's his eyes that do me in. Those sky-blue eyes that always seemed to see straight into my soul. What, I wonder, are they seeing now?

As if in answer, he takes a step toward me. "I think I must be a masochist," he says. "Soaking up these memories. It's like drawing acid into my veins."

"Good. I hope it burns." I allow myself one tight smile. "And thank you."

His brow furrows. "For what?"

"For showing me who you really are. You ripped the bandage off back then. It just about killed me, but that was better than the alternative." I take a step toward him. "Imagine how stupid I'd feel right now if I still believed you'd ever loved me."

Though it's probably a trick of the light, I think he actually winces at my words. But all he says is, "You called me. Why?"

I let my eyes roam over him. Toe to head, head to toe. "We made a good team back in the day, didn't we?"

He slides his hands into the pockets of his slacks. "We did."

"I think we can again."

He tilts his head, studying me. "I'm listening."

"Not now. Meet me in the bar at my hotel in an hour. We can talk there."

"You haven't told me which hotel."

I flash him my sweetest smile. "Sugar, if you can't figure that out, then you aren't even close to good enough for me." And then, even though I know he's dangerous, I turn my back on him, and I walk away.

Chapter Eleven

The charming little bar off the lobby of my hotel does a brisk business, and I can only assume that it's a hangout for folks who live and work in the area. I tried to get a stool at the actual bar, but all the seats were taken, so I'm standing near a stone column, sipping club soda and deflecting interest from several of the men who pass by.

I'd popped up to my room to change, and apparently the sleeveless top, body-hugging skirt, and fuck-me-heels were the right choice for catching a man's eye. But it's not these random bar-goers I'm interested in catching. I want Maxim to see me at my best, not in the jeans and tee I'd worn to wander the streets.

I need him to trust me. And maybe it's a cliche, but I'm more than willing to use sex to get what I want.

And my deep, dark secret? I'm actually looking forward to that whole Sex For The Mission thing. He may be an evil, scum-sucking creep who I'll never forgive for ghosting me, but I can't deny the twinge of arousal that seeing him earlier shot through me. The way my pulse had quickened when I became certain he was tailing me. The way my memory became a physical thing, all touches and caresses, lips and hands. On the one hand, I despise the way my body had reacted. But more than that, I want him to fully understand what he walked away from. I'd been a girl when he left. I'm a woman now. And I want him to regret the hell out of leaving me.

Still, it's not payback or emotional castration that's truly running this show. That's just a bonus. Right now, all I need is for him to get his ass to this bar so I can start the work of worming myself into Killion Lambert's operation.

Frustrated, I check my watch again. I'd told him one hour, and it's five minutes past that.

He's ghosting you.

The possibility makes me anxious. All we know is that Killion Lambert is planning to deploy a weapon, and he's using the water treatment plant project as cover. But as for details, we know nothing. Not what his timetable is, not the nature of the weapon, not even if the water treatment plant is part of the delivery method, or merely acted as a cover during the manufacture of the device.

For all we know, it's nothing more than a functioning water treatment plant, and has been a red herring all along.

Since the only way to get that information is to get close to Maxim, this entire mission is riding on me. But it's not just about a mission. It's about lives. One or a million or even more—we don't know, and it doesn't matter. If Killion Lambert takes even one innocent life it's too many.

I can't let that happen. But unless and until I come up with a Plan B, my access point to Lambert is through Maxim. And if he doesn't show up, I don't know what the hell I'm going to do.

And, honestly, why wouldn't he show up? He followed me around all night; you'd think he'd follow me here, too.

I order another club soda, then sip it as I meander through the bar, hoping he'll sidle up beside me.

He doesn't.

I step out onto the little patio that opens to a sitting area and koi pond.

No Maxim.

I go back inside and chat with the bartender, going so far as to ask if he noticed a guy fitting Maxim's description in the last hour.

No luck. And now he's more than fifteen minutes late. Either something happened or he never intended to meet me in the first place. Which means I need to figure out where he's staying and go to him.

Or find another pathway for getting close to Killion Lambert.

I walk the perimeter of the bar one more time, and when I still don't see him, I go into the lobby, then fidget until it's my turn at the concierge desk. Perhaps he left a message.

But the concierge confirms what I already know. No message. Moreover, this hotel has no second bar or secret executive club room where he might be instead.

The son-of-a-bitch blew me off. Which, frankly, irritates the shit out of me.

There's nothing I can do tonight, though. I don't even want to try. I'm physically exhausted from the travel and emotionally exhausted from

my trip down memory lane. I need sleep, and my plan is to crash now, then check in with Brax and the rest of the team the minute the sun rises over Los Angeles.

I'm still seething about Maxim's no-show when I exit the elevator onto my floor, and despite the fact that it would probably be wise to grab my iPad from the hidden lockbox and give the research file another read, I promise myself that all I'm going to do once I get inside my room is glom a mindless movie, drink whatever wine is in the minibar, and think absolutely zero thoughts about Maxim Wilder.

I need that man out of my head.

Armed with my no-Maxim plan, I swipe my card key with a much lighter heart, then push open the door, step inside, and scream.

Chapter Twelve

Or I try to scream.

I can't manage it with the hand over my mouth, and I can't struggle free from the strong arms holding me from behind. I've had training in hand-to-hand combat, but right now, my skills are about as useless as a Nerf football.

"I probably should have killed you on the street." His words are flat. Matter-of-fact. "I'm seriously considering remedying that right now."

His breath is warm behind my ear, but the words are as cold as ice. I tremble in his arms, then want to kick myself for showing fear. Hell, for getting caught at all. I'm better than that. And the only excuse I have is that I let my attention slip. Part of my mind had veered away from safety and the mission and my training.

Part of my mind had gone to Maxim. The man who may kill me right now.

"You shouldn't have come," he says. "I'd almost gotten over hating you."

"Mmmph!" The sound erupts from me before I can help myself. *He* hates *me*? I haven't just been captured, I've been catapulted down the freaking rabbit hole.

"Now that we have some privacy, we should probably have a little talk. Much more productive than me watching you wander the city."

His lips brush the back of my ear, and his breath flutters my hair as his arm remains at my neck. "What do you think? Shall we do some catching up between old friends?"

As he speaks, his arm tightens. One quick move, and he can break my neck. He doesn't bother to tell me. He knows that I know.

But it's not the death grip that truly frightens me. It's what he's doing with his other hand. Which is exactly what I'd intended as part of my plan

to entice him to add me to his team. In that scenario, though, I'd been the one with the power. Right now—as his fingers slip under my fuck-me skirt and begin slowly tracing their way up—he's definitely claimed the upper hand.

I try to hold myself straight. To fight a traitorous, rising desire. He's a dangerous man, I know that. But more than that, he's dangerous to me.

This is a man who knows what turns me on. What gets me off. Who knows all the little secrets that I shared with him in our bed. Hell, most of those are secrets we learned together.

How I like it hard. Not tender or sweet. How I get off on danger. How every time we were almost caught, the sex when we got home was incredible. Sometimes, we couldn't even wait until we got home.

Which is why even though I hate myself right now, my breathing is hard and shallow. My skin is tingling. And my core is so wet that when he thrusts his fingers inside, his low moan harmonizes with mine, and in that moment a wave of fury crashes through me. Fury against him, because he betrayed me. Betrayed *us*. And against myself, because despite his treason, all I want right now is him. His touch, his mouth, his cock.

All of him. I want it. I want *him*.

This man I'd once loved is at the center of a god-only-knows what kind of nefarious plot. He's holding hands with evil and he knows its name.

And right now, I don't give a damn about any of that. This is Maxim. The only man I ever loved. A man who doesn't know the real reason I've come to New York.

A man who believes my hate for him stems only from him leaving me, and not because of the vile master he now follows.

A man I will destroy if I have to.

But not yet.

Not until he makes me come.

"There she is," he says, keeping two fingers in my pussy and teasing my ass with another as he tumbles us both onto the bed. He ends up on top of me, his cock hard beneath his slacks. I reach for him, wanting him inside me. Wanting this one last fuck even though I know what he is and that we can never, ever do this again.

"Not yet," he says, then bends over me, his fingers playing me, bringing me higher and higher. "Kiss me," he demands, and as I arch up to meet his mouth, I see a familiar heat in his eyes. A gleam that sends a slurry of sparks cascading through me. Because I know that look. This may have started as a hate fuck. An anger fuck. An I'm-Beating-my-nemesis fuck.

But it's more than that now. This is us. This is the us we used to be. And though I hold no illusions that we'll ever get that back—I know that once the passion fades, we'll be enemies again—I can't help but thank whatever gods there are that I get to have this man one more time.

With more grace than should be possible, he strips off his tailored slacks and jacket as I rip his shirt open, sending buttons flying. His mouth is on mine, his hands on my breasts, his cock right there. Then he shifts, rolling us without warning so that I'm on top of him. "Now," he says, and I take him in, arching back as I rock my hips, taking him deeper and deeper until it feels as though he's touching everything inside me.

I ride him hard, not caring that he's the enemy, not knowing what he'll do after. Right now, I'm simply chasing an orgasm, thrusting myself back to a past when he belonged entirely to me. When we'd discovered the pleasures of our bodies together.

When we hadn't had any secrets.

"Stop," he demands, and I whimper in protest as his fingers tease my clit. "Stop," he repeats as I continue to rock my hips, just a little, wanting to keep fueling the explosion.

I sit up straighter, feeling smug that he's no longer protesting. I'm still grinding against him, and he's still hard inside me. He has one hand on my hip and his eyes are locked on mine. It's a dangerous game we're playing. We both know it. Absent a blade at my throat, it doesn't get more dangerous than this. And right now, Maxim is a living, breathing blade.

"Tell me why you're here," he says, his fingertip still teasing my clit.

"I want to join you." I have to force the words out on a gasp of exquisite pleasure. "I know you're planning something big. I want in."

"Why?"

"I'm tired of being fucking broke. The FBI pays a shit wage, and most of my bosses are assholes. And I don't work that well having a boss anyway."

The corner of his mouth curves into a knowing smile and he moves his fingers in a slow, deliberate motion even as he pistons his hips. "FBI? Aren't you giving away too much?"

I'm having a very hard time focusing on his words.

"*Cami.*"

"Yes. I mean no. Don't try to bullshit me, Maxim. You must have checked me out. You know they recruited me."

"I did. That's a nice little program they have going. Recruiting all those bad girls and boys who already have such interesting skill sets."

"Yes." The word is a moan, more in response to the play of his

fingers than what he's saying to me.

He cups the back of my head, then pulls me down so that his mouth captures mine. The kiss reverberates through me, and I have to fight the urge to let go, to quit thinking, to simply be with this man I love.

No.

I jerk myself upright, unsettled by my thoughts. By that word. By how much his touch has pushed me back into the past. I don't want this man any more. If I want anything from him, it's to land his ass behind bars.

"What?" he asks, but I dodge the question by easing off of him, then rolling onto my side. "I want out," I say as I stroke his cock. "But right now, my job is the last thing I want to talk about. For that matter, I don't want to talk at all." I'm playing a game—a dangerous one. All the more dangerous because although the words are meant to be a ploy, I mean them.

His eyes narrow, and for a moment I think the gig is up. Then I see that slow, sexy grin I know so well. He presses a fingertip to my lips as if acknowledging my plea, then rolls us over once again so that I'm straddling him, his cock filling me.

"Is that what you want?" His hands are on my hips and he lifts me easily, then brings me back down over and over and over in a rhythm that has all sorts of wildness riding through me. That has me brushing up against that sweet, dangerous edge.

"Do you want me to take you over?"

I gasp. I'm close. So damn close.

"Say it, baby."

"Yes."

"Come here," he says, lifting his head as if to kiss me. I bend over, and his lips brush over mine. "Too fucking bad."

In a heartbeat, he shifts, then pivots at the waist so he's sitting up. In that same moment, he lets me see the syringe in his hand. I don't know where it came from—and it doesn't matter. That metaphorical blade I'd felt earlier? That was nothing.

This is fear.

That unknown clear liquid?

It could be death

"That's all folks," he says in a cartoon voice. Then the needle is at my throat and I'm struggling, but it's no use, because the plunger is in and whatever this stuff is, it works fast. The room spins, then goes black.

And my last thought is that I hope I'm not going to wake up dead…because I really want the chance to kill that man.

Chapter Thirteen

The monsters are everywhere. Needle-like teeth. Razor-like claws. They slice and cut. They lash, they sting.

The venom...oh, god, the venom...

It's in my blood.

"Tell us, Cami. Just whisper your secrets..."

Can't talk.

Can't tell.

"Quit fighting. It will all be okay if you just listen to the voice. Just answer the question. How will the agent be introduced? Into what population?"

Yes! Yes! That's the question. Need to wake up. But the monsters, the monsters, oh, god, the monsters!

"Does he suspect a traitor? Who? What does he think he knows?"

Can't breathe, can't breathe, can't—

My eyes fly open, and I try to sit up. I can't. I'm weighted down, my arms and legs spread, my body trapped.

Monsters and needles.

Was it a dream? Was it real?

Maxim!

Was he real? Is he one of the monsters?

Has my cover been blown?

I draw a breath, then another. Then, slowly, I realize that I'm not tied down at all. That was a remnant of the dream. But I am in a bed in a small, dark room.

And—oh, joy—I'm naked.

There's a single sheet on the dingy mattress, and I slide off the bed, then wrap the sheet around myself as a make-shift toga. I'm alone, so it's not so much for modesty—though I can't discount the possibility of peepholes or spy cameras—but because I'll think better if I'm at least

semi-clad.

The first thing I need to think about is getting the hell out of here.

I glance around, taking a fast assessment of the place. A bed. A wooden chair. A boarded-up window. A narrow beam of early-morning light has snuck through, and dust dances in the light. Across the room, there's an open door through which I can see a sliver of a sink, and a closed door locked with six deadbolts.

I don't have to be a genius to know they can't be unlocked from this side. Even so, I go over there and check.

Just that short walk is exhausting, and I scrub my hands over my face, then lean against the wall. I'm a little dizzy, but other than that, I don't seem to have any lingering effect from whatever drug he injected me with.

So far so good.

That, however, is about the only thing that's good. For one thing, I don't have my phone. Which means that I have no way of calling Brax at the number he made me memorize. Or anyone else, for that matter.

Worse, while a quick check reveals I'm still wearing the small opal stud earrings I habitually wear when I travel, the stud I wear in the second hole in my right earlobe is missing. Which means that Maxim discovered—and removed—the tiny location beacon that, when activated, would have sent the emergency SOS to Zane Parker.

Still, I wasn't tied to the bed, despite the fact that I see handcuffs attached to the wrought-iron bed posts. So that's a plus. More, the door to the bathroom is open, so even if they manage to keep me in here for days, I'll have water and facilities.

I'm trapped, yes. But I'm not being tortured.

Why?

The only reason I can think of is that Maxim is too busy getting ready for whatever it is that Killion has planned. All the chatter we've been able to pick up indicates that D-Day is going down soon, but if I can't get out of this room, I sure as hell can't do anything to stop it.

Dammit, dammit, dammit.

Time is slipping away and not only am I still a zillion miles away from being any use whatsoever, but I have no way of contacting anyone at Stark Security to let them know I'm fucked. And, to top it off, I can't even begin to figure out how to go about stopping it…because I still don't know what *it* is.

Shit.

My only consolation is that I'm probably not the only agent currently

working on this. With a threat this hot, Ryan probably sent at least one other team to New York. On top of that, all of Stark Security is most likely working with the SOC, MI6, Interpol, and a half dozen other organizations all over the world.

All true, but it doesn't make me feel better. My past with Maxim gives me unique access. And somehow, I blew it. I have no idea what I did to make him suspicious, but considering I'm trapped in a tiny room, I'm thinking the odds of him letting me join the mission are slim.

Still, he's my best bet, and time is running out.

With that clock ticking down in my head, I start pounding on the door and shouting his name. "Dammit, Maxim! You come talk to me! You owe me, and you fucking know it!"

I have no idea if my shouts will entice him. Or, for that matter, if he can even hear me. But at the moment, I'm all out of other options.

I pound again. "Maxim! Maxim! You answer me right now!"

"Back away from the door." I jump as Maxim's voice fills the room, and my heart is pounding like a hammer as I look up, searching for the hidden speakers. I don't find them, but I do see a glimmer that is probably the refection off a camera lens.

I flip it the bird.

"Now," he says, "or I flood this room with tranq. You really want to take another nap? It's not the kind of drug that makes for easy sleep."

I want to stand my ground, but I also need to not only stay awake but to get him in this room. Right now, I'm completely impotent. But once Maxim opens that door... Well, unfortunately, I'm not Ethan Hunt, and neither is any real person working in espionage. But there still might be an opportunity. At the very least, I have to hope.

I step back, hands up, just a girl following instructions. As I do, I notice a shiny little gleam on the floor, and my heart does a happy dance.

Maybe I'll get lucky after all...

I don't have time to think about that, though, because the door's opening and Maxim is stepping over the threshold.

He's changed out of the suit and into jeans and a pale blue button down over a white T-shirt. He looks so much like the man I once loved that I feel my heart hitch, and I hate myself for that little bit of traitorous weakness.

Determined to keep my control, I wrap the sheet tighter around me as I perch on the edge of the bed. I say nothing, but I note that he hasn't locked the door behind him. It doesn't matter, though. I don't know what building we're in, how many guards are stationed outside, or even if we're

still in New York.

I'll fight to get free when I have a legitimate chance. Right now, I just want to gather as much intel as I can for when that chance appears.

"What's the matter?" I ask. "Didn't like my room?"

"Those little boutique hotels are just too dainty for me," he says, then sweeps an arm to encompass this tiny space. "So much more character here."

I keep my eyes only on him. "Is this why you left me? So that you could work with a maniac like Killion Lambert?"

His eyes narrow, and his voice is cold as ice when he says, "Do not make the mistake of thinking you can fool me again."

I force myself not to react, but my mind is racing, trying to figure out what the hell he means by that. Instead of asking, I say, "Why did you leave me?"

"I told you—I had to. I didn't want to. Considering what I know now, I should have walked away a hell of a lot sooner."

"Had to," I repeat, thinking of that terse note he'd mailed me. "What? Someone had a gun to your head?"

"It might as well have been." He makes a raw scoffing noise. "I loved you, you know. I actually loved you. It ripped me apart to leave you. But I didn't have a choice."

I glance around the room. "If this is how you treat someone you love…"

"Things change," he says. "Or, actually, they don't. But things reveal themselves. You know the saying—the more you know…"

There's no disguising the harshness in his tone, and I don't understand it. I'm the one who has reason to be harsh. He not only fucking left me, he turned evil. So what the hell does he think I did to him?

His gaze skims over me from head to toe, and though I'm covered by the sheet, I feel completely exposed.

"Drop it," he says.

"What?"

"The sheet."

"Screw that," I say. "You lost the right to see me naked when you skipped out on me."

"Drop it," he repeats, "or you're not getting out of this cell, much less getting a payday."

"Why? You think I have a weapon stashed?" I tilt my head and offer him a sultry smile. "You already searched me quite thoroughly."

"You drop the sheet," he says, his voice pitched in a way that brings back all sorts of decadent memories, "because I'm telling you to."

My mouth is suddenly very dry. The truth is, I have no choice.

The darker truth is that I want to.

I'm holding the sheet toga-style with one hand on a clump of material gathered between my breasts. Now, I open my hand and let the material fall to the ground. There," I say, standing naked in front of him. "Paid in full."

"You want in?" He takes a step toward me, then another. He's so close, but I'm tempted to lean closer. Maybe I could sneak that key from his pocket...

But then his palms are cupping my bare ass, and he's pulling me to him. My hands have no place else to go, so I reciprocate, his very fine ass under my hands feeling so painfully familiar.

He bends his head until his lips are close to my ear, and when he whispers, I can feel his breath stir my hair. "What will you give me in return?"

"Whatever you want," I answer, and the horrible truth is that I mean it. I should hate this man—I do hate him.

But I crave him all the same.

"I'm very glad to hear it." His voice is as soft as his palm when he caresses the curve of my rear. Then his fingers slip between my butt cheeks. "But that doesn't mean you're in."

"Then no," I say, trying to pull away.

He yanks me closer. "Do you really think you have a say? Do you think I give a shit about what you want anymore?"

As he speaks, his thumb teases my ass while two fingers slip into my core. I'm wet—so wet—and I hate my body for reacting this way. For craving a touch that he wants to be torture.

He thinks he has the upper hand. That he's punishing me for some crime he won't even reveal. This isn't love or affection—it's hate sex. It's power sex. It's Maxim trying to get his way sex.

And now it's me turning all that shit around on him. Me taking the power as he throws me back onto the bed, then straddles me.

"Yes," I say, telling myself this is *my* Maxim as my fingers fumble at his fly. "Fuck me," I beg, refusing to concede. Taking the power. Claiming this moment. "Please, Maxim. I want you."

The words are rough and raw, and I see the frustration on his face. He didn't expect this. Didn't expect me to crave him. To need him.

I don't.

It's an act. The bastard locked me up. He's trying to use sex to make me small.

Except you do like it. You want him. You know the horrible truth about him, and you want him anyway.

So what does that make you?

Broken. It makes me broken.

And when I tilt back my head and find his eyes looking back into mine, I know that he's broken, too.

I wonder vaguely if we broke each other, but the thought barely has a chance to form before he's spreading my legs, his fingers dancing over my clit, sliding into my very wet core, readying me even though I don't need readying at all.

I hear myself whimper, and hate myself. But I can't worry about what that means right now. I'll have to worry about the state of my soul tomorrow.

Right now, I just want him. I've missed him so damn much, and we never had closure, and as I spread my legs and hear myself begging, I tell myself that's my excuse. Closure. Release.

Just sex.

Sex so that he doesn't have the upper hand.

But as his hands slide up to cup my breasts—as he thrusts his cock inside me, then bends my knees so that we rock together—as he pounds harder and deeper in a way that brings back all the sweet memories of the years with him—I don't care who is in control. I don't care about the mission. For just this slice of time, it's me and Maxim again. Something I never thought I'd ever have again. Something I've craved.

Something I need to soak up now, because it's all about to disappear. Because I'm going to take the bastard down.

At the very least, I'm going to die trying.

Chapter Fourteen

Her eyes were closed, her lips parting as she cried out in pleasure. Each cry made his cock harder, and when those sweet sounds were interspersed with whimpers of, "Please," and "Oh, yes, yes," Maxim wasn't sure if he wanted to come right then or stay inside her forever.

He wanted her.

She was a lying, scamming bitch. He knew that. And yet he couldn't wrap his head around it. Not when he'd first learned about her duplicity so many years ago. Not when she'd called him out of the blue, intent on shoving her way onto this operation. And not now, when she was here, completely at his mercy.

He'd tried to pry the truth from her while the drug had pulsed in her veins. To identify the population Killion intended to contaminate and how. He was frustrated as hell that Killion hadn't yet revealed the full plan to him—and he couldn't help but wonder if Killion had somehow discovered that Maxim wasn't loyal. Not by a fucking long shot.

Considering that Killion still hadn't revealed to Maxim the soon-to-be recipients of the D-Day bacteriophage, he had to at least consider the possibility that his cover was blown.

Except if that was the case, why wasn't he dead? Either through the same method as the senator or from a bullet through the brain.

More, he hadn't caught even a hint that Killion had lost faith in him.

And yet the bastard still hadn't shared the Phase One and Two details. Which most likely meant that there was someone above Maxim in the hierarchy. Someone Killion trusted more than Maxim.

Someone duplicitous enough to be Killion's true right hand, and to have no one in the world suspect a thing. Someone who just happened to appear in New York right as the time was drawing near.

Camilla.

As much as he hated to believe that the woman he'd once loved would willingly commit mass murder, he couldn't escape the facts. Hadn't Killion himself once told Maxim how essential Cami had been to the very creation of the D-Day project.

True, he never saw her in the office space, but that didn't surprise him. Cami was supposed to appear to be a straight arrow with the FBI. So of course, it made the most sense for her to keep her distance.

"Maxim, please."

She struggled beneath him, and he was certain that though part of her wanted him off, another part of her wanted him to take her. To make her linger at the edge with no satisfaction.

He should release her. Should walk away. Should leave her locked alone in this goddamn tiny room.

But he couldn't. He wanted her, dammit. And not to punish her or himself. He wanted the woman he'd never truly had. The woman who still lived in his memories, corrupt though they might be.

He'd let himself feel the self-loathing tomorrow. Right now, he had to have her. Had to touch her. Had to lose himself in the memories of when life was good. When he'd believed they were a team. When he'd known he would never love another woman like he loved her.

That still held true. He never had. Never would.

Before, he thought that was a good thing.

Now, he knew better. He understood the woman he'd fallen for.

Hell, maybe they deserved each other after all.

The thought made him even harder. *His.* She'd been his for years, and now she was back again. He'd punish her—for everything she'd done, for the lies she'd told, for the evil she wanted to wreak on the world.

Oh, yes, he'd punish her.

But right now, all he wanted was to feel her beneath him again. To feel her shatter from the pleasure he gave, even if it was mixed with pain.

To watch that beautiful face when it went over.

He wanted to lose himself in the memories. To go back to a time before he knew of her deceit. To hold her. To fuck her. To love her.

"Cami," he murmured, and her eyes fluttered open. He expected to see hate. What he saw was desire. His cock stiffened even as he felt a surge of pure lust laced with anger from her betrayal. "I'm going to make you scream," he murmured, coming undone from her responsive cry of *yes, yes, oh, please yes.*

That's where he lost himself. It was no longer revenge. No longer punishment. It was Maxim and Cami. It was power and passion, building

and building until it exploded with an intensity he hadn't experienced since the night he left her.

Then the glow faded and he remembered the betrayal. With a low groan of disgust, he pulled out of her, then went into the bathroom to clean up. When he returned, she was wrapped in the sheet, her back against the wall.

"Was it good for you, too?" He hadn't meant to speak, but the words had burst out laden with sarcasm.

For a moment, he thought she would ignore him. Instead, she lifted her chin, met his eyes, and said, "Yes."

He heard the truth in the word, and felt the sting of it like a slap.

And for the first time since he'd received her phone message, he wished there was a way to scale the wall of betrayal that stood between them. But it was only a passing thought, and he'd learned the hard way that wishes never came true.

Chapter Fifteen

"Well?" I say when the sheet is once again wrapped tight around me. I try to keep my voice steady, but inside, I'm trembling. Because, damn me, this isn't a man I should want. He hates me, that much is clear.

I want to hate him, too. He's aligned himself with evil, and I can't want a man like that.

But I do. I want him even more desperately now.

And I hate myself for it.

"Well, what?"

"Did I pass your test?" My words are laced with real contempt, but I'm not sure if it's for me or for him.

He looks me up and down. "That wasn't a test. It was a fuck. A nice one—don't get me wrong—but it hardly qualifies as an exchange of currency. Besides," he adds in a voice that is caramel-sweet, "I don't know what the hell you're talking about."

"Bullshit."

"Your cursing vocabulary hasn't improved," he says mildly. "You really should work on your repertoire."

"Get me in with Killion, and I'll hire a comedian to write me material," I say. "Please, Maxim. I need the money. If you have ever loved—"

"Don't."

I stiffen. His voice had been as sharp as a knife, and now his finger is right in my face.

"Don't you dare go down that road."

I nod. I don't understand what's triggered him, but I'm confident the trigger is real. And I'm not willing to risk him blowing.

His brow furrows as he studies me. "What kind of game are you

playing?"

I shake my head. "Game?"

"Get you in with Killion? Do you really think that I don't know the truth? That you're already years deep with that man? That you're his go-to girl?"

"That's not truth. That's delusion."

His eyes narrow. "Bullshit."

I shake my head, racking my brain to figure out why he would think I know Killion Lambert.

"Fine," he says after the silence lingers. "You say you don't know Lambert personally. Why are you here?"

"I told you. I'm looking for a payday."

"And you just happened to think he has a big one coming up."

I tilt my head, studying him. Something's off, and I can't figure out what it is. "Doesn't he?"

"Where's your intel coming from?"

I smile. "A girl has to have some secrets."

"A girl tells her secrets, or she hangs out in this room alone indefinitely. Your choice."

"Fine." The word is clipped, and I don't even have to act to play the part of a frustrated prisoner. "I heard from a guy I used to hang with after you bailed on me. He'd heard about Group Ultra and a guy named Maxim."

I shrug, hoping he buys the bullshit story. "Not that common a name, right? Anyway, he heard something about a big job. And then I poked around and realized it really was you..." I trail off. "I figured maybe you'd give me a job. To make up for the way you walked out on me."

"Me? What about how you—"

He cuts his words off, and I fight a frown. That's not the first time he's danced around an accusation. But I have no idea what I've done that's pissed him off. Which, unfortunately, puts me at a significant disadvantage.

When he continues to say nothing, I press the point. "You owe me."

"How do you figure that?"

"Because you left me, you prick. If we were still together, we'd still be a team, and I'd already be on this job."

His whole body goes visibly stiffer. "Do we really want to compare the way we injured each other? Because I'll win."

I shake my head. I truly don't have a clue what he is talking about.

"How about this. I tell you what I know about you. You tell me what you know about me. Clear the air."

For a moment, he says nothing. Then he moves across the room and leans against the wall. "You first."

I nod, then get settled more comfortably on the bed, once again wearing the sheet like a toga. "After you abandoned me, you ended up in England. Turns out you had dual-citizenship. I never knew."

"Neither did I," he said. "Not back then."

"And just like in a storybook, you went back home and ended up working for MI6. Pretty typical story, really. Happens all the time." I am practically dripping with sarcasm.

"I was recruited," he says. "It doesn't happen all the time, but it did happen to me."

"And then you decided to be a bad boy. You had a real chance to go straight after the life you and I led, but you flipped off your country and became a double-agent. I don't know why I'm surprised considering all the scams we ran. But somehow I thought you'd have more integrity."

A muscle in his cheek twitches. "Coming from you, that's rich."

I brush his words away, confident that everything I've said about his history is true. "You're still in MI6. But here you are working for Killion Lambert. They think you're gathering intel, but I know better. You've gone rogue, Maxim Wilder. You flipped King and country the bird. You're pretending to be undercover for MI6. But you're really in bed with Killion. I doubt it's for some grand principle. Which means you signed up for the money. How am I doing so far?"

He doesn't answer, but his eyes hold fast to mine.

"Yeah, I thought so. Nailed it straight down the line. And the ironic kicker? All I want is for you to add me to the team so I can get a nice payday. Which you should understand, since you're only in it for the money, too."

I watch his face, but can read nothing. So I shrug, then manage a fake pout. "Seems mean you won't let me have a piece of that pie, too. We used to be so good at sharing." I shift so that I've spread my legs under the sheet, then lower the top so he can see a bit of cleavage. "You share with me, I'll share with you…"

I trail off, letting the words hang in the air as I watch his face.

But I can't read a damn thing.

"Go on," he says, after I let the pause hang a few uncomfortable moments.

"That's pretty much it," I say, acknowledging failure by adjusting the

sheet back to where it was. "Except for the grand plan. A new weapon. I figure Killion's planning to sell it to the highest bidder. He's going to arrange a demonstration. Kill a few innocents, then take protection payments from those governments that want their people to stay alive." I meet his eyes. "How am I doing?"

"Not bad," he says. "But you forgot the part where he brings you in as a partner. Sharing in the proceeds as payment for indispensable help you gave him early in the game. Not to mention your relationship."

"And what help would that be?"

"I know how he got access to the keystone. I know what you did. How you helped him. And I know that if he succeeds, all of those deaths will be on your traitorous shoulders."

Since I have no idea what the fuck he's talking about, I start to protest, but he holds up a finger as he takes a step toward me, then another, and another. When he's just inches from me, he leans forward. "All those years you spent saying you hated him—that you fantasized about killing him—was that just your way of establishing a cover?"

"Dammit, I don't know what—" But my words are cut off by the sharp sting of his palm against my face.

"Don't you dare," he says, his voice like death. "From the first day I met you, you said you despised your father, and I saw the reasons why. You got away from him. I helped you get away. You had a new life. A better life. And what did you do? You rolled over and joined him. You used your job—your clearance—to give him access to the thing he needed most. The keystone. The details of the genetic research at the heart of everything that son-of-a-bitch is doing now."

"I don't know what you're—"

"People are going to die, dammit. And that's on your head." He looks me up and down with disgust. "I loved you. Dammit, Cami, I loved your heart. I loved who you were, good and bad. I knew you were a good liar and a good thief. So was I. But never once did I think you'd slide into mass murder. And I sure as hell never thought that you'd ever help that man. You aren't the woman I once loved. And good job playing me for the fool."

"Maxim, I—"

But he's out the door. And I don't have a single clue what he's talking about.

* * * *

Keystone? Genetic research?
My fault?

The words swirl around in my head, but I have no idea what he's accusing me of. I can worry about that later, though, and I toss the question aside as I hurry to where I saw that little glint, terrified that it's disappeared into a crack in the floor, or that it isn't my earring at all.

But there it is. The small, fake diamond stud that's really an emergency contact beacon.

I pick it up, use my thumb to pry off the post, then use one end of the now-free post to puncture the fake gem through one of the facets. For a split second, there's a tiny flash of blue light to indicate the signal was sent, and then I drop the stone and the stem. They're useless now. Nothing but a broken piece of costume jewelry.

I draw in a breath, then exhale noisily. By now, Zane Parker should have received the notification of an incoming distress message. With luck, he'll be zeroed in on my position within the next minute, and I'll be extracted within the next fifteen.

I pace the room, anxious to be free, Maxim's words swirling in my head. *On your traitorous shoulders.*

Traitorous…

My knees go weak as the realization hits me—Maxim thinks that *I* helped Killion Lambert. He believes that I'm a traitor.

And the only reason that would bother him is if he's not.

I realize I'm braiding my hair, and I toss it back over my shoulder as the inescapable conclusion hits me: Maxim is undercover.

My heart leaps. Our chances of stopping Killion have just increased exponentially.

But only if I can get him to believe the truth about me.

Why, why, why does Maxim think I'm a traitor? Have I been framed? I don't understand what he's talking about. I have no idea what *the keystone* refers to, and I've never done any mission that centers around genetic research, so how—"

Except I have.

Only tangentially, but when I was with the SOC, we ran a top secret op in conjunction with FBI agents who were undercover at the CDC. I was still young and green, and because of that, my role in the mission was miniscule. All I did, in fact, was test security for an off-book division of the CDC that focused on next-gen research. And even then, my role was limited to entering and exiting the Q-wing of the facility using various key cards so that the tech team could tweak the access programs.

There was nothing sexy about it, and I never had direct access to any biological material. But there was some very sexy information stored in the Q-wing. Information on genomes and gene modification and CRISPR-Cas9 tech, and I don't know what else.

Still, it was only two days of work, and the work consisted of me walking back and forth through the entrance. Hardly national security. After all, the keycard never left my person unless it was being locked in the safe.

I shake my head, still baffled. And even more confused by Maxim's suggestion that I've had any contact with my dad since we ran. Hell, he should know I haven't, because how do you contact a dead man?

When I was seventeen, I decided to look him up. I don't know why—some masochistic need for closure, maybe. But I'd called the college where he'd taught, and they told me that Professor Gregory Green had killed himself. He'd taken a boat out into the Atlantic, left a suicide note, then jumped into the water.

Surely Maxim remembered that, because it was one of the happiest days of my life.

"He wanted to kill the fucking lions?" Maxim had sneered that day. "All he killed was a sniveling, cowardly worm of a man. And a shit father, too."

But had he?

I realize I've been pacing, as if I'm racing to catch up with the nascent idea trying to hatch in my mind. Something about my father. About his duplicitous nature. His overbearing belief that he was the only person who mattered on Earth. That the lambs and the lions should be struck down so that he—

Oh, shit.

Killion. Kill. Lion.

Lambert. Lamb.

He hadn't committed suicide at all. My father had faked his own death.

He'd become Killion Lambert.

He'd changed his appearance. He'd watched me.

Somehow he must have gotten close enough to clone the CDC card key.

He's vile. Evil. As twisted as he ever was. Only now he's a hell of a lot more powerful.

And Maxim is working side-by-side with him. But is Maxim a good guy ... or is he truly loyal to the man who is my father?

Chapter Sixteen

Maxim dodged the early afternoon traffic as he hurried to the coffee shop three blocks from the Squire. That was the standard protocol when any member of Killion's security team needed to report a potential breach, and Zane Parker had just requested a meet.

He stepped into the shop, breathing in the scent of coffee and pastries as he scanned the room. No customers except for the one familiar face in the back booth.

Zane might be a member of Killion's security team and a rising star as far as Killion was concerned, but Maxim personally didn't care for the man. As a general rule, he didn't care for anyone who pretended to serve one leader while really serving the other. Ironic, since he'd spent most of his own life doing undercover work. But then again, it all depended on where the loyalty lay.

As of right now, that was an open question with Zane.

"Tell me," he said, sliding into the booth across from the man.

"The girl. The bitch in Interrogation A."

Maxim leaned back, careful to show no emotion. "What about her?"

"She works for Stark Security."

Of everything that Zane could have said, that was the last thing Maxim expected.

Over the course of the last year, Maxim had learned that Zane had been affiliated with the world-renowned private agency. He'd assumed that Zane had, in fact, been assigned to infiltrate Killion Lambert's operation.

Maxim also knew that the paycheck Zane drew from Killion had increased over time. And over those same months, Maxim had assumed that Zane's loyalty had shifted.

Today, Zane had confirmed that.

The bastard was now one hundred percent Killion's man.

Now, it was Cami who was the question mark.

"Cami Green," Maxim said, forcing a knife-edge into his voice. "You're telling me that bitch is with Stark Security?"

"Covert ops," Zane confirmed.

"And you know this how? Have you worked with her before?"

Zane shook his head, then pulled out his phone. "Stark Security agents are tied into an emergency response network. She must have activated a beacon, because I just got pinged."

He turned his phone so that Maxim could see the map display. Sure enough, there was a beacon signal...and it was coming from her holding cell.

"You informed Stark Security?"

Zane tilted his head. "Who pays you better? Killion or MI6?"

Maxim nodded in acknowledgement and disgust. But he kept the latter off his face. "Good work, Parker," he said. "We're done here. And keep this between us. Killion has enough on his plate with D-Day approaching."

Zane nodded, then slid from the booth. Maxim stayed behind, sipping his coffee and contemplating his next move. He now knew with certainty where Zane's loyalties lay.

He'd thought he understood Cami's. Now, however, he wasn't so sure. After leaving a twenty on the table and putting in his headphones, he left the coffee shop and started strolling the neighborhood, taking care to ensure he wasn't followed. When he was certain he was alone, he placed a call, then grinned when the familiar voice answered.

"Maxim Wilder," Quincy Radcliffe said. "It's been a long time. You still working retail in Manhattan?" It was a coded question, meant to ask if Maxim was still working as a double agent for MI6.

"Same old, same old," Maxim said. "I had some free time. Thought we'd catch up." And that was code to confirm that the call was end-to-end encrypted. Not that he'd take chances, but the more precautions, the better.

"Love to," Quincy said, as Maxim took another look around. Just to be sure he wasn't overheard.

"Cami Green," he said. "Tell me about her."

"Not sure I'm familiar with that name."

Maxim frowned. *Interesting.* That suggested Cami worked deep cover. Which definitely made sense. "Yeah, you are. And we may need help soon. How fast could you put a team together in Manhattan? You have those resources?"

"We do. What do you need?"

"Unsure. Two vehicles at least. A helicopter if you can get one. Sharpshooters."

There was a pause, then Quincy said, "How fast?"

"Possibly fifteen minutes. Possibly fifteen days."

"Roger that. I'll confirm when I've pulled the package together."

"Good. I'll follow up with a text or a call as soon as I know more."

"Anything else?"

"Cami," he said. "If you did know her, what would be your take?"

"I'd say that anyone who works at Stark Security is a stellar agent. Well-vetted. Skilled. Trustworthy."

"That's a solid endorsement. Of both the organization and the team."

"Yeah," Quincy said. "It is."

They ended the call, and Maxim pinched his nose between his brows.

Could he really have gotten it so horribly wrong? Was Cami here to take down her father? Not to align with him?

And if that was the case, did Killion himself know that his daughter was locked in a cell?

* * * *

Maxim was on his way to see Cami—to hear her story, to tell his own—when Killion Lambert summoned him to the main conference room.

"Sir?"

Lambert looked up from a mess of papers scattered across the surface of one of the conference tables. "Ah, Maxim. My good right hand. Come here, come here."

"You're in a good mood, Sir," Maxim said, working to keep his tone light even though the fact of Killion's mood disturbed him greatly.

"Action, my boy. A man is always at his best when there is action."

"I agree. What action are we talking about?"

"Tonight. We move forward with D-day tonight."

"Delivery Day," Maxim said, pretending to sound excited. "And what will be the delivery method?"

Killion chuckled. "Ah, yes, well that has already been taken care of. Tonight, D-Day will be death."

"Sir—that's...that's incredible." He hoped his voice sounded excited and not sickened. "I wish you would have told me. I would have liked to have been involved from the start."

"Oh, but you were. The juice and snack boxes we delivered to those

children last week. I believe it was you that put together that donation?"

He felt his body grow cold. "Yes. After you donated a hundred thousand to build an indoor playground on the Children's Haven top floor. I thought it would be nice to send something tangible for those poor kids."

"An excellent thought. And one I have built an entire campaign off of."

Maxim swallowed. "I see. So when do you plan—"

"Tonight, of course. The fundraiser. The children will be there. The press will be there in spades. A refuge for abused and abandoned children? What newsman would turn his back on that? And what better time to demonstrate our power? Anonymously, of course. A minor, but necessary, downside, but those children will be remembered."

"Can I assume that means you won't be pulling the trigger yourself?"

Killion shook his head. "Sadly, you assume correctly. With over two dozen infected children dying on site in front of the inevitable news cameras, that would be inadvisable. We'll use the Jeep."

"With a long-range activation transmitter," Maxim said, recalling that with a long-range transmitter mounted on a vehicle, the frequency burst to trigger the deadly bacteriophage could take place up to a full kilometer from the infected victim.

He fought a shudder. "So, the children who ate the cupcakes or drank the juice…"

"They'll bleed," Killion said. "First from their noses, then their eyes, then from under their fingernails. It will be quite a show, and a much better advertisement for our future services than one dull-witted senator."

"You really are a genius, sir," Maxim said, with what he hoped sounded like respect and not disgust.

"You flatter me. The event starts at seven. Be on time, Maxim. I may need you."

* * * *

"Killion cloned your card key."

The voice pulls me from sleep, and it takes me a minute to realize that not only is it coming from the door of my cell, but that the speaker is Maxim.

"You," I say, then roll over to face the wall and the single beam of light sneaking in from outside. "Go away."

"I'm sorry. Cami, I'm so, so sorry."

I stay as I am, my knees tucked up near my chest, my eyes watching the dust dancing in that thin beam. And I force myself to say nothing.

"Did I ever tell you why my father went away? It was because they found out he was a double agent. He'd betrayed his country. That meant he'd betrayed me, too. All the stuff about honor and patriotism he'd ever spoken of had turned out to be a lie."

I hear the rustle of his clothes as he moves closer.

"I didn't know that when he left home," he continues. "I found out the night I had to leave you. They came to take me away. I wasn't given a choice. My father had tried to find me during those years we were on our own. He never did, but MI6 thought he had. So they took me in. They interrogated me. They trained me. But it was years before they trusted me. Before I even had the chance to reach out to you."

His words wash over me. I tell myself they mean nothing. That they are just water sluicing over my skin.

I roll over, intending to tell him so.

That's when I see the pain on his face.

I steel my resolve and speak. "You should have tried harder."

He nods. "I should have, yes. And I should have figured out a way to get a message to you when they took me. And the moment I got back, I should have started a campaign of roses and flowers and heartfelt grovels. I didn't. I fucked up."

"Yeah," I say. "You did."

"I'm sorry."

I frown, remembering where we are, and I turn my head just a bit so that I can flick my eyes up toward the camera.

"I disabled them. Anyone looking will think they need regular maintenance."

I sit up. "Is he really my father?"

Maxim nods. "I'm sorry."

"He cloned the access keycard to the CDC," I say, even though he clearly already knows that. "I only just realized. I don't know for certain how he managed, but he used me, Maxim. Just like he always used me." I swallow, then stare him down. "I never expected you to use me, too."

"I fucked up." He holds his arms out to his sides. "I love you, Cami," he says, and the words crash through my soul. "Even when I hated you— even when I was so sure that you'd fallen in with Killion—I still loved you."

I taste salt, then realize that I'm crying. I start to wipe it away, but he's there first, his thumb brushing the tears out from under my eyes.

"You have no reason to forgive me," he says. "The things I convinced myself you did—I never should have believed that. Not even for a second. I betrayed you. No," he corrects. "I betrayed us."

"You kinda did," I say. "But so did I. I read the file. It said you'd fallen in with Killion. Not once did I think that you might have been undercover. Not once did I give you the benefit of the doubt. You'd disappeared on me, and that made you evil." Tears are streaming now. "I betrayed you by thinking that."

"No—"

"Yes," I say. "Who in this world knew you better than me? We loved each other—we *knew* each other. More than that, we both know that things aren't always what they seem. But I looked and I believed. And I betrayed you in my heart."

I can barely see him now through the tears that are flowing. My nose is running, too.

I laugh, the sound a little bit pathetic. "Hell of a reunion, huh? I'm a snotty mess."

"Just a little bit," he says, using his shirt tail to dab my eyes and wipe my nose.

"Gross," I say.

"You're worth it."

I tilt my head up to look at him. "*We're* worth it." It's a statement, not a question. Because this time, I'm not giving him up without a fight.

He strokes my cheek, then brushes a lock of hair behind my ear, his eyes never leaving mine. "Are you okay? With—well, with finding out about your father?"

"Yes. No." I shrug. "I don't know." I scrub my hands over my face and draw in a deep breath. "It'll hit me harder later, but right now I feel..." I trail off searching for the right word.

"Hurt?"

I shake my head. "Vindicated."

He frowns. "What do you mean?"

"That man...and he's *not* my father. Sperm provider is as far as I'll go, but he was never a father. He was a monster. I always knew he was, and that he was a hell of lot worse than anything he ever showed me or my mother. He broke her. He wanted to break me."

"He won't," Maxim says, his voice gentle.

"No, he won't," I confirm. "But I'll break him. You and I will break him together." I draw in a breath, then give a little shrug. "It sounds pretty woo, I guess, but I think this is the reason I got stuck with that

man. And the reason I found you right across the street. Because Fate knew I couldn't end him by myself. Together, we can."

"We will," he confirms, then holds out his hand.

I take it, relishing the warmth. The comfort of his touch. "Maxim? Will you do something for me?"

"Anything."

"Will you kiss me?"

His grin is slow and a little devious as he draws me toward him. His fingers slide into my hair as he cups my head. "Baby," he says, leaning forward, "it would be my pleasure."

The kiss is slow and long and deep, and by the time he pulls away from me, I'm certain that I've partially melted. "Hi," I say.

"I've missed us," he says.

"Me, too." I tilt my head, then grin. "I've missed sex, too. Not that the kidnapping-revenge fuck wasn't incredible—it actually kinda was—but I'm looking forward to something a little less…criminally oriented."

He laughs. "I will be very happy to accommodate. Right now, let's concentrate on getting you out of here."

"I like that plan."

He has a bag hanging over his shoulder, and he passes it to me. I open it and find sweat pants and a T-shirt. Immediately, I start dressing.

"We'll get you into a safe house," he says. "And then I need to go to the children's benefit."

I pause in the process of tightening the cord around my waist. "What the hell are you talking about?"

"Short version," he says, then fills me in, ending with the horrible takeaway that the bastard who fathered me is planning to kill at least a dozen kids.

"And you think I'm going to hide away in a safe house?"

"Yes."

I shake my head. "Not happening."

"We can argue later. We'll get you out of here now."

Since he's right, I shut up. He opens the door and we step out together. We move down the hall, foregoing the main elevator for the service one. He pushes the button, and I hear the rumble of the car rising up toward our floor. The *clank* as it settles in place, and the then the soft *swish* as the door slides open.

I'm expecting it to be empty. What I find is my father.

"Cami, my precious," he says, looking between me and Maxim. "Where exactly do you think you're going?"

Chapter Seventeen

"I'm taking her to get dressed," Maxim says. "You want her at the benefit, right? She's going to need some real clothes."

"Actually, I don't see the need to have her there. Why add the burden of having to watch her? It's not as if you can trust her not to misbehave."

"With all due respect, Sir," Maxim says, "I think Camilla knows just how much I'll enjoy punishing her if she steps out of line."

"You always speak about my dear daughter with such vitriol. One day, you must tell me what is behind the venom."

"Happy to, Sir. Today, though, she needs an outfit. I'll return her to her room if you disagree, but don't you think she should understand what could happen if she misbehaves? It's going to be quite a show."

I remained stone-faced, but inside, I'm silently cheering Maxim's acting skills.

A look of cunning crosses Killion's face. "You have a point. And it's only fair. After all, once you tranqed her and brought her here, she became part of our happy family. His smile is wide and cheerful and absolutely terrifying. "Shall I offer you a word of wisdom for tonight, daughter dear?"

I remain silent. He leans in so close I can smell his breath. "Don't misbehave this evening. A little tip from your doting father."

I fight a shiver as his he turns his attention to Maxim, his tone light and breezy. "Ask Sasha to run out to Macy's and get her something appropriate."

"Right away." Maxim pushes the button for the elevator again, and when the doors open, we slip on as Killion continues down the hall. It's not until the doors close that I can breathe again, but I dare not show any relief. The elevator cameras probably function just fine. And I need to remember that I'm a prisoner, downtrodden, and undoubtedly marked for

death.

Honestly, even with my glee from having reconciled with Maxim, the downtrodden thing isn't hard to pull off. Especially after Maxim explains to me exactly what my father has planned.

"Give me your phone," I say once we're back in my cell with a dress fetched by Sasha.

He passes it over without question. I open his text app, type in the number Brax gave me, put a question mark in the text box, and then hit send.

"What was that about?" he asks, and I'm suddenly struck by the fact that he didn't ask that question before I sent the message. He'd let me use his phone. He'd let me send a random message. And he hadn't hesitated for a second.

I pull him close and kiss him. "Thank you," I say.

His brow furrows. "You're welcome? But seriously. Who are you texting question marks to, and why?"

I explain about Brax and the promise to contact him, a little bit afraid that Maxim is going to worry that any action by Brax might interfere with whatever plan we come up with.

Which leads me to the next question. "Have we got a plan?"

"I texted Quincy after Killion told me what he has planned. A team is on the way, and he's also calling in favors from a group he used to work with in this area, as well as contacts from the SOC and some other covert agencies."

"There's another Stark Security agent who knows I'm here. Zane Parker. I used an emergency beacon to contact him."

"I know," Maxim says.

"How—*oh*."

"I told Quincy. By now, Zane should be detained."

"So what exactly is the plan?" I ask.

He drags his fingers through his hair. "The key is to locate the RF transmitter. It's mounted on a Jeep, so part of the trick is finding a moving target before it gets in range."

"What is the range?"

"About a kilometer," he says. "The transmitter's keyed to the frequency of the bacteriophage those kids ingested. If the pulse goes out anywhere within a one-kilometer radius, and those children are dead."

I shudder. "So the trick is to take out the Jeep and its driver before they break the one-kilometer mark."

"Exactly."

I nod, but I hate that I don't know who's going to be on that. From what Maxim has told me, there are going to be a lot of children at risk this afternoon.

I take a deep breath, forcing the worry away. "And you and me? What's our task?" I know perfectly well that we'll just be party guests. Maxim can't break cover, and I can't go off and be something other than a prisoner. But I hate having no control.

Gently, Maxim tugs my hair from my fingers, then kisses my hand.

"We'll just be at the party, keeping our eye on Killion. As soon as I get confirmation that the Jeep's transmitter is out of commission and those kids are safe, all teams not involved in locking down the transmitter and its handlers will storm the building, providing backup so you and I can take out Killion."

I smile. "I like the sound of that."

"It's a good plan," he says. And he's right.

But we both know that good plans can go to hell. And this night might completely go to shit.

* * * *

I'm standing by the window sipping a glass of Chardonnay when Killion steps up beside me. He looks me up and down, then nods. "You look lovely, *daughter*." He reaches out and I have to force myself not to shudder as he brushes his palm against my upper arm, left bare by the thin straps of my dress. No way am I giving him the satisfaction of a reaction.

"It's been so long since I left, I almost forgot how much I had planned for the two of us to enjoy when you got older."

"Sorry to have ruined your plans," I say. "Oh, wait. No. I'm not."

I turn, then start to walk away.

"One pulse," he says. "One pulse from a pocket transmitter, and I can take you out, girl. You remember that."

He turns and walks away as I stand there fighting an urge to tremble as I try to make sense of his words.

"What is it?" Maxim asks, coming to stand behind me with the plate of food he's gathered, the better to camouflage his real purpose in walking the perimeter of this room.

"Killion," I say, then repeat what that vile monster had said to me.

"He's being an ass," Maxim says. "Trying to scare you."

I'm not so certain. The one thing my father has never done is make idle threats. "Is a pocket transmitter really a thing?" The only transmitter I

know of is the one Killion has strapped to a Jeep.

"It would be short range, but yeah."

"Short?"

"Ten meters max."

I consider that. "Then why doesn't he use it for the kids?"

Maxim shakes his head. "For one, the kids could scatter. This room is huge. For another, no way will he want to be carrying a transmitter. The Jeep's on the street, so—"

I nod. "Plausible deniability. I get it. It's just weird that he mentioned the pocket version."

I shake it off, turning instead to look at the kids. The fifteen darling children playing on a jungle gym who have no idea the danger they're in. The whole indoor playground was provided courtesy of Foundational Tech, and I tell myself not to be sickened. Rather, I need to be glad that something good has come out of something so bad.

"The Children's Haven owns this whole building?" I ask as I wander with Maxim toward the window.

"They do. Dorm style rooms for homeless kids on the first three floors. Then medical facilities, then classrooms above that. Office space, a few as-yet-un-purposed floors, and then this in-the-sky playscape."

We're on the eleventh floor, and as we stand by the window and look down, we can see the roof of the gym and swim center that shares an entire exterior wall with this building.

It's Manhattan, after all.

There's nobody in the rooftop pool right now, but I remember going there once many years ago to watch a diving competition. And I can't help but think how much I'd like to be over there right now, rather than standing over here waiting and waiting and trying to make small talk.

"We'll know soon," Maxim says, obviously reading my mind. "Nothing yet, but—" He looks at me. "Wait."

He tilts his head, and I know he's fighting the urge to press his fingers to his ear to make it easier to hear, since doing so might reveal to Killion that Maxim has some reason to be on coms.

"It's on," he whispers. "Our vehicles are forcing a perimeter. The transmitter's on a Jeep. They'll keep him blocked."

"Thank God," I say, though I won't believe it until it's over. I glance back at the adorable children playing tag on the far side of the room. I fight a shiver as I try not to think what will happen if that signal gets through.

If Killion's monstrous plan actually goes into effect.

I remember my little KelTec pistol and wish that I'd asked Maxim to get it back for me. But considering my tiny dress, I'm not sure where I would have stashed it. And if Killion had discovered that Maxim had armed me...

Well, that would be what we in the covert ops biz call very, very bad.

I sigh, take a sip of my wine, and tell myself that Maxim has a gun. And that it doesn't matter anyway, because he won't need it.

But the truth is that I fear he will. Because sooner or later Killion is going to realize that his transmitter is stuck outside the perimeter. And when that happens, I have no idea what a crazy, fucked up man like my father is going to do.

The thought makes me shiver, and I instinctively seek out Maxim. The realization makes me smile. For so long, he'd been the enemy. But we were back now. Fully and completely. All we have to do is save these kids, take down Killion, and manage to stay alive.

Do that, and we can go live happily ever after.

I'm really, really looking forward to that part of my personal fairy tale. I've been the beaten down Cinderella for far too long.

"Hey," Maxim says, hurrying to my side. He bends close, as if kissing my cheek, and whispers, "Done."

I pull away so that I can look at him straight on. "You're sure?"

He nods. "Some of the team are on their way here right now. Backup. It's time, Baby. We're going to take this fucker down."

My grin is so wide it hurts my face. "You say the sweetest things."

A huge clatter comes from the far side of the room, and I turn in that direction only to see my father in a fury, sweeping some of the charming tables free of their drinks and appetizers.

"You," he says, his finger pointing straight at me. "I should have killed you in the womb."

He opens his jacket, and I immediately imagine him pulling out a gun.

He doesn't.

Instead, he pulls out some sort of freakish gizmo.

"What the hell—" I begin, as Maxim cries, "Oh, fuck! The injection!"

Then he's pulling out the gun he's holstered under his jacket and he's firing at my father. Grabbing my arm. Tugging me toward him. Everything is happening so fast I barely have time to notice that he's shot out the window.

And I definitely don't have time to scream when he pulls me toward it even as the glass is still falling. We go sailing through, then we're falling,

falling, falling until we land with a splash in the rooftop diving pool.

I paddle furiously in the water, working to stay up as my soggy dress tries to drag me down. I lean back and look up as I see someone—Brax?—drag my father away.

I turn, to look at Maxim. "What the—"

"The injection. The tranq I gave you. It had a bacteriophage, too. One triggered by a different frequency than the kids. I didn't know. Not until I thought about what he said to you. And when he realized that we'd foiled his plan to take out the kids—"

"—my father decided to take me out."

"I'm sorry," Maxim says, holding out a hand and pulling me toward the side of the pool. He hugs me close. "I'm so, so sorry."

"I'm not," I say, then smile at the way his brow furrows in confusion. "I got you back, didn't I?"

His smile blooms wide, and he leans closer. "Yes," he says. "And I got you."

And then, thank heavens, he kisses me.

Chapter Eighteen

"I guess he'll do," Brax says, swinging one arm around me as he nods toward Maxim, who's on the far side of the pool ordering my third drink of the afternoon.

"Oh, yeah, he will," I say.

We're on the roof of the Stark Century Manhattan, and Maxim is appropriately dressed for the occasion. Or undressed, depending on your point of view, and I'm thoroughly enjoying the view of his exceptional ass in a pair of navy-blue swim trunks.

Beside me, Brina snorts with laughter, though I don't understand why until Brax starts to protest. "I did not mean it that way," he says. "I meant he's a good match for Cami in general. Not because he looks good in a bathing suit."

"But he really does look good," Brina adds, giving me a thumbs-up.

"Oh, believe me," I say. "I know."

Brax just rolls his eyes.

"You do, too, sweetie," Brina says, reaching over to pat his hand as we both crack up again.

"So do I pass?" Maxim asks, returning from the bar and passing me a fresh glass of wine. Then he slides his arms around my waist and kisses the side of my neck as I sigh with pleasure.

Brax cocks his head. "From what I can tell, all you need to do for approval from these two today is deliver drinks and look good in swim trunks."

"Which I will happily do," Maxim promises. He releases me long enough to nod toward an oversized chaise, then to pull me down beside him. As I snuggle close, he glances at his watch. "What time is this party starting?"

"Ryan said four," I say, lifting his arm so I can look at his watch. "So another forty-five minutes. I can't wait for you to meet everybody."

We didn't have to come early, but with Brax and Brina being in town and pretty much saving the world, de-stressing seemed like a wonderful idea. Especially since I also want to celebrate the fact that the kids and I all received an antiviral injection this morning. The antidote was specifically engineered by Killion's team to neutralize both bacteriophages—the one I'd been dosed with and the one that had contaminated the children. Killion had kept the cure in a refrigerated lock-up on the off-chance that he'd ever need it himself.

Of course, the odds were slim that the kids or I would ever stumble across the particular deadly frequencies. But I still feel a lot better knowing that I could swim in a sea of radio frequencies and still be just fine.

"And Ryan's really making a formal announcement?" Brina asks, turning my attention back to the main reason for this party.

"That's the rumor," Brax says. There's been mumbling about a New York office of Stark Security opening up. Now there's a rumor that, today, Ryan is going to formally share that news and either tell us who's staffing the place or ask for volunteers.

"I wonder if he's talked to Curtis Blaze," I say. Blaze is the former Green Beret whose skill behind the wheel of a Porsche managed to not only keep the Jeep that was carrying the RF transmitter far enough away, but also sent it tumbling into a construction site, ripping the transmitter to shreds in the process.

"I think Ryan's chatting with him tomorrow," Brax says. "He seems like a good guy. Quiet, but good."

Maxim squeezes my hand. "And what about you? Are you hoping for the transfer up here? Or are you and Gimble happy at the beach?"

I prop myself up and brush a kiss over his lips. "I love the beach," I tell him. "But I love you more. So let's just play it by ear and see where we land."

"That's a plan I can live with," he says, and as Maxim draws me closer, I meet Brax's eyes. He smiles back at me, and I know he's thinking about how lucky he and I are. We both lost the loves of our lives early on. And then we both found them.

And now we're all living our happily ever afters.

* * * *

Thanks so much for reading! I hope you enjoyed *Craved By You!* Want all the scoop on Stark Security? Be sure to sign up for my newsletter so

you don't miss a thing!

* * * *

Also from 1001 Dark Nights and J. Kenner, discover Touch Me, Tangled With You, Charmed By You, Memories of You, Cherish Me, Indulge Me, Please Me, Hold Me, Tease Me, Tempt Me, Tame Me, Damien, Justify Me, Caress of Darkness, Caress of Pleasure, and Rising Storm.

Sign up for the 1001 Dark Nights Newsletter
and be entered to win a Tiffany Key necklace.

There's a contest every month!

Go to www.1001DarkNights.com to subscribe.

**As a bonus, all subscribers can download
FIVE FREE exclusive books!**

Discover 1001 Dark Nights Collection Eleven

DRAGON KISS by Donna Grant
A Dragon Kings Novella

THE WILD CARD by Dylan Allen
A Rivers Wilde Novella

ROCK CHICK REMATCH by Kristen Ashley
A Rock Chick Novella

JUST ONE SUMMER by Carly Phillips
A Dirty Dare Series Novella

HAPPILY EVER MAYBE by Carrie Ann Ryan
A Montgomery Ink Legacy Novella

BLUE MOON by Skye Warren
A Cirque des Moroirs Novella

A VAMPIRE'S MATE by Rebecca Zanetti
A Dark Protectors/Rebels Novella

LOVE HAZARD by Rachel Van Dyken

BRODIE by Aurora Rose Reynolds
An Until Her Novella

THE BODYGUARD AND THE BOMBSHELL by Lexi Blake
A Masters and Mercenaries: New Recruits Novella

THE SUBSTITUTE by Kristen Proby
A Single in Seattle Novella

CRAVED BY YOU by J. Kenner
A Stark Security Novella

GRAVEYARD DOG by Darynda Jones
A Charley Davidson Novella

A CHRISTMAS AUCTION by Audrey Carlan
A Marriage Auction Novella

THE GHOST OF A CHANCE by Heather Graham
A Krewe of Hunters Novella

Also from Blue Box Press

LEGACY OF TEMPTATION by Larissa Ione
A Demonica Birthright Novel

VISIONS OF FLESH AND BLOOD by Jennifer L. Armentrout and
Ravyn Salvador
A Blood & Ash and Fire & Flesh Compendium

FORGETTING TO REMEMBER by M.J. Rose

TOUCH ME by J. Kenner
A Stark International Novella

BORN OF BLOOD AND ASH by Jennifer L. Armentrout
A Flesh and Fire Novel

MY ROYAL SHOWMANCE by Lexi Blake
A Park Avenue Promise Novel

SAPPHIRE DAWN by Christopher Rice writing as C. Travis Rice
A Sapphire Cove Novel

EMBRACING THE CHANGE by Kristen Ashley
A River Rain Novel

IN THE AIR TONIGHT by Marie Force

LEGACY OF CHAOS by Larissa Ione
A Demonica Birthright Novel

Discover More J. Kenner

Touch Me: A Stark International Novella

Former wild child Jamie Archer can't believe how amazing her life has become. Not only is she married to the sexiest man on the planet, Stark Security Chief Ryan Hunter, but she's also set to star in a big budget blockbuster that is sure to send her career soaring into the stratosphere.

Everything is perfect until Jamie, the least maternal person on the planet, finds out that not only is she pregnant, but that her due date interferes with the film's production schedule.

Ryan has always supported his wife's ambition, but he never expected to learn that they were having a baby from the shouts of paparazzi. Hurt, angry, and afraid that Jamie will choose her career over their family, Ryan tries to pull her closer, but only succeeds in pushing her away.

Now, as the pillars of their once fairytale marriage begin to crumble, Jamie and Ryan must find a way to outshine the glitter of stardom and rediscover the strength of their bond.

* * * *

Tangled With You: A Stark Security Novella

He never expected to feel this kind of heat again...

FBI agent Ollie McKee is burned out on relationships. After a head-spinningly on-again/off-again relationship with his former fiancée, he's been out of the dating pool for years. Now he's focused on his career—and it's getting more intense. Because Ollie's ex was just kidnapped, and despite the rules, he's resolved to work the case and find her.

Stark Security agent Trevor Barone knows better than to fall for a friend, especially one who's straight. But there's no denying the way his heart and body react around Ollie, especially after the last quick mission they worked together. He swore to himself to keep his distance. But now Ollie's begging for his help. The woman he once loved—maybe still loves—has been kidnapped, and Ollie's determined to bring her home alive. Trevor's not about to let his friend down, but as they work the case together, the attraction and connection between them can't be denied.

When the kidnappers turn deadly, Ollie and Trevor put their lives in each other's hands. But can they trust the passion that threatens to consume them both?

* * * *

Charmed By You: A Stark Security Novella

Former vigilante-for-hire Simon Barré has one steadfast rule: stay far away from celebrities. Too bad Simon's first assignment at Stark Security is to protect A-list actress Francesca Muratti. He can't even turn down the assignment, as that would be violating his second rule—never fail a woman. Now he finds himself up-close-and-personal with a high-maintenance diva whose flash and sass drives him crazy—but whose touch he undeniably craves.

The world might believe that Francesca Muratti leads a fairy tale life, but the truth is far darker. For years, she's kept a horrible secret about her best friend's death. Now someone is threatening to kill Francesca if she doesn't reveal all. She needs protection, but there's no way she's going to tell the sexy Stark Security agent what she did or why she's being threatened. Which means that in order to survive and protect her secrets, Francesca must pull off the biggest acting job of her career: she's going to have to let Simon close, but not let him see her true heart.

* * * *

Memories of You: A Stark Security Novella

Hollywood consultant Renly Cooper is fed up with relationships. His recent breakup with a leading lady played out across the tabloids, and the former Navy Seal is more than ready to focus on his new position as an agent at the elite Stark Security agency. He's expecting international stakes. Instead, his first assignment is to protect one of Damien Stark's friends from a stalker. A woman who, to his delight, turns out to be one of his closest childhood friends.

After a foray into online dating puts tech genius Abby Jones in danger, she needs a bodyguard, and her business partner, Nikki Fairchild Stark, enlists help from Stark Security. When the assigned agent turns out to be her best friend from junior high—and her first crush—she's thrilled to discover he's even more delicious now. She hopes one sexy night can

turn into more, but Renly is firmly in the friends-with-benefits camp.

As the threat to Abby increases, she tries to keep her growing feelings for Renly at bay. But as the sparks between them burn even hotter, can they go from friends to lovers when the first order of business is simply to keep Abby alive?

* * * *

Cherish Me: A Stark Ever After Novella

My life with Damien has always been magical, and never more so than during the holidays, a time for us to celebrate the hardships we've overcome and the incredible gift that is our family. Over the years, he has both protected and cherished me. He has made my life more rich and full than I could ever have imagined.

This year, he's treating me and our daughters to a holiday in Manhattan. With parades and ice skating, toy displays and candies. And, most of all, with each other.

It's a wonderful gift, a trip I will always cherish. But this year, I'm the one with the surprise. And I can't wait to see the look of delight and awe when I finally share my secret with Damien.

But I'm terrified that when danger strikes, it will take a holiday miracle for me to even get the chance.

* * * *

Indulge Me: A Stark Ever After Novella

Despite everything I have suffered, I never truly understood darkness until my family was in danger. Those desperate hours came close to breaking both Damien and me, but together we found the strength to survive and hold our family together.

Even so, my wounds are deep and wispy shadows still linger. But Damien is my rock. My hero against the dark and violence.

When dark memories threaten to consume me, he whisks me away, knowing that in order to conquer my fears he must take control. Demand my submission. Claim me completely. Because if I am going to find my center again, I must hold tight to Damien and draw deep from the spring of our shared passion.

* * * *

Please Me: A Stark Ever After Novella

Each day with Damien is a miracle, each moment with our children a gift. And yet I cannot escape the growing sense that a storm is gathering, threatening to pull me away, to rip us apart. To drag me down, once again, into a darkness to which I swore never to return.

I have to fight it—I know that. And I am waging the battle with of all my heart. But it is Damien who is my strength, and we both know that the only way to push away the darkness is for him to fold me in his arms and claim me completely. And for me to surrender myself, once again, to the fire that burns between us.

* * * *

Hold Me: A Stark Ever After Novella

My life with Damien has never been fuller. Every day is a miracle, and every night I lose myself in the oasis of his arms.
But there are new challenges, too. Our families. Our careers. And new responsibilities that test us with unrelenting, unexpected trials.
I know we will survive—we have to. Because I cannot live without Damien by my side. But sometimes the darkness seems overwhelming, and I am terrified that the day will come when Damien cannot bring the light. And I will have to find the strength inside myself to find my way back into his arms.

* * * *

Tease Me: A Stark International Novel

Entertainment reporter Jamie Archer knew it would be hard when her husband, Stark Security Chief Ryan Hunter, was called away for a long-term project in London. The distance is difficult to endure, but Jamie trusts the deep and passionate love that has always burned between them. At least until a mysterious woman from Ryan's past shows up at his doorstep, her very presence threatening to destroy everything that Jamie holds dear.

Ryan never expected to see Felicia Randall again, a woman with whom he shared a dark past and a dangerous secret. The first and only woman he ever truly failed.

Desperate and on the run, Felicia's come to plead for his help. But while Ryan knows that helping her is the only way to heal old wounds, he also knows that the mission will not only endanger the life of the woman he holds most dear, but will brutally test the deep trust that binds Jamie and Ryan together.

* * * *

Tempt Me: A Stark International Novella

Sometimes passion has a price…

When sexy Stark Security Chief Ryan Hunter whisks his girlfriend Jamie Archer away for a passionate, romance-filled weekend so he can finally pop the question, he's certain that the answer will be an enthusiastic yes. So when Jamie tries to avoid the conversation, hiding her fears of commitment and change under a blanket of wild sensuality and decadent playtime in bed, Ryan is more determined than ever to convince Jamie that they belong together.

Knowing there's no halfway with this woman, Ryan gives her an ultimatum – marry him or walk away. Now Jamie is forced to face her deepest insecurities or risk destroying the best thing in her life. And it will take all of her strength, and all of Ryan's love, to keep her right where she belongs…

* * * *

Tame Me: A Stark International Novella

Aspiring actress Jamie Archer is on the run. From herself. From her wild child ways. From the screwed up life that she left behind in Los Angeles. And, most of all, from Ryan Hunter—the first man who has the potential to break through her defenses to see the dark fears and secrets she hides.

Stark International Security Chief Ryan Hunter knows only one thing for sure—he wants Jamie. Wants to hold her, make love to her, possess her, and claim her. Wants to do whatever it takes to make her his.

But after one night of bliss, Jamie bolts. And now it's up to Ryan to not only bring her back, but to convince her that she's running away from the best thing that ever happened to her--him.

* * * *

Damien: A Stark Novel

I am Damien Stark. From the outside, I have a perfect life. A billionaire with a beautiful family. But if you could see inside my head, you'd know I'm as f-ed up as a person can be. Now more than ever.

I'm driven, relentless, and successful, but all of that means nothing without my wife and daughters. They're my entire world, and I failed them. Now I can barely look at them without drowning in an abyss of self-recrimination.

Only one thing keeps me sane—losing myself in my wife's silken caresses where I can pour all my pain into the one thing I know I can give her. Pleasure.

But the threats against my family are real, and I won't let anything happen to them ever again. I'll do whatever it takes to keep them safe—pay any price, embrace any darkness. They are mine.

I am Damien Stark. Do you want to see inside my head? Careful what you wish for.

* * * *

Justify Me: A Stark International/Masters and Mercenaries Novella

McKay-Taggart operative Riley Blade has no intention of returning to Los Angeles after his brief stint as a consultant on mega-star Lyle Tarpin's latest action flick. Not even for Natasha Black, Tarpin's sexy personal assistant who'd gotten under his skin. Why would he, when Tasha made it absolutely clear that—attraction or not—she wasn't interested in a fling, much less a relationship.

But when Riley learns that someone is stalking her, he races to her side. Determined not only protect her, but to convince her that—no matter what has hurt her in the past—he's not only going to fight for her, he's going to win her heart. Forever.

* * * *

Caress of Darkness: A Dark Pleasures Novella

From the first moment I saw him, I knew that Rainer Engel was like no other man. Dangerously sexy and darkly mysterious, he both enticed me and terrified me.

I wanted to run—to fight against the heat that was building between us—but there was nowhere to go. I needed his help as much as I needed his touch. And so help me, I knew that I would do anything he asked in order to have both.

But even as our passion burned hot, the secrets in Raine's past reached out to destroy us … and we would both have to make the greatest sacrifice to find a love that would last forever.

Don't miss the next novellas in the Dark Pleasures series!

Find Me in Darkness, Find Me in Pleasure, Find Me in Passion, Caress of Pleasure…

* * * *

Storm, Texas.

Where passion runs hot, desire runs deep, and secrets have the power to destroy…

Nestled among rolling hills and painted with vibrant wildflowers, the bucolic town of Storm, Texas, seems like nothing short of perfection.

But there are secrets beneath the facade. Dark secrets. Powerful secrets. The kind that can destroy lives and tear families apart. The kind that can cut through a town like a tempest, leaving jealousy and destruction in its wake, along with shattered hopes and broken dreams. All it takes is one little thing to shatter that polish.

Rising Storm is a series conceived by Julie Kenner and Dee Davis to read like an on-going drama. Set in a small Texas town, Rising Storm is full of scandal, deceit, romance, passion, and secrets. Lots of secrets.

About J. Kenner

J. Kenner (aka Julie Kenner) is the *New York Times*, *USA Today*, *Publishers Weekly*, *Wall Street Journal* and #1 International bestselling author of over one-hundred novels, novellas and short stories in a variety of genres.

JK has been praised by *Publishers Weekly* as an author with a "flair for dialogue and eccentric characterizations" and by *RT Bookclub* for having "cornered the market on sinfully attractive, dominant antiheroes and the women who swoon for them."

In her previous career as an attorney, JK worked as a lawyer in Southern California and Texas. She currently lives in Central Texas, with her husband, two daughters, and two rather spastic cats.

Visit JK online at www.jkenner.com
Join JK's Patreon for bonus content, exclusive stories, and more!
Subscribe to JK's Newsletter
Text JKenner to 21000 to subscribe to JK's text alerts
Twitter: http://www.twitter.com/juliekenner
Instagram: http://www.instagram.com/juliekenner
Facebook Page: http://www.facebook.com/jkennerbooks
Facebook Fan Group: https://www.facebook.com/groups/jkenner/

On Behalf of 1001 Dark Nights,
Liz Berry, M.J. Rose, and Jillian Stein would like to thank ~

Steve Berry
Doug Scofield
Benjamin Stein
Kim Guidroz
Chelle Olson
Tanaka Kangara
Asha Hossain
Chris Graham
Suzy Baldwin
Jessica Saunders
Stacey Tardif
Dylan Stockton
Kate Boggs
Richard Blake
and Simon Lipskar